THE PLACE OF RELIGION IN FAMILY LAW: A COMPARATIVE SEARCH

European Family Law Series

Published by the Organising Committee of the
Commission on European Family Law

THE PLACE OF RELIGION IN FAMILY LAW: A COMPARATIVE SEARCH

Edited by

Jane Mair
Esin Örücü

intersentia
Cambridge – Antwerp – Portland

Intersentia Ltd
Trinity House | Cambridge Business Park | Cowley Road
Cambridge | CB4 0WZ | United Kingdom
mail@intersentia.co.uk

Distribution for the UK:
Hart Publishing Ltd
16C Worcester Place
Oxford, OX1 2JW
UK
Tel.: +44 1865 51 75 30
Email: mail@hartpub.co.uk

Distribution for the USA and Canada:
International Specialized Book Services
920 NE 58th Ave. Suite 300
Portland, OR 97213
USA
Tel.: +1 800 944 6190 (toll free)
Email: info@isbs.com

Distribution for Switzerland and Germany:
Stämpfli Verlag AG
Wölflistrasse 1
CH-3001 Bern
Switzerland
Tel.: +41 0 31 300 63 18
order@buchstaempfli.com

Distribution for other countries:
Intersentia Publishers
Groenstraat 31
2640 Mortsel
Belgium
Tel.: +32 3 680 15 50
Email: mail@intersentia.be

The Place of Religion in Family Law: A Comparative Search
Edited by Jane Mair and Esin Örücü

ISBN 978-1-78068-015-6
NUR 822

British Library Cataloguing in Publication Data. A catalogue record for this book is available from the British Library.

PREFACE

The increasing role of religion in the growing international discussion on diversity and multiculturalism led us to inquire into the legal frameworks in which religion is approached in a number of jurisdictions in order to find out what the scope and impact of the principle of religious freedom is. This concern was specifically related to the legal parameters affecting the influence of religion in family life and law. How did European states deal with the increasing interest in religion and the role of religion in the predominantly secular family laws of our day?

Our curiosity as to the true picture of the extent of law tolerating, accommodating, reconciling or even merely recognising the existence of religions and traditions in the area of family relationships, led us first to organise a one day Workshop to search for the place of religion in family law in March 2010. A number of scholars from various jurisdictions and interests were invited to participate in this Workshop, which was supported by Seedcorn Funding from the Adam Smith Research Foundation, University of Glasgow. We had a series of short presentations in the morning followed by a round-table discussion in the afternoon with the aim of incorporating a broad range of interests and opinions and highlighting the various ways in which religion and religious belief may influence or affect family relationships.

When it came to the production of this volume, we decided to fill the remaining gaps, as we saw them, by inviting some additional contributions from other scholars known to be involved in this field. Thus this volume now has 12 essays covering jurisdictions from the secular states with predominantly Muslim populations to Catholic and Jewish societies with semi-secular legal systems; from secular to Catholic and Jewish states. The search is for the place of religion in each of these both in historical and contemporary contexts. We hope that a diversity of countries and regions, and a number of different approaches our contributors take, will reflect a useful picture of recent, as well as historical, developments. This collection of essays highlights the religious dimension of law, the legal dimension of religion and the interaction or otherwise between secular law and religion in the field of family law, and, at the same time, also considers practical and topical issues.

The final part of the volume is a general and comparative assessment of our findings.

Jane Mair and Esin Örücü
30 March 2011

LIST OF AUTHORS

Prof. Masha Antokolskaia
Professor of Private and Family Law at VU University of Amsterdam, The Netherlands

Prof. Janeen M. Carruthers
Professor of Private Law, School of Law, University of Glasgow, Scotland

Prof. Elizabeth B. Crawford
Professor of International Private Law, School of Law, University of Glasgow, Scotland

Dr. Matthijs de Blois
Senior Lecturer at the Institute of Legal Theory, Department of Law, Utrecht University, The Netherlands

Dr. Ruth Farrugia
Advocate and Senior Lecturer in Civil Law, University of Malta, Malta

Dr. John Finlay
Senior Lecturer, School of Law, University of Glasgow, Scotland

Dr. Maebh Harding
Senior Lecturer, University of Portsmouth, England

Prof. Maarit Jänterä-Jareborg
Professor of Private International Law and International Civil Procedure at Uppsala University, Sweden; Former Dean of the Faculty of Law, Uppsala University, Sweden

Dr. Frankie McCarthy
Lecturer, School of Law, University of Glasgow, Scotland

Dr. Jane Mair
Senior Lecturer, School of Law, University of Glasgow, Scotland

Prof. Werner Menski
Professor of South Asian Laws, SOAS, University of London, England

Prof. Kenneth McK. Norrie
School of Law, University of Strathclyde, Scotland

Prof. Esin Örücü
Professor Emerita of Comparative Law and Honorary Senior Research Fellow, University of Glasgow, Scotland; Professor Emerita of Comparative law, Erasmus University Rotterdam, The Netherlands

Dr. Michael Rosie
Senior Lecturer in Sociology; Deputy Director, Institute of Governance, School of Social and Political Science, University of Edinburgh, Scotland

Prof. Fran Wasoff
Emeritus Professor of Family Policies, Social Policy, School of Social and Political Science and Centre for Research on Families and Relationships, University of Edinburgh, Scotland

CONTENTS

INTRODUCTORY OVERVIEW

INTRODUCTION TO THE PLACE OF RELIGION IN FAMILY LAW: A COMPARATIVE SEARCH

Esin Örücü

There have been steady and significant moves towards more secular forms of legal regulation in the area of family law, though religion and religious beliefs continue to play an important role, overtly or covertly, in the development, reform and regulation of family relationships. With shifting populations, religious diversity and issues of multiculturalism are becoming increasingly significant in all legal systems. We believe that recent debates about the nature of sacred and secular law and about the interplay between them come to light most profoundly in the area of family law. So we, as the editors of this volume, wanted to inquire not only into the relationship and connection of the different legacies of monotheism and legal traditions but also into such relationships in the increasingly multi-faith societies in the Europe of our day.

Our thoughts first turned to the fact that, traditionally, family law in Scotland, as in many other European countries, was based on Canon law but since the Scottish Reformation in 1560, there have been significant changes bringing in first secularism and then human rights as the predominant value systems underlying all the reforms introduced. Though our starting point was Scotland, our gaze naturally turned beyond Scotland. History of social change has been marked by restrictions and limitations imposed by the law on certain groups, especially religious communities, on the freedom "to act in accordance with their beliefs". This was clearly the case in family law.

We then questioned, however, secularism in view of religious diversity and multiculturalism in our day, hence the loss of homogeneity in the populations of, for instance, European countries, juxtaposed to the duty of the State to satisfy the needs of the people. We were also aware that State-religion systems have undergone profound changes in the last two decades, as a result of such developments.[1] In addition, there was the case of multi-cultural families, which challenged established approaches to family law, bringing to the fore legal pluralism, minority religious communities and customary and indigenous laws.[2] After all, individuals tend to create their own identity around symbols of faith and law in complex ways. These problems now existed in the context of European countries as they never did before.

Our awareness of the importance and increasing role of religion in the growing international discussion on diversity and multiculturalism led us to inquire into the legal frameworks in which religion is approached in a number of jurisdictions and to find out what the scope and impact of the principle of religious freedom is in this relationship. This concern was specifically related to the legal parameters affecting the influence of religion in family life and law. We were curious as to how European States deal with the increasing interest in religion and the role religion does or can play in the predominantly secular family laws of our day.[3]

This awareness and curiosity as to the true picture of the extent of law tolerating, accommodating, reconciling or even merely recognising the existence of religions and traditions in the area of family relationships, led us first to organise a one day Workshop to search for the place of religion in family law in March 2010. We invited a number of scholars from various jurisdictions and interests to participate in this Workshop with the intention to have a series of short presentations in the morning followed by a round-table discussion in the afternoon. The aim was to incorporate a broad range of interests and opinions highlighting the various ways in which religion and religious belief may influence or affect family relationships – involving both adults and children – and the way in which they are regulated. This would lead us also to provide, we thought, an overview of current issues in State-religion relations.

Following the Workshop, when it came to the production of this volume, we decided to fill some of the remaining gaps, as we saw them, by inviting additional contributions from other scholars known to be involved in this field. Thus this volume now has 12 essays covering jurisdictions from Scotland to Sweden and Turkey; from the secular states with predominantly Muslim populations to Catholic and Jewish societies with semi-secular legal systems; from secular to

1 Relations between States and Religious communities in various fields have been explored in a recent collection. See FERRARI, S. and CRISTOFORI, R. (eds.), *Law and Religion in the 21st Century* (Ashgate, 2010).

2 See the essays in LAQUER ESTIN, A. (ed.), *The Multi-Cultural Family* (Ashgate, 2008).

3 See for instance, a recent volume of the *International Encyclopaedia of Law* on religion law, a loose leaf publication that looks in Part X at Matrimonial and Family Law, each country following the same elaborate outline comprising 11 Parts: TORFS, R. (ed.) *International Encyclopaedia of Law: Religion Law* (Kluwer law International, 2010).

Catholic and Jewish states. The search is for the place of religion in each of these both in historical and contemporary contexts. The hope is that a diversity of countries and religions, and a number of different approaches our contributors take, will reflect a more thorough picture of recent, as well as historical, developments. Our aim is to gain, through these essays, theoretical, historical, legal and religious insights into the issue under consideration by highlighting the religious dimension of law, the legal dimension of religion and the interaction or otherwise between secular law and religion in the field of family law, and, at the same time, also to consider practical and topical issues.

Some of the jurisdictions under survey, show a gradual and incremental evolution towards secularism in family law, such as Scotland; some, abrupt and revolutionary, such as Russia. Nevertheless, in all of the jurisdictions, whether secular or not, religion has an impact on family law, overtly or covertly. Secular legal systems such as Sweden, by allowing an "either or" in secular and religious marriage, succumb to the existence of religious sentiments; others such as Turkey, do not, but show some toleration to life-styles based on belief systems, under the guise of equating them with custom and tradition and then accepting them in that guise. All jurisdictions also encounter belief or faith systems as a consequence of their private international law rules, even when they do not accept such life-styles for their own citizens. One thing is sure. There is pressure on the legal systems from individuals to be accepted for who they are.

A number of questions were important to us. For instance, what could be the role of religion in the public order? Was accommodating religion in family law relationships part of facilitation and protection of individual and institutional religious freedom in Western law? What could be the means through which law could facilitate, if at all, religious input and influence over itself? What would be the limitations?[4] Could there be a choice as to which rules specific for a particular region, religion or culture need to be preserved in a Western secular State? Did family law have inherent legal pluralism and, if so, should private "opting out" be allowed, in spite of the fact that nearly all the legal systems under consideration, were not "multijural"?

Family law in European legal systems, even when there is a State religion, is now dogma-neutral. This fact raises additional questions: To what extent could citizens be permitted complete freedom of belief and practice within the general law in a modern legal system? Since no one could escape being governed by the general law – which would act at worst as an overarching framework – how far could claiming of the freedom to act on a religious belief, be upheld? Or, could a

4 These issues have been comprehensively covered in the context of the EU. See McCREA, R., *Religion and the Public Order of the European Union* (Oxford University Press, 2010).

believer, for instance, withdraw from the general law on the basis of his/her particular code of beliefs? Was there a dichotomy between religion and secular law? Should not the rules of a legal system apply generally to all, particularly in societies of diverse cultures and belief systems, which more and more European countries are becoming? Would the essays presented in the Workshop and after, challenge our established positions on these issues?

With these concerns we can now turn to a brief introduction to the essays in this volume.

After lamenting the fact that European legal practitioners are not prepared by education and training for complex pluralistic challenges, Werner Menski, who also acts as an expert in English courts in the family laws of Pakistan, Bangladesh and India, wonders "whether we really do not know any better, or if we just do not wish to know". Although his essay predominantly presents the English scene, he is adamant that lawyers and judges everywhere should "understand" the pluralising effects of "the now deeply manifest cultural and religious normative pluralities all around us". Menski challenges the prevalent "modernity-centric" positivist modes of thought, and makes a case for taking into account the "living law" in our times of "superdiversity". He exposes various assumptions that surround this issue. Menski undertakes here a critical legal pluralistic approach as a legal methodology, rather than a traditional legal analysis, and advocates "equity in multicultural contexts", stemming from his experiences, by highlighting three case studies in which he has been involved. Since the consideration of our topic is also tied up with a closer look at broad issues of multiculturalism, secularism, immigration, settlement and security, we chose to start the volume with Menski's essay which takes the widest angle of all the essays by setting the tone not only for religion's implications for multiculturalism but also for legal pluralism.

In contrast, Elizabeth Crawford and Janeen Carruthers advocate traditional legal analysis, reject twin or multi-track versions of private law rules, and show that in Britain, it is only the international private law rules that can accommodate and resolve issues of cross-cultural diversity, including religious diversity. Crawford and Carruthers state that, "UK law does not permit bespoke application of a party's religious laws" otherwise. The authors illustrate the attitude of the courts in the United Kingdom which is secular, and offer "some examples of the manner in which the courts in Scotland and England, applying conflict of laws principles as part of the civil law of the land, treat parties' religious beliefs and cultural traditions". The essay views the issues in the framework of international private law and does not attempt to discuss the place of Christian beliefs in family law. The issues the authors deal with cover polygamy, legal capacity to marry, extra-judicial divorces and annulments, recognition of overseas divorces and annulments, transnational divorces, nullity and forced marriages. We are then offered an analysis of the Family Law (Scotland) Act 2006 and the Forced Marriage etc. (Protection and Jurisdiction) (Scotland) Act 2011; both examples of legislation being used to address some of the problems encountered. The essay also looks into child custody and child abduction.

Maarit Jänterä-Jareborg, talks of the "myth of Sweden being the most secular country in the world" by showing us how in Sweden – a revealing site for contemporary studies on our subject – religion is tolerated not only through the private international law rules, which is the expected norm in all jurisdictions, but also in the form of religiosity of the Swedish population and its impact on marriage. Today, for historical reasons, Sweden has a "double track system of marriage conclusion", secular (civil) and religious marriages being regarded as equal alternatives by the legal system. In this essay, Jänterä-Jareborg considers what she calls "the Swedish paradoxes", such as the high level of church membership with continued popularity of church rituals in celebrating marriage, though without active participation in other church activities; the reality of the presumed impact of secularisation and neutrality as regards the majority religion; and the new presence of Islam in the country and the ensuing challenges of multiculture which impacts the relationship between what is regarded as "law" and as "religion". The author also highlights the tension created by same-sex marriages within this context. Some aspects of a united Nordic approach are also assessed in this essay.

The past and present Russian perspective proves to be an intriguing example of an interaction between religion and family law that shows a zigzag movement rather than a gradual, evolutionary one, swayed by strong political and ideological winds. In spite of the various periods in the development of family law, from exclusive competence of the Orthodox Christian Church in the Middle Ages to the strictly secular one of the "militant atheism", and in spite of the radicalism of the Soviet period, Masha Antokolskaia's essay indicates that Russian developments follow the same pattern as those of other European countries. Her conclusion is that in Russian family law today, law and religion "co-exist in near perfect harmony" without much interaction.

In Turkey, another State where revolutionary changes took place after 1924, we see that there is virtually no official interaction between law and religion. Neither is there near perfect harmony, since in this country of a mainly Muslim population, the legal system is strictly laic/secular. From the legally pluralist, though Islamic, Ottoman Empire, the Republic was born, which adheres to total "laicism", dubbed as "assertive laicism", with State control over religion, yet, with no interference of religion allowed into the laws of the country. One important fact to note is that secular (civil) and religious marriages are not regarded as equal alternatives by the legal system, with the possibility of religious marriage only arising after the conclusion of the civil marriage. Nevertheless, as demonstrated by Esin Örücü, in family law, the courts try to navigate, though always within the laic legal framework, in order to respond, to a certain extent, to the belief system of the majority Muslim population. This essay covers, in this context and predominantly through court cases, religious marriages, legitimacy of children, religious instruction, adultery, and various aspects of the position of the wife as the equal spouse.

In Catholic Ireland, pre-1937 there were two separate functioning systems, with Catholics being subject to the doctrines and jurisdiction of the Church in family law matters, and since that time, article 41 of the 1937 Constitution protects marriage and Catholic values. Maebh Harding analyses judicial attitudes to Catholic values and the constitutional review of 1967, concentrating on nullity grounds, which she dubs, "the high tide-mark of canon law". The reforms of 1989, bringing in judicial separation rather than divorce, is assessed as the beginning of a new secular age and provides for us serious possibilities of comparison with the situation in Malta, for instance. Finally, and incrementally, we see civil marriage and no-fault divorce making an entry in 1996. In this new context, the constitutional protection of marriage is questioned by Harding.

Ruth Farrugia provides for us a portrait of Maltese family law, where family values and the (civil) law are painted with the brush of the Catholic faith. To start with, the Constitution proclaims the Roman Catholic Apostolic Religion as the religion of Malta, and this faith has shaped Maltese family values and family law. This essay, looked at in conjunction with the one on Ireland, shows how strong this hold of religion in family law is. The "understanding and interpretation of basic definitions of 'family' and the well-defined responsibilities" between family members, the care givers and the dependants, are all determined by the Roman Catholic Church. In addition, Malta is the only EU Member State where, for the time being, there is no divorce, since marriage is a sacrament and can only be dissolved by death. The essay considers marriage, annulment, divorce and cohabitation. Finally, the author considers the influence of the Catholic Church in Malta today. Farrugia shows how various laws and policies "decreasingly reflect the position" of the Church, and that, "when determining particular social support such as housing allocation and access to social assistance", the State responds by humanitarian considerations rather than religious ones.

How does Jewish family law fare in Israel and in secular legal orders? The example of *get* refusal is the special issue addressed by Matthijs de Blois. De Blois approaches generally, Jewish law on marriage and divorce, and specifically, the problems arising from *get* refusal. His first stop is Israel, where religious law is the law of the State and where legal pluralism as to personal laws has been incorporated into the legal system by legislation. The Israeli approach to the *get* problem is discussed with reference to case law. The next stop is Western secular jurisdictions. In this context, de Blois considers Canada, England, France, Germany and the Netherlands. Both legislative and judicial approaches in these jurisdictions are discussed. The tackling of the problems arising from *get* refusal seems to be through civil divorce proceedings, breach of contract or tort, with some courts refusing such claims altogether. The integration of religious and secular laws is complex and marriage and divorce are a concern of both religious and secular laws. The *get* refusal illustrates the tensions between the two laws, even in Israel. The tension that we see here is not only between the secular and the religious, but also between the orthodox and liberal interpretations emanating from "the factions of the same religions as to the right interpretation of the divine prescriptions". Finally, de Blois clearly shows that in a secular State, human rights arguments can be used both "in favour of the recognition of religious law" and "against the recognition of religious law". Thus the complexities cannot be reduced, let alone solved, by human rights arguments either, especially when the two laws collide.

Frankie McCarthy's contribution bears witness to how "the rapid development of the law of human rights in the UK and Europe more generally has allowed for an examination of the intersections between religion and education to take place within a new framework". Issues such as human rights, education law, equalities legislation, faith schools and the place of secular education, state neutrality, curriculum content and sex education, school uniform and religious dress, and conflicts of rights between parents and children are fully considered in this essay, in the legal systems of the UK which have "never embraced a secular system of education". Though it is mainly the UK position and cases that are discussed, there is ample juxtaposition to and comparison with cases from other jurisdictions and the position taken by the European Court of Human Rights.

The place of religion in the history of family law in Scotland is analysed in detail by John Finlay. Here we also encounter an inquiry into the relatively novel concept of family law, as it developed over the years, from humble beginnings of being part of the law of persons. Finlay illustrates how, from a very strict religious starting point, the law evolved, again incrementally, towards secularism, based "almost entirely on statute". The story begins with the 1560 Protestant Reformation. The reader is taken through the centuries, from the influence of Canon law, the Reformation, the significance of Roman law, to post 1800 "when the local kirk sessions declined in significance". Although the impact of religion in family law has not totally disappeared, it "did not ever remain static". Finlay remarks that throughout time, religion, which "has been an important force in the development of family law in Scotland," "has both offered a moral framework and occasionally imposed specific legal rules". We are reminded especially of the existence of the social control aspect of religion in an otherwise secular society.

Now we can turn to gay equality in family law, with an assessment of the position of same-sex couples, vis-à-vis religion, analysed by Kenneth Norrie. After indicating that the two competing rationalities – one secular, the other revelatory – are alien to each other, Norrie then juxtaposes the Catholic Emancipation Act of 1929 to the 2004 Civil Partnership Act. This shows the profound cultural change and radical reversal in attitudes towards homosexuality. At the time when religious bodies totally rejected the legitimacy of same-sex relationships, they were not out of line with social attitudes and the law, since the limited definition of "family" excluded same-sex couples. Today, the developing consensus is that "sexual orientation is morally neutral". The law follows this consensus. Some progressive religious groups and individuals draw on "the strand of Christianity that emphasises the virtues of love, forgiveness and tolerance" and accommodate their beliefs with the legal developments. Some others, however, do not. Norrie's essay first illustrates Christian approaches to gay and lesbian equality, assesses the changing law accommodating religious concerns, identifies the underlying principles upon which the accommodation is based and then offers an assessment of how family law is likely to develop in the light of such accommodation. The way forward points to same-sex marriages.

The only essay that presents an empirical survey is by Michael Rosie and Fran Wasoff, and it throws intriguing light on the relationship between religion, family values and family law. The authors focus on secular/religious social divisions and "examine the extent to which there is an association between religion and views on obligations and attitudes towards family life". The trend towards secularisation, the voice of faith groups in family law reform, religious affiliation and practice, views on marriage and cohabitation, the effect of age and gender, the relationship between religious adherence and sexual morality, attitudes on gay and lesbian adoption and familial obligations are analysed within 20 Tables, and the Scottish Social Attitudes Survey of 2004 is elaborated on. A number of questions were posed, tested and evidenced. The findings were then analysed and assessed. Although the study is Scottish based, we believe that its findings have valuable indications for other European jurisdictions.

In the final essay Jane Mair tries to reach a clear and comprehensive comparative overview of the legal position on religion in the field of family law and draws a conclusion to this comparative search for the place of religion in family law.

Hitherto, comparative lawyers hardly ever mentioned the relationship between law and religion, mainly because the emphasis of comparisons has largely been between the civil law and common law worlds and these are assumed to be fundamentally based on the same belief system: Christianity. Neither did they study family law in depth, partly due to the fact that until recently, family law was not seen to be a field of private law where comparisons could be meaningfully undertaken. The emerging common features of the major legal systems may be seen as being founded on common beliefs concerning the nature and the functions of law. There may also be truth in that the major cultures of the world share a common faith in law as a process of just and orderly resolution of conflicts. But, faith in law may be part of religious faith. In family law, in historical terms, this was definitely the case everywhere. Today, following secularisation movements, this may have lost its significance for some. The comparative search undertaken here indicates that this has not happened for all. Until recently, those studying the secular-rational model of law tended "to neglect elements of law that transcend secular rationality, elements that law shares with religion."[5] If it can validly be said that, "the development of a body of world law is sustainable only if the belief system that underlies it and nourishes it also continues to be sustained and to develop,"[6] then, since there is not one world belief system, there can not be one worldwide legal system. Does this put paid to the attempts to create a unified or even meaningfully harmonised family law system, even in the Western world? If we are talking of eras of convergence followed by divergence, can we then look at the future and talk of a new era of convergence ahead, based on similar moral principles constituting a global ethics on which social cohesion can be built, and that, together with a human rights approach, can reflect itself into various family laws?

5 BERMAN, H.J., "Comparative Law and religion" in REIMANN, M. and ZIMMERMANN, R. (eds.), *The Oxford Handbook of Comparative Law* (Oxford University Press, 2006), p. 745.

6 *Ibid.*, p. 747.

PART ONE

ACCOMMODATING A PLACE FOR RELIGION?

ISLAMIC LAW IN BRITISH COURTS: DO WE NOT KNOW OR DO WE NOT WANT TO KNOW?

Werner MENSKI

1. INTRODUCTION

This revised and enlarged paper for the Workshop "The Place of Religion in Family Law", held at the School of Law, University of Glasgow on 12 March 2010, explores first of all major reasons why British and more generally European family law scholarship does not appear to wish to "understand" the pluralising legal effects of the now deeply manifest cultural and religious normative pluralities all around us. The main reason could of course simply be that legal scholarship remains mentally imprisoned by modernity-centric positivist modes of thought. Quite surprisingly, this happens even in relation to family law, where recent pluralising developments in the form of growing "superdiversity",[1] leading to informal "ethnic implants",[2] and new research on "living law",[3] are not properly taken into account. Because such developments are not reflected well enough in the specialist literature, absence of knowledge about "others" leads currently to certain bottlenecks of justice when it comes to decision making about Muslims and other "others" in British courts. Legal scholarship and practice – this confirms again – are closely linked, but their connections remain tenuous and subject to many subjectivities. While judges are much closer to the coalface of justice than (often highly politicised) scholars of family law, mainstream family law scholarship simply refuses to acknowledge certain aspects of such new dilemmas that have arisen. This is clearly reflected in

---

1 See VERTOVEC, S., "Super-diversity and its implications" (2007), *Ethnic and Racial Studies*, 30.6 (November), pp. 1024–1054.

2 On the important distinction between formal transplants and more informal but no less powerful "ethnic implants", see MENSKI, W., *Comparative law in a global context. The legal systems of Asia and Africa* (2nd ed.) (Cambridge University Press, 2006), pp. 58–65.

3 Apart from his general work on law and culture, see specifically COTTERRELL, R., *Living law. Studies in legal and social theory* (Ashgate, 2008).

important new cases which indicate the direction in which developments appear to be moving, using now a new form of equity in multicultural contexts.[4]

In the absence of global agreement of what we mean by law,[5] the old question thus remains as difficult as ever: Can and should state-centric law really regulate all aspects of family law, and what can legal systems and their personnel do when new groups of migrants bring in their own forms of family regulation and predictably, as we should also know by now,[6] begin to order their legal universes on their own terms even though they are living in Britain? Simplistic assumptions about assimilation of migrants like "salt into water" are manifestly wishful thinking, because simple common sense suggests that the water itself changes its quality when the salt dissolves. Family law issues, this confirms, remain quite evidently subject to strongly felt value judgments, making the whole field discussed here even more volatile in relation to specific ideologies and perceptions about law and practice. This discussion also illustrates then that law and life cannot ever be separated and that law and morality, at least when it comes to family law, have always been uneasy cohabitants in the same space.

While we may attempt to stick to now outdated assumptions about legal centralism and its powers that remain quite fictitious, as several well-known writers have clearly told us, it cannot be discounted that wider political agenda also play a role here. Gordon Brown's reaction to the speech of the Archbishop of Canterbury, discussed further below, was symptomatic of positivist positioning. Of course, we need state control, and of course someone has to have the ultimate power to make decisions – we cannot have limitless plurality. However, motivated by certain ideologies, we often simply do not wish to know to what extent these new ethnically and ethically pluralising developments in our midst have actually intruded into the legal arena by now and have created new legal hybrids that we urgently need to study to keep up with recent developments and to understand the world around us.

---

4 For England, see *Chief Adjudication Officer v Kirpal Kaur Bath* [2000] 1 FLR 8 CA and note how the Court of Appeal was forced, simply to avoid plain injustice, to resort to equity and thus to acknowledge the legal validity and legal effects of an unregistered Sikh religious marriage in London some 40 years earlier. See also the unreported *mahr* case of *Ali v Ali* in 2000, first discussed in MENSKI, W. (2002), "Immigration and multiculturalism in Britain: New issues in research and policy", *KIAPS: Bulletin of Asia-Pacific Studies*, Osaka, XII: pp. 43–66.

5 See on this MENSKI, *supra* note 2, p. 32, which identifies the central challenge as "the absence of any worldwide agreement, in theory as well as in practice, about the central object of globalised legal studies, namely 'the law' itself". This is also found and elaborately confirmed by TAMANAHA, B.Z. in the entry under "Law" in KATZ, S.N. (ed.), *The Oxford International Encyclopedia of Legal History* Vol. 4 (Oxford University Press, 2009), pp. 17–23.

6 See especially BALLARD, R. (ed.), *Desh pardesh. The South Asian presence in Britain* (Hurst & Co., 1994).

The key issue for lawyers may well be that the growing divergences between what Masaji Chiba's writing so sharply identified as various forms of "official law" and "unofficial law" continue to cause a lot of headache to the legal fraternity, a term which has itself become outdated and evidently reflects lack of gender-consciousness.[7] The world around us has clearly moved on and has diversified in more than one way. We should have become more perceptive of the need to account for such differences within a framework of seeking to secure equality, or at least equity. But instead we often instinctively desire more uniformity and certainty. One must wonder whether such desires are part of the "bone marrow", as some people call it now, specifically of lawyers and legal scholars.

While legal scholarship has not been totally silent about such key issues, oddly enough legal pluralism studies remain treated as polluted and polluting interventions that one can all too easily sweep under the carpet, or may simply throw out and discard without further consideration. In Britain of the twenty-first century, I suggest, such dismissive thinking, which fails to account for certain types of "others", and thus is blatantly and inherently discriminatory, is spelling deep trouble for maintaining fairness and justice, especially when it comes to the regulation of family law in emerging scenarios of "superdiversity",[8] and even of "plutopia",[9] an emerging condition where no single community has absolute control.

The message that also lawyers have to account for various pluralisms as a fact of life is thus increasingly loud and clear. But such echoes are still widely resisted, even by mainstream social science, which oddly cultivates a state-centric image of law, and particularly by most mainstream legal scholarship itself. It seems we still need to be reminded that, certainly not as the first voice in this field,[10] John Griffiths stated powerfully in 1986:

> "Legal pluralism is the fact. Legal centralism is a myth, an ideal, a claim, an illusion. Nevertheless, the ideology of legal centralism has had such a powerful hold on the imagination of lawyers and social scientists that its picture of the legal world has been

---

7 CHIBA, M. (ed.), *Asian indigenous law. In interaction with received law* (KPI, 1986) excerpted in MENSKI, *supra* note 2, pp. 119–128.

8 See VERTOVEC, *supra* note 1.

9 SPENCER, N., "The price of diversity" (2010), *Third Way. Christian Comment on Culture*, 33.7 (September), p. 19.

10 On evidence of struggles over legal pluralism in ancient India, thousands of years ago, see now MENSKI, W., "Sanskrit law. Excavating Vedic legal pluralism", (2010) *SOAS School of Law Research Paper*, No. 05–2010 [available at SSRN: http://ssrn.com/abstract=1621384]. I would also refer readers to the highly instructive preface by LLOYD, D. of 1959, reprinted in FREEMAN, M.D.A., *Lloyd's Introduction to Jurisprudence* (7th ed.) (Sweet & Maxwell, 2001), pp. vii-xi.

> able successfully to masquerade as fact and has formed the foundation stone of social and legal theory."[11]

Similarly, William Twining summed up his critical analysis of uniformisation trends in 2000 by saying that lawyers continue to have problems with legal pluralism in practice and that "legal pluralism is generally marginalised and viewed with scepticism in legal discourse".[12] Significantly, a major study of jurisprudence candidly admitted around the same time that when the first edition of that study appeared in 1959, "jurisprudence was still something of a 'dirty word'".[13] Today, we see, in turn, that legal pluralism studies and particularly ethnic minority legal studies are being dismissed as "dirty". These are consequences of the fact that "law" and "culture" still struggle to find mutually acceptable forms of co-existence in terms of legal regulation.

When it comes to assessing the place of Islamic law in English or British courts today, therefore, it is quite unsurprising that we continue to face huge turbulence in management of legal issues, which I now illustrate in a more recent set of lectures and articles as the highly dynamic activity of kite flying.[14] I remain agnostic about whether in the UK we do not wish to know or do not know any better, but it is evident that the continuing messiness of allowing unsystematic exceptions and granting occasional exemptions from the general law that prevails is widely and increasingly perceived to be unsatisfactory and itself discriminatory. The tempting question whether this messy scenario can ever be fully regulated raises issues too large and far too philosophical for the present paper. But let us not forget that all law "lives" and is culture-specific. Hence Sally Falk Moore sagely advised decades ago that formal law-making is always a piecemeal form of legal intervention:

> "The piecemeal quality of intentional legal intervention, whether legislative, executive or judicial, is due to its construction as a response to particular circumstances at particular moments. The accretion of many such responses over time makes for a composite, unplanned, total result. Even though, at various times and places, there have been attempts to codify everything once and for all, in the long term all legal 'systems' are built by accretion, not by total systematic planning."[15]

---

11 GRIFFITHS, J., "What is legal pluralism?", (1986) *Journal of Legal Pluralism and Unofficial Law*, 24, 1 at pp. 4–5.

12 TWINING, W., *Globalisation and legal theory* (Butterworths, 2000), p. 232.

13 FREEMAN, *supra* note 10, p. 3.

14 See MENSKI, W., "Fuzzy law and the boundaries of secularism". Lecture for RELIGARE, London, 24 June 2010 [www.religareproject.eu]. MENSKI, W., "Flying kites in Pakistan: Turbulences in theory and practice" (2009–2010), *Journal of Law and Social Research*, Vol. 1, No. 1, pp. 41–57. MENSKI, W., "Plural worlds of law and the search for living law" in GEPHART, W. (ed.), *Recht als Kultur* (Vittorio Klostermann, 2011) (forthcoming).

15 MOORE, S.F., *Law as process: an anthropological approach* (Routledge & Kegan Paul, 1978), p. 9.

Demonstrating that there are several types of law being operated in the world today, especially when it comes to family law, I argue here mainly that the present reluctance to incorporate Islamic aspects of family law into British legal practice is evidence of continuing myopia, with more than a hint of Islamophobia, and probably some kind of colonial tummy ache that we should learn to overcome. The issue is not just the extent of formal recognition of *shari'a* law as part of "our" legal systems, it is a much bigger and indeed global problem, as some examples from recent cases will help to illustrate. Nobody should assume that such issues only arise in relation to matters of Islamic law, though the present paper focuses on this particular legal system's place within the legal systems of the UK.

2. THE CORE ISSUE: BARRIERS FOR KNOWLEDGE

We have not moved forward at all when Brian Tamanaha now polemically challenges the concept of "living law" as a key image of legal pluralism but suggests simplistically that it is safer to assume that all law is dynamic.[16] We knew that all along. Such polemics simply seek to belittle realistic pluralist analysis and obstruct pluralist reconstructions in emerging conditions of socio-legal superdiversity. It shows that even major legal theorists and of course many practising lawyers still do not wish to accept that law may indeed at all times be its own "other" in various ways. Since it is hardly new that law is not only about state-made rules, we have long known that many aspects of human life import dynamic and inherently messy legal dimensions that lawyers may struggle to regulate and to acknowledge as legally relevant. But we do not wish to know this.

There are some deeper reasons for this than mere obstinacy or racist exclusionism. It appears that we remain too closely wedded to Maine-style evolutionist thinking and refuse to accept, somehow, that no single legal theory on its own can explain the totality of the global or, as Emmanuel Melissaris put it, the ubiquitous phenomenon of law.[17] Legal codification, as Sir Henry Sumner Maine argued much earlier, is not simply the epitome of legal development, it remains just one of its major elements.[18] We see that all around us today when we "rediscover" ADR, the interactions of formal and informal laws, the boundary crossing of private and public laws, and so on – none of this is really new at all. In reality, the constant interaction of different types of law with their many fuzzy

16 TAMANAHA, B.Z., "A vision of socio-legal change: Rescuing Ehrlich from 'living law'" in *Legal Studies Research Paper Series* (2010), Washington University in St. Louis, School of Law, Paper No. 10-10-05 [http://ssrn.com/abstract=1689669].

17 MELISSARIS, E., *Ubiquitous law. Legal theory and the space for legal pluralism* (Ashgate, 2009).

18 MAINE, H.S., *Ancient law* (John Murray, 1861).

boundaries has constantly been challenging humans to live and work together in the never-ending search for justice and for "the right law", an image for which there are indeed many culture-specific terms all over the world.

Islamic law with its key notion of the right path (*shari'a*) should hardly be a new subject for English lawyers today and for the courts in England, Wales and Scotland. But knowledge of such "foreign" subjects, which are no longer so outlandish in this multicultural globalising age, seems to remain thin and is still deeply unsatisfactory, a situation not helped by much Muslim positioning about the alleged inherent superiority of this particular legal system. Much of the published work on Islamic law is now simply out of date. Many existing studies, including my own practice-focused work,[19] are often not detailed enough to tackle specific questions that lawyers or judges may have today.[20] A few specialised contributions exist, here and there, if one can find them,[21] but even the latest books on the subject seem to leave more questions than answers.[22]

After 30 years of involvement with such laws (the same goes largely for Hindu law and African laws) I am thus noting some disappointment about current levels of engagement with international dimensions of family law.[23] It seems as though many judges and lawyers within the English legal system are simply unwilling to learn about subjects like Islamic law and other "foreign" legal systems. Academics and activists have not been helping them as much as one might expect. Significant barriers of communication continue to block progress. Notably, it also makes a difference whether one reports and discusses what the law is, or what scholars think it should be.[24]

---

19 PEARL, D. and MENSKI, W., *Muslim family law* (3rd ed.) (Sweet & Maxwell, 1998).

20 On earlier efforts to provide such guidance, see especially PEARL, D., "Islam in English family law" in NIELSEN, J.S. (ed.), *Islam in English law and administration.* A symposium (= Muslims in Europe, No. 9, March 1981), pp. 6–10; PEARL, D., *Family law and the immigrant communities* (Jordan & Sons, 1986); PEARL, D., "South Asian immigrant communities and English family law: 1971–1987" (1987), *New Community*, 14.1–2 (Autumn), pp. 161–169.

21 Some of the essays in SHAH, P., *Legal pluralism in conflict. Coping with cultural diversity in law* (Glass House, 2005) are useful for practitioners, especially chapters 5 and 6 on "Attitudes to polygamy in English law" and "Bangladeshi legal pluralism and English law".

22 See now ARSHAD, R., *Islamic family law* (Sweet & Maxwell, 2010). If this particular book was expected to supplement and update PEARL *et al.*, *supra* note 19, it achieves that objective only partially. Significantly, this new book does not even mention the earlier text and seems to start *de novo*, which makes the tasks of drawing lines and realising connections even more complicated, both for scholars and practitioners.

23 See on this topic especially MURPHY, J., *International dimensions in family law* (Manchester University Press, 2005). This is a much better effort than an earlier edited volume of articles, MURPHY, J. (ed.), *Ethnic minorities, their families and the law* (Hart Publishing, 2000). Murphy brought out (especially pp. 71–76) that the topic was hardly studied, was held back by cultural imperialism and incomplete theorisation, and largely wrapped in deliberate silence.

24 I have been particularly disappointed about some writing from a network under the heading "Women Living Under Muslim Law" (WLUML), which often fails to report truthfully what

Such barriers, then, have partly to do with professional ethics and boundary drawing. But conflicts go much deeper, resenting admission that there should even be a legitimately recognised space for subject matters like Islamic law within English law. In the quite culture-specific Scottish context of secular orientation, as the Glasgow Workshop clearly brought out, multiple resistances towards pluralising tendencies in today's legal practice obstruct clear-cut realisation that we have to learn to practise law as an intensely plural field of activity if we want to achieve just and equitable outcomes. Banning certain perspectives and blacklisting certain views, while allowing certain others in a spirit of liberalism and progressive thinking, will not resolve anything. We have to remain more aware of the fact that there are multiple disagreements about and within law itself, especially about the role of Islamic laws in relation to Western legal systems today. The still widely prevailing trend to assume that adherence to Islamic law (and other culture-specific systems of law) is inherently violative of human rights, goes a little too far, to put it diplomatically.

There are at least five reasons for the continuing and quite remarkable resistance towards more plural perspectives; there may well be some more. Firstly, as noted above, most English (and Scottish) lawyers seem to carry now in their DNA an inbuilt reluctance to apply anything that is not seen as proper "law". In late modernity, that may be unsurprising. However, such negative and exclusionary positioning arises from the rather proud but misguided presumption that we actually know or agree on what we mean by "law".[25] In a globalised environment, it is depressingly bad news if eurocentric lawyers continue to be parochial positivists rather than skilful and versatile cosmopolitan pluralists. My long experience in teaching comparative law and different legal systems suggests that turning plain positivists into skilled legal navigators and consummate professionals in a global context is a tough task, but can be achieved.[26] Merely by birth into the modern age, our students seem to be primed today to privilege rationality and secularism, failing to realise without some guidance that law cannot be studied in black boxes.[27] We have also somehow forgotten that everywhere law and values remain deeply connected; Chiba's tripartite model of legal theory reinforced the realisation that there is simply no value-free jurisprudence.[28] The continuing Eurocentric orientation of most British legal

---

the law is and instead engages in politics. However well-meaning, this confuses legal practitioners and Muslims, too. See e.g. WARRAICH, S.A. and BALCHIN, C., *Recognizing the un-recognized: Inter-country cases and Muslim marriages & divorces in Britain* (WLUML Publications, 2006) and my review in *Immigration, Asylum and Nationality Law*, 20.4 (November 2006), pp. 307–10.

25 See *supra* note 5.

26 On good practice and a relevant model of legal education, see MENSKI, *supra* note 2, pp. 66–81.

27 TWINING, *supra* note 12, discusses this problem in depth.

28 CHIBA, *supra* note 7.

education, however, means that only few students benefit from such deeper jurisprudential exposure and analysis. Most legal education remains focused on black letter law and what one may call "legal plumbing", failing to empower future legal professionals in the competent handling of non-Western legal systems; there are few but notable efforts to make significant change.[29]

Secondly, and closely linked to this, since legal education simply does not prepare most law students for global and thus of necessity plural legal practice, comparative lawyers, often led by Professor Őrűcű, are and continue to remain really rare creatures. Many specialists in this field have recently retired or are soon due to relinquish their positions and one must worry about the next generation of scholars. Young academics do not normally secure jobs as experts in subjects like comparative law or Islamic law, even today; they are first of all hired for teaching bread-and-butter subjects of domestic law or maybe now in international law and/or human rights. Current austerity measures will make this worse. Regional experts and comparativists like Professors Cotterrell, Őrűcű, Woodman and myself, have always had to do at least two jobs to secure employment in the first place. Quite understandably, such raised barriers put many young people off.

Thirdly, Islamic law is still widely seen as irrelevant to our lives, even after the thoughtful speech by the Archbishop of Canterbury in 2008,[30] which was instantly attacked by a hostile press and a dishonest British government that claimed simply that we operate one law for all, and relied on the *status quo*. No admission was made, no hint was dropped, that sophisticated legal systems like English law indeed cultivate formal adherence to the Diceyan principle of "one law for all", but at the same time make targeted allowances and thus often quite rational exceptions for differences of all kinds. So we co-opt Islamic law – but only when it suits us – and doubts are in order whether the long-term implications of such exception-focused policy have been thought through by anyone so far. Thus the wider message of that important speech, which was not simply concerned about the place of Islamic law, but rather about the voice of religion and ethics at the global table of post-Enlightenment legal and political discourse, has not even been registered in sufficient depth in the minds of people who ought to know better. The proceedings of the Glasgow Workshop confirmed that, also north of the border between England/Wales and Scotland, a radically secular

29 See ÖRÜCÜ, E. and NELKEN, D. (eds.), *Comparative law. A handbook* (Hart Publishing, 2008).

30 See WILLIAMS, R., "Civil and Religious Law in England: A Religious Perspective", the now famous Foundation Lecture, delivered on 7 February 2008 by the Archbishop of Canterbury, which seemed to upset a lot of people not only because he talked about Sharia law in Britain, but brought natural law perspectives back into the arena of ongoing jurisprudential discussions. See www.archbishopofcanterbury.org/1575 [last accessed 20 June 2010].

perspective is assiduously at work to deny the right to freedom of speech for value-based discourses the moment they indicate any closeness or allegiance to religion.

Since we largely remain intellectually dishonest about the fact that religion *per se* (which in my understanding includes atheism and agnosticism) has continued to have a rather plural voice also in the post-Enlightenment world, it is easy to blacklist allegedly "fundamentalist" and "other" religions as the enemy and engage in hurtful positioning akin to Islamophobia. This seems to make things worse rather than opening avenues for liberal discourse. Seeking to ban religiously grounded talk about law, in an effort to be rational, neutral and subjective, we claim that as enlightened Western people, freed from the yoke of religion and the *diktats* of popes and other pompous figures, we are closer to finding truth and justice than anyone who uses moral or religious arguments. What this really still means is that natural law perspectives are deemed to be outdated. Engaging in such power plays, however, tends to overlook the inherent pompousness of self-serving rational secularity and all too easily comes across as secular fundamentalism. We are engaged, it is claimed, in a scientific discourse of law and its powers and effects. But in the process many players have become quite accustomed to simply silencing other voices that we have chosen to declare either non-existent or simply irrelevant for our day and age.

But since "we" are no longer just modern English or Scottish people, wishing to privilege concepts like secularism and even atheism over all other modes of thought, we seem to be running into trouble not only in discussions but also in legal regulation. Clearly, many people living among us now are Muslims, Hindus and members of many other minority ethnic or faith communities with their own religious and cultural traditions and perceptions. They will not abandon their ways of life just because they have come to live among us. Moreover, these ways of life are not just religious; they are in turn composed of religious-cum-secular elements, which the respective languages clearly demarcate as interlinked entities.[31] For such people, then, as we are told loud and clear in the new multicultural classrooms of the twenty-first century, not only in London or at SOAS, realisation of dynamic interlegality and recognition that legal pluralism is a fact are intrinsic parts of their personal identity. Of course this then impacts on how such people perceive "law" as a living entity rather than a mechanistic tool kit. What is also becoming clearer in today's postmodern discourses is that rejection of the denial of a place for religion does not mean one automatically becomes a rabid fundamentalist who bows to, or imposes on others, various

31 See on this issue the various articles in HUXLEY, A. (ed.), *Religion, law and tradition: Comparative studies in religious law* (Routledge Curzon, 2002).

forms of religious *diktat*. There is simply no real and necessary contradiction between being liberal and being religious.

While we should have known this all the time, it seems that we chose to dream about Enlightenment as an accomplished act of autonomisation and individualisation rather than a continuing challenge in surfing and managing multiple competing expectations.[32] In the same vein, many "white" Europeans, in particular, still continue to presume that persons who have come to live in the UK should just assimilate and "do as the Romans do", as Sebastian Poulter, so supposedly liberally, suggested some decades ago in the first major legal textbook on the subject.[33] The growing divergence between current patterns of increasingly strict legal imposition of such assimilation policies in various European countries and various counteracting tendencies among ethnic minority communities has meanwhile become deeply worrying. In family law, we see more recently – and with particular clarity in many unreported cases – that such conflicting trends lead to yet more skilful navigation and an increase in informal legal regulation patterns. Another navigation technique to manage such conflicts is simply recourse to familiar overseas jurisdictions, which then in turn creates new problems of formal recognition. New research on how British settlers in Turkey handle this challenge is eye-opening, to say the least.[34] Of course the concept of extraterritoriality is rather familiar to comparative lawyers, but we have conveniently forgotten that, too.

In socio-legal reality, this begins to indicate, we have failed to track and account for the emerging superdiversities in the living laws of the UK and elsewhere in Europe. Disappointed that unrealistic Eurocentric dreams have turned sour, various official laws almost everywhere in Europe now vigorously resist and oppose acceptance of such new legal realities, creating new injustices in the process and sparking off lively debates among academics. There is now a whole new literature on this mushrooming topic, again mainly focused on Muslims,[35]

32 See BORRADORI, G., *Philosophy in a time of terror. Dialogues with Jürgen Habermas and Jacques Derrida* (The University of Chicago Press, 2003).

33 POULTER, S., *English law and ethnic minority customs* (Butterworths, 1986). See also, with an explicit human rights argumentation, POULTER, S., *Ethnicity, law and human rights: The English experience* (Clarendon Press, 1998). I had several intense debates with Poulter before his untimely death. It became clear that we could not agree on these issues because as a quite radical secularist he refused to acknowledge a role for religion as a legally sanctioned force in our days, while I saw secularism as another form of religion or ethics.

34 BAYIR, D. and SHAH, P., "The socio-legal adaptation of British immigrants in Turkey: A theoretical puzzle". Paper presented at the International Conference on Transnationalism and Migration, 4–5 November 2010 in Stockholm.

35 See FERRARI, S. and CRISTOFORI, R. (eds.), *Law and religion in the 21st century: Relations between states and religious communities* (Ashgate, 2011). FOBLETS, M.-C., GAUDREAULT-DESBIENS, J.-F. and RENTELN, A.D. (eds.), *Cultural diversity and the law. State responses from around the world* (Bruylant and Éditions Yvon Blais, 2010). GRILLO, R., BALLARD, R.,

so that another reminder becomes necessary that this is not just a Muslim issue. Such new strains and stresses concern every aspect of our knowledge of how law as an internally plural entity functions globally and glocally in different cultural, socio-economic, ethical and more formally legal contexts.

Presently, most lawyers and judges still hide behind stiff formal definitions of law and thus end up officially denying certain individuals the right to use their "living law" as fully as they wish. Wishing to draw strict boundaries of "official law" and other forms of regulation in the interest of certainty, safety and much else, we claim, with increasing vigour these days, that such "others" do not really know what they are doing when they argue for a blurring of boundaries between "law" and other forms of management of life.[36] We claim to protect such perceived "children", as the new term "vulnerable adults" so clearly indicates, but quite who is to be classed as "vulnerable" remains to be seen.[37]

So we find that, blinded by the supposedly dangerous threats of "tradition" and "religion", many legal systems in Europe now seem to impose "ethnic penalties" in new forms. If the Danes are demanding that foreigners must marry only in their mid-twenties, and other nations follow suit,[38] we have strong evidence of such a trend. It has long been known that the British jail population, and more recently also mental health institutions and childcare homes, include many more – and now also new kinds of – non-white individuals than before. As in colonial times, we invent new legal categories and then skilfully hide behind such constructs to intervene in matters of Islamic law on our terms, failing to respect in the process the views and rights of Muslims and of other people. I am not saying there are no problems in what Muslims actually do when they engage in forced marriages, cousin marriages and "honour"-related killings, but there is much evidence of lack of full and open discussions to understand better what the various options for amelioration and legal management might be.[39]

FERRARI, A., HOEKEMA, A., MAUSSEN, M. and SHAH, P. (eds.), *Legal practice and cultural diversity* (Ashgate, 2009). MEHDI, R., PETERSEN, H., SAND, E.R. and WOODMAN, G.R. (eds.), *Law and religion in multicultural societies* (DJØF Publishing, 2008).

36 The most recent example of such resistance to legal pluralist perspectives is TAMANAHA, *supra* note 16.

37 Acting as an expert, I have begun to come across deeply disturbing cases of official misuse of this category in decisions behind closed doors.

38 Apparently Denmark increased the age limit to 24 in 2002, while the Netherlands followed suit in 2004 by increasing the age limit to 21 years. With effect from 27 November 2008, Rule 277 of the Immigration Rules (HC1113) was amended under English law to require that both spouses were 21 years of age. For details see the important case of *Diego Andres Aguilar Quila and Amber Aguilar v SSHD* [2010] EWCA Civ 1482 which challenged the proportionality of those legal measures. It was held that the new rule was a disproportionate inhibition on family and private life.

39 See e.g. HASAN, K., "The medical and social costs of consanguineous marriages among British Mirpuris", *South Asia Research* (2009) 29.3 (November), pp. 275–298.

A closely linked bigger issue is the ongoing battle over secularism, the prescription that law and religion should be strictly separated, and the dominant view that what one does in the public sphere should be subject to legal control. *Verstaatlichung*, as one calls it in German, more state intervention, battles everywhere with trends of *Entstaatlichung*, the trend for less state involvement, efforts to search for informal regulatory mechanisms. Most lawyers, however, and many judges, are simply not prepared to allow space for more informal regulation, perhaps fearing competition and loss of business and control. Indeed, one frequently hears the assertion that without formal laws there would be chaos. From that perspective, we still insist, for example, that all marriages and divorces must be registered to be legally valid. Such chains of arguments fail to notice – or maybe simply deny – that in many jurisdictions all around the world such state-centric forms of regulation are simply not practised and that the art of not being governed by state-centric laws is a highly prized survival skill not only among some remote communities.

The fifth and final ground for confusion to highlight here is not just lack of education and information, or control freakism, but a latent desire among English lawyers in particular to keep everything somewhat open and floating. It seems better for business not to clarify the law, to work from case to case, to litigate *de novo* rather than to rely on precedent. So we systematically do not report highly instructive cases that ought to be reported to educate lawyers and the public.[40] Since we do not share existing knowledge as efficiently as might be done, it becomes quite difficult for people, lawyers and judges to understand what is actually going on in relation to new developments within vast and complex fields like Islamic law. We also deliberately misrepresent what forms and patterns of "ethnic minority laws" actually exist and play politics with labelling. For example, using convenient stereotypes such as blanket reference to unilateral *talaq* divorce strategies among Muslims, while in reality many other forms of Muslim divorce exist and are being practised, serves the agenda of scholarly politics about systematic cultural damage inflicted on Muslim wives. Such bad-mannered politics even extend to jealousy over who should be working as an expert on Islamic law. Should this field be reserved only to Muslims or can indeed anyone become an expert in Islamic law?

3. METHODOLOGICAL BARRIERS

As a theorist of legal pluralism, informed also by frequent activity as an expert on South Asian laws in British and other court proceedings, I have over time developed a model of law that emphasises the co-existence and constant

40 For example, see the dower case of *Ali v Ali* (2000), discussed further below.

competition of different types of law. We are indeed dealing with intercultural conflicts of law here, not merely the standard concept of private international law. Such combination of theory and practice constantly reinforces the message that legal pluralism is a fact. It also illustrates all the time in various new culture-specific combinations that the earlier domination of natural law methodologies and perspectives did not result in their demise once state-centric positivism took over the main field of legal regulation. New forms of pluralism constantly develop, of course traversing the formal/informal and official-unofficial boundaries. This pluralist experience in practice has clearly helped me develop the theoretical models that I now use to teach about legal pluralism.

Starting from a decidedly socio-legal stance, this marked co-existence of different methodologies and types of law was at first represented as a triangular structure, in which legal positivism competes with forms of natural law and socio-cultural norms.[41] At that stage, the potential competition and intervention of international laws and human rights norms as new forms of natural law were still kept outside the model, but were beginning to make their presence felt as threats to the claims of the other three corners, even as dangerous monsters that might ruin the self-controlled ordering efforts of local patterns.[42] More recently, I have developed a kite model, in which the fourth corner is now clearly represented by international law, human rights and globalising pressures.[43] I now argue that these kite structures as mental constructs or actual regulatory mechanisms are potentially of four types: every individual can be viewed as a kite, and we can perceive whole societies as kites, too. Thirdly, every state can be seen or depicted as a kite structure, and fourthly there is also one huge global kite floating in the sky. One major analytical element for understanding this complex kite flying exercise is that all of these competing pulls exist and operate at the same time. This demonstrates that the older Maine-type evolutionary thinking, according to which one type of law replaced the other over time, is certainly not an appropriate approach for understanding the actual operation of pluralist legal regulation and competitive ordering.

Of course this also means that none of these models is a closed entity, since there are always going to be multiple boundary crossings between the various types of legal navigation depicted here; they occur at the same time, in the same cultural context, and they are thus bound to clash and rub against each other. Ideally such conflicts and tensions should not lead to crashes of the kites, but generate a state of symbiotic and more or less altruistic co-existence. The underlying pattern appears to be, one realises, that any one type of law actually needs the others to

41 See MENSKI, *supra* note 2, pp. 185–189 and p. 612.

42 *Ibid.*, pp. 3–24, and especially on "monsters" at p. 13.

43 See MENSKI, *supra* note 14 and other references in the same note.

achieve its objectives. Masaji Chiba, in another highly significant set of research articles from the 1980s, spoke in this context of different kinds of dichotomies, conflicts and tensions in other words, that are therefore probably an integral part of all legal navigation.[44]

I suggest that another theoretical model is helpful particularly for understanding why we may find certain difficulties in English and Scots law to handle matters of Islamic family law and other ethnic minority laws. We generally assume in Europe and North America that according to Diceyan principles we are operating one legal system for all persons present in a particular state, whether based on the linking factor of residence, domicile or citizenship. However, this image of uniformity is remarkably different from what happens in daily reality and in terms of practical application. So in theory the prevailing technique and methodology is to claim that there is one law for all, and we then seem to imagine a kind of closed box. In reality such a state-centric legal system constantly makes exceptions for certain scenarios. I wrote about this a few years ago, including pictures of those boxes, contrasting at that time the Eurocentric model of a uniform law with exceptions with the Asian/African model of the co-existence of general laws and personal laws.[45]

It is the latter system that most ethnic minorities living in our midst now, and certainly most Muslims, are deeply familiar with. It is this pattern which they often seek to reconstruct, frequently without realising this or being able to explain it. In many parts of the world, and most Islamic countries, too, there is indeed a pluralist structure of law in operation which bifurcates into a cluster of general laws applicable to all and various personal laws that apply to certain groups of people. These personal laws are mostly allocated on the basis of religion or community membership, giving rise in many current debates to human rights concerns about freedom of choice for individuals. However, some plurality-conscious states like India have added into this already plural structure a specific secular option, so that individuals can indeed choose and can opt out of their traditionally allotted system if they wish to or feel they have to. Such optional rules often apply to mixed marriages and other relationships between people from different communities and they may be the appropriate or even required law when a foreign party is involved. Awareness of the fact that different people may have different laws applied to them is thus part of the remembered history and probably also the "bone marrow" of many migrant communities. Again, we see that local English or Scottish populations have been left uneducated about

[44] See CHIBA, M., *Legal pluralism: Towards a general theory through Japanese legal culture* (Tokai University Press, 1989).

[45] See MENSKI, W., "Law, religion and South Asians in diaspora" in HINNELLS, J.R. (ed.), *Religious reconstruction in the South Asian diasporas. From one generation to another* (Palgrave Macmillan, 2007), pp. 243–264.

the presence of such pluralist patterns. Centuries of legicentric domination clearly hid the message that certain exceptions continue to be made, for example for Jews and Quakers when it comes to marriage law.[46]

Notably, the official Eurocentric claim that there is just one law for all was rapidly asserted by Gordon Brown in response to the Archbishop's speech of February 2008. But given the presence of exceptions, this dominant Diceyan axiom, though constantly reiterated, is actually an amazingly powerful fiction. The quote from John Griffiths, produced at the start of this article to state that legal pluralism is "the fact", while legal centralism is a fiction, makes even better sense in light of such comments.

When it comes to matters of Islamic law in the UK, therefore, such competing models of legal regulation clash, and have given rise to some rather interesting writing that may not be on most people's reading lists – if indeed it ever was.[47] I can conclude at this point that most lawyers in England and in Scotland, too, are simply not educated enough about legal pluralism to handle such clashes, so that many mistakes are being made in managing such legal diversities. The three case studies provided below convey a bittersweet message, therefore. Despite the absence of sound knowledge, in some cases, justice is delivered at the end of the day, but only after some near-disastrous legal turbulences, which more often than not are very costly in every respect.

4. THREE CASE STUDIES

These recent case studies illustrate the continuing insecurities and doubts with regard to the question whether in legal practice in the UK today we do not know about Islamic laws, or may not wish to know. The first case concerns an informal adoption of a young boy among Muslims in Azad Kashmir, a part of Pakistan with its own laws, a basic fact which until recently was not officially acknowledged and gave rise to much injustice. This is a horrible case concerning a young child being taken into care. It ended ultimately with the right result because fortunately I got involved as an expert and the Court was willing to listen to my detailed advice. The second case concerns marriages among Ahmadis in Pakistan, where my expert knowledge is simply not liked, as will become obvious, for multiple political reasons. The third legal problem focuses on continuing serious confusions over the formal legal recognition of Muslim divorces in Pakistan and Bangladesh. This continues to be a really messy area of the law in which even

46 For details see HAMILTON, C., *Family, law and religion* (Sweet & Maxwell, 1995).
47 KING, M. (ed.), *God's law versus state law. The construction of an Islamic identity in Western Europe* (Grey Seal, 1995).

South Asian lawyers are seen to be confused about their own laws, so we should not be surprised to find that English and Scottish lawyers and judges struggle to handle such conflicts.

4.1. THE ADOPTION CASE OF LITTLE ANAS

A childless Muslim couple living in Stoke-on-Trent made regular visits to their extended family in Azad Kashmir over several years. The wife's brother in Kashmir had many children, altogether ultimately seven. One day in 2004, the two women, who were also cousins, discussed that it would be rather nice if the next child born to the fertile sister-in-law would be given to the childless UK couple. The fertile woman discussed this with her husband, who readily agreed to help his sadly childless sister. The next child, a boy named Anas, was then born as the sixth child of his parents on 23 December 2005. At the age of only three days, he was informally transferred to his new mum and dad from Stoke-on-Trent. Of course he stayed with his birth mother, who seems to have nurtured him until he was weaned. In due course, questions were to arise whether this was a customary transfer of custody of the child or a full-fledged adoption in accordance with local custom. Or was it even a case of private surrogacy?

Entirely typical for Kashmiri local practice, no paperwork was prepared to document this family arrangement at the time and there is also no birth certificate for Anas. When he was about two years old, his new mother took Anas from Kashmir to Pakistan, declared him her own child and applied for a Pakistani passport for her child in Islamabad. This request was granted without much questioning, and Anas was taken to the UK in mid-2008. In February 2009, when a social worker in Stoke-on-Trent found out that the child had been adopted, Anas was immediately taken away from his parents, on the grounds that Islamic law does not permit adoption. The mother was accused of child trafficking and Anas was put into foster care. The distraught parents filed a case for recovery of the child and I became involved in July 2009 as an expert on Islamic law.

After considerable and disconcerting delay, I eventually received the case papers, including a set of Affidavits from the birth parents, dated 4 April 2009, which candidly explained the background to this family arrangement. It was obvious from these documents that the birth parents had entirely given up their rights over Anas; for all intents and purposes, his new parents were fully and irrevocably his parents now. Clearly, informally managed local Kashmiri Muslim customary norms had prevailed in this case over the standard rules of traditional Islamic law regarding adoption.

I explained this in detail in my Expert Report, and was relieved to find in November 2009 that the judge had given Anas back to his parents in Stoke-on-Trent, together with a recommendation that the child should now be formally adopted by both parents under English law, also because that would instantly give him British citizenship. So this adoption had and had not been accepted under English law. It was also noted by the judge that the adoptive father in Stoke had not directly been involved in the informal adoption process, so it seems that well-considered directions were made to safeguard the legal position of Anas. Everyone concerned was of course aware by then that English law knows the concept of "Special Guardianship" since 2002.

What should worry us, though, is that English lawyers and social workers can today simply snatch a child from a Muslim family on the basis of rather superficial knowledge of Islamic law and a rather general and broad presumption that adoption is prohibited among Muslims. Jumping to certain presently fashionable conclusions about child trafficking among Pakistanis or Kashmiris, it seems that quick-footed expert involvement, in this case, could protect the child's human rights and the human rights of the adoptive parents. The Kashmiri dimension of this case with its interplay of local custom and Islamic doctrine is of course highly intriguing. I have since had other cases, also from Africa, where locally arranged Muslim adoptions were the key issue. There is growing recognition worldwide that the traditional reservations of Islamic *shari'a* law about the fiction of adoption need to be analysed on a case-by-case basis.[48] Pluralism, here too, is the fact.

4.2. AHMADI MARRIAGES IN PAKISTAN

I have recently encountered a number of cases where an Ahmadi couple with links to Pakistan faced immigration problems, mostly for the wife, because the marriage had not been registered in accordance with certain formal processes that are deemed to apply. Such cases throw up the continuing lack of knowledge among English lawyers and even Home Office or UKBA staff abroad about the specific legal position of Ahmadis, who have since 1974 been treated as non-Muslims in Pakistan, are prohibited by criminal law from declaring themselves to be Muslims, and are prevented from using the provisions of the 1961 *Muslim Family Laws Ordinance* (MFLO) of Pakistan.

The brief facts in one specific case were that the husband lived with his prosperous parents in London and a marriage was arranged with a well-off

48 See O'HALLORAN, K., *The politics of adoption. International perspectives on law, policy & practice* (2nd ed.) (Springer, 2009).

Ahmadi girl from Lahore and was contracted in Lahore in September 2002. An indicator of the middle class status of the spouses is the *mahr* (dower) of 200,000 Rupees. The couple then lived together in London and in Pakistan, moving back and forth. Two sons were born in London, in December 2003 and March 2007. The mother then made an application to join her husband as a spouse for settlement in the UK in 2009 and in October 2009 was refused entry clearance on the basis that her marriage certificate of 18 September 2002 had not been registered by the Union Council in Pakistan. Thus the marriage was held to be invalid and the family was separated.

I expressed my surprise (at the risk of being seen as partisan) that the Home Office still should not know that unregistered marriages from Pakistan are perfectly legally valid, provided the required religious rituals had been followed. But what is the expected religious ritual in an Ahmadi marriage? And how would Ahmadis produce any form of marriage documentation if they cannot follow the Islamic law of Pakistan without risking criminal prosecution?

My Expert Report laid out what actually happens in practice these days. Given that a "normal" Muslim marriage contracted under Islamic law in Pakistan is first of all recorded in a private document, a *nikahnama*, and that such a marriage is legally valid in Islamic Pakistan as soon as offer and acceptance have been completed in the expected form, to insist on marriage registration amounts to the imposition of formal English legal rules on Pakistani law. That is clearly a *mala fide* act of official "gracelessness", as Professor Hanne Petersen from Copenhagen called it in a recent discussion. An important reported case, *Allah Rakha v Federation of Pakistan*, PLD 2000 FSC1, has clearly held that unregistered and properly contracted Muslim marriages in Pakistan are legally valid, so that the little word "shall" in section 5 of the MFLO is to be read as "should ideally", but certainly not as "must".

Since Ahmadis have been declared non-Muslims in Pakistan, how would they prove the existence of a legally valid marriage? They cannot simply claim that they had an Ahmadi wedding in accordance with custom, as the English courts are likely to reject such assertions of the emergence of a new custom. This kind of scenario, then, opens a can of worms and throws the matter into the hotbed of politics. While "normal" Muslims do not wish to know what Ahmadis are doing to cope with their officially imposed status as non-Muslims, Ahmadis themselves – including their leaders – are extremely nervous about disclosing what transpires from legal practice on the ground in Pakistan. Here again, legal pluralism raises its confusing head.

The position appears to be that, first of all, Ahmadi couples produce a private marriage certificate, which they cannot really call a *nikahnama*, but they still do.

Secondly, such couples may then register their marriage with the Marriage Section of the Sadr Anjuman Ahmadiyya Pakistan in Rabwah, an Ahmadi organisation based in a town in Pakistan that is known to be the centre of that country's Ahmadi community. This organisation thus acts now virtually as the equivalent of the local Union Council for all Ahmadis of Pakistan, a legal position that I found vigorously opposed by all sides, each for their own political reasons. Of course an Ahmadi *nikahnama* document by itself does not make the marriage legally valid, since the marriage was already legally validated when the offer and acceptance in accordance with Ahmadi customary rituals were completed. Some Ahmadis now appear with Affidavits from Pakistani lawyers (who may themselves be Ahmadis), certifying that the marriage in question "is true and according to the Rules and Regulations of Pakistan". Such odd wording hides the fact that there is no formally acknowledged marriage law for Ahmadis in Pakistan, but of course some form of legal regulation must exist for a community of probably several millions.

In another recent case of the same kind, I saw a registration document prepared under Pakistan's *Special Marriage Act* of 1872, an old colonial Act that is available to all kinds of odd couples and in cases of mixed marriages. Such documentary evidence confirms that Ahmadis in Pakistan, and as members of a global diaspora, are presently engaged in constructing a new personal law for themselves and, faced with hostile immigration laws abroad, are forced to become plurality-conscious, to use my pluralism tool kit terminology. Exploring all possible avenues for official documentation, knowing that this is what is expected by officials who do not understand that different Islamic laws have been developing in South Asia and elsewhere, they nevertheless run the risk, whether in London or Glasgow, to be treated as "dodgy Asians" rather than skilled legal navigators who must find acceptable solutions to document their marital relations. The result, as I see it now, is the gradually more visible full-fledged emergence of a new personal law in Pakistan, which will of course face multiple resistance in terms of formal legal recognition. But there is no alternative, given the way these people are treated by Pakistani law. British courts must learn to accept and formally recognise such new legal facts if we want to avoid piling blatant injustice on top of the injury inflicted on Ahmadis by Pakistani state law. Again, only recognition of legal pluralism can help judges and lawyers to disentangle this dangerous mess and to find a semblance of justice.

4.3. MUSLIM DIVORCE CASES FROM PAKISTAN AND BANGLADESH

There are many cases coming to English and also Scottish courts in which either a Muslim wife or a Muslim husband claims to be divorced under the law of

Pakistan or Bangladesh, i.e. the *Muslim Family Laws Ordinance* (MFLO) of 1961. But how does one read the provisions of section 7 MFLO, and quite how does one get validly divorced in those countries under Muslim law?

Two prominent kinds of court battle have given rise to repeated huge wastage of time and money, since nobody seems to wish to understand the law as it stands in Pakistan. As we saw earlier, in relation to the Ahmadi example, if an unregistered Muslim marriage is legally valid according to Pakistani law, the same by analogy also applies to divorce. So if there was any form of Muslim divorce, and certainly when there is evidence that the third and final *talaq* was pronounced, the couple are irrevocably divorced under Muslim law. Whether this is formally registered or not is not relevant, since the case of *Allah Rakha v. Federation of Pakistan*, PLD 2000 FSC 1, indicates the latest position, namely that in cases of doubt the *shari'a* law prevails in Pakistan over the provisions of the MFLO of 1961. But even most Pakistani lawyers do not wish to know or acknowledge this.

The resulting legal insecurities give rise to two kinds of pleadings before English and sometimes Scottish courts. Either a Muslim husband claims that he divorced his wife validly under the MFLO and has no further responsibility for his ex-wife, or a Muslim wife claims that she was not validly divorced under the MFLO, despite evidence that the divorce did take place. Fighting over the assumed requirement of formal "notice" as an aspect of "judicial or other proceedings", these are often extremely complex and deliberately convoluted cases, generally with one party hoping that nobody will know anything about legal practice in Pakistan. Normally one of the two parties is deliberately dishonest, but who? Much detective work is often required on the part of experts to get to the bottom of such cases.

Such case scenarios demand that lawyers and judges take account of relevant protective provisions of the English *Family Law Act* 1986, on the one hand, and of the MFLO 1961 on the other. Finding the right balance has continued to be a most difficult challenge. This kind of case, in particular, has often made me wonder whether we really do not know any better, or if we just do not wish to know. Clearly, maintaining this messy gold digging field is a brilliant source of additional revenue for lawyers and keeps the courts occupied, too.

5. CONCLUSIONS

The previous sentence may have said it all, but maybe it is totally wrong as an explanatory model. Perhaps it is indeed just too difficult for English or Scottish lawyers and judges to navigate the mentality and rules of Islamic law and of the even more complicated formal and informal regulatory frameworks of Pakistani and Bangladeshi Muslim family laws, in particular. British and other European legal practitioners are simply not prepared by their educational backgrounds and professional training for such complex pluralist challenges. The few experts that exist are in constant demand and complain of stress. As experts have finally begun to talk a bit more to each other, we discover – unsurprisingly, I suggest – that experts are to some extent exploited and victimised for the confusions that exist in this particular legal field.[49]

Two things are certain: Firstly, whether we actually do not know or do not wish to know about Islamic law in British legal practice today, the prevailing insecurities and lack of certainty are massively contributing to costs and human suffering in this field. Secondly, unless practitioners and judges become more plurality-conscious about the emerging super-diversity in family law litigation all over Europe, and also in North America now, this suffering will continue and there is a risk that everywhere Muslims will be blamed for our official systems' inability to hear their concerns and to take account of their specific legal needs.

Finally, in the current European legal systems and in North America, such needs do not necessarily extend to full-fledged recognition of *shari'a* as a personal law system, because that would not match the historical trajectory of European or North American legal regulation as it stands today. But that does not prevent clear-cut acknowledgement, in theory and in practice, that Muslims continue to have their own, internally plural and often highly sophisticated methods of dealing with family law matters and that they can expect respect for such concerns, if they are taken to our courts as *bona fide* matters. As it stands at present, however, far too many cases as brought to our courts attempt to exploit the opposing party by banking on the official system's ignorance of Islamic family law regulation, whether formal or informal. It is for this reason, too, that in the UK several Muslim self-help mechanisms such as the various Sharia Councils and the Muslim Arbitration Tribunal have been brought into the fray. The increasing diversity of available dispute settlement, and thus increased scope for forum shopping, suggests that awareness of legal pluralism as a fact will remain a key element for good decision making in this highly complex field. Whether we like it or not, Muslim law in its various forms is now inevitably part of new Europe's patterns of legal pluralism. Better levels of knowledge would be desirable, but better knowledge by itself does not guarantee a higher quality of justice, since knowledge can also be exploited for the wrong reasons. Judicial alertness, this suggests, will remain absolutely necessary. Hence more culture-

---

49 See HOLDEN, L. (ed.), *Cultural expertise and litigation: Patterns, conflicts, narratives* (Routledge, 2011).

specific training for judges may be a useful final suggestion to bring about approximation to best practice. If we can trust Jacques Derrida, who famously claimed that justice is always "in the making", that is anyway all we can hope for.

THE PLACE OF RELIGION IN FAMILY LAW: THE INTERNATIONAL PRIVATE LAW IMPERATIVE

Elizabeth B. CRAWFORD and Janeen M. CARRUTHERS

1. INTRODUCTION

Since it is one purpose of a legal system's international private law rules to accommodate and resolve issues of cross-cultural diversity, it is fundamental that any treatment of the place of religion in family law should take full account of conflict of laws rules, common law and legislative, which address the interface between religion and law in the private law sphere.

While legislative provision in the UK (domestic, conflict of laws, or both) dealing with the impact of religion on any given legal issue is disparate, the accumulated whole is notable for its width, subtlety, and detail. Additionally, the growing case law reveals the sensitivity of UK courts in matters of family law where religion may impinge. Family law is not the only subject area in which religious and cultural issues may be met with,[1] but currently it is the major one. The fact that, at the option of the parties whether or not to plead and prove foreign law, full use is not always made of the potential of conflict of laws rules to provide a satisfactory outcome,[2] does not detract from the essential role which Scots and English private international law rules play in recognising and upholding cross-cultural diversity. The attitude of UK courts in this regard is expressed in the words of Munby J., as he then was, in *Sulaiman v Juffali*[3] as follows:

> "Although historically [England] is part of the Christian west, and although it has an established church which is Christian, I sit as a secular judge serving a multi-cultural

1 See also, e.g., in the commercial arena: *Shamil Bank of Bahrain EC v Beximco Pharmaceuticals Ltd* [2004] 1 WLR 1784; *Halpern v Halpern (Nos 1 and 2)* [2008] QB 195; *Musawi v R.E. International (UK) Ltd and ors* [2008] 1 Ll's Rep 326; and *Jivraj v Hashwani* [2009] EWHC 1364.

2 E.g. *Mahmood v Mahmood* 1993 SLT 589; *Mahmud v Mahmud* 1994 SLT 599; *Sohrab v Khan* 2002 SLT 1255. Contrast *Singh v Singh (sub nom. Kaur v Singh)* 2005 SLT 749.

3 [2002] 2 FCR 427, at p. 439; and see further *R (on the application of Johns) v Derby City Council* [2011] EWHC 375) (Admin), per Munby L.J. at paras. [32] – [45].

> community of many faiths in which all of us can now take some pride, sworn to do justice 'to all manner of people'. Religion – whatever the particular believer's faith – is no doubt something to be encouraged but it is not the business of government or of the secular courts. So the starting point of the law is an essentially agnostic view of religious beliefs and a tolerant indulgence to religious and cultural diversity. A secular judge must be wary of straying across the well-recognised divide between church and state. It is not for a judge to weigh one religion against another. All are entitled to equal respect, whether in times of peace or, as at present, amidst the clash of arms."

This essay offers some examples of the manner in which the courts in Scotland and England, applying conflict of laws principles as part of the civil law of the land, treat parties' religious beliefs and cultural traditions.

2. MARRIAGE

2.1. POLYGAMY

The classic definition of marriage in the view of Scots and English law derives from the 19th century case of *Hyde v Hyde & Woodmansee*, where Lord Penzance conceived that, "... marriage, as understood in Christendom, may for this purpose be defined as the voluntary union for life of one man and one woman, to the exclusion of all others."[4]

The requirement that the relationship of married persons be exclusive presents obvious problems for UK courts in considering the validity, in the "UK" view, of polygamous marriages.[5] Polygamous relationships are special cases. Polygyny and the much less commonly found polyandry may be said to be rooted in culture rather than in religion per se, but nonetheless it is apt to include them in this account.

Polygamous marriages now are recognised for practically all purposes in Scots and English law, but such recognition is of relatively recent origin. The older view was that such "marriages" should not be recognised at all.[6] Lord Penzance in *Hyde*[7] remarked that, " ... it is obvious that the matrimonial law of this country

4 *Hyde v Hyde & Woodmansee* [1866] LR 1 P & D 130, per Lord Penzance at p. 133.

5 CRAWFORD, E.B. and CARRUTHERS, J.M., *International Private Law: A Scots Perspective* (3rd ed.) (W. Green, 2010), paras. 11–02 – 11–08.

6 *Hyde v Hyde and Woodmansee* [1866] LR 1 P & D 130; *Armitage* (1866) LR 3 Eq 343; *Re Bethell* (1888) 38 ChD 220; and *Brinkley v Att.-Gen* (1890) 15 PD 76. Recognition depended on status of marriage as monogamous or not.

7 *Ibid.*, at p. 135.

is adapted to the Christian marriage, and it is wholly inapplicable to polygamy". But his Lordship tempered that declaration with the words,

> "[t]his Court does not profess to decide upon the rights of succession or legitimacy which it might be proper to accord to the issue of the polygamous unions, nor upon the rights or obligations in relation to third persons which people living under the sanction of such unions may have created for themselves. All that is intended to be here decided is that as between each other they are not entitled to the remedies, the adjudication, or the relief of the matrimonial law of England."[8]

After 1945, it was realised that there was a growing case for the recognition, for some purposes, of polygamous marriages if permitted by the *lex loci celebrationis* and by the personal law(s) of the participants, and it began to be appreciated that the question was not whether such a marriage should be recognised in general or in the abstract, but whether it should be recognised for the particular purpose before the court; that is, it came to be appreciated that the problem concerned the incidents of the status, not the status itself. This change was seen first in *The Sinha Peerage Case*,[9] in which, in a peerage claim without aid of precedent, the son of a Hindu marriage was held entitled to succeed to the title. The marriage at its inception was potentially polygamous, but was never actually polygamous and had changed in nature through a change of religious sect by the parties before the birth of the son and, obviously, therefore, before the litigation.[10] From 1945, polygamous marriages began to be recognised by UK courts gradually over an increasingly wide field, including for the purposes of certain social security benefits, albeit on a benefit-specific basis.[11]

Though the consistorial remedies provided by Scots and English law were not available until 1972 to parties to a polygamous marriage,[12] prior to that time such a marriage was regarded as conferring upon the parties thereto the status of married persons, to the effect that, being married, they could not enter into subsequent monogamous unions. Annulments were granted of purported monogamous unions entered into by persons who previously had entered into

---

8 *Ibid.*, at p. 138.

9 1939, reported [1946] 1 All ER 348.

10 Hence, mutability of nature of a marriage received recognition as a concept; and the importance of *tempus inspiciendum* is clearly seen. See CRAWFORD and CARRUTHERS, *supra* note 5, paras. 11–09 – 11–11.

11 *Ibid.*, para. 11–08.

12 *Mehta* [1945] 2 All ER 690; *Risk* [1951] P 50; *Sowa* [1961] P 70; *Ohochuku* [1960] 1 WLR 183; and *Muhammed v Suna* 1956 SC 366; WEBB, P.R.H., "Potentially Polygamous Marriages and Capacity to Marry" (1963) 12 *ICLQ* 672; COWAN, Z., "A Note on Potentially Polygamous Marriages" (1963) 12 *ICLQ* 1407. See also ANTON, A.E., "The 'Christian Marriage' Heresy", 1956 *SLT (News)* 201.

marriages polygamous in nature.[13] To this extent, therefore, polygamous marriage was recognised.

The position with regard to the availability of consistorial remedies in UK courts was altered materially by the Matrimonial Proceedings (Polygamous Marriages) Act 1972,[14] section 2 of which provides that the fact that a marriage was entered into under a law which permits polygamy shall not preclude a British court from entertaining proceedings for divorce, nullity, separation etc. Since 1972, the issue of a marriage's character (that is, whether it is actually or potentially polygamous, or monogamous) has been less important since, for jurisdiction in matters of status to exist in the UK, it is no longer necessary for a marriage to bear the character of monogamous as it comes to court. According to the balance of authorities, the character of a union is determined initially by the *lex loci celebrationis*,[15] though later, for the particular purpose before the court, the decision upon classification is for the forum.[16] A marriage bears a mark, but not an indelible mark. Characterisation rests, therefore, on a territorial connecting factor in the first instance, and then on the discretionary power of the forum. Initial characterisation by the law of the place of celebration is likely to be influenced, in turn, by the tenets of the religion there prevalent.[17] The nature of any marriage celebrated in Scotland necessarily is monogamous despite the scope for a wide variation in locus and form of ceremony,[18] and regardless of the personal law(s) of the parties thereto.

As regards the question of capacity to enter a union which, at the outset, is characterised as non-monogamous, it is clear that no Scottish or English domiciliary has legal capacity by his or her personal law to enter an *actually* polygamous marriage, in Scotland or abroad.[19] Ingenuity of argument was deployed in *Hussain v Hussain*,[20] at a particular point in the development of the subject, to persuade the Court of Appeal that the nature of a marriage at the

13 *Srini Vasan* [1946] P 67; *Baindail* [1946] P 122.

14 As amended by Divorce Jurisdiction, Court Fees and Legal Aid (Scotland) Act 1983, s. 6(2); Law Reform (Husband and Wife) Act 1984, s. 9(1); Family Law (Scotland) Act 1985, s. 28(1). The equivalent English provisions are contained now in the Matrimonial Causes Act 1973, s. 47.

15 *R. v Hammersmith Superintendent Registrar of Marriages, ex p. Mir-Anwaruddin* [1917] 1 KB 634; *R. v Naguib* [1917] 1 KB 359; *Lendrum v Chakravarti* 1929 SLT 96; *MacDougall v Chitnavis* 1937 SC 390; *Qureshi v Qureshi* [1971] 1 All ER 325 (*obiter*).

16 *Lee v Lau* [1967] P 14, *per* Cairns J. at p. 20. It is for the forum to determine whether a multi-party relationship is an instance of polygamy or merely concubinage.

17 *Cheni (otherwise Rodriguez) v Cheni* [1965] P 85, *per* Sir Jocelyn Simon P, at pp. 86–87.

18 Marriage (Scotland) Act 1977, extended by Marriage (Scotland) Act 2002.

19 Scots law: *McDougall v Chitnavis* 1937 S 390; Marriage (Scotland) Act 1977, s.2(3)(b) and s.5(4)(b). English law: see Matrimonial Causes Act 1973, s. 11(d), and *Hussain v Hussain* [1982] 3 All ER 369, now subject to Private International Law (Miscellaneous Provisions) Act 1995, ss. 5, 6 and 7.

20 [1982] 3 All ER 369.

point of celebration in Pakistan could not be potentially polygamous since the man, being of English domicile, lacked legal capacity by his personal law to enter into such a union, and the woman, although of Pakistani domicile, lacked capacity as a female ever to take an additional, concurrent spouse. This decision served to solve a particular problem[21] to which now there is a statutory solution. The Private International Law (Miscellaneous Provisions) Act 1995 made provision[22] to the effect that a person of Scots domicile may enter into a *potentially* polygamous marriage, which marriage shall be treated as a monogamous marriage for every day that it remains so. This removes doubt about the validity of marriages entered into abroad by persons of British residence and uncertain domicile, where, by the *lex loci celebrationis* (e.g. Pakistan), the nature of all marriages at the point of celebration is potentially polygamous (i.e. giving one spouse, normally the husband, the legal entitlement to take concurrently more than one wife).[23] Capacity so to marry rests therefore on the personal law of the parties ascertained at the point of marriage, and in accordance with the content of that/those law(s) at that date.[24]

The UK position is one of tolerance and recognition of polygamy, therefore, for those whose personal law(s) permits it, and where the marriage took place abroad, but to withhold approval (subject to the 1995 Act) for those whose personal law, established by means of domicile, is Scottish or English. This bifurcated approach can be seen also in the Scottish and English conflict rules pertaining to recognition of foreign extrajudicial consistorial decrees. While such (polygamous) marriages and (religious) divorces are capable of recognition in the UK, care is taken to protect, or inhibit, those individuals having personal law links with the UK through domicile or residence, for whom secular norms (for this purpose exemplified by monogamous marriage and civil divorce) are appropriate.

---

21 See, in English law, Matrimonial Causes Act 1973, original wording of s. 11(d) (now amended in light of Private International Law (Miscellaneous Provisions) Act 1995, s. 5) which provided that a marriage should be void in the case of a polygamous marriage entered into outside England and Wales where either party at the time of the marriage was domiciled in England and Wales. The provision extended to potentially polygamous marriages. For background, see NORTH, P.M. and FAWCETT, J.J., *Cheshire and North's Private International Law* (13th ed.) (Butterworths, 1999), pp. 752–755.

22 S. 7 for Scotland; as to England and Wales, see ss. 5 and 6 (retrospective effect, subject to conditions therein contained).

23 Unlike the equivalent English provisions, the rule in s. 7 of the 1995 Act is not retrospective.

24 Contrast *Starkowski v Attorney General* [1954] AC 155, in which the House of Lords felt able to give effect to changes in the content of the *lex loci celebrationis*, so as to rectify a flaw in the formalities of the ceremony, *i.e.* to ratify retrospectively civil registration of a purely religious marriage ceremony.

2.2. LEGAL CAPACITY TO MARRY

More generally, the question whether a person has legal capacity to enter into a marriage is regulated in Scots law, by virtue of section 38(2) of the Family Law (Scotland) Act 2006, by the law of the place where, immediately before the marriage, that person was domiciled. This is a statutory crystallisation of the pre-existing, favoured dual domicile theory at common law.[25] Being cumulative in effect, it operates to insist upon the application of the more stringent rule as between the personal laws of the parties intending to marry. In the case of non-Scottish domiciliaries, application of the dual domicile theory has resulted in the recognition in Scotland of marriages which have taken place abroad[26] between persons related more closely in blood or by affinity than is permitted by domestic Scots law, where such marriages are valid by the law(s) of the domicile(s) of the parties. That which is applied, subject to public policy,[27] is the civil law of the domicile(s) of the parties, not their religious law(s), but the municipal legal system of the domicile occasionally may be found to be coincident with the religious rules of some particular denomination.[28]

An important common law authority is *Cheni (otherwise Rodriguez) v Cheni*[29] which came before Sir Jocelyn Simon P. The case is rich in interest, and relevance, for it concerned not only a matter of consanguinity, but also the nature of a union as potentially polygamous at its inception, but capable of changing irrevocably to monogamous in character in accordance with Sephardic Jewish law upon the birth of a child within ten years (which event happened). The parties, who were uncle and niece, married in Cairo according to Jewish rites in 1924. They lived in Egypt until 1957, when they moved to England where the husband established a domicile of choice. In 1961 the wife sought from an English court a declaration that the marriage was null and void on the ground of consanguinity, or in the alternative, that it be dissolved on the ground of the husband's cruelty. The forum, satisfied that it had jurisdiction, the marriage being monogamous in character by the date of the proceedings,[30] thereafter proceeded to address the issues of its essential and formal validity. In the matter of formal validity of marriage, expert evidence was offered that the municipal law of Egypt applied the religious law of the parties. There was no provision for civil marriage in Egypt. The locus would accept a marriage valid by the parties'

---

25 CRAWFORD and CARRUTHERS, *supra* note 5, paras. 11–18 and 11–19.

26 The dual domicile theory is further fortified in Scots law by s. 38(3), which requires capacity according to the *lex loci celebrationis* where the locus is Scots.

27 S. 38(4), 2006 Act. See below, pp. 43-45.

28 *Russ v Russ* [1964] P 315; *Cheni (otherwise Rodriguez) v Cheni* [1965] P 85. Cf. and contrast *Sottomayor v De Barros (No 2)* (1879–80) LR 5 PD 94.

29 [1965] P 85.

30 CRAWFORD and CARRUTHERS, *supra* note 5, para. 11–03.

Jewish or other religious law. Consequently, by Egyptian law, the marriage was formally valid and so also by English law, through the operation of its choice of law rules.

The marriage being formally valid, the court considered the question of legal capacity to marry, and public policy issues arising in connection therewith. Although the judgment contains much interesting discussion of biblical text concerning the propriety of uncle-niece marriages in Christian churches of all denominations, and evidence was given that uncle-niece marriage (but not aunt-nephew marriage, which is deemed to reverse the natural order of authority) is in accordance with Jewish law, the crucial point was that the marriage was valid by the law of the parties' Egyptian domicile, "which is the proper law by which capacity to marry is to be tested".[31] Thereafter, the question was whether such a marriage was incestuous in the view of the forum to the point where it so offended English public policy that the rule of the law of the domicile could not be accepted. An interesting question is whether, or to what extent, the policy of the English court as expressed in its own domestic law is influenced by religious texts. In the matter of prohibited degrees, the basis of Scots law is biblical.

Counsel for the wife argued that such unions being incestuous by the general, though not by the universal, consent of Christendom (or, as he preferred to put it, by "the general consent of civilised nations"), annulment should be granted. Sir Jocelyn Simon P said that he believed the true rule to be,

> "that the courts of this country will exceptionally refuse to recognise and give effect to a capacity or incapacity to marry by the law of the domicile on the ground that … it … would be unconscionable in the circumstances in question."[32]

In the instant circumstances, the judge concluded that non-recognition of the marriage on this ground was not justified. In handling the public policy challenge, the court will "seek to exercise common sense, good manners and a reasonable tolerance."[33] Further, he took the view that the validity of marriages in this respect require to be considered not as a generality, but in relation to a particular marriage. In the instant case, the marriage was valid by the religious law of the parties' common faith, and by the municipal law of their common domicile at the point of the marriage. Moreover, the marriage had stood unquestioned for 35 years,[34] and had produced a child whose status would be

---

31 [1965] P 85, at p. 89.

32 *Ibid.*, p. 98.

33 *Ibid.*

34 But is this a logical consideration, or a self-serving rationalisation? What weight should be given to this factor? Does a policy in favour of the upholding of a longstanding, apparently valid marriage arise, and be required to be ranked by the forum, against its notions of

prejudiced by the grant of an annulment. This latter point raises an important point of different policy, namely, the importance (then) of the legitimacy or otherwise of the child.[35] While the combination of policies assisted Sir Jocelyn in coming to his conclusion, such decisions rest upon the discretion of the forum, and of the individual judge seized. The judge, in striking language, remarked that,

> "If the general consent of civilised nations were to be the test, I do not think that the matter can be resolved by, so to speak, taking a card-vote of the United Nations and disregarding the views of the many civilised countries by whose laws these marriages are permissible."[36]

It is a feature of his opinion that Sir Jocelyn received and considered evidence of the religious stance on such unions taken by certain Protestant traditions and by Roman Catholicism.

In Scots conflict rules, the public policy challenge to the dual domicile theory has always been available, and remains available under the statutory scheme in section 38(4) of the Family Law (Scotland) Act 2006. In earlier years, Scots and English courts on occasion were required to deal with public policy objections to incapacity to marry, under the head of "penal incapacities". In *MacDougall v Chitnavis*,[37] a woman of Scots domicile purported to marry in Scotland an Indian domiciliary, Hindu by religion. Subsequently she sought to have the marriage declared null by the Court of Session, arguing that the defender had no legal capacity to enter into the marriage in question since, by the law of his Indian domicile, he was incapable of marriage with a non-Hindu for as long as he remained of Hindu religion. The case presents an interesting example of the inter-relationship between a party's personal law and religious law; as a matter of Indian municipal law, the prohibition or incapacity affected only those persons domiciled in India who adhered to the Hindu religion, and not to all persons domiciled in India. Lord President Normand followed the English authority of *Chetti*[38] in holding that a personal disability imposed on a man by the laws of his Indian domicile and Hindu religion does not prevent him from entering into a valid marriage in the UK. The Lord President noted the religious and temporal restriction on the incapacity, observing that the restriction was not in *pari casu* with, for example, the incapacity of nonage in Scots law, which applies universally

---

propriety? Cf. *Radwan (No 2)* [1972] 3 All ER 1026. Contrast *Administrator of Austrian Property v Von Lorang* 1927 SC (HL) 80, in which for financial reasons, a marriage which had stood unquestioned for 30 years was declared null and void as a result of defect in formalities.

35 A policy which arose also in *Gray (otherwise Formosa) v Formosa* [1963] P 259, e.g. *per* Lord Denning M.R., at pp. 268–269.

36 [1965] P 85, at p. 98.

37 1937 SC 390.

38 *Chetti v Chetti* [1909] P 67.

to all persons "within Scotland".[39] Moreover, it was a disability of which the defender of his own volition could have rid himself. His Lordship found no case in Scotland or England where a disability of this type had founded an annulment; rather was the opposite conclusion reached in *Chetti*. The Scottish court concluded in *MacDougall* that, "[i]t is certainly a disability of a kind alien to our own law."[40] Such a conclusion in effect disapproves on policy grounds the foreign imposed disability (as opposed to disapproving on policy grounds a foreign conferred capacity). So too, although there are few cases to vouch the point, would be treated incapacities upon marriage such as vows of celibacy imposed by religious orders. The 2006 Act makes no express reference to the common law exception of penal incapacity, and it is likely that such a prohibition would fall to be treated now within the terms of section 38(4).

More recently in England, the Court of Appeal was required to consider issues of capacity and public policy in *Westminster City Council v C*.[41] The circumstances were that C, a 25 year old man of severely impaired intellectual functioning, and suffering from autism, was found to have taken part, at the instigation of his parents, in a Muslim marriage ceremony. C was domiciled in England and the other party to the ceremony, K, was of Bangladeshi domicile. The Court of Appeal found that the application of the dual domicile rule (to the effect that C had no mental - and therefore legal - capacity to enter into marriage by the English law of his domicile, leading to non-recognition of the purported marriage in the view of English law) did no violence to the general policy *in favorem matrimonii*. Rather, C's incapacity rendered the marriage sufficiently offensive to the conscience of the court that it should on public policy grounds refuse to recognise it. That this result would receive nothing but approbation from a UK private law and policy perspective indicates a "profound difference in culture and thinking between domestic English notions of welfare and those embraced by Islam".[42] The unchallenged expert evidence was that to the Bangladeshi mind the marriage was perceived as a protection for C, guaranteeing him a safe future when his parents could no longer look after him. To the English mind, however, the purported marriage was exploitative and abusive not only of C, but also of K, notwithstanding that she apparently consented in the full knowledge of C's disability.

It can be seen that in this instance a combination of the fortuity of English jurisdiction and the application of an English personal law secured a result which

---

39 *I.e.*, presumably, those persons purporting to marry in Scotland and/or persons of Scots domicile. See Marriage (Scotland) Act 1977, s. 1(1) and (2).

40 *MacDougall v Chitnavis* 1937 SC 390, at p. 403. But see different approach taken in *Lendrum v Chakravarti* 1929 SLT 96.

41 [2009] Fam 11. See also *X City Council v MB* [2006] 2 FLR 968.

42 *Ibid.*, *per* Wall L.J. at para. 44.

satisfied English notions of propriety and policy. If the personal law safeguard were removed, and supposing that C had been of Bangladeshi domicile at the date of purported marriage, there would remain only the shield of territorial link and the exercise of discretion within an admittedly debateable jurisdiction,[43] to protect, as English law would see it, the vulnerable person.

Though the form of marriage by telephone seems inappropriate and inadequate against the background of Scots and English domestic marriage law, it is one which, according to expert evidence in *Westminster City Council*, is a "form of celebration of marriage ... increasingly common and accepted as entirely valid in Islamic practice."[44] Since the marriage foundered on the absence of consent, the matter of identification of the *lex loci celebrationis*, providing the connecting factor by which to judge the formal validity of the marriage, was left undecided by the judge at first instance, and not debated in the Court of Appeal. However, *obiter*, it appears to have been accepted that the locus of the marriage celebration was Bangladesh. The groom, his siblings, and an imam were present in London, while the bride, her family and a *khazi* (Sharia judge), who officiated at the ceremony and issued the certificate of marriage, were present in Bangladesh, and the dowry was paid over in Bangladesh. In effect, on the analogy of contract, it was agreed by counsel that the marriage was concluded in Bangladesh. Were the locus to have been regarded as English, the marriage would have been defective in form. The conflict of laws reasoning is recognisable.[45]

In terms of section 38(3) of the 2006 Act, Scots law insists upon its own application in the matter of capacity to marry where the *locus celebrationis* is Scotland.[46] Where the *locus* is overseas, or deemed to be so, and if neither party to the purported marriage has a Scottish personal law, Scots law cannot insist on its own application in the matter of capacity. Rather, its influence is limited to a refusal to apply the law of the domicile on the grounds of policy if an issue of recognition of that overseas marriage should arise in Scotland. Inevitably, and properly, the authority or *vires* based upon territoriality recedes as the link with the territory diminishes, and the *vires* based upon domicile exists only so long as one party at least is of Scots domicile.

---

43 *Re S (Hospital Patient: Court's Jurisdiction) (No 2)* [1995] 4 All ER 30. There is an inherent jurisdiction of the English court to protect the welfare of incapable adults, based upon presence within the jurisdiction.

44 Para. 34.

45 *Apt v Apt* [1948] P 83; *Ponticelli v Ponticelli* [1958] P 204; *Brinkibon v Stahag Stahl* [1982] 1 All ER 293. Cf. *McCabe v McCabe* [1994] 1 FLR 410.

46 As to which see Marriage (Scotland) Act 1977, s. 5.

3. EXTRA-JUDICIAL DIVORCES AND ANNULMENTS

3.1. BACKGROUND

It has been said that the apparent simplicity of a policy of cross-border recognition of divorce and of annulment hides a multiplicity of underlying tensions of different types, e.g. political tensions; moral tensions; tensions between the religious and the secular viewpoints; between regionalism and internationalism; between liberalism and conservatism.[47] This is particularly true in relation to divorces obtained extra-judicially.

For example, under Jewish Rabbinical law, and under the law of the state of Israel,[48] a husband may dissolve a marriage to which he is a party by delivering to his wife a letter of divorce, called a *ghet* (or *gett* or *get*). The *get* is a form of bilateral consensual divorce, executed by the husband in a court of Jewish law in the presence of three *dayanim* (ecclesiastical judges) and delivered to the wife in person, in the presence of two qualified witnesses, with the husband declaring, in a prescribed formula, the import of the instrument of divorce. The *get* represents the spouses' joint free will to bring their marriage to an end. Under Israeli civil law, divorce is obtained solely by the religious *get* procedure. Though the procedure necessitates a husband's appearance before a Rabbinical court, the proceeding is a formality and is not accompanied by a judicial finding and pronouncement.[49]

Under Islamic law,[50] a husband is permitted to divorce his wife without any reference to a civil court. Such a divorce, by *talak* (or *talaq)*, merely requires him to state unequivocally three times his intention to repudiate the marriage. In some countries, no further formality is required than this "bare" *talak*.[51] In other Islamic law jurisdictions, it is necessary also either to register such a divorce with a court or administrative body or, as under the Pakistan Muslim Family Laws

47 NI SHUILLEABHAIN, M., *Cross-Border Divorce Law: Brussels II Bis* (Oxford University Press, 2010), Preface.

48 See BERKOVITS, B., "Transnational divorces: the Fatima Decision" (1988) 104 *LQR* 60.

49 E.g. *Har-Shefi v Har-Shefi (No 2)* [1953] P 220; *Broit v Broit* 1972 SLT (Notes) 32; *Maples v Maples* [1988] Fam 14; *Berkovits v Grinberg* [1995] Fam 142; and *O v O (Jurisdiction: Jewish Divorce)* [2000] 2 FLR 147; and see BERKOVITS, *ibid.*, pp. 81–93. See pp. 54–56, below.

50 See generally REHMAN, J., "The Sharia, Islamic Family Law, and International Human Rights Law: Examining the Theory and Practice of Polygamy and Talaq" (2007) 21 *International Journal of Law, Policy and the Family* 108, at p. 118 *et seq.*; and *El Fadl v El Fadl* [2000] 1 FCR 685, per Hughes J. at p. 694 *et seq.*

51 E.g. *Sharif v Sharif* (1980) 10 Fam Law 216 (Iraq); *Zaal v Zaal* (1982) 4 FLR 284 (Dubai); *Chaudhary v Chaudhary* [1985] Fam 19 (Kashmir); and *Sulaiman v Juffali* [2002] 2 FCR 427.

Ordinance (VIII) 1961,[52] to go through supplementary procedures giving the opportunity of reconciliation proceedings.[53] Islamic law also provides other forms of divorce, such as by *khula*, a form of divorce by agreement on the suggestion of the wife.[54]

Examples of extra-judicial annulments are much less easy to provide, but there are instances of annulment by an ecclesiastical rather than civil tribunal.[55] It may matter for the parties' religious sensibilities that an annulment rather than a divorce is granted; or, more commonly, that a canon law annulment be granted after a civil divorce, in order that remarriage can take place in a Roman Catholic church. An ecclesiastical annulment may be recognised in the UK, but not if the status of the marriage has already been adjudicated upon, to contrary result, in a British court, an outcome which illustrates the principle of *res judicata*, the desirability of avoiding irreconcilable judgments, and the supremacy within the UK of the secular law in matters of status.

3.2. RECOGNITION OF OVERSEAS DIVORCES AND ANNULMENTS

At common law English courts originally were reluctant to recognise the effectiveness and validity of extra-judicial divorces;[56] but attitudes changed over time and became less strict. It has been accepted, on a statutory footing since 1971, that extra-judicial divorces will be recognised if the general jurisdictional criteria for recognition have been established. Policy objection may require recognition to be withheld, but this is true of divorces judicial and extra-judicial. Recognition in Scotland of a divorce, legal separation or marriage annulment granted by a court of an EU Member State (apart from Denmark) depends upon the scheme of recognition contained in Brussels II*bis*.[57] Recognition of Danish decrees, and non-EU decrees, is regulated, however, by the Family Law Act 1986.

52 See *Qureshi v Qureshi* [1972] Fam 173; *R v Registrar General of Births, Deaths and Marriages, ex p Minhas* [1977] QB 1; *Quazi v Quazi* [1980] AC 744; *R v Secretary of State for the Home Department, ex p Fatima* [1986] AC 527.

53 See *Radwan v Radwan* [1973] Fam 24 (Egypt).

54 *Quazi v Quazi* [1980] AC 744.

55 *Di Rollo v Di Rollo* 1959 SC 75; *Butterley v Butterley* (1974) 48 DLR (3d) 351. See now Family Law Act 1986, s. 46(1), set out at pp. 49-50, below.

56 E.g. *R v Hammersmith Superintendent Registrar of Marriages, ex p Mir-Anwarrudin* [1917] 1 KB 634. See generally CRAWFORD and CARRUTHERS, *supra* note 5, para. 12–33.

57 Council Regulation (EC) No 2201/2003 concerning Jurisdiction and the Recognition and Enforcement of Judgments in Matrimonial Matters and Matters of Parental Responsibility, repealing Regulation (EC) No 1347/2000.

3.2.1. *EU divorce, legal separation or marriage annulment*

The position with regard to the recognition of religious divorces granted in a country of the EU requires to be considered. If membership of the EU continues to expand, and comes to include, e.g. predominantly Muslim countries, the applicability of the Brussels II*bis* Regulation to religious divorces will become an important issue.[58] In view of the EU family law harmonisation programme, it is necessary to determine the extent of application, if any, of Brussels II*bis* to the matter of recognition of extra-judicial divorces.

Article 1.1 of Brussels II*bis* states that the Regulation shall apply "whatever the nature of the court or tribunal, in civil matters relating to divorce, legal separation or marriage annulment." The system of recognition depends upon jurisdiction having been assumed in terms of Article 3 of the Regulation, which states that jurisdiction shall lie with the *courts* of a Member State, broadly speaking, on the grounds of habitual residence of one or both parties.[59] For a religious divorce to fall under Brussels II*bis*, therefore, the religious tribunal would have to satisfy Article 1.1 (scope), which *ex facie* it would seem to do. The terms of the Regulation are somewhat ambivalent, and might be apt to include divorces involving the participation by a religious court or tribunal, such as the Jewish *get* issued by the Rabbinical court. A case could be presented that Article 1.1 can be interpreted so as to include religious divorces, but arguably this was not the intention of the EU draftsmen. A reported case is awaited.

3.2.2. *Non-EU divorce, legal separation or marriage annulment*

The law on recognition in the UK of non-EU, overseas divorces, annulments and legal separations is to be found in the Family Law Act 1986. In terms of section 46:

> "(1) The validity of an overseas divorce, annulment or legal separation obtained by means of proceedings shall be recognised if–
>
> (a) the divorce, annulment or legal separation is effective under the law of the country in which it was obtained;[60] and
> (b) at the relevant date either party to the marriage–
>
> (i) was habitually resident in the country in which the divorce, annulment or legal separation was obtained; or

58 Cf. note 111 *infra*.

59 See CRAWFORD and CARRUTHERS, *supra* note 5, para. 12–07.

60 See *Kellman v Kellman* [2000] 1 FLR 785; *Emin v Yeldag* [2002] 1 FLR 956; *H v H (Validity of Japanese Divorce)* [2006] EWHC 2989 (Fam), [2007] 1 FLR 1318; and *H v H (talaq divorce)* [2007] EWHC 2945 (Fam).

(ii) was domiciled in that country; or
(iii) was a national of that country.

(2) The validity of an overseas divorce, annulment or legal separation obtained otherwise than by means of proceedings shall be recognised if–

(a) the divorce, annulment or legal separation is effective under the law of the country in which it was obtained;
(b) at the relevant date–

(i) each party to the marriage was domiciled in that country; or
(ii) either party to the marriage was domiciled in that country and the other party was domiciled in a country under whose law the divorce, annulment or legal separation is recognised as valid; and

(c) neither party to the marriage was habitually resident in the United Kingdom throughout the period of one year immediately preceding that date.

(3) In this section "the relevant date" means–

(a) in the case of an overseas divorce, annulment or legal separation obtained by means of proceedings, the date of the commencement of the proceedings;
(b) in the case of an overseas divorce, annulment or legal separation obtained otherwise than by means of proceedings, the date on which it was obtained."

The subject of recognition of extra-EU, extra-judicial religious divorces[61] resolves itself into a consideration of whether the divorce can be said to be a "proceedings" divorce or an "otherwise than by means of proceedings" divorce. With regard to the latter, the Act requires evidence of a stronger connection between both parties to the marriage and the territory whence the divorce emanates than is the case with the former. Furthermore, by section 46(2)(c), neither party[62] to the marriage must have been habitually resident in the UK for one year preceding the date on which the "otherwise than by means of proceedings" divorce etc was obtained.

What constitutes "proceedings" is the question central to most reported cases on this topic.[63] Opinion in the religious communities from which such divorces

61 Or annulments.

62 The prior rule had withheld recognition only if both parties had been habitually resident in the UK for one year before pronouncement of divorce (Domicile and Matrimonial Proceedings Act 1973, s. 16) and so the current formulation of this rule is stricter.

63 See, e.g. *Chaudhary v Chaudhary* [1984] 3 All ER 1017. See also *El-Fadl v El-Fadl* [2000] 1 FLR 175; *Ahmed v Ahmed* 2006 SLT 135; *Abbassi v Abbassi* [2006] EWCA Civ 355 (Fam); and *H v H (talaq divorce)* [2007] EWHC 2945 (Fam).

spring may not be convinced of the rightness of the "proceedings" distinction enshrined in UK legislation, nor of the feasibility of obtaining official certificates to demonstrate that the divorce etc was effective under the law of the country in which it was obtained. There has been no amendment in the intervening years of this latter requirement; its insertion and continued existence may be thought to evidence cross-cultural misunderstanding.

Additionally, certain safeguards, in the way of adequate notice and procedural justice,[64] operate to justify denial of recognition, where necessary in the view of the forum. These differ according to whether the divorce is "proceedings" or otherwise, which is a sensible acknowledgment of reality.[65] Perhaps most importantly in the context of extra-judicial divorce etc, recognition can be withheld on the grounds of public policy.[66] Section 51 of the 1986 Act permits non-recognition if the divorce is "manifestly contrary to public policy". It is noteworthy that this sweeper provision applies indiscriminately to proceedings and non-proceedings divorces, i.e. to judicial and non-judicial divorces, and within non-judicial, to the relatively formal and the bare dissolution.

It is speculated that the introduction of the Matrimonial and Family Proceedings Act 1984 (which permits a Scottish or English court to supplement a foreign award, judicial or extra-judicial, with an order for financial provision, if it is deemed that the original provision is lacking) has resulted in a reduction in the number of cases brought in the UK querying the validity of an overseas religious divorce, where the overarching purpose of the action was to secure financial provision otherwise absent or deficient.[67] Leaving aside the 1984 Act, on occasion English courts have given effect to Sharia law in the context of applications in England for ancillary relief after an English divorce. This may require giving effect, at least in part, to a marriage contract. In *A v T (Ancillary Relief: Cultural Factors)*[68] the spouses, who both were nationals of Iran, and Muslims bound by the code of Sharia law, had entered into a marriage contract in Iran, in terms of which the husband supplied the wife with a marriage portion of approximately £60,000, which portion the wife was entitled to retain if her

64 1986 Act, s. 51.

65 Whereas (s. 51(3)(a)) in the case of divorces obtained by means of proceedings, recognition may be refused if insufficient notice was given of the proceedings to a party to the marriage, or without a party being given for any other reason a reasonable opportunity to take part in the proceedings, in the case of divorces obtained otherwise than by means of proceedings, recognition may be refused (s. 51(3)(b)) if there is no official document certifying the effectiveness of the divorce etc. under the law of the country in which it was obtained or of the recognition of the divorce as valid by the law of the domicile of the other party.

66 1986 Act, s. 51(3)(c).

67 Cf. and contrast *Quazi v Quazi* [1979] 3 All ER 897 and *Tahir v Tahir* 1993 SLT 194 and *(No 2)* 1995 SLT 451.

68 [2004] EWHC 471 (Fam).

husband divorced her by *talaq*, or failed to give her a divorce; if the wife sought divorce, the percentage of the portion which she could keep would require to be negotiated. Upon dissolution sought by the wife in England of a short-lived marriage, Baron J. appears to have decided the matter of ancillary relief in light of the manner in which the question would have been dealt with by the courts of Iran. The judge was anxious to comply with what it appeared the cultural background of the parties would have required.[69]

3.3. TRANSNATIONAL DIVORCES

Section 44(1) of the Family Law Act 1986 provides that no divorce or annulment obtained in any part of the British Islands shall be regarded as effective in any part of the UK unless granted by a court of civil jurisdiction. This is the position, irrespective of parties' domicile(s) and religion.[70] However, by contrast, as has been seen, divorces obtained outside the UK in a variety of extra-judicial ways (divorce by mutual consent,[71] by administrative process[72] or under religious laws) may be accorded recognition in the UK dependent on circumstances.

A relatively recent example, vouching the difference in treatment accorded to religious divorces obtained outside the UK, on the one hand, and those purportedly obtained inside the UK, on the other, is *Sulaiman v Juffali*,[73] which came before the Family Division of the English High Court. Both parties to the marriage were nationals of and domiciled in the Kingdom of Saudi Arabia. They were married in Saudi Arabia in accordance with Sharia law in 1980. The husband pronounced *talaq* in England on 23 June 2001. Expert evidence was to the effect that by Saudi law the marriage was dissolved as soon as the *talaq* was pronounced, and its validity was not dependent in any way upon the participation of judicial authorities in Saudi Arabia, even though these authorities were involved according to the factual evidence.

---

69 Cf. *Shahnaz v Rizwan* [1965] 1 QB 390. Contrast *Phrantzes v Argenti* [1960] 2 QB 19 (where the English court declined to exercise a discretion as to dowry, a discretion it thought more properly exercised by a Greek court).

70 The same is true with regard to marriages celebrated in Scotland, which as to form and nature must comply with Scots law. The Marriage (Scotland) Act 1977, s. 9, makes provision for religious marriages, but such marriages are not exempt from the formal requirements applying to marriages generally.

71 *National Insurance Decision No R(G) 1/72*; and *H v H (Validity of Japanese Divorce)* [2006] EWHC 2989 (Fam), [2007] 1 FLR 1318 (divorce by "*kyogi rikon*", that is, by agreement, under Article 763 of the Japanese Civil Code).

72 *Manning v Manning* [1958] P 112.

73 [2002] 2 FCR 427, at p. 439.

The wife made an application for summary determination as to whether her husband's pronouncement of a *talaq* in England amounted to an overseas divorce within the meaning of the Family Law Act 1986, section 45(1). It was held that the *talaq* was not worthy of recognition from a UK perspective: having been pronounced within the UK, it was not an overseas divorce, and so breached the terms of section 44(1) of the 1986 Act.

In order for a transnational divorce (that is, one the religious and/or legal procedure of which is seen to have taken place in two countries) to qualify for recognition in the UK, it is essential that no part of the "proceedings" shall have taken place in the UK.[74] This policy applies indiscriminately to all divorces, regardless of the nature of parties' religious or other beliefs. The reality, however, is that where transnational divorces have presented before courts in the UK, the form of divorce has been extra-judicial, notably, the Islamic *talaq* or Jewish *get*.

The paradigm case is *In re Fatima*.[75] The House of Lords was required to determine whether Mohammed Afzal, a UK resident since 1968, had been divorced, in the view of English law, from his first wife by virtue of a *talaq* which he pronounced in England in 1978, and in respect of which he made a statutory declaration before a solicitor in England. Copies of the *talaq* were sent to Pakistan, to Afzal's wife and to the chairman of the relevant Union Council. No reconciliation having been effected within the 90 day period necessitated by the Pakistan Muslim Family Laws Ordinance 1961, the marriage was duly dissolved according to Pakistan law. In England Afzal wished to marry Ms Fatima, a Pakistani national, whose leave to enter the UK was dependent upon her satisfying the Heathrow immigration officer that her intended marriage would take place within a reasonable time. That, in turn, was dependent upon recognition in England of the *talaq* pronounced by Afzal. Recognition fell to be decided according to the then applicable Recognition of Divorces and Legal Separations Act 1971, sections 2 and 3(1). The House of Lords held that sections 2, 3(1) and 16, when read together, made it clear that the "proceedings" must be a single set of proceedings, instituted in the same country as that in which the divorce was ultimately obtained.[76] Since the pronouncement of *talaq* in the instant case had taken place in England, the requirement of section 2 was not met, namely, that the divorce have been obtained by means of judicial or other proceedings in any country outside the British Isles.

---

74 *R. v Secretary of State for the Home Dept, ex p. Fatima; ex p. Bi (transnational talaq)* [1984] 2 All ER 458.

75 [1986] AC 527.

76 See CRAWFORD, E.B., *International Private Law in Scotland* (W. Green/Sweet&Maxwell, 1998), para. 10.19.

Where part of the proceedings takes place in the UK, as in *Berkovits v Grinberg*,[77] transnational divorces will not be recognised. In *Berkovits* the spouses, who were both Israeli citizens, were married in Israel in 1975. Later, the husband became habitually resident and domiciled in England. When he wished to remarry, he had a Jewish *get* written in England and delivered to his wife in Israel. By this procedure, the Grinbergs' marriage was dissolved by the law of Israel. Subsequently, the English Registrar-General advised Mr Grinberg that the divorce would not be recognised in England, prompting a petition by Rabbi Berkovits, Dayan of the Beth Din Ecclesiastical Court of the Federation of Synagogues in London, for a declaration that the divorce be recognised as valid in England and Wales. This was a matter of importance to the Jewish community, Dayan Berkovits having received a number of applications similar to that of the Grinbergs, and so the Grinbergs' application was regarded as a test case.

The matter fell to be regulated by the Family Law Act 1986. Wall J. held that a *get*, written in England but delivered in Israel, was not worthy of recognition in England under section 46 of the 1986 Act, even though it was effective under the law of Israel to dissolve the marriage. It was accepted that the writing of the *get* was an important part of the proceedings by which the divorce ultimately was obtained; that which had taken place in London was an integral part of the proceedings, and rendered the divorce transnational in character.

Rabbi Berkovits submitted that the sole requirement for recognition under the 1986 Act was that the divorce was "obtained" (i.e. granted, rather than initiated) in a country outside the British Islands; he argued that for the Act to be satisfied, all that is necessary is that some event (i.e. the final event) take place abroad. Wall J., however, considered that it was not the intention of Parliament in passing the Family Law Act 1986 to alter the law relating to transnational divorces. His Lordship's interpretation of section 46(1) is that an overseas divorce will be recognised only if the proceedings have been instituted in the country where the divorce was obtained.

It might have been expected that, upon the coming into effect of the 1986 Act, section 46 of which suggests that the test is whether the divorce is valid where it is *obtained* (i.e. rather than where it is initiated), a less strict approach would be taken in cases of transnational divorce where no component of proceedings can be said to have taken place in the UK. Such expectation, however, so far has been disappointed. In Wall J.'s view, the word "obtained" connotes a process, rather than a single act – comparable to obtaining a University degree. "The mere fact that it is 'obtained' in the sense of 'finalised' or 'pronounced' in one country

77 [1995] Fam 142; McCLEAN, D., "The Non-Recognition of Transnational Divorces" (1996) 112 *LQR* 230.

cannot … dissociate the process of 'obtaining' it from the proceedings in which it was obtained."[78] Further development of a more liberal attitude towards the transnational divorce appears to have been stalled by this single judge decision.

3.4. FAMILY LAW (SCOTLAND) ACT 2006, SECTION 15

A further legislative development, separately in England and Scotland, is the recognition that although determination of matters of marital status are a civil law issue in the UK, UK legal systems acknowledge that in the view of certain religions, civil determination of status is insufficient. Adherents to such religions who are domiciled or habitually resident in the UK may petition a UK court for a consistorial decree in order to achieve civil dissolution, as required by Scots or English law, but nonetheless may find themselves still of married status according to their religious law and beliefs. In response to this, there was enacted in Scotland the Family Law (Scotland) Act 2006, section 15, which amends the Divorce (Scotland) Act 1976, section 3, so as to permit postponement of the grant of a decree of divorce by a Scots court, where religious impediment to re-marry exists.[79]

The background to this legislation was the importance attached to religious divorce under certain religious laws, especially those of Judaism, and in particular the difficulty caused by the refusal of a man to grant to his wife a *get*. Under Jewish law, civil divorce does not end the religious marriage, and a marriage can be dissolved only by the voluntary granting by the husband to the wife of a religious bill of divorce, and by the wife's voluntary acceptance thereof. If the *get* is not obtained, the wife, in the view of her religion, has the status of a "chained woman" (*agunah*), a status which forbids her re-marriage under Orthodox Jewish law, and by which any issue of a subsequent union would be regarded by Jewish law as illegitimate unto the tenth generation.

The Jewish community worked with the Scottish Executive, as it then was, to secure this legislative remedy. The issue affects only a very small number of

[78] [1995] Fam 142, at p. 157.

[79] See also the Divorce (Religious Bodies) (Scotland) Regulations 2006 (SI 2006/253). Further, LEVINE, D., "Divorce Law, the Jewish client and the *Get*"' 2009 *SLT (News)* 61. Equivalent legislation for England was implemented by Divorce (Religious Marriages) Act 2002, by s. 1 of which an insertion is made, qua s. 10A, in the Matrimonial Causes Act 1973, to the effect that if a decree of divorce has been granted but not made absolute, and the parties to the marriage were married in accordance with Jewish or other religious usages and must co-operate if the marriage is to be dissolved, then the court may postpone, on the application of either party, the granting of a decree absolute until a declaration made by both parties that they have taken such steps as are required to dissolve the marriage in accordance with those usages is produced to the court.

people in Scotland each year, but the positive effect on those few will be significant. In terms, if in any Scots divorce action in which irretrievable breakdown of a marriage has been established, one party ("the applicant") is prevented from entering into a religious marriage by virtue of a requirement of the religion of that marriage, and the other party to the divorce can act so as to remove, or enable or contribute to the removal of, the impediment which prevents that marriage, that Scots divorce court, upon application by the applicant, and if satisfied that it is just and reasonable to do so, may postpone the grant of decree until it is satisfied that the other party has so acted to remove the impediment.

This legislative measure exemplifies, for the first time, amendment of the domestic law of the forum (indeed potential denial of a civil remedy) in response to proven difficulty stemming from religious beliefs. In order for a party to be able to invoke the benefit of section 15, *ex hypothesi*, that party must be capable of finding, in addition to a substantive ground of divorce available under the *lex fori*, a ground of consistorial jurisdiction which clothes the Scots courts with jurisdiction in the instant case, that is to say, in terms of sections 7 or 8 of the Domicile and Matrimonial Proceedings Act 1973, which, in turn, refer, in the first place, to jurisdiction under Article 3 of Brussels II*bis*.[80] Article 3 sets the qualification upon the alternative bases of domicile (in its classic sense) or the habitual residence of one or both spouses such as satisfies any one of the seven indents in Article 3. While ostensibly the benefit of the section 15 postponement remedy is limited to those having some connection of a personal nature with Scotland, the consistorial jurisdiction of the Scots court is quite easily seized because of the range of bases contained in Article 3. From the perspective of a religious adherent, the availability of the postponement remedy in a Scots court may be good reason to resort to a Scots court.

4. CHOICE OF LAW IN NULLITY

Scots domestic and international private law of marriage requires that there be "an agreeing mind" to marry. In domestic law, failure of this requirement will render a marriage void; whether annulment is sought by either party is a matter for decision by that party, for strictly speaking, that which is void need not be annulled. As a result of the vagaries associated with proof of foreign law, namely, that failure by parties to plead and prove foreign law will result, by default, in application of the content of the *lex fori* (that is to say, in a Scots forum, of Scots domestic law), it may sometimes be the case that the question of applicable law is not addressed by the court. In consequence, the *lex fori* will apply. In Scots domestic law there are many subtle gradations on the precise nature of the

80 CRAWFORD and CARRUTHERS, *supra* note 5, paras. 12–06 – 12–10.

deficiency of consent which will found annulment.[81] A Scots court hearing a nullity petition must apply these subtleties of the domestic law to a case having (unfulfilled) conflict of laws potential, in which the parties only arguably are of Scots domicile,[82] but it is observable that where the religious background is Muslim, the Scots courts have been mindful of that background in their application of Scots law.

Parties may marry out of a sense of family duty if that is the pattern of their cultural background. In each of the two cases of *Mahmud v Mahmud*[83] and *Mahmood v Mahmood*,[84] on evidence that family pressure had been brought to bear on the pursuers, respectively, to enter into arranged marriages, the Court of Session granted annulments. The pursuers argued respectively that s/he had entered into marriage without the (Scottish) requisite of free will and rather out of a sense of family loyalty or under threat of being cut off from the family.[85] It does not appear that in either case was the issue of domicile raised; nor did the Scots court make any reference to foreign law. In both cases the parties were of Pakistani culture living in Scotland. It was appreciated that their wills would be more easily overborne as a result of the family piety which formed part of their tradition. Had the content of Pakistan law *qua* domicile of allegedly non-consenting party been required to be proved in the matter of matrimonial consent, a different outcome might have been reached. Equally, had a petition on similar facts been raised by parties of western background, would the court have been so readily persuaded that the parties' will(s) had been overborne? But since arranged marriages are not part of western tradition, even the query seems artificial.

In *Sohrab v Kahn*,[86] a 19 year old Muslim woman sought declarator of nullity of her marriage, which had taken place when she was aged 16 years. The marriage had been arranged between the parties' parents, without the pursuer's prior knowledge or consent, and she was notified of the wedding plans a week before the ceremony. The absence of a marriage schedule was held by Lord McEwan to be fatal to the marriage's formal validity, even where there had been subsequent

81 E.g. *Lang v Lang* 1921 SC 44.

82 The point of domicile being rarely argued: *Mahmood v Mahmood* 1993 SLT 589; *Mahmud v Mahmud* 1994 SLT 559; and *Sohrab v Kahn* 2002 SLT 1255.

83 1994 SLT 559.

84 1993 SLT 589.

85 A more extreme variation is exemplified by parental wishes to take a daughter out of a UK jurisdiction in order to arrange a marriage in Pakistan: *M v B* [2005] EWHC 1681 (consent to remove refused where the (adult) daughter had learning difficulties such that she was incapable of understanding the meaning of consent to marry); or where the party who, it is surmised, may be induced to marry, is under the age of 16 years, in which event the case may present as an abduction or wardship case: *Re KR (a child) (abduction: forcible removal by parents)* [1999] 4 All ER 954. See also *Singh v Singh* 2005 SLT 749.

86 2002 SLT 1255.

registration. On that ground, and because of the pursuer's lack of consent to the pretended marriage, induced by duress, decree of nullity was granted. In that case, Lord McEwan heard much evidence on the detail of the Muslim wedding ceremony and marriage customs. Although his Lordship's decision on lack of consent was reached after careful consideration of factual evidence of Muslim practice and parties' actings and statements in relation thereto, there is no indication that Lord McEwan applied any law other than Scots to determine the quality of consent which he deemed requisite for a valid marriage.

By contrast, Temporary Judge R.F. Macdonald Q.C. (as he then was) in *Singh v Singh*,[87] examined the conflict implications which might be expected to attend such a case, and held that the law governing the issue of consent to marry is the law of the domicile of the party alleging lack of consent. The pursuer, a UK citizen, had been brought up in Edinburgh and expressed the intention to live in Scotland for the foreseeable future; there was no challenge to the inference of Scots domicile. She had accompanied her mother to India to visit relations, only to be coerced into marriage at the mother's insistence during the holiday in India. The judge applied Scots law, being the law of the pursuer's domicile, in the matter of the requirement and content of consent to marry.[88]

A different paradox, exhibited in cases such as *Akram v Akram*[89] and *Hakeem v Hussain*,[90] is that the application of Scots law to the facts of a given case may produce an affront to Scots domestic law, in the areas of constitution of marriage, dissolution of marriage, and potentially in public law areas. This occurs where parties who have utilised Scots civil marriage procedures later deny that a marriage has taken place between them, citing mental reservation by one or both, and lack of true matrimonial consent; these deficiencies are attributed to the religious mindset of the participants, which is said to preclude true acceptance of the marriage contract despite there being present every *indicia* required by Scots civil law.

Scots law does not favour giving legal effect to unilateral mental reservation by one party, yet in 1979 Lord Dunpark in *Akram* was required by the facts of the case to grant an annulment to Muslim parties who had "married" in a civil

---

87 2005 SLT 749.

88 Making reference to *Mahmood* and *Mahmud*, *supra* note 82.

89 1979 SLT (Notes) 87. See also *Orlandi v Castelli* 1961 SC 113, which is comparable in terms of the parties' states of mind, the marriage having been entered into by means of a registry office ceremony in Scotland between two Roman Catholics for the purpose of extending the man's residence permit to remain in the UK. Since the parties, by reason of their religion, did not regard a civil ceremony as a marriage, Lord Cameron concluded, with reference to Scots domestic law (FRASER, P., *Husband and Wife*, I (Edinburgh, 1876–1878) p. 435), that there was no true matrimonial consent, and the marriage being a sham could be set aside.

90 2003 SLT 515, and on appeal, *sub nom SH v KH* 2005 SLT 1025.

ceremony in Glasgow, upon evidence given that neither had considered the formalities to amount to marriage from the viewpoint of their religion. His Lordship asked the vexed question,

> "whether it is right to allow parties, who have voluntarily participated in a civil ceremony of marriage provided by Scots law in the full knowledge of its legal effect, to have that ceremony declared null and void on the ground that their religious faith did not recognise a civil ceremony. In presenting themselves to a marriage registrar for marriage when they do not intend marriage, they are deceiving the registrar and abusing the law. I have found that the law permits itself to be abused in this way, and I cannot change it. It must be for Parliament to decide whether this abuse should be made a statutory offence or whether legislation should preclude parties from challenging the legal effect of any formal ceremony of marriage on the ground that they knowingly but tacitly withheld their true consent to marriage."[91]

Many years later, Parliament not yet having intervened, facts presented which permitted Lord Clarke the chance to essay a judicial solution. In *Hakeem v Hussain*, Saira Hakeem, a Muslim woman, sought declarator of nullity of her marriage to her husband, Khalid Hussain, a Pakistani national. The parties had been married in a civil ceremony at a registry office in Scotland in 1998, their private agreement being that they would go through a civil ceremony of marriage, as an extension to Hussain's visa could be granted if immigration authorities were satisfied that he was married to Hakeem; but that they would not live together as husband and wife until a religious ceremony had taken place between them when the pursuer finished school. False information having been given to the authorities that the parties were living together, Hussain's leave to remain in the UK was extended, and it was subsequently confirmed that he might remain indefinitely in the UK. Thereafter, Hussain expressed reluctance to enter a religious marriage with Hakeem. Hakeem, in seeking annulment, argued that the civil ceremony was simply a precursor to a true marriage prescribed by the Muslim faith, and that neither party had consented to being married by means of a registry office ceremony. Hussain defended the action, arguing that declarator of nullity should not be pronounced, the marriage not having been entered into without the consent of either party.

Lord Clarke, at first instance, held that a civil marriage was not void merely because the parties to it did not regard it as having any religious significance. His Lordship drew a distinction between consent to marriage for the purposes of the civil law, and the parties' private views on the relationship of a Scottish civil marriage ceremony and a religious marriage prescribed by their own faith. His Lordship placed reliance on a statement by Professor Clive that,

---

91 1979 SLT (Notes) 87, *per* Lord Dunpark at p. 89.

> "[e]verything turns on the distinction between an intention to assume the legal relationship of husband and wife and an intention not to get married at all. If the parties intended to get married... then they will be married even if their marriage was for a limited purpose and they had no intention of living together or assuming the normal social roles of husband and wife. If they intended not to get married at all, but merely to go through an empty ceremony they will not be married."[92]

Clive's central distinction is difficult to grasp; the difference between marrying without the intention of assuming the normal roles, on the one hand, and, on the other, merely going through a ceremony with no intention to get married at all, is one which may not convince. The distinction is a fine one.

Lord Clarke noted that as from the date of the civil ceremony, both parties wanted to be held to be man and wife according to the law of Scotland,

> "that is why they went through the ceremony in question ... I have no difficulty in accepting their evidence [of the pursuer and her mother] that, as far as their religion was concerned, it was not a valid marriage. But sitting as a judge in a secular court what I have to decide is whether or not it was a valid civil marriage."[93]

Did the parties intend to be married for the purposes of the civil law? Since his Lordship thought the answer to that question was in the affirmative, he could not hold the marriage void. Lord Clarke noted that in none of the authorities of *Orlandi v Castelli*, *Mahmud v Mahmud*, and *Akram v Akram*, did the other party to the marriage contradict the pursuer on the question of whether the parties had consented to be married.

However, in a long and careful judgment on appeal, Lord Penrose, while agreeing with Lord Clarke that parties' motives on entering into marriage are not a determinative factor, nevertheless held that "there may be cases in which the religious convictions of the parties may affect the consent exchanged in a regular marriage ceremony to the extent of wholly undermining it."[94] Lord Penrose was in no doubt that the parties wished it to be understood that the registry office ceremony was a formal marriage; but the critical question in an annulment is whether at the moment of seeming acceptance of/acquiescence in the civil ceremony, they intended to become husband and wife. Since, in the view of the appellate court, an agreement that the parties would not become husband and

---

92 CLIVE, E., *Husband and Wife* (4th ed.) (W. Green, 1997), para. 07.047. A further variation is that the argument is advanced that one or both parties believed that the ceremony was merely an engagement ceremony: *Alfonso-Brown v Millwood* [2006] All ER (D) 420.

93 2003 SLT 515, para. 31.

94 Para. 36. Lord Penrose made reference to *Brady v Murray* 1933 SLT 534.

wife in any real sense until some further condition was satisfied in the indefinite future was not a marriage, the appeal was allowed, and decree of nullity granted.

Insofar as the appeal decision in *Hakeem* reverted to a criterion of assessing the existence of matrimonial consent on a subjective basis, it is in line with earlier Scots law marriage precedents.[95] Yet in policy terms it is unreasonable: if the parties register themselves as married persons, having utilised Scottish marriage procedures, they have purported to consent to enter the institution of marriage in Scots law, for which the formalities were designed. Such marriage has public law and private law consequences. It is unacceptable that parties should hope to enjoy the public law consequences of the married status in Scotland, but should choose not to recognise the private law consequences. In these cases, the parties appear to wish to have the benefit of the incidents of marriage without acquiring the status of married parties. The judicial attempt to solve the problem having failed, responsibility passed to Parliament.

4.1. A STATUTORY RESPONSE

The Family Law (Scotland) Act 2006 seeks, inter alia, to address the problems encountered in this area. Section 38(2) directs the question whether a person has consented to enter into a marriage to the law of the domicile of that person immediately before the marriage. This provision will make clear the basic rule in the general case, but the inclusion in section 2 of the Act of a particular rule concerning void marriages[96] represents an attempt to address the problems described above, viz.:

> "*20A Grounds on which marriage void*
>
> (1) Where subsection (2) or (3) applies in relation to a marriage solemnised in Scotland, the marriage shall be void.
> (2) This subsection applies if at the time of the marriage ceremony a party to the marriage who was capable of consenting to the marriage purported to give consent but did so by reason only of duress or error.
> (3) This subsection applies if at the time of the marriage ceremony a party to the marriage was incapable of –
>
> (a) understanding the nature of marriage; and
> (b) consenting to the marriage.

95 Such as *Akram* 1979 SLT (Notes) 87 (*per* Lord Dunpark at p. 88) and *Brady v Murray* 1933 SLT 534.

96 Inserted as s. 20A of the Marriage (Scotland) Act 1977.

(4) If a party to a marriage purported to give consent to the marriage other than by reason only of duress or error, the marriage shall not be void by reason only of that party's having tacitly withheld consent to the marriage at the time when it was solemnised.

(5) In this section "error" means –

(a) error as to the nature of the ceremony; or

(b) a mistaken belief held by a person ("A") that the other party at the ceremony with whom A purported to enter into a marriage was the person whom A had agreed to marry."

Section 2, in establishing a criterion of consent, objectively construed,[97] to marriage lays down a rule which insists upon its own operation so long as the marriage, the validity of which is in question, was solemnised in Scotland.

4.2. FORCED MARRIAGE ETC. (PROTECTION AND JURISDICTION) (SCOTLAND) ACT

On 29 September 2010, the Forced Marriage etc. (Protection and Jurisdiction) (Scotland) Bill was introduced before the Scottish Parliament. The Bill, at its Stage 3 legislative proceedings, was approved by the Scottish Parliament on 22 March 2011. The date of its implementation is not yet known. The purpose of the legislation is, principally, to make provision to enable the Court of Session and sheriff court to make a forced marriage protection order in order to protect persons from being forced[98] into marriage without their free and full consent and to protect persons who have been forced into marriage without such consent; and, subsidiarily, to extend the jurisdiction of the sheriff court in relation to actions for declarator of nullity of marriage. It is intended that such a forced marriage protection order may be made by the court *ex proprio motu*,[99] or upon application[100] by the protected person or a relevant third party.[101] Significantly, section 13 (interpretation) defines marriage for this purpose as "any religious or civil ceremony of marriage (wherever carried out and whether or not legally binding under the law of Scotland or any other place)"; and by

97 Cf. "Commercial contracts cannot be arranged by what people think in their inmost minds. Commercial contracts are made according to what people say" (*Muirhead & Turnbull v Dickson* (1905) 7 F 686, *per* Lord President Dunedin at p. 694).

98 "Force", defined in s. 1(6) of the Act includes (a) to coerce by physical, verbal or psychological means, threatening conduct, harassment or other means; and (b) knowingly to take advantage of a person's incapacity to consent to marriage or to understand the nature of marriage.

99 S. 4(1).

100 S. 3(1).

101 That is, a local authority, the Lord Advocate or person specified by order of the Scottish Ministers (s. 3(7)).

section 2 the terms of a forced marriage protection order may relate to conduct outwith, as well as, or instead of, conduct within Scotland.[102] Further, such an order may require a person, inter alia, to refrain from taking the protected person from, or to, such place (undefined territorially) as the court may specify, and to facilitate or otherwise enable the protected person or any other person to return or go to such place (whether in Scotland or another part of the UK) within such period as the court may specify. Notably, any person who, knowingly and without reasonable excuse, breaches a forced marriage protection (civil) order commits an offence and becomes liable to imprisonment and/or fine.[103]

The legislation is not intended to detract from any other protection or remedy available to persons under the existing law, and in particular any criminal liability, any claim in delict, or the law of marriage.[104] Since section 13 of the Act defines marriage in a very broad manner, and is not limited to marriages legally binding under the law of Scotland, existing protections under the "law of marriage" must be construed equally broadly to encompass protection and/or remedy available under Scots domestic private law, and international private law, and potentially beyond.

This hybrid civil/criminal legislative provision will echo the Forced Marriage (Civil Protection) Act 2007, which applies in England and Wales.[105] In Scotland, it will render the remedy of annulment more accessible from a technical point of view by clothing the sheriff court with jurisdiction to grant decree of nullity. In other respects, although not per se a piece of conflict of laws legislation – being, indeed, tangential thereto – it has conflict of laws implications and, paradoxically, is bolder than many international private law provisions in taking to itself power to regulate conduct outside Scotland. This raises issues of the territorial operation of UK statute law, providing an example of the principle of intra-territoriality being honoured more in the breach than in the observance.[106]

As with a number of modern Scottish legislative enactments, this measure does not make clear the constituency of persons for whom it is intended to provide protection. The Policy Memorandum states that, "The Scottish Government believes that *all people in Scotland* who are eligible to marry ... have a right to do so freely and without coercion".[107] In common with the Family Law (Scotland)

102 S. 2 (2)(a).

103 S. 9.

104 S. 12.

105 See FAWCETT, J.J. and CARRUTHERS, J.M., *Cheshire, North & Fawcett's Private International Law* (14th ed.) (Oxford University Press, 2008), pp. 976–977.

106 CRAWFORD and CARRUTHERS, *supra* note 5, para. 3–07.

107 Para. 3. Emphasis added.

Act 2006, sections 25–30 whereof seek to regulate property rights arising from *de facto* cohabitation, the Forced Marriage legislation does not specify the scope of its operation,[108] or seek to identify spatially – i.e. in conflict of laws terms – those persons who may invoke its protection.

Whereas section 2 of the Family Law (Scotland) Act 2006 is principally territorial in its operation, section 38 of that Act reiterates in statutory form the common law rule, referring questions of capacity and consent to marry to the law of the ante-nuptial domicile, a rule which being personal in nature transcends territorial boundaries. The Forced Marriage legislation clearly is tailored to assist in alleviating a social problem which arises acutely in certain religious communities. Rather than providing merely territorial protection, the proposed provisions are more ambitious, intending also to apply extra-territorially, with the aim of curing, by means of Scots court order, a mischief visible within Scotland, but not necessarily entirely contained therein, and having cross-border characteristics.

5. CHILDREN

In the UK, the subject of international child abduction is regulated by the Child Abduction and Custody Act 1985, bringing into operation in the UK the 1980 Hague Convention on the Civil Aspects of International Child Abduction and the 1980 European Convention on the Recognition and Enforcement of Custody Decisions, and complemented, where applicable, by Article 11 of Brussels II*bis*. Although the 1980 Hague Convention, in particular, has been extremely successful, one measure thereof being its international acceptability,[109] Thorpe L.J. remarked in *Osman v Elasha*,[110] that there has been an obvious limitation to its success: "The member states by and large all derive their sense of law and justice from the Judaeo-Christian root. No state that settles civil and family disputes according to Islamic law has joined the club".[111] His Lordship recognised that, "The further development of international collaboration to combat child abduction may well depend upon the capacity of states to respect a variety of concepts of child welfare derived from differing cultures and

108 Cf. CRAWFORD and CARRUTHERS, *supra* note 5, paras. 13–13 – 13–14.

109 As of 1 March 2011 there are 84 Contracting States.

110 [2000] Fam 62.

111 *Ibid.*, at 69. Cf. *Re J (A Child) (Custody Rights: Jurisdiction)* [2005] UKHL 40, [2006] 1 AC 80, at para. 21, where Baroness Hale of Richmond noted that three states where the predominant religion is Islam (Turkey, Turkmenistan, and Uzbekistan) are Contracting States to the Hague Convention. She commented that the cultures and legal systems of the Contracting States will vary widely, but that one group of states, viz. states which adopt some form of Sharia law, is conspicuous by its absence.

traditions".[112] While this is, in principle, a desideratum, there is a limit to the degree of variation from any given forum's own concept of welfare which can be accommodated or tolerated by that forum. Therefore, it seems that the most that can be hoped for is that agreement be pursued between countries on a bilateral basis.[113]

Where a case is not regulated by international Convention or Regulation or bilateral agreement, it falls to be determined by common law principles.[114] The interesting question is in what circumstances, if any, a court in the UK might or might not feel inclined to apply to a non-Convention case, by analogy, Hague Convention principles. Early indications suggested that an English court in its discretion would follow Hague principles where it felt it appropriate so to do in a particular case,[115] but in *Re A (Abduction; non-convention country)*,[116] where the non-Convention country was the United Arab Emirates, the Court of Appeal drew back from that approach, reverting to application of the welfare principle.[117]

In *In re J (A Child) (Custody Rights: Jurisdiction)*[118] Baroness Hale of Richmond stated firmly that,

> "There is no warrant, either in statute or authority, for the principles of the Hague Convention to be extended to countries which are not parties to it... This is so even in a case where a friendly foreign state has made orders about the child's future."[119]

---

112 *Ibid.*, at 70.

113 E.g. collaboration on a UK–Pakistan basis only is evident from the conclusion of the UK–Pakistan Judicial Protocol on Child Contact and Abduction [2003] Fam Law 199. See also *Guidance Note from the President of the Family Division* at [2004] Fam Law 609; and [2006] Fam Law 5. See also *A v A (unreported)*, 2 February 2004; *A v A (unreported)*, 25 February 2004, discussed by Binns at [2004] Fam Law 359; *Re Z (A Child)* [2006] EWCA Civ 1219, *per* Wilson L.J., at para. 31; and in Scotland, *A v N* 2007 GWD 01–2.

114 CRAWFORD and CARRUTHERS, *supra* note 5, paras. 14–63 and 14–64.

115 E.g. *Re F (Minor; Abduction; Jurisdiction)* [1990] 3 All ER 97; *D v D* [1994] 1 FLR 137, CA; *Re A (Minors; Abduction)* [1996] 1 All ER 24; *Re S* [1994] 1 FLR 297; and *Re Z (Abduction: Non-Convention Country)* [1999] 1 FLR 1270.

116 [1998] 1 FLR 231. See also *Re P (A Minor: Abduction) The Times*, 19 July 1996.

117 The mantra of 20th century UK domestic legislation relating to children has been to stress that the paramount consideration is the best interests of the child. By contrast, the rationale of the Hague Convention is that the interests of children in general are best served by the creation of a predictable and consistent system operating internationally, in terms of which, in the majority of cases, substantive custody issues shall be determined by the legal system of the child's habitual residence.

118 [2006] 1 AC 80.

119 Para. 22.

The House of Lords held that,

> "[I]n all non-Convention cases, the courts have consistently held that they must act in accordance with the welfare of the individual child. If they do decide to return the child, that is because it is in his best interests to do so, not because the welfare principle has been superseded by some other consideration... the specialist rules and concepts of the Hague Convention are not to be applied by analogy in a non-Convention case."[120]

In the instant case, the House of Lords allowed the appeal, and in refusing to order the return of the child to Saudi Arabia, effectively restored the decision of Hughes J.

In *In re J*, the mother had dual British and Saudi Arabian citizenship, and had been educated mainly in Saudi Arabia, but also in Britain. In Saudi Arabia, she married the child's father, a Saudi national, in accordance with Sharia law. The child spent his early years in Saudi, but with the father's consent accompanied the mother to the UK while she studied for a further degree. During the course of her studies, the marriage failed and the mother decided she did not wish to return to Saudi Arabia. She presented a divorce petition in England, and the father applied to the English court for a specific issue order under the Children Act 1989, that the child be summarily returned to Saudi Arabia. The judge of first instance refused to return the child, being aware that allegations made by the father against the mother, if raised before a Sharia court, would have disastrous consequences for the mother, and thereby, in the judge's view, would seriously damage the child's interests. This decision having been reversed by the Court of Appeal, the mother appealed successfully to the House of Lords. It was against this background that Baroness Hale's remarks were made. The House of Lords held that any court determining a question concerning the upbringing of a child had a statutory duty to hold the welfare of the child as the paramount consideration. The fact that the welfare principle might be specifically excluded by statute, as for example by the Child Abduction and Custody Act 1985, did not remove in non-Convention cases the duty of the judge to focus on the individual child in the particular circumstances. In reaching this decision, it cannot be said that the parties' religious principles, and the outcome which their application would be likely to produce in a Saudi court, were absent from the minds of the Bench. It was a relevant factor that the courts of Saudi Arabia had no choice but to do as the father wished.

---

120 Para. 25.

A contrasting outcome was produced by the Court of Appeal in *Osman v Elasha*,[121] concerning a couple, both Sudanese citizens and practising Muslims, who married in the Sudan in 1986. Between 1987 and 1991 they lived in the UK, where two sons of the marriage were born. A third son was born following the family's return to the Sudan in 1993. The father returned to the UK in May 1993, but the mother continued to reside in the Sudan, although she visited the UK with her children between December 1993 and April 1994. In 1995 the parties divorced and the mother remarried. In November 1995 the local Sudanese court, applying Islamic law, ordered that the children should reside with their paternal grandmother, but that the mother should be able to visit them at any time. In 1997 the father remarried but continued to live in the UK. In May 1999 the mother brought the three children to the UK, and was granted an *ex parte* residence order and an injunction preventing the father from removing the children from the jurisdiction of the English court. The father applied for the children to be made wards of court and for their immediate return to the Sudan, which was not party to the Hague Convention. Expert evidence was to the effect that Sudanese personal law provided for the maternal grandmother (whom failing, the paternal grandmother) to have care of the children of a divorced mother who remarried; and that the Sudanese court normally would take full account of a range of factors including, above all, the best interests of the children according to Sudanese culture.

It was held by the trial judge that it was the father's intention to return soon to the Sudan to live; that the children spoke very little English, had habitually resided in the Sudan until May 1999 and had been removed by the mother from familiar surroundings to an uncertain future in the UK, where they lived in temporary accommodation. In ordering return of the children to the Sudan, he concluded that in determining any residence application the Sudanese courts would apply Islamic law, an outcome which he deemed appropriate and acceptable in all the circumstances of the case. The mother appealed this decision unsuccessfully. The Court of Appeal, in affirming that the welfare principle should apply, nonetheless held that the welfare principle is not an absolute standard, and it is not for an English court to criticise the standards of, or paramount principles applied by, the family justice system in such a country, save in exceptional circumstances, such as persecution or ethnic, sex or other discrimination. To the western mind, the taking of children from their mother after her re-marriage, in order to place them with the paternal grandmother, is exceptional, in the absence of compelling facts. On the other hand, the wife had flouted the order of the Sudanese court. This is an example of a true cultural clash.[122] However, in the circumstances of this family, the welfare principle was

121 [2000] Fam 62.

122 Cf. *Westminster City Council v C* [2009] Fam 11, discussed above at pp. 45-46.

looked at in the context of Sudanese custom and culture, which applied Islamic law and which was familiar and acceptable to a practising Muslim family.

While the *Osman* decision demonstrates willingness by the English court (sometimes) to respect, after enquiry, the family traditions and concepts of non-Judeo-Christian communities, UK courts will not allow the forum's own conception of what is best for the individual child to be subordinated.[123]

6. CONCLUSION

The proper business of any legal system's international private law is to deal with diversity, principally legal diversity, and subsidiarily cultural and religious diversity, and to accommodate that diversity as the forum from time to time sees fit. There is an important temporal dimension, in that there are observable in the UK changing social mores, greater familiarity with different cultures, and growing receptiveness to different religious and cultural traditions. This essay set out to offer some examples of the manner in which the courts in Scotland and England, applying conflict of laws principles as part of the civil law of the land, treat parties' religious beliefs and cultural traditions. The exposition has been done in the contexts of marriage, divorce, nullity, and child custody. It has been seen that attitudes within the UK legal systems have changed with the passage of time, generally in the direction of becoming more tolerant of norms different from those native to the forum's legal system.[124] Yet even in a Europe which is undergoing a process of harmonisation of international private law, the legal systems of the UK retain control of the extent to which non-secular norms, in family law in particular, are to be recognised and given effect. Sometimes this control is exercised on a criterion of territoriality,[125] frequently on the basis of Scots/English influence *qua* personal law,[126] and always with the tool of public policy as longstop.

---

123 Cf. Singer J. in *Re KR (a child) (abduction: forcible removal by parents)* [1999] 4 All ER 954.

124 See, for example in the UK, the changing approach to the recognition of religious divorces, beginning with *R v Hammersmith Superintendent Registrar of Marriages Ex p. Mir-Anwaruddin* [1917] 1 KB 634, and currently represented by the Family Law Act 1986, s. 46 and cases thereunder as detailed, *supra* at notes 60 and 63. Similarly, see *supra* at section 2.1 the tale of recognition in the UK of polygamous marriages.

125 E.g. prohibition of religious divorces in the UK *per* s. 44, Family Law Act 1986; and mandatory monogamous nature of marriages celebrated in the UK. The Family Law (Scotland) Act 2006, s. 2 is a territorial protection rather than a personal protection, the policy being to protect the institutions of Scots law.

126 E.g. in the matter of age, or consanguinity, or incapacity to enter an actually polygamous marriage.

The question which remains to be addressed is whether UK courts applying conflict of laws principles could and should further accommodate parties' religious beliefs and cultural traditions. In international private law, religious law typically has been encountered under the banner of "foreign law." This assumes that foreign law starts at the border. If it be argued that in a multi-cultural Britain, this assumption can no longer be made, what answer shall the conflict of laws branch of Scots law return? The conflict lawyer must transmute into a domestic lawyer and, in the interests of fairness to all, of whatever creed, and in the interests of certainty, insist that the domestic legal systems of the UK remain secular, and reject twin or multi track versions of private law rules in areas such as marriage, divorce, custody (or debt or any other commercial area). Likewise, it is not wise to speculate that religious courts might co-exist with the civil courts of the land in any more significant way than currently is tolerated. "UK" law does not permit bespoke application of a party's religious law;[127] reference to an individual's personal law is, and in the submission of the authors must remain, a reference only to the civil law. This must mean, despite judicial lipservice paid to the respect due to all faiths and beliefs,[128] that in the event of conflict between the civil (i.e. secular) law of the forum and an individual's religious beliefs, the former must prevail:

> "... it is important to realise that reliance upon religious belief, however conscientious the belief and however ancient and respectable the religion, can never of itself immunise the believer from the reach of the secular law. And invocation of religious belief does not necessarily provide a defence to what is otherwise a valid claim."[129]

Therefore, while the inner life may be regulated by any number of religious beliefs, or by none, an attempt to substitute religious views for secular outcomes, so as to permit them to operate in place of the latter, would be to undermine the universal application of private law. Acceptance of the principle of party autonomy in domestic private law should not extend so far as to permit a party to evade the operation of civil law, by opting in to the religious law of his/her choosing. The civil (secular) law has demonstrated sensitivity to religious issues, but ultimately only the secular judge in the multi-cultural society can administer justice even-handedly to all manner of people.

---

127 "... we live in this country in a democratic and pluralistic society, in a secular state not a theocracy." *R (on the application of Johns) v Derby City Council* [2011] EWHC 375) (Admin), per Munby L.J. at [36]. Contrast Indian law (*McDougall v Chitnavis* 1937 SC 390); and Egyptian law (*Russ v Russ* [1964] P 315 and *Cheni (otherwise Rodriguez) v Cheni* [1965] P 85).

128 See *R (on the application of Johns) v Derby City Council* [2011] EWHC 375) (Admin), *per* Munby L.J. at paras. [34] – [41].

129 *Ibid.*, at para. [43].

PART TWO
DENYING A PLACE FOR RELIGION?

THE LEGAL SCOPE FOR RELIGIOUS IDENTITY IN FAMILY MATTERS – THE PARADOXES OF THE SWEDISH APPROACH

Maarit JÄNTERÄ-JAREBORG

1. INTRODUCTION

1.1. THE MYTH OF SWEDEN AS "THE MOST SECULAR COUNTRY IN THE WORLD"

If anyone asked "What is the place of religion in Swedish family law?" I believe that the standard answer by any Swedish lawyer, and delivered without hesitation, would be "None". If any explanation be provided it would, most likely, refer to the (allegedly) secular nature of Swedish family law, reflecting exclusively secular values. This answer might be further developed by claiming that the main legal actors in Sweden, namely the legislator – Parliament – and the courts, do not count religious arguments as factors of relevance in drafting laws or in adjudicating cases. The Swedish State is, furthermore, not only secular but also neutral in matters of confession.[1] The consulted lawyer might even point out, with certain pride in her voice, that Sweden, by reputation, is one of the most secularised countries in the world, if not even "the most secular country in the world". Until only a few years ago, when I initiated a multidisciplinary research project in Sweden on the impact of religion on family law,[2] I would essentially have shared this view. Today, I am less convinced, for several reasons.

1 The Swedish Constitution does not contain any explicit provisions on State neutrality on religious issues. Nevertheless, confessional neutrality is implied. See JÄNTERÄ-JAREBORG, M., "Religion and the Secular State in Sweden" in *Religion and the Secular State: National Reports, under the direction of J. Martinez-Torrón & W. Cole Durham. Jr. Interim Reports, XVIIIth International Congress of Comparative Law, Washington D.C.*, The International Center for Law and Religion Studies, Brigham Young University, Provo Utah 2010, p. 676.

2 The IMPACT of Religion: Challenges for Society, Law and Democracy. This multidisciplinary research programme is founded as a "Centre of Excellence" at Uppsala University for the period 2008–2018 and is largely funded by the Swedish Research Council. One of the six themes of the programme focuses on families, law and society.

First, statistics reveal high rates of Church membership within the Swedish population. Statistics also reveal that most marriages in Sweden are still concluded by using religious rites. This may appear surprising, considering Sweden's self-image and reputation as a secular State. Therefore, it is important to immediately point out that for historical reasons Sweden has a double track system of marriage conclusion, the law of marriage permitting both secular (civil) marriages and religious marriages as equal alternatives, both carrying full civil law effects if officiated by a person qualifying as "marriage authority" under Swedish law. Still, why do so many couples in Sweden choose to marry in a religious ceremony? This question has primarily interested theologians but should be of interest also from a legal point of view. I will return to the issue in Section 3.2.3, below.

Second, the reactions in Swedish society towards a proposal in 2007, by a government appointed commission,[3] to transform the legal institution of marriage into a gender-neutral concept, thus permitting also same-sex marriages, clearly demonstrated how deeply intertwined marriage is with religion. It became evident in public discussion that marriage is not only a legal (secular) institution but also has a deep religious dimension. Two questions dominated the debate. Should not the State abstain from a law reform that would collide with all the leading world religions' notion of marriage as a heterosexual relationship? Alternatively, is it not high time to cancel the delegation of powers from the State to religious communities? If, namely, the religious communities cannot share the legislator's notion of "marriage" and marry all who qualify according to (secular) law, then their state-authorisations to marry people should be drawn back, the argument went. The faith communities' role should instead be reduced to offering "blessings" to a marriage in line with their religions, without any legal implications. Interestingly enough, this argument was advocated both by members of the clergy (from different religious communities) and non-believers advocating a full separation of powers between the State and Church. Although the proposal was subsequently adopted by Parliament and the revised legislation came into force on 1 May 2009, the final word concerning the faith communities' role in marriage celebration had not yet been said. An explicit provision was, nevertheless, added to the Marriage Code stating that no faith community or clergy would be under any obligation to officiate at same-sex marriage ceremonies. I will return to these issues in Section 3.2.4, below.

Third, through global immigration to Sweden during the last decades, new cultures, traditions and religions have been brought to Sweden. Not least the new presence of Islam and Muslims in Sweden is striking, with Islam having become

---

3 Äktenskap för par av samma kön, Vigselfrågor, Statens Offentliga Utredningar, Report SOU 2007:17.

the second largest faith[4] in Sweden, after the Evangelical Lutheran Church of Sweden. The Islamic understanding of family law as religious by origin, laying down the basis for a Muslim's personal and family life, raises new challenges. To what extent and under what conditions can Islamic (or other religious) family law be enforced in Sweden? To what extent is Swedish law in line with any religion? These issues raise direct concerns of whether multiculturalism also can include a normative dimension, opening up for application of, for example, religious norms forming part of a culture. In the on-going debate about multiculture, tolerance and democracy in Sweden and elsewhere in Europe it is, on the contrary, often emphasised that a secular democracy can exist only on condition that the same laws apply to everybody and are followed by all, irrespective of religion or faith. In this contribution, it is not possible to look closer at this important aspect. I restrict myself to stating that a co-existence between law and religion is within certain limits possible. Sweden's example, as demonstrated in this essay, shows that law can confirm religion, as well as contradict it.

1.2. DEMARCATIONS

All these aspects raise questions such as what does being "secular" mean within the context of family law. Above all, how does "secular" in family law relate to religion? In addition, how do we define "religion" and "religious"? Should law be drafted in such a manner as to leave scope for a person's religious identity in family law matters, or should we strive at keeping all religion out of family law? And what does State "neutrality" in matters of confession mean in a family law context?

Family law reforms in Sweden have stirred much interest all over the world, due to the radicalism of the adopted laws. This applies not only to Sweden's *avant-garde* marriage and divorce law reforms of the 1970s, but also to previous and subsequent law reforms in particular in these two fields. As Max Rheinstein saw it, the development in Swedish family law demonstrated "the shift of social change from Christian traditionalism to fully established liberalism".[5] Consequently, Rheinstein included Swedish law in his last major research project *Marriage Stability, Divorce and the Law*, published in 1972. The developments in Swedish family law received much attention also in Mary Ann Glendon's internationally celebrated work *The Transformation of Family Law – State, Law*

4 Describing Islam as the second largest faith in Sweden is, nevertheless, a simplification, since no regard is had to the different schools and orientations on Islam among the "Muslims" in Sweden.

5 RHEINSTEIN, M., *Marriage Stability, Divorce and the Law* (Chicago University Press, 1972), p. 152.

and Family in the United States and Western Europe, from 1989.[6] The Swedish developments are central also in David Bradley's works, in particular his book *Family Law and Political Culture. Scandinavian Laws in Comparative Perspective*, from 1996.[7] More recently, they have attracted the attention of Masha Antokolskaia, in her huge comparative study *Harmonisation of Family Law in Europe: A Historical Perspective. A Tale of Two Millenia*, published in 2006.[8]

The focus of this contribution will be on the law of marriage and divorce, and how these fields of law relate to religion on the one hand and secularism on the other hand. In addition to analysis of statistical data, these issues will be approached from the point of view of Swedish substantive family law regulation and its underlying ideology. Private international law, which in Sweden serves as the primary tool for normative multiculturalism, falls outside the scope of this contribution.[9]

2. RELIGIOUS AFFINITY IN SWEDEN – STATISTICS AND EXPLANATIONS

2.1. THE DOMINANCE OF THE CHURCH OF SWEDEN

As already mentioned, Sweden is popularly regarded as one of the most secular countries in the world,[10] and the "place of religion" is defined to be limited to the private sphere of life. Nevertheless, an absolute majority of the population – 73 per cent in 2008 – are members of the Church of Sweden, which is an Evangelical Lutheran (Protestant) church and the former (until 2000) State Church of Sweden. More than 40 per cent of all marriages celebrated in Sweden in 2008 were officiated within the Church of Sweden. When regard is had to marriages

6 GLENDON, M.A., *The Transformation of Family Law. State, Law and Family in the United States and Western Europe* (Chicago University Press, 1989).

7 BRADLEY, D., *Family Law and Political Culture (Scandinavian Laws in Comparative Perspective* (Sweet & Maxwell, 1996). See also, BRADLEY, D., "Radical Principles and the Legal Institution of Marriage: Domestic Relations Law and Social Democracy in Sweden" (1990) *International Journal of Law and the Family*, pp. 154–185.

8 ANTOKOLSKAIA, M., *Harmonisation of Family Law in Europe: A Historical Perspective, A Tale of Two Millennia* (Intersentia, 2006).

9 Private international law "localizes or coordinates justice" in cross-border cases. In many cases, the Swedish rules of this discipline refer to the application of foreign law or require the recognition of foreign decisions or a foreign family law status. Normally, however, the rules of private international law only capture situations where at least one of the concerned parties at a relevant point of time had a connection to a foreign state, such as its citizenship, or domicile or habitual residence there.

10 See, e.g., Staten och imamerna, Statens Offentliga Utredningar, Report SOU 2009:52, 86; PETTERSSON, T., "Sekularisering" in SVANBERG, I. and WESTERLUND, D. (eds.), *Religion i Sverige* (Dialogos, 2008), pp. 34–38.

officiated, upon State authorisation, by other religious communities in Sweden, religious marriages amount to more than half of all recently celebrated marriages. In 2008, of all new-born children in Sweden, approximately 60 per cent were baptised and 83 per cent of all the dead were buried according to the rites of the Church of Sweden.[11]

2.2. "THE SWEDISH PARADOXES"

2.2.1. High Church membership without active participation

On the other hand, the high church membership rates are not reflected in the everyday lives of the citizens. According to statistics by the Church of Sweden, only 2 per cent of its members regularly attend worship services.[12] Furthermore, according to a European Barometer Study, only 23 per cent of the Swedish population admit believing in God.[13] Other available figures indicate that as much as 85 per cent of the population identify themselves as non-believers.[14] In these figures, 90.1 per cent of the population are classified as being of "Christian Protestant origin", 1.8 per cent are Catholics, and 8.2 per cent are classified as of "other" religious belief. The category "other" consists mainly of Muslims.

In sociology of religion, reference is made to "the Swedish paradox". This description refers to a situation where the majority population have a weak church-associated belief in God, but remain members of the dominating church and continue to make use of its rites in important situations in life.[15] In other words, "What in normal everyday life is *religiously abnormal* in Sweden, is considered *religiously normal* in *abnormal* situations."[16] This, in turn, is interpreted to mean that people still feel a "sense of belonging" and "identification" with the Church of Sweden.[17] Sweden's early transformation into a social welfare state – from the 1930s onwards – has been regarded as an important explanation of the low rates of church activity. When, namely, the

11 See JÄNTERÄ-JAREBORG, *supra* note 1, p. 669 f.

12 Www.svenskakyrkan.se/SVK/eng/liturgy.htm.

13 *Special Eurobarometer 225/Wave 63.1*, European Commission January – February 2005, 9. These results are rather similar to those of a World Value Survey, carried out in the 1990s and 2006 and described by PETTERSSON, *supra* note 10, pp. 34–38. See also R. Nygren's figures comparing Japan, Sweden and the United States in his article "Can We Predict the Future of Family Law?" in SCHEIBER, H.N. and MAYALI, L. (eds.), *Japanese Family Law in Comparative Perspective* (The Robbins Collection, 2009), pp. 24–29.

14 See JÄNTERÄ-JAREBORG, *supra* note 1, p. 669.

15 BÄCKSTRÖM, A., EDGARDH BECKMAN, N. and PETTERSSON, P., *Religious Change in Northern Europe, The Case of Sweden* (Verbum, 2004), pp. 87–88.

16 *Ibid.*, p. 139. The situation is very similar in the other Nordic countries.

17 *Ibid.*, pp. 88–90 and pp. 139–140.

State takes over the collective responsibility for the welfare of its population, church members become less engaged and the role of religious denominations in society is "diminished" to providing religious services.[18] The members expect the right to be married or buried in Church, as a form of remuneration for the annual Church fees.[19]

As a lawyer I am inclined to emphasise other factors which also could explain the above-mentioned "paradox". The high membership rates reflect, above all, the recent history of a Church to which, with few exceptions, all citizens of Sweden were born as members until as late as 1996. From the sixteenth century onwards, when the Protestant Reformation was carried out in Sweden, until 2000, this Church was the national State Church of Sweden; unity of faith (and membership in the Church of Sweden) being the common denominator of society. It was not until the 1860s that it became possible for Swedish nationals to leave the Church, but only if they became members of another congregation approved by the State. An unconditional right to leave the Church of Sweden, without entering into another congregation, became possible only in 1951, when the Freedom of Religion Act (*Religionsfrihetslagen, 1951:680*) was adopted.

I would claim that, from a citizen's perspective, to *renounce* one's membership in the Church to which one was born and which continues to be well-established in society, requires taking a position on what religion is about. Few people seem to actively reflect upon the views of the Church or what the Evangelical Lutheran faith is about. The popularity of religious rites may find an explanation in the traditions of the country and in the beautiful and dignified settings that Sweden's thousands of old church buildings offer for events such as marriage ceremonies and burials. But when people truly identify themselves with religion, religious beliefs may form unexpected lines of division, in situations where societal developments challenge traditional outlooks with links to religion. In Sweden, the gender neutral marriage reform is the latest example of religion's latent impact on public opinion and legislation.[20]

---

18 See SULTÁN SJÖQVIST, M., "*Vi blev muslimer, Svenska kvinnor berättar, En religionssociologisk studie av konversionsberättelser* (Universitetstryckeriet, 2006), p. 39.

19 In connection with the separation of the State and the Church of Sweden, church tax was replaced by a church fee. The State continues to levy this fee, on behalf of the Church, just as it levied the church tax prior to the separation. A novelty brought forth by the separation is that the same right to be assisted by the State in levying church fees is now available to all denominations that are registered as religious communities under Swedish law. This fee constitutes approximately 1% of an individual's annual income in most of the registered communities which make use of this service. The procedure for levying of church fees is regulated by Act (1999:291) concerning fees to registered religious communities. See further, JÄNTERÄ-JAREBORG, *supra* note 1, p. 680.

20 Similar developments are visible in Denmark, Iceland, Norway and Finland. The Norwegian, Swedish and Icelandic positions with regard to the introduction of a gender-neutral marriage concept, in 2008, 2009 and 2010, respectively, are discussed in JÄNTERÄ-JAREBORG, M.,

2.2.2. The impact of secularisation on society and religion

Since 1 January 2000, the State and the Church of Sweden are separated from each other and the Church of Sweden has been put on a more equal legal footing with other (registered) religious communities in Sweden. Nevertheless, the position of the Church of Sweden is still regulated in a special enactment (concerning only this Church).[21] The Church's self-image, sanctioned by this enactment, is that of a nation-wide, "open" "Folk Church",[22] although membership rates have gone down since the State-Church separation.[23] The Church has successively also lost its earlier privileges, and many of its previous State-delegated functions, such as keeping the official records concerning the population of Sweden, have been taken over by other bodies.[24] Its dominance and influence, compared with all other religious communities in Sweden, remain nevertheless unique in Swedish society.[25]

Martin Scheinin, a Finnish human rights specialist, identifies a new paradox which in his opinion is visible in all the Evangelic Lutheran Nordic States.[26] This consists of the combination of the traditional special status of the Lutheran Church together with the secularisation of society. The core of the paradox is that "the majority population and public authorities do not take seriously the fact that Lutheran Christianity still is a religion and not merely a cultural and

---

"When 'marriage' becomes a religious battlefield – Swedish and Scandinavian experiences at the dawn of same-sex marriages" (forthcoming). In Finland, a debate on the issue was initiated in 2010 and, essentially, follows the same lines as those previously in Sweden or Norway. See HALLAMAA, J., "Parisuhde ja sen sääntely uskonnollisena kysymyksenä" *Lakimies* 2010, pp. 1222–1248. Both Finland and Denmark still adhere (2011) to the institution of registered partnership for same-sex couples and have not adopted a gender-neutral marriage concept. In the other three Nordic countries, it is no longer possible to register a partnership since the entry into force of the gender-neutral marriage legislation.

21 See Act (1998:1591) concerning the Church of Sweden.

22 The vision of the Church as a Folk Church can be seen as a counterpart to the Swedish Social Democrats' idea, launched in the 1930s, of Swedish society as the "Folk Home".

23 Compared to 1999, which is the last year when the Church of Sweden was the State Church of Sweden, the Church has lost more than 10% of its members. Interestingly, in his study, *supra* note 5 at p. 127, Rheinstein, without referring to any particular year or source, states that "at least nominally" 99% of the population belong to the Lutheran State Church of Sweden. This must reflect the situation in the early 1950s before the Freedom of Religion Act, enabling all Swedes to freely leave the Church.

24 Since 1991, the Swedish Tax Registration Offices (*Skatteverket*) is in charge of the population records.

25 A striking example is that, according to the Ordinance of Succession, originally dating back to 1810, the Head of the State, officially the King or Queen of Sweden, must be of "pure Evangelical faith", that is a member of the Church of Sweden.

26 SCHEININ, M., "Secular Human Rights Perspectives. As a Challenge to Nordic Law & Religion Solutions" in CHRISTOFFERSEN, L., MODÉER, K.Å. and ANDERSEN, S. (eds.), *Law & Religion in the 21st Century – Nordic Perspective* (Djof Publishing, 2010), pp. 547–548.

historical phenomenon".[27] It follows that "adherents of other religions or of the non-religious world views may experience that the State, due to its traditional links with Christianity, is involved in or at least condoning religious indoctrination".[28] Scheinin points out that the majority religion, "often in a secularized or symbolic form, may be present in the law and in public institutions to the extent that individuals not belonging to the Lutheran Church may experience as a lack of respect for their own freedom of thought, conscience and religion".[29] According to Scheinin, these kinds of misgivings exist not only among religious communities that take religion seriously, such as the new Muslim communities, but also among active atheists and active agnostics. This is the second "paradox", of relevance for our topic.

2.3. THE NEW PRESENCE OF ISLAM IN SWEDEN

Until quite recently, the population of Sweden was extremely homogeneous as regards ethnicity, language, and religion. During the last 60 years, Sweden has transformed from a country of emigration[30] into a country of immigration with a resulting ethnic, cultural and religious diversity. Today, more than two million inhabitants, of a population of 9.3 million (2009), are of foreign origin, if regard is had to their own or their parents' place of birth in a foreign country. This number can be compared to the situation in the early 1900s when 0.7 per cent of the population was foreign-born.[31] Today, more than 200 languages are spoken in Sweden, to be compared with the previous total dominance of the Swedish language. Sweden has also become a multi-confessional society. Considering the topic of this contribution, it is also of interest that marriage to a person habitually resident in Sweden is one of the most common grounds for the granting of a residence permit in Sweden.[32]

27 *Ibid.*, p. 548.

28 *Ibid.*

29 In the above-mentioned article (*ibid.*), Scheinin focuses on decisions of international human rights bodies in cases, originating from the Nordic States, which concerned the conformity of government regulated curricula in religious education with the human rights of children and parents.

30 Between the mid 1800s and the 1930s, more than half of Sweden's population emigrated to the New World, mainly to the United States of America. See SOU 2009:52, 22.

31 SOU 2009:52, 21.

32 According to available information, in 2006, 15,000 persons from abroad received a residence permit in Sweden on the basis of marriage to a Swedish citizen or a person with a residence permit in Sweden. This number is to be compared with the total number of marriages that year in Sweden; approximately 45,000.

A new challenge in Sweden, as well as in Denmark and Norway, is that Islam has become the second largest faith in the country,[33] after the Evangelical Lutheran faith exercised within the Church of Sweden. (Denmark and Norway have corresponding Evangelical Lutheran Folk Churches, to which the majority of their population belong.) The number of "Muslims" in Sweden, with a total population of 9.3 million inhabitants (2009), is normally estimated to lie between 50,000 and 300,000,[34] but could, according to some sources, be as high as 400,000.[35] Of these, approximately 100,000 are believed to be religiously active.[36] Since no statistics are kept in Sweden regarding a person's faith, it follows that all the estimates remain inaccurate and disputed.[37]

Much of religion's current visibility in Sweden is in fact a result of Islam's new presence in Sweden. Religion is increasingly experienced as a problem because it challenges the majority's understanding of the scope of the allegedly secular – not least, in family law. But as Scheinin above points out, there is also another side to the coin. New demands, based on the right to exercise one's religion (or conscience) but with a direct link with matters of the family, also challenge the notion of the State's neutrality in respect of religion. Is the allegedly "secular", in fact, "concealed religion"? Likewise, one should also ask what qualifies as "religion" or as a "religiously motivated practice", compared to traditions and customs of a particular geographical region.

A general experience all over the world is that "exile" strengthens traditions and customs and puts the concerned individuals under increased pressure to live accordingly, in a totally different kind of societal environment. These traditions and customs are often labelled by their followers as "religion", irrespective of the historical origin, and even claimed to be "law". The Danish-Pakistani scholar, Rubya Mehdi, emphasises that Muslims in the Nordic States usually have limited

33 Nevertheless, the origin of the "Muslim" population differs between the countries. In Sweden, the first big groups came from Turkey in the 1960s and 1970s. In the 1980s, immigrants from Iran and Arabic speaking countries dominated. In the 1990s, the biggest groups came from Somalia and Bosnia. In the first years of the 21st century, Iraq and Afghanistan have stuck out. In Norway, on the contrary, Muslims from Pakistan constitute the largest group. See SAYED, M., *Islam och arvsrätt i det mångkulturella Sverige, En internationellt privaträttslig och jämförande studie* (Iustus Förlag, 2009), p. 69 f.

34 See BÄCKSTRÖM *et al.*, *supra* note 15, p. 83. According to Sultán Sjöqvist, the estimation is 250,000 Muslims, but with regard to "ethnical Muslims" in respect of background and not faith. See SULTÁN SJÖQVIST, *supra* note 18, p. 42.

35 See SAYED, *supra* note 33, p. 81.

36 See BÄCKSTRÖM *et al.*, *supra* note 15, p. 83.

37 One can, for example, raise the issue, who qualifies as a "Muslim"? The fact that a person is born in a predominantly Muslim country is, evidently, not sufficient as a criterion. On the contrary, there is reason to believe that the religious minorities from these countries are represented above average among those who have emigrated. In addition, in particular as regards Iran, people may have emigrated also to "escape religion".

knowledge of Muslim laws; in particular women lack knowledge of their rights under Islamic law.[38] The religious leaders, in turn, are often educated abroad and have little knowledge of the Nordic societies and their languages.[39] We encounter here a third "paradox" of relevance, namely confusion on both sides concerning what is "religion" and what is "law".

3. MARRIAGE AND RELIGION

"Matters of marriage, as of old, belonged to the sphere of religion."[40]

3.1. VARIOUS STAGES OF DEVELOPMENT

Swedish marriage law demonstrates, more clearly than any other field of (family) law, how legislation progressively became free from the "chains of religion" and, correspondingly, secularised. Or at least, it is popular in Sweden to regard the country's legislation on family law as secularised. Still, in accordance with the "paradox" identified by Scheinin, this understanding can today also be disputed.[41] Under all circumstances, there are nuances as regards the level of secularisation. It may be partial, as is the case concerning the legislation on marriage conclusion, or total at least on the surface level of law, as is the case concerning the rules on divorce. In the following, I will touch upon the relevant concerns and "forces" behind the various stages of legal development by using marriage and divorce as examples.

---

38 Also, according to Mehdi, when Muslims migrate to the Nordic countries they bring with them a mixture of classical *sharia*, the state family laws of their countries of origin and their customs and traditions. See MEHDI, R., "Facing the enigma: talaq-e-tafweez, a need of Muslim women in Nordic Perspective" in MEHDI, R. (ed.), *Integration & Retsudvikling* (Jurist- og Økonomforbundets Forlag, 2007), p. 140 f.

39 In 2008, the Swedish government set up a commission (under the leadership of a professor of government studies) to investigate and propose special education measures for Imams in Sweden, about Swedish society, its traditions, language, institutions and laws. The purpose of this commission was to create means to facilitate the integration of new immigrant groups in Sweden. Nevertheless, in its final report, the commission abstained from delivering any such proposals with reference, inter alia, to constitutional rights and to the official, confession-neutral stance of the Swedish State. All religious communities should be treated on equal terms and the State should not interfere with their exercise of religion. The generally available education in Sweden should be sufficient and should strive to make all citizens share the fundamental values of a democratic society. See SOU 2009:52, 12 f. The report is at present under consultation. Among the Muslim communities in Sweden, the reaction to the idea of special education measures, focused on the communities' religious leadership, has been mixed.

40 RHEINSTEIN, *supra* note 5, p. 153, with reference to the impact of the religious reformation and the Evangelical Luterhan outlook in Sweden.

41 See above, Section 2.2.2.

The *first* stage of special importance is the enactment of the 1734 Marriage Code of Sweden, a codification of family law which for the first time in history covered the whole of Sweden.[42] This codification carried with it a breakthrough of Evangelical Lutheran values and, in that sense, also strengthened the role of the Church of Sweden and the influence of its clergy in the everyday lives of the ordinary people.[43]

The *second* significant stage is a result of Nordic legal cooperation, initiated in the late 1800s and bringing forth almost identical laws on marriage and divorce during the first decades of the twentieth century in the five Nordic countries. The aim was to create a modern law, guided by ideas of humanism and the Enlightenment, at a period of time when the Nordic rural societies were transformed to industrial societies. The importance of religion and Christian ideology decreased.[44]

The *third* stage is still pending. In many ways, it is a follow-up of Sweden's transformation, since the 1930s, into a social welfare state, adjusting legislation to democratic and progressive values, in particular gender equality and related goals. Legislation has also been responding to societal changes. A certain developing European human rights' impact is also visible. These developments have paved the way for the gender-neutral marriage concept adopted in Sweden in 2009. On the other hand, Sweden's transformation into a multicultural, multi-faith society is hardly visible at all in the prevailing substantive family law regulation. An explanation is that the "newcomers" have been expected to be subject to and follow Swedish laws in all respects, unless otherwise provided by the rules of private international law.[45] In certain cases, more restrictive rules have been enacted, in order to prevent practices that are considered harmful, such as the conclusion of child marriages or forced marriages.[46] The contrary

42 Previously, different provincial rules applied for cities and for rural areas.

43 See INGER, G., *Svensk rättshistoria* (Liber, 1980), p. 140.

44 See MODÉER, K.Å., "Secularization, Liberalization and Modernization: Family Law in Scandinavian Welfare States in the 1960s and 1970s" in SCHEIBER, H.N. and MAYALI, L. (eds.), *Japanese Family Law in Comparative Perspective* (The Robbins Collection, 2009), p. 209.

45 See JÄNTERÄ-JAREBORG, M., "Family Law in a Multicultural Sweden – the challenges of migration and religion" in *De lege, Juridiska fakultetens årsbok 2009, Uppsala-Minnesota Colloquium: Law, Culture and Values* (Iustus Förlag, 2009) pp. 145–172, in particular pp. 149–150.

46 See JÄNTERÄ-JAREBORG, M., "Combatting child marriages and forced marriages – the prospects of the Hague Marriage Convention in the Scandinavian 'multicultural' societies" in EINHORN, T. and SIEHR, K. (eds.), *Intercontinental Cooperation through Private International Law, Essays in Memory of Peter E. Nygh* (T.M. Asser Press, 2004), pp. 163–175. See also JÄNTERÄ-JAREBORG, M., "Barn- och tvångsäktenskap i Sverige – finns det utrymme för olika kulturer och tolerans?" in FRANTZEN, T., GIERTSEN, J. and CORDERO MOSS, G. (eds.), *Rett og toleranse, Festskrift til Helge Johan Thue 70 år* (Gyldendal, 2007), pp. 304–320.

trend of striving to open up for a normative multiculturalism is, yet, missing.[47] On the other hand, an increasing number of religious denominations have been authorised by the Swedish State to officiate at marriages. Catholic, Jewish and Muslim denominations are well represented among them.

3.2. MARRIAGE CONCLUSION

3.2.1. The 1734 Marriage Code: Obligatory religious ceremony

A requirement for the legal validity of any marriage, brought forth by the 1734 Marriage Code, was an obligatory religious marriage ceremony, to be conducted by a priest belonging to the Church of Sweden. Until then it had been possible to conclude legally valid marriages also in the form of a secular marriage ceremony. The introduction of an obligatory religious ceremony might appear strange considering that, according to the Evangelical Lutheran approach, officially followed in Sweden since the reformation in the sixteenth century, marriage is not a sacrament but belongs to the "worldly sphere" ("*weltlich Ding*").[48] Although religious reasons were also given in support of the mandatory church ceremony, for example, the particular value of marital status in the Lutheran doctrine,[49] the solution was above all practical with clear administrative advantages. The Church being represented all over the country, everyone had access to its services. The uniform form requirement brought legal clarity concerning whether a man and a woman living together were married to each other or not, and in respect of children's legitimacy.[50] Towards the end of the eighteenth century, Catholics and other "alien (Christian) faiths" were permitted to form congregations in Sweden and to perform marriages within the congregation in accordance with their rites. Also Jews received similar rights. Intermarriage between Christians and those of Mosaic faith was forbidden until 1863, when a special "non-religious" ceremony was introduced for such couples by a special Ordinance. The Muslim presence in Sweden is of much later origin. Hence, in 1930 when for the last time, in connection with the population census, a person's religious affinity was also registered, altogether 15 persons were recorded as Muslims.[51]

47 A natural "testing field" should, in my opinion, be those areas of family law which grant party autonomy, for example the law of inheritance. To the extent that party autonomy prevails, there should also be scope for multicultural normativism. See also SAYED, *supra* note 33.

48 MODÉER, K.Å., "Marriage and Cohabitation in the History of Law" in *Love, Cohabitation and Marriage*, The Theological Committee of the Church of Sweden, Report from a public hearing September 6–9 (Church of Sweden, 2005), p. 55 f.

49 According to Luther, marriage was a "remedium peccati" towards man's inclination to sin. See SCHMIDT, F., *Äktenskapsrätt* (Femte upplagan, Norstedts 1976), p. 14.

50 Nevertheless, so-called incomplete marriages where a man had promised to marry a woman and then had sexual intercourse with her, continued to be acknowledged.

51 See SAYED, *supra* note 33, p. 68 f.

3.2.2. *A united Nordic approach – freedom of choice between ceremonies*

In 1908, a secular "civil marriage ceremony" was introduced as a fully equivalent legal alternative for those couples who otherwise could not marry each other, being of different faiths, or who were not willing to be married within the Church, for example for reasons of conscience.[52] Similar pressures had arisen also in the other Nordic countries, and joint legislative actions were taken. In Sweden, this resulted in the 1915 enactment on the conclusion and dissolution of marriage, which confirmed the two options to enter into a legally valid marriage. In Sweden, as well as in the other Nordic countries, any Church opposition to the reform was overruled. Most importantly, the church wedding ceremony became subject to the rules of civil law. As expressed by the Swedish legal historian Kjell Åke Modéer, "The priest is obliged to establish the marriage by means of a legally effective church wedding under such conditions and prerequisites for the marriage as are to be regulated solely in civil law".[53] That a "religious marriage", conducted under proper state authorisation within a religious denomination in Sweden, also qualifies as a "civil law marriage" in Sweden, appears not to be fully understood among Sweden's religious minorities.

3.2.3. *The present situation and challenges of multiculture*

Until 2010, all ministers of the Church of Sweden were *ex lege*, through an explicit provision in the Marriage Code, authorised to conduct legally valid marriages. This competence followed simply from ordination as a priest of the Church and reflects the Church's former position as the State Church. Today, the right of the Church and its ministers to officiate at marriage ceremonies is subject to the same rules that apply to all religious denominations.[54] This means that both the religious community wishing to celebrate legally valid marriages and its individual officials performing such services, need a special authorisation from the State, to be granted by Swedish Legal, Financial and Administrative Services Agency (*Kammarkollegiet*).

In 2010, such authorisations were granted in relation to approximately 40 religious communities (Free Protestant, Muslim, Mosaic, Roman Catholic, Greek Orthodox, etc.). An authorisation means a delegation of a State law function; therefore it is conditional. The conditions include, inter alia, that the

52 In both cases, special enactments had, nevertheless, been adopted in 1863 and 1873, respectively, enabling a secular marriage.

53 MODÉER, *supra* note 48, p. 58 f.

54 The legal ground follows from a special provision in the Ordinance of Government (*Regeringsformen*), Ch. 11 §6. This provision is a general clause concerning delegation of administrative duties of a public law nature from State to other bodies.

denomination is registered as a so-called faith community in Sweden[55] which gives it legal personality. Furthermore, the denomination's activities must be organised in such a manner that there is reason to expect that it – and the officials authorised for the purpose – will be willing and able to follow the requirements of the Swedish Marriage Code when conducting marriages. This means, in particular, that the impediments to marriage and the form requirements as regards the ceremony, set up in the Marriage Code, must be respected.[56] The spouses-to-be must, for example, be of at least 18 years of age and unmarried, both must be present at the ceremony in addition to witnesses, and both must consent to the marriage. Once the authorised official has declared them to be married to each other, the marriage is legally valid. The authorisation requires in addition, that any marriage must immediately be reported to the national agency in charge of the population records.[57]

Although conditional, this State delegation of powers (to create a legally valid civil status) can be seen as recognition of religion and religion's impact on marriage.[58] The religious community is free to follow its own rites, subject to the mandatory requirements of the Swedish Marriage Code which it has undertaken to follow. This solution also gives scope for a person's religious identity. Consequently, even if religious marriages are no longer as popular as they used to be,[59] the majority of marriages in Sweden continue to be celebrated in a religious form. The reasons for this choice may consist of truly religious concerns – to include God's participation in the marriage – the church building being regarded as a holy place and the priest as God's representative upon earth.[60] Or instead the choice may be motivated by access to a solemn setting for the marriage ceremony, without any particular religious motives.[61] In 2008,

55 To qualify for such registration, the denomination must aim to be a community for religious activities, it must have at least 3.000 members and a required form of organisation. See Act (1998:1593) on Religious Communities and Regulation (1999:731) on Registration of Faith Communities. See also Act (1993:305) on the Right to Officiate at Marriages within Faith Communities.

56 See Marriage Code (1987:230), Ch. 4 §2 and §§5–8.

57 The legal validity of a marriage in the Swedish legal system is, however, not dependent on a subsequent registration of the marriage.

58 "When the legislator recognizes a religious marriage ceremony, he also sanctions the religious norms connected to marriage." And, on the contrary, in those States with mandatory civil marriage, the legislator signals that the secular order prevails and religion is a private matter. See SCHMIDT, *supra* note 49, p. 39.

59 For many years a trend has been visible in Sweden to celebrate big marriages, requiring a lot of festivities. Civil wedding arrangements have become on the level of romantic church weddings, which can explain why church weddings have lost some of their earlier popularity. The couple is also free to choose the site of their wedding; castles, mansions and home-gardens have become popular places for the marriage ceremony.

60 See Church of Sweden, "Information on a possible decision by the Church of Sweden regarding same-sex marriages", Report 17 September 2009, p. 10.

61 See HALLAMAA, J., *supra* note 20.

altogether 44.1 per cent of all marriages concluded that year were celebrated within the Church of Sweden. Nevertheless, ten years earlier in 1998, the corresponding figure was 61.9 per cent. The figures from the other Nordic countries, all with similar Evangelical Lutheran Folk Churches, are in line with the Swedish development. In 2008, more than 10 per cent of all marriages that year were celebrated within other religious communities in Sweden, under proper authorisation.

For reasons of clarity, it should be emphasised that everybody in Sweden has access to the same secular marriage ceremony, irrespective of one's faith. Even "believers" may for one reason or another choose a secular ceremony instead of a religious one. The parties are free to confirm an informal religious marriage by a secular marriage ceremony in Sweden, rendering the marriage a legal validity. Access to a religious wedding, on the contrary, is not fully a matter of choice for the parties but dependent on the consulted religious denomination's willingness to officiate at the marriage.[62]

The Swedish legal system refuses to recognise religious marriages celebrated in Sweden when the religious community or the person conducting the ceremony lacked the authorisation required by Swedish law. In these cases, the denomination/marriage official had no legally recognised "jurisdiction" to conclude the marriage, with the result that no legally valid marriage has come into existence and it cannot be registered as a marriage in Sweden's population records. The "marriage" remains informal but the parties may still qualify for the protection provided by the Swedish Cohabitee Act (2003:376) for couples cohabiting out of marriage, on condition that neither of them is married (to somebody else).[63] The non-recognition of the "marriage" in a case like this is not a matter of discrimination or lack of respect for one's religion, but about respecting the law.

Nevertheless, it appears that this distinction between "purely religious marriages" and "marriages celebrated in a religious ceremony but qualifying as civil law marriages" as well, is not clear to everybody. *One the one hand,* there are cases where an informal religious marriage has been chosen intentionally. For example, according to an investigation by the Swedish Youth Agency (*Ungdomsstyrelsen*) concerning the period between 2005–2007, 25 per cent of the persons under the

---

62 In Sweden, for example, the Catholic Church refuses to officiate at marriages where the parties or one of them has, previously, divorced.

63 This enactment provides, upon separation, for a certain basic protection regarding the family home and joint house hold goods. See, for example, JÄNTERÄ-JAREBORG, M., "Schweden" in KROPPENBERG, SCHWAB, HENRICH, GOTTWALD and SPICKHOFF (eds.), *Rechtsregeln für nichteheliches Zusammenleben*, Beiträge zum europäischen Familienrecht, Band 12 (Gieseking, 2009), pp. 207–226 (in English).

age of 18 who applied for a special dispensation to marry before that age were already "married" in the form of a "religious" or other "traditional marriage ceremony".[64] These figures have raised concerns in Sweden and they are part of the public debate linked with "involuntary marriages" against the wishes of the child; legislative counter measures towards such informal "child marriages" are at present under consideration. *On the other hand*, there have also been cases where both adult parties have been mistaken regarding the legal validity of their religious marriage. In such cases, on exceptional grounds, the Swedish Ministry of Justice may, upon application of the parties or one of them, decide that the marriage is to be regarded as legally valid in Sweden.[65] Such applications are rare, approximately one per year.

3.2.4. The tension of same-sex marriages

The State may stipulate the conditions upon which it is willing to delegate the exercise of an official power. But it cannot force religious communities or their officials to marry people against the community's or the official's own notion of religion. In this respect, the freedom of religion, sanctioned by the Constitution of Sweden and the European Convention on Human Rights, sets limits for measures by the State. As a result, the position of religious denominations authorised to celebrate marriages differs from that of *civil marriage authorities* who by law, in their office, are obliged to marry everybody qualifying for marriage. In a double track system of marriage conclusion, such as the Swedish one, issues of (alleged) discrimination arise, when some couples are denied the right to a legally valid religious ceremony whereas others have access to it. Should not everybody's religious identity be recognised on the same terms?

This issue has recently been much debated in Sweden as a result of the new gender-neutral marriage concept, in force since 1 May 2009.[66] The faith

64 See: *Gift mot sin vilja,* Ungdomsstyrelsens rapport 2009:5, p. 269. The application is to be made to the competent county administrative board. The required permission for the marriage may be granted by the board only if there is a special reason for doing so, following a restrictive practice. See JÄNTERÄ-JAREBORG, *supra* note 45, pp. 158–160.

65 A requirement is that the parties should be in agreement that they intended, from the beginning, to conclude a legally valid marriage and that there is no contradictory evidence. If one of the parties was aware of the purely religious nature of the marriage, the marriage is not recognised. It is not sufficient for recognition in Sweden that the parties have registered their marriage in Sweden, having concluded an informal marriage in their country of origin. See SOU 2007:17, 301 and JÄNTERÄ-JAREBORG, M., "Transnationella familjer ur ett internationellt privaträttsligt perspektiv – särskilt avseende äktenskap" in SINGER, A., JÄNTERÄ-JAREBORG, M. and SCHLYTTER, A. (eds.), *Familj – Religion – Rätt, En Antologi om kulturella spänningar i familjen – med Sverige och Turkiet som exempel* (Iustus Förlag, 2010), pp. 215–217.

66 See JÄNTERÄ-JAREBORG, M., "Sweden: The Same-Sex Marriage Reform with Special Regard to Concerns of Religion" in *Zeitschrift für das gesamte Familienrecht* 2010, pp. 1505–

communities in Sweden made it clear that from their point of view it would be better to relinquish the right to officiate at marriages than to contribute to the constitution of marriages which are in conflict with the communities' own notion of marriage.[67] The double track system was, nevertheless, maintained with reference to the importance of people's preferences and the freedom of choice, the customs of Sweden and the desirability of avoiding two ceremonies, when people find it important to give their marriage a religious recognition.[68] To meet the concerns of the freedom of religion, an explicit provision was added to the Marriage Code stating that no faith community or its marriage official would be under any *obligation* to celebrate a marriage.[69] On the other hand, all religious communities authorised by the State to celebrate marriages have the *right* to marry same-sex couples. So far, among Sweden's numerous religious communities, only the Church of Sweden has taken the decision to marry same-sex couples.[70] This Church is, however, split on the issue, and it is up to each of its ministers to decide whether to officiate at a same-sex marriage or not.[71] A couple of small religious communities have relinquished their state-authorised right to officiate at marriages. According to critics, official powers should not be delegated by the State when they are exercised in a discriminatory manner. Consequently, religion should be seen as incompatible with any exercise of public powers.

An important aspect which has received much less attention is the following. The religious denominations' right to officiate at marriages is one of the few expressions of family law explicitly recognising a person's religious identity. Furthermore, the authorised religious communities and their authorised officials have undertaken to respect the provisions of the Swedish Marriage Code when celebrating marriages. This, if anything, is an example of the kind of

1508 and JÄNTERÄ-JAREBORG, *supra* note 20. For a broader overview on the law's development towards permitting same-sex marriages, see SÖRGJERD, C., *Reconstructing Marriage in a Changing Legal and Societal Landscape, Challenges of New Cohabitation Models in Sweden* (Uppsala University, 2011), pp. 185-235.

67 In debate articles in leading Swedish new papers, this view was advocated also by several bishops of the Church of Sweden.

68 See SOU 2007:17, p. 41.

69 Marriage Code, Ch. 4 §3.2. It follows, that the authorised marriage officials of the faith communities are free to follow their faith in deciding who do not qualify for a church marriage, for example due to sexual orientation, a previous divorce, or other grounds.

70 This decision was taken by the highest decision-making body of the Church of Sweden, *the General Synod*, four months after the new legislation had entered into force. Prior to the decision, theological committees within the Church analysed whether it was possible to combine the new marriage concept with the Evangelical Lutheran understanding of marriage. See JÄNTERÄ-JAREBORG, *supra* note 66, p. 1506 f.

71 According to Church Order, the senior priest of each parish is responsible for ensuring that those willing and qualifying to get married in the Church are also able to do so and to appoint a minister who is willing to conduct the ceremony.

"accommodation" needed in multi-faith societies. It can, therefore, be argued that to abolish this right would contradict the spirit of a late post-modern society striving to give scope for freedom of choice and a plurality of options.[72] But it has also been argued that this right cements patriarchic values, transforms individual rights into collective rights and contributes to "politics of difference", where each concerned community can claim a unique identity.[73]

4. DIVORCE AND RELIGION

4.1. DIVORCE UNDER THE 1734 MARRIAGE CODE

In accordance with the Evangelical Lutheran interpretation of the New Testament, the 1734 Marriage Code recognised two grounds for divorce, namely adultery and malicious desertion.[74] In addition, the King had the power to grant divorce upon dispensation, in order to enable both spouses to remarry, but only after both spouses had been warned by the Church and after a decree of separation.[75] In practice, those with financial means achieved divorce through an arranged "malicious desertion" whereby one spouse, usually the husband, travelled to the nearest foreign city (normally Copenhagen). The wife then sued him in court claiming divorce on the ground that he maliciously and wilfully had deserted her, the defendant admitting the circumstances of the case and divorce was granted.[76] The shortcoming of the system was that it gave the clergy considerable influence (warnings to spouses) or, alternatively, was very easily set aside (arranged malicious desertion).[77]

4.2. A UNITED NORDIC APPROACH TO DIVORCE

The divorce provisions of the 1734 Marriage Code were set aside by the above-mentioned 1915 Act on the conclusion and dissolution of marriage, as a result of

72 See JÄNTERÄ-JAREBORG, *supra* note 66, p. 1507.

73 See ROALD, A.S., "Vigselrättens symbolvärde", *Invandrare & minoriteter* 2010, pp. 30–33.

74 Statements in Matthew XIX and Paul's First Epistle to the Corinthians VII were considered to legitimise divorce. See SCHMIDT, F., "The 'leniency' of the Scandinavian divorce laws", *Scandinavian Studies in Law* 1963, pp. 110–111.

75 In an Ordinance of Divorces issued in 1810, this royal prerogative was explicitly recognised. The procedure remained, nevertheless, cumbersome and time-consuming. See SCHMIDT, *ibid.*, pp. 111–112.

76 See SCHMIDT, *ibid.*

77 In the more poetic words by Rheinstein, "The demand was for a law that would no longer favor the rich over the poor, that would no longer expose the parties to the 'humiliating indignity' of public admonition in church, that would instate truthfulness in place of hypocrisy of feigning desertion to foreign parts". See RHEINSTEIN, *supra* note 5, p. 136 f.

Nordic legal cooperation. This enactment introduced irretrievable ("deep and permanent") breakdown of the marriage as a divorce ground, after a decree of legal separation, in addition to various primarily fault-based divorce grounds,[78] and directed all divorces to ordinary courts. Joint application by the spouses for a decree of separation became sufficient proof of the breakdown of the marriage. Having lived apart for one year after the decree of separation, each spouse had the right to apply for divorce. A few years later, the provisions of this Act were a transferred into the 1920 Marriage Code and remained in force, with some minor changes, until 1974. The prominent Swedish family law scholar, Anders Agell, described this legislation as very liberal at the time of its enactment; it was followed by corresponding rules in other European countries only 50–60 years later.[79]

It is a commonly held opinion in Nordic legal literature that the uniform Nordic divorce rules were designed as secular statements, to do away with religious constraints. It has also been claimed that, for example in Sweden, the Church did not object to the reform; liberalism having achieved an early foothold among the leadership of the Church.[80] On the other hand, religion's continued impact on the new divorce rules has been recognised alongside the ideas of the Enlightenment. Of importance was, not least, that mediation remained obligatory,[81] and normally was carried out by the clergy within their office as ministers of the Church. Yet, as expressed by the Swedish law professor Folke Schmidt, in essence, the new enactments meant an emancipation of the law of marriage from the Church and women's emancipation from men.[82] Nevertheless, a common opinion in Sweden is that Swedish society affirmed to solid conservative family ideals until the 1960s.[83]

78 These consisted of adultery, malicious desertion, bigamy, threatening the life of the other spouse, sentence to hard labour for more than three years, addiction to excessive use of alcohol, contagious venereal disease, incurable insanity and presumption of death.

79 See JÄNTERÄ-JAREBORG, M., "National Report of Sweden" (Question 2) in BOELE-WOELKI, K., BRAAT, B. and SUMNER, I. (eds.), *European Family Law in Action, Volume I: Grounds for Divorce* (Intersentia, 2003).

80 See RHEINSTEIN, *supra* note 5, p. 153.

81 This has also been claimed to be "the last successful demand regarding family law coming from the Swedish church". See MODÉER, *supra* note 44, p. 213 with reference to SUNDBY, O., *Luthersk äktenskapsuppfattning: En studie i den kyrkliga äktenskapsdebatten i Sverige efter 1900* (Lund, 1959).

82 See SCHMIDT, *supra* note 49, p. 16.

83 See NYGREN, R., "Legal Culture and World Value Mapping", in *Europäische Rechtsgeschichte und europäische Integration, Heinz Mohnhaupt von seinen skandinavischen Kollegen gewidmet* (Rönnells, 2002), pp. 116–117.

4.3. THE PRESENT SITUATION

> "Sweden is a society where the need to marry, remarry or remain in an unhappy marriage for reasons of status, economic security, or for the sake of children, would appear to have been reduced as a result of social welfare, labour market and equality policies. This has been a conscious objective."[84]

The prevailing rules on divorce originate from a law reform in 1973, carried out by Sweden on its own.[85] A guiding principle of the law reform was to remove from law all moral and ethical evaluations.[86] An unconditional right to divorce was introduced, and all particular grounds for divorce were abandoned.[87] A spouse's wish to dissolve the marriage, demonstrated in the form of a divorce application to court, alone became decisive. "Fault" in the breakdown of marriage lost all legal relevance; also in respect of any ancillary claim. All requirements of mediation preceding a divorce were abandoned, as an unjustified public interference within spousal autonomy to freely dissolve a marriage. The assessment of any ancillary issues could be postponed until a divorce decree. The institutions of legal separation and marriage annulment[88] were abolished from legislation as redundant.

Although the preparatory works preceding this reform explicitly focused on the desirability of emancipating law from all moral and ethical evaluations, the abandoned values were also part of Sweden's religious heritage, which in the case of legal separation and marriage annulment originated from the Canon law era. If secularisation means abandoning the law's religious heritage, then the decisive step in Sweden was taken in connection with the 1973 reform. It was only then that "secular rationality" replaced "traditional rationality", in the words of the Swedish legal historian Rolf Nygren.[89] According to Nygren, traditional rational

---

84 BRADLEY, D., "Radical Principles and the Legal Institution of Marriage: Domestic Relations Law and Social Democracy in Sweden" (1990) *International Journal of Law and the Family*, p. 178.

85 From the point of view of Nordic legal co-operation, the new legislation meant Sweden's unilateral departure from the above described principles agreed by the Nordic states to govern divorce. BRADLEY, *ibid.*, p. 156, connects this law reform with an aim of "social engineering" at a (nation State) political level. The new rules entered into force on 1 January 1974. In 1987, when the new Marriage Code was enacted in Sweden, these rules were transferred, unaltered, into the new Code.

86 The 1973 law reform was not limited to issues of divorce, but covered also, *inter alia*, marriage conclusion – reducing marriage impediment to a minimum. In addition, certain basic protective rules were introduced regarding cohabitation outside of marriage.

87 See JÄNTERÄ-JAREBORG, *supra* note 79.

88 During the period between 1959–1970, altogether 29 marriages were annulled in Sweden. See SCHMIDT, *supra* note 49, p. 42.

89 See NYGREN, *supra* note 83, p. 114. See also BRADLEY, *supra* note 84, p. 161 and pp. 164–167.

authority appreciates religion, patriarchal and multi-child family structures and promotes confidence in authorities and hierarchic systems. Secular rational authority, on the other hand, negates such values and prefers the opposite. Secular rational authority is based on individualism, is open to alternative life-styles and is suspicious of hierarchic institutions and family patterns. Through the 1973 enactments, Swedish legislation on family law took the lead of modernity in family law.[90]

4.4. DIVORCE AND MULTICULTURE

In a multicultural context the present Swedish divorce law raises two primary concerns.

The *first* relates to the confusion existing among many religious communities (and believers) in Sweden as regards marriages validly celebrated within a religious community in Sweden and marriages celebrated in a "secular order" in Sweden.[91] Under the divorce rules of the Swedish Marriage Code, applicable to everybody falling under Swedish jurisdiction,[92] a *legally valid marriage* (irrespective of whether it was concluded in a religious or a secular ceremony, in Sweden or abroad) can, in Sweden, only be dissolved by decree of a court. Religious denominations do not have jurisdiction to validly dissolve a marriage in Sweden. In particular, Muslim believers may insist on a Muslim divorce, as well. Cases are reported where a divorce decree, by Swedish court, upon initiative of the wife and without the husband's consent, is not recognised in the couple's Muslim congregation – or in their country of origin.[93] Conflicts like this[94] would require a proper dialogue between the Swedish State and, in particular, those religious denominations which have been authorised by the Swedish State to conclude legally valid marriages in Sweden.[95] The Norwegian solution, requiring

90 NYGREN, *supra* note 83, p. 117. See also MODÉER, *supra* note 44, p. 215.

91 Confusion exists also in relation to religiously celebrated marriages, see above Section 3.2.2.

92 In addition, since the 1973 reform, the Swedish private international law rules concerning the law applicable to divorce are also based on the *lex fori* principle.

93 See JÄNTERÄ-JAREBORG, *supra* note 65, pp. 235 f. and JÄNTERÄ-JAREBORG, *supra* note 45, pp. 164–167.

94 Beneath the divorce conflict can also lie a dispute concerning the wife's right to receive whatever "mahr" is yet to be paid. Swedish courts have examined several disputes on "mahr". See SAYED, M., "The Muslim Dower (Mahr) in Europe – With special reference to Sweden" in BOELE-WOELKI, K. and SVERDRUP, T. (eds.), *European Challenges in Contemporary Family Law* (Intersentia, 2008), pp. 187–208.

95 These denominations have, namely, undertaken to respect the provisions of the Swedish Marriage Code and related provisions, when officiating at marriages in Sweden. Due to the recent origin of Muslim presence in Sweden, the level of organisation among Swedish

each state-authorised marriage authority in Norway (whether secular or religious), in the marriage ceremony itself, to also request whether the parties consent not only to the marriage but also to each other's unilateral right to dissolve the marriage is, naturally, one way out,[96] but it cannot be combined with all religions.[97]

The *second* concern relates to the exclusivity of divorce as the only available instrument to dissolve a marriage in Sweden, save death. This raises concerns of religion, as illustrated by the following case: A woman of Catholic faith raised a petition in a Swedish court in 2006 for a nullity decree of her marriage, validly celebrated in Sweden in 1992 within a Catholic congregation, on the ground that she had been forced into the marriage. The marriage had been dissolved by divorce decree of a Swedish court in 1993; furthermore it had been declared void by decree of a Canon law court in 1997, but such decrees have no civil effects in Sweden. She motivated her petition by reference to her Catholic faith and the importance for her well-being of the society recognising the nullity of the marriage. Her petition was rejected by the court as unfounded.[98] Other cases involve polygamous marriages, which also must be dissolved by divorce in Sweden.[99] It is to be hoped that reintroduction of marriage annulment into Swedish legislation – or the possibility to apply for a nullity decree – will be considered in the near future.

Muslims is low and no Sharia councils exist. The problem relates not only to Muslim denominations but also to several others, for example the Catholic Church in Sweden.

96 Norwegian Marriage Act 1991, Article 7.1. See MEHDI, *supra* note 38, pp. 144–145. According to Mehdi this solution is inspired by the sharia concept of *talaq-e-tafweez*, enabling the spouses-to-be at the time of the marriage contract to also stipulate in the contract that both parties shall have equal right to divorce.

97 In Norway, the primary opposition has come from the Catholic denominations in Norway. From Islamic perspective, on the other hand, this solution is not problematic.

98 See the judgment of the Court of Appeal, *Hovrätten för Övre Norrland*, T 689–06, 20 December 2006. Both the first instance court and the court of appeal shared the conclusion. Of relevance for the courts' reasoning seems to have been that the marriage had already been dissolved by divorce in Sweden. Divorce is the all-inclusive remedy under Swedish law also in cases of defect in the act of consent to the marriage and in cases where a marriage is concluded in breach of an absolute marriage impediment.

99 See JÄNTERÄ-JAREBORG, M., "Kan polygami vara laglig i Sverige? Thuréusföredrag den 31 augusti 2010" in *Kungl. Vetenskaps-Societeten i Uppsala Årsbok 2010* (Universitetstryckeriet Uppsala, 2010), pp. 83–96.

5. THE "PARADOXES" – A SUMMARY OF THE INTER-RELATION BETWEEN FAMILY LAW AND RELIGION IN SWEDEN

Through enactments adopted in the 1970s, Swedish legislation has been claimed to have taken "the lead of modernity" in family law.[100] The idea that Swedish family law would, at the same time, be sensitive to concerns of religion and faith might not fit well with this understanding. In this contribution, three paradoxes relating to family law and religion in Sweden have been identified.

The *first* one relates to the high church membership rates in Sweden and the continued popularity of church rites, for example as a form of celebrating a marriage, while at the same time the majority population does not participate in any other church activities. In spite of recent heavy criticism of church marriages, in connection with the same-sex (or gender-neutral) marriage reform in 2009, Swedish legislation continues to be based on a double track model, permitting religious marriages and secular marriages, both with full civil law effects. At the same time, the freedom of the religious communities and their officials to choose whom they are willing to marry is respected. Approximately 40 faith communities in Sweden have at present a State-authorisation to conclude legally valid marriages. Marriage dissolution in the form of divorce is concentrated in secular courts; death being in Sweden the only "divine method" of legally dissolving a marriage.

The *second* paradox is a more complicated one, and has not yet been subjected to any close analysis. It is based on the allegation that Swedish family law legislation is not as secular and neutral in relation to the majority religion – the Evangelical Lutheran faith of the Church of Sweden – as is commonly assumed. Instead, it expresses the values of that faith, which may violate other people's faith or conscience, irrespective of whether the latter are believers or non-believers. On the other hand, it is also claimed that legislation does not take religion and religious concerns seriously. This, in turn, may be experienced by followers of other faiths or even atheists as a lack of respect for, or even violation of, their own outlook. Again, the Swedish legislative solutions in connection with the same-sex marriage reform can be given as an example. It may well be possible to justify this reform with reference to Lutheran theology, as the Church of Sweden has done when taking the decision to officiate at same-sex marriages.[101] But one

100 Characteristic of this was that the legislation "promoted an attitude of allowing whatever to be permissible". See NYGREN, *supra* note 83, p. 117.

101 See Church of Sweden, "Information on a possible decision by the Church of Sweden regarding same-sex marriages", Report 17 September 2009, 14. The decisive line of argument for the decision taken was to answer whether same-sex marriage would harm or benefit

can hardly expect all other religions communities of Sweden to follow suit. Same-sex marriages and the continued double track system of marriage celebration are nails in the eye for both believers and non-believers, although for diametrically opposed reasons. More generally, the legislator's dilemma is how to contribute to an increased "feeling of belonging" and inclusion in society.

The *third* paradox is the experience that traditions and customs are strengthened in diaspora and extensively regarded as parts of religion and also law. This increases not only the confusion regarding what qualifies as "religion" or as "law" but also concerning what the legal system should protect as part of freedom of religion or, for example, as part of a person's right to private life and family life under the European Convention of Human Rights. The legal-religious mix of norms, originating from other cultures, may be in contradiction of established values of the Swedish legal system, in particular those of gender equality and sexual equality.

The identified paradoxes make Swedish legislation on issues of the family an interesting object of study. Future law reforms will need to pay more attention to these paradoxes. We are heading towards a challenging future which will require a clear stance on how Swedish family law relates to religion.[102]

people. The conclusion drawn was that same-sex marriage is a good way for society to support people and, therefore, in line with Evangelical Lutheran doctrine. This is also in line with Lutheran understanding of the biblical commandment of love. It was also pointed out that religious traditions must undergo changes. Otherwise, the Church would still prohibit the priesthood of women, and advocate the death penalty, slavery and men's superiority over women.

102 To a certain extent, this development will most probably be guided by the European Court on Human Rights.

FAMILY LAW AND RELIGION: THE RUSSIAN PERSPECTIVE, PAST AND PRESENT

Masha ANTOKOLSKAIA

1. INTRODUCTION

Russia is a rather interesting case for studying the interactions between religion and family law. For centuries Russia had no family laws other than religious ones. Then after the Bolshevik Revolution of 1917 it faced one of the most sudden experiences in European history of a radical break with religion. One of the first things the Bolsheviks did after they seized power was to vigorously purge the family of every bit of religious influence. Subsequently, Russia entered a 70-year-long period of "militant atheism". After the collapse of the Soviet system the secular character of family law has been preserved, but relations between family law and religious rules have changed from hostile to benevolent.

Thus, the history of Russian family law could be roughly divided in two major periods: the period of religious family laws before the Revolution of 1917 and the period of secular family law thereafter. Both periods will be looked at in this essay. In the first section, the period of religious family law will be addressed from the historical perspective and set against similar developments in the Western Europe. In the second section, the period of radical transformation from religious to strictly secular law and the subsequent period of "militant-atheism" will be dealt with. Thereby the puzzling issue of the limits of the use of (family) law as an instrument of social engineering will be addressed. In the final section the current benevolent co-existence between family law and religion will be briefly depicted.

2. THE PERIOD OF RELIGIOUS FAMILY LAW

The "religious" period of the history of Russian family can be in turn divided into two parts: the early period of pure canon family law, which lasted from the adoption of Christianity in 988 to the reforms of Peter the Great in the first part of the eighteenth century; and the late period of a mixture of canon and secular laws, which commenced with the reforms of Peter the Great and ended with the Revolution of 1917.

2.1. MIDDLE AGES: THE PERIOD OF PURE RELIGIOUS FAMILY LAW

Russia was Christianised in 988 and received the Eastern Orthodox Christendom from Byzantium, rather then the Western Roman Catholic Christendom from Rome. This major event was accompanied by the complete reception of the Orthodox canon law. The codification of Orthodox canon law – *Nomocanon*[1] became fully applicable in Russia. After the great schism of 1054, that formally divided the Orthodox and the Roman Catholic Churches, Russia remained within the Orthodox realm. Notwithstanding the schism, many developments in the domain of family law in the East and the West during the Middle Ages were surprisingly similar.

In both parts of Europe, the Church acquired all but exclusive competence in family matters. In Russia the competence of the ecclesiastical authorities in family matters became even broader than in Western Europe. Church law came to govern marriage, divorce, nullity of marriage and illegitimacy. Special ecclesiastical courts were established for adjudicating marriage and divorce cases. In contrast to Western Europe, the Russian Church also acquired competence in all matrimonial property disputes.[2] Matrimonial property cases were dealt with by special Church courts. Those courts applied canon law, but their judges were mainly recruited from among laymen.[3]

The sets of canon family laws developed on both sides of the Orthodox-Catholic divide were in many ways strikingly similar.[4] Around the eleventh century, marriage was proclaimed a sacrament and came to be seen as a sacral symbol of the unification of Christ and the Church. In the same period, the impediments to marriage were made rather severe in both parts of the Christian world. Two councils of Rome (721 and 744) ruled that a man could not marry those to whom

1 From Greek *νομος* and *κανων*. Made by John the Scholastic, Patriarch of Constantinople (565–577), who has digested all known canons of Councils, supplemented with the sentences of the Fathers, as early as the sixth century.

2 ZAGOROVSKII, I., *Kurs semeinogo prava* (*Course of Family Law*) (Zertzalo, 2003: Reprint of the 1909 edition), p. 198.

3 METROPOLITAN MAKARIY, *The History of the Russian Church*, book IV, pt II book IV (Spaso-Preobragenskiy Monastery, 1996), p. 106.

4 See ANTOKOLSKAIA, M., *Harmonisation of Family Law in Europe: A Historical Perspective. A Tale of Two Millenia* (Intersentia, 2006), pp. 101–115.

he was related in the third and fourth degrees (niece or first cousin).[5] In the mid-eighth century, the prohibited degree of consanguinity was extended to the seventh degree. The Church equally extended this prohibition to the spiritual kinship created by baptism or confirmation.[6] Peculiarly enough, at the same time, the Eastern Church independently extended the impediments up to the seventh degree of consanguinity, affinity and spiritual kinship.[7] Marriage-as-sacrament came to be seen as principally indissoluble. Concubinage and illegitimate children, largely tolerated during the pre-Christian and early Christian periods, were entirely outlawed.

Along with these major similarities, rather significant differences between the two systems of canon family law can also be distinguished. The chief differences were twofold: the rejection of the consensual theory of marriage and of the doctrine of absolute indissolubility of marriage by the Orthodox Church.

In the course of the eleventh century the Catholic Church adopted a consensual theory of marriage as its doctrine. In short, this meant that a marriage based purely upon consent of the parties was valid, even if all other elements such as consummation, parental consent and Church solemnisation were lacking. In line with the consensual theory, it was considered that it was not the priests, but the parties themselves that gave sacrament to each other. In the Orthodox East, the consensual theory never managed to prevail. Around the twelfth century, Church solemnisation of marriage was made compulsory for all marriages in the Orthodox East.[8] Around the same time parental consent also became a requirement for the validity of marriage. Consensus of the parties was regarded as an indispensable element of the formation of marriage but, unlike in the Catholic West, it was not the consensus but the priestly blessing that made the marriage a sacrament. Therefore, in the Orthodox law the priestly blessing acquired the status of the second constitutive element of marriage alongside the consensus.[9] In Russia, however, the law in action differed from the law in the books. Although the Russian Church always insisted on the free consent of the parties to a marriage, it was unable to implement this rule in practice. The practice of arranged marriages was facilitated by the usage of betrothing children

5 GIES, F. and GIES, J., *Marriage and the Family in the Middle Ages* (Harper & Row, 1989), p. 84.

6 GOODY, J., *The European Family, An Historico- Anthropological Essay (*Blackwell, 2000), p. 28.

7 In fact these restrictions went less far as the Eastern Church kept counting according to the Roman method.

8 TROITSKII, S., *Khristianskaia filisofia braka* (Christian Philosophy of Marriage) (Put, 1995), p. 192.

9 NEUHAUS, P. *et al.*, "The Family in Religious and Customary Laws" in, GLENDON, M.-A. (ed.), *International Encyclopaedia of Comparative Law,* Vol. IV *Persons and Family* (Martinus Nijhoff Publishers, 1983), pp. 16–17.

in their infancy and the custom that a groom should not see a bride before the wedding.[10]

The second important difference was the attitudes of the Churches toward divorce. The Roman Catholic Church interpreted the scripture in the way that marriage ought to be rendered indissoluble. With the acknowledgment of the sacramental nature of marriage, the doctrine of indissolubility gained in strength. Consequently divorce with the possibility of remarriage was no longer permitted. The only way of terminating marriage was annulment: nullification with retroactive effect upon violation of the validity requirements such as consent of the parties and the prohibited degrees of relationship. The Orthodox Church also rendered marriage indissoluble as a rule, but nonetheless allowed divorce and remarriage in case of adultery,[11] choosing to enter the religious life, and a few other instances. The Orthodox example shows that the development of the concept of marriage as a sacrament did not necessitate rendering marriage indissoluble. The Byzantine theologians managed to reconcile the sacred character of marriage with a limited admissibility of divorce.[12] Still, divorce in the Orthodox countries was almost as rare as annulment in the Catholic part of Europe. After Christianisation, the Byzantine divorce law was received in Russia, however, the grounds for divorce under Russian canon law, identical to the Byzantine ones in the books, were not the same in practice. For instance, divorce for the wife's adultery, compulsory under Byzantine law, was only compulsory for priests under Russian law. Some grounds, like a wife's attendance at a theatre or circus without her husband's consent, were never applied in Russia due to the absence of both theatres and circuses. At the same time, divorce on the ground of choosing monastic life became very popular in Russia and acquired rather excessive forms, as for the purposes of divorce wives were often forced by their husbands into nunneries against their will.[13]

Byzantine law already forbade concubinage altogether in 887.[14] After its accession to Christianity, Russia imported this prohibitive attitude towards concubinage as a part of its transplanted Byzantine law. In addition, differing from Western

---

10 ZAGOROVSKII, *supra* note 2, p. 214.

11 It is interesting to note that the double standards regarding male and female adultery that developed in Roman law came to prevail in Russian canon law over the teaching of the Church regarding the equality of spousal duty of fidelity. ZAGOROVSKII, *supra* note 2, p. 104.

12 Their reasoning was that marriage was a gift of God's grace and not a magic action. Being only human, the parties to a marriage could make mistakes and ask for this grace while they were not yet ready to receive it. Therefore the Church accepted that the sacrament could in exceptional cases be regarded as not properly received and the Church authorities could dissolve such marriages. TROITSKII, *supra* note 8, p. 244.

13 ZAGOROVSKII, *supra* note 2, pp. 105–110.

14 VOLTERRA, E., *La conception du mariage d'après les juristes romains* (La Garangola, 1940), p. 676.

and Byzantine laws, Russian canon and secular law did not allow legitimisation by the subsequent marriage of the parents.[15]

It should be mentioned that, after Russia became Orthodox, the requirements of the Orthodox canon family law were for a long time obeyed only by the nobility. In Northern Russia where Christianisation was weaker, instances of polygamy and keeping a concubine among common people were recorded even in the thirteenth century. The population also continued to marry according to pagan customs, considering the Church solemnisation only relevant for "princes and barons".[16]

2.2. NEW TIMES: RELIGIOUS FAMILY LAW WITH SOME SECULAR FLAVOUR

2.2.1. *Reforms of Peter the Great*

After the fall of Byzantium in 1453, Russia became by far the most important country of Orthodox Christendom. Until the eighteenth century, the Russian Orthodox Church enjoyed exclusive jurisdiction in an even broader scope of family matters than the Roman Catholic Church during its hey day. This came to an end in the early eighteenth century when Peter the Great transformed the half-oriental Russia into the westernised Russian Empire. The impact of Peter's reforms on family law was fairly comparable to that of the Protestant Reformation in Western Europe. Peter the Great's ecclesiastical reforms were clearly inspired by the State churches of the Reformed countries. He did away with the independence of the Russian Church and abolished the position of the Patriarch. Consequently, the Russian Orthodox Church became a kind of State church with the Tsar as its head and the *Holly Synod* as its highest authority. The ecclesiastical jurisdiction in family matters was diminished, and secular laws replaced some parts of the canon family law.

Modern time was also characterised by the "Westernisation" of Eastern Europe; thus, Eastern Europe came to be influenced by the same developments and ideas as Western Europe. Peter the Great, eager to "westernise" Russia, reformed family law in line with contemporary European trends. At the time of his accession to the throne, Russia was a patriarchal, oriental country, where family life of nobility and common people alike was guided by the influential sixteenth-

15 It was explicitly forbidden in an important 1648 Code (Vol. X, 280). See: ZAGOROVSKII, *supra* note 2, p. 333.

16 SOLOV'EV, C., *Istoria Rissii 1054–1462*, in *Istoria Rissii s drevneishih vremen (History of Russia from the Ancient Times)*, book II (Astrel, 2001), p. 89.

century handbook *Domostroy*,[17] which contained detailed instructions on how the husband should rule the household by chastening his wife, children and servants. The notion of courtly love and the cult of fair lady which profoundly influenced the perception of women in Western Europe, did not reach Russia until the times of Peter the Great. From the High Middle Ages till the times of Peter the Great, a Russian upper class woman would spend her life under conditions resembling those of a harem, hardly ever seeing any man that did not belong to her close family.[18] Marriages were arranged by the parents, and the future spouses often did not even see each other before the day of the wedding.[19] Peter the Great put a rapid end to this situation by forcing the nobility to let their wives and daughters to leave the confinement of their home, put on Western clothes and take part in balls and other entertainment of the newly established courtly life.[20] Secular law reinforced the previously widely neglected canon law requirement of free consent of the parties to a marriage.[21] At the same time, family control over marriages was strengthened. Although the absence of parental consent did not make a marriage invalid, children of any age married without consent of their parents could be punished through disinheritance.[22] As everywhere in Europe after the Council of Trent,[23] the requirements for the solemnisation of marriage became stricter. After due announcement, the solemnisation of marriage had to be conducted in public in the presence of the parties and witnesses. From 1775 on, the solemnisation had to be performed in the parish church of the bride or the groom. Other innovations were also similar to those in Western Europe. For instance, the degrees of consanguinity and affinity impeding marriage were limited to the fourth degree.[24]

Even in the Middle Ages the Orthodox law always allowed divorce, albeit under rigid conditions. The reforms of Peter the Great did not make divorce easier.

---

17 The literal meaning of this title is: "how-to-build-up-a-household". The second part of this handbook contained guidelines on how "to live in peace with wife, children, and servants" according to the patriarchal ideal, and "how to punish and to teach them". So "a wife should submit herself to her husband, and do everything that he orders her with fear and love" (chapter 29). Next followed the advice to punish the wife without witnesses. The oldest known version of *Domostroy* was compiled in the first half of the sixteenth century. Later this popular manual was re-edited and amended many times. For more details see: METROPOLITAN MAKARIY, *supra* note 3, pp. 445–449.

18 SOLOV'EV, *supra* note 16, p. 197.

19 KARAMZIN, N., *The History of the State of Russia* (Eksmo, 2003), p. 593.

20 *Ibid.*, p. 999.

21 A short-lived Ukase of Peter the Great required a sworn statement of the parents that they had not forced their children into marriage. Later Article 12 of the *Svod Zakonov* repeated the requirement of "free and unforced" consent of the parties to a marriage.

22 Article 6 of the *Svod Zakonov*.

23 The Council of Trent held in 1563 made public church solemnisation a legal requirement for the validity of marriage.

24 Ukas of the Synod of 1810.

Divorce by mutual consent was explicitly forbidden.[25] The number of grounds for divorce was diminished.[26] Granting divorce remained the prerogative of the ecclesiastical courts. Divorce by Royal dispensation, resembling the Nordic practice, was briefly introduced during the reign of Peter the Great.[27] As everywhere in the Europe of those days, divorce remained rare and very difficult to obtain due to the intricate procedure and the notorious reluctance of the ecclesiastical courts *Duhovnaia Consistoria*.

Due to the reforms of Peter the Great, the adjudication of illegitimacy cases passed into secular hands. Legitimisation by subsequent marriage and by royal dispensation (*per rescriptum principis*) became possible. Illegitimate children followed the status of their mother, unless she was of nobility.[28] The mother was obliged to maintain her unlawful children, but could not pass property to them upon death.[29] The establishment of paternity was possible under a criminal procedure, with the sole purpose of claiming "damages": maintenance for the child and the mother.[30]

The importance of the reforms of Peter the Great could hardly be exaggerated. In a life-time of one generation he managed to make Russia a western and, for that time, fairly modern country. His reforms can in some ways be compared with the reforms endeavoured by Kemal Atatürk in the first part of the twentieth century[31] in order to secularise and westernise what was left of the Ottoman Empire.[32] The reforms of Peter de Great, however, did not in fact penetrate any deeper than the upper layer of Russian society. Russian nobility adopted Western patterns of life, habits, attitudes, and even language: in the eighteenth-nineteenth century, Russian upper class society was predominantly French-speaking. In contrast, the great majority of the Russian population remained rural, illiterate, patriarchal and oriental. The difference between these two groups was so great that in a way, Russia could be said to have been inhabited by two different "peoples". As a result, the elite and the peasantry could hardly understand each

25 Article 46 *Svod Zakonov*.

26 ZAGOROVSKII, *supra* note 2, p. 114.

27 *Ibid*., p. 111.

28 *Ibid*., p. 419.

29 *Ibid*., p. 346.

30 *Ibid*., pp. 336–338; 345–350. Russian law knew no civil maintenance claim on behalf of an illegitimate child. Instead a begetter had to pay "damages" caused by the crime of illicit cohabitation. *Ibid*, p. 348.

31 See ÖRÜCÜ, E., "Turkey: Change Under Pressure" in ÖRÜCÜ, E. *et al.* (eds.), *Studies of Legal Systems: Mixed and Mixing* (Kluwer, 1996), pp. 89–111.

32 ANTOKOLSKAIA, M., "Development of Family Law in Western and Eastern Europe: Common Origins, Common Driving Forces, Common Tendencies", *28 Journal of Family History* (2003), pp. 52–69.

other, and had a rather different mentality and different ideas about family, marriage and divorce.

2.2.2. *Russia "misses the train" of Enlightenment*

Thus, on the eve of the Enlightenment, the reforms of Peter the Great brought Russian family law and the family practices of the upper class elite in line with developments in Western Europe. Since that time Russia has been influenced by the same ideas, trends and pursuits as Western Europe. Still, Russia almost completely missed the following wave of reforms of the late eighteenth and nineteenth centuries, inspired by the ideas of the Enlightenment. Until the very end of Imperial Russia, marriage and divorce law were neither uniform nor secular. The population was subordinated to the ecclesiastical rules of different religions and confessions. Until the fall of the monarchy in 1917, Russia resolutely rejected even the possibility of introducing civil marriage.[33] As everywhere in Europe, a married woman was under the power of her husband, who was considered the sole head of the family.[34] The particular Russian oddity was that throughout the whole of the nineteenth century, parents still had the legal ability to imprison disobedient children by means of the so-called *Lettres de cochet*.[35] Eventually this measure became so much at odds with the common perception of the personal rights of children[36] that by the end of the century the magistrates refused to enforce such requests.[37] Divorce was also regulated by religious rules of various religions: it was not possible for the Catholics, but allowed for Protestants, Jews, Muslims and Russian Orthodox Christians (by far the largest religious denomination). The latter could divorce on fault grounds such as adultery, bigamy, desertion for more than five years, attempt on the life of the other spouse, and certain no-fault grounds, such as impotency and choosing to enter the religious life.[38] Divorce by mutual consent was still explicitly forbidden.[39] Divorce suits were dealt with by ecclesiastical courts, which applied medieval procedure rules based on formal assessment of evidence. Their practice can be well illustrated by an early-twentieth century case in which a man on his

---

33 Even the Legislative Commission in charge of the drafting of the Russian Civil Code that worked, with some interruptions, from 1882 until the Bolshevik revolution, considered the introduction of civil marriage as a "rush and dangerous innovation". WAGNER, W., *Marriage, Property, and Law in Late Imperial Russia* (Clarendon Press, 1994), p. 160.

34 Article 107 is illustrative of the "Digest of the Laws of the Russian Empire", which stated that: "the wife should unconditionally obey the husband as the head of the family, love him, be devoted to him, and serve him as he is the chief of the household" (author's translation).

35 Letters of arbitrary arrest.

36 SHERSHENEVICH, G., *Russkoe grazgdanskoe pravo* (*Russian Civil Law*) (Spark, 1995), p. 458.

37 ZAGOROVSKII, *supra* note 2, p. 243.

38 For a comprehensive account see *ibid.*, pp. 115–127.

39 Article 46 *Svod Zakonov.*

return from long-standing military service discovered that his wife was working in a brothel as an officially registered prostitute. Notwithstanding this, his suit for divorce on the ground of adultery was rejected by the ecclesiastical court because, according to the formal rules, the adultery could only be proved by a testimony of two eyewitnesses.

Against the background of a lack of political freedom and the absence of legal reforms, liberalisation of family law became, in the late nineteenth century, one of the most pressing issues on the agenda of the diverse political forces that sought modernisation of Russian society. The liberalisation of divorce was advocated by persons with various political inclinations – as different as radical socialists and Leo Tolstoy. An influential feminist movement gained much public support in its pursuit of the emancipation of women. This was the legal and political setting in which the new secular period of development of Russian family commenced.

3. THE PERIOD OF SECULAR FAMILY LAW IN THE MILITANT ATHEISTIC ENVIRONMENT

3.1. RADICAL BREAK WITH RELIGIOUS LAW

When the Bolsheviks seized power in October 1917 they declared "militant atheism" as one of the pillars of their ideology. The Church was separated from the State, *Sinod* was abolished and religion was declared to be a private matter for the citizens. At the same time a massive campaign against "religious superstitions of the population" was set off.

Secularisation of family law was one of the first reforms carried out by the Bolsheviks. One could wonder why it was that civil marriage and divorce was rendered so much of a priority that, just two months after the *coup d'état* in the middle in the turmoil of the Civil war, civil marriage[40] and divorce[41] had to be introduced. This haste becomes more understandable, if one considers that the main purpose of this reform was to roll back the influence of religion – the Bolsheviks' greatest ideological rival.

This was only the beginning. The scope and radical nature of the family law reforms carried out in the Soviet Union were virtually without precedent. These innovations could be seen as heralding the pan-European "family law revolution"

40 Decree of 18 December 1917 *O grazhdanskom brake, detiakh. u vedenii knig aktov grazhdanskogo sosnoiania* (On Civil Marriage, Children and the Act of Civil Status).

41 Decree of 19 December 1917 *O rastorzhenii braka* (On divorce).

that would take place at the end of the twentieth century. The diversity of religious family laws of the Russian Empire was swiftly replaced by a uniform civil law of unprecedented libertarianism; marriage and divorce were completely purged from religious influence and largely deformalised. As part of the general progressive attitude towards sexual morality, Soviet Russia introduced the most liberal law in Europe in regard to same-sex relationships. Neither the criminal code of 1922 nor of 1926 contained sanctions for same-sex acts between consenting adults. The age of consent was set at 16 for both homosexual and heterosexual acts.[42]

Civil marriage became the only valid form of marriage. Celebration of religious marriages was not forbidden, but rather produced no legal consequences henceforth. However, religious marriages concluded before 18 December 1917 remained valid. The first Russian Family Code of 1918[43] proclaimed total equality between men and women within the family and in public life.[44] The Second Family Code of 1926[45] gave de facto, durable cohabitation the legal status of marriage.[46] For the first time since it was banned in the Middle Ages, concubinage returned to the European legal stage. The reasons for this far-reaching innovation were manifold. In the first place, the deformalisation of marriage simply followed on from the consensual theory of marriage, which again came to the surface after marriage was released from its theological straitjacket. The registration of marriage was preserved,[47] but no longer treated as a constitutive element of the formation of marriage.[48] As in Roman and pre-Tridentine Europe, consent alone was sufficient to create a valid marriage. Marriage therefore became a private informal transaction. Another, rather utopian, motive behind the deformalisation was the urge to enter the communist future, where marriage was supposed to "die out". A more down-to-earth incentive to equate registered and unregistered marriage was the aim of

---

42 ALEKSEEV, N., *Pravovoe regulirovanie polozgenia sexual'nikh men'shinstv. Rossia v svete praktiki mezgdynarodnikx opganizaii I natsional'nogo zakonodatel'stva stran mipa (Legal Regulation of the Status of Sequel Minorities. Russia in the light of the perceives of the International organisation and national legislation of the foreign countries)* (Beck, 2002), p. 197.

43 *Kodeks Zakonov ob Aktah Grazhdanskogo Sostoiania, Brachnom, Semeinom i Opekynskom Prave* (Code on Civil Status, Marriage, Family and Guardianship) of 22 October 1918.

44 Articles 100–132 Family Code of 1918.

45 *Kodeks zakonov o brake sem'e i opeke* (Code on Marriage, Family and Guardianship) of 19 November 1926.

46 The Code as such did not treat both institutions as equal, but this result was reached by virtue of case law.

47 The registration of marriage was regarded by one of the drafters of the Code as "a remnant of the past that is doomed to disappear, but at the moment is temporally maintained largely as a measure against church marriages". BRANDENBURGSKII, J., "Presentation at the dispute on the family in the House of Soviets", *48–49 ECU* (1925), p. 1504 (author's translation).

48 RAEVICH, S., "Brarnoe i semeinoe pravo" in MAGEROVSKIi, D. (ed.), *Osnovy sovetskogo prava* (Gosudarstvennoe Izdatel'stevo, 1927), p. 426.

protecting "proletarian" de facto wives from "exploitation" by their usually more economically powerful de facto husbands.[49]

Divorce law was simultaneously liberalised with the law on marriage.[50] Divorce cases passed into the competence of civil courts. Religious courts were abolished. Already in 1917, the fault grounds for divorce had been removed. The Family Code of 1918 introduced an administrative procedure without inquiry which was established for divorce by mutual consent. Until 1926, judicial divorce was retained for contested cases but, even in the court procedure, no proof of the irretrievable breakdown of marriage was required.[51] The deformalisation of marriage in 1926 drastically affected the law on divorce. Formal divorce was preserved, but came to be regarded as just a subsidiary means of termination for both registered and unregistered marriage.[52] There was general consensus that spouses could not be kept in a marriage, even if only one of them wanted out of it. The State declined to decide upon the dissolution of marriage, leaving the floor to the autonomous decisions of the spouses themselves. Marriage was dissolved upon the demand of one or both of the spouses; the registration of divorce was, therefore, merely a formality. In light of this approach, the administrative procedure without any inquiry was extended to all divorce cases. The deformalisation of divorce went so far that the presence of a contesting spouse at the time of the registration was not considered essential. This was only logical, in the light of the fact that his or her defence was of no relevance in any case. The absent spouse was then to be informed by a letter, which caused the procedure to be nicknamed "divorce by postcard".[53]

Illegitimate children were equalised with legitimate issue in every legal aspect. The very concept of illegitimacy was done away with. The voluntary recognition of paternity and the winning of a paternity suit against a reluctant biological father became extremely easy. The Family Code of 1918 (Articles 140–141) introduced the so-called "establishment of paternity by registration". Accordingly, a mother during her pregnancy could declare before the civil servant that a certain man was the father of her child. The putative father could deny his paternity before the court during a short period of two weeks. If the paternity was not denied in time, it was presumed to be established. The Code of 1926 (Article 32) went even further. The putative father was no longer allowed to evoke the *exceptio congressus cum pluribus*. This rather unbalanced character of

---

49 GENKIN, D., NOVITZKII., I., RABINOVICH, N., *Istoriia sovetskogo semeinogo prava 1917–1947* (Juridicheskaia Literatura, 1949), p. 443.

50 Decree of 19 December 1917 *O ra storzhenii braka* (On divorce).

51 SEMIDVORKIN, N., *Sozdanie pervogo brachno-semeinogo kodeksa*, Sozdanie pervogo brachno-semeinogo kodeksa (MGY, 1989), p. 50.

52 Article 19 Family Code of 1926.

53 GENKIN *et al.*, *supra* note 49, p. 441.

the paternity legislation became the subject of justified criticism.[54] The reasons for these "woman-friendly" rules were partly the influence of feminist ideology, and partly the Bolsheviks' urge to protect unmarried mothers who were often of humble origin and therefore considered as an "exploited class" whose weak position could be abused by socially more privileged men.[55]

The existing matrimonial property regime of separate property was initially preserved after the Revolution. However, as divorce became easier, separate property came to work to the disadvantage of women, the majority of whom at that time did not have any independent income. Thus, in 1926, a limited form of community property, the community of acquests, replaced the separate property regime.[56] Two features distinguished the newly introduced Russian community from those in Western Europe. First, the community in Russia was administered by both husband and wife on an equal basis.[57] Secondly, Russian law did not allow any contractual deviation from the legal matrimonial property regime.

3.2. RADICAL REFORMS OF FAMILY LAW AS AN EXAMPLE OF SUCCESSFUL SOCIAL ENGINEERING

The Soviet Union stands for a case of radical social engineering by means of family legislation, undertaken by a dictatorial regime that knew little, if any, restraint when it came to the use of coercion. In the Soviet Union, the reforms were carried out by the Bolshevik dictatorship, although in regard to the liberalisation of family law and the emancipation of women, the Bolsheviks shared the ideals of the whole of the progressive elite of the Russian Empire. As often occurs at the time of social disruption, the Bolsheviks were engulfed in a kind of instrumentalist fanaticism. They did not hesitate to impose their vision of the future on the rest of the predominantly traditional and religious population, whether it liked it or not. Despite their undemocratic and top-down character, the reforms did produce lasting social change. The social impact of the Soviet reforms differed, depending on the particular area of family law. Some long awaited and broadly supported changes, like the emancipation of women and easy divorce, were an immediate success. The effect of the divorce reform was as if the prison gates had suddenly been opened: during the first months some 5,000 divorce petitions were filed in Moscow alone.[58] In contrast, the abolition of Church marriages did not initially take root. The majority of the population was deeply religious. Reading between the lines of the manipulated

54 *Ibid.*
55 *Ibid.*
56 *Ibid.*, pp. 433–440.
57 *Ibid.*, pp. 439–440.
58 *Ibid.*, p. 419.

statistics of that time, it is possible to discern indications that the rural population continued to solemnise marriages in the Church, ignoring the prescribed civil registration.[59] The Bolsheviks considered the secularisation of marriage an important weapon in the battle with their ideological opponents. They did not hesitate to use terror and repression against the clergy and the religious population in order to implement civil marriage. The extent of the pressure can be illustrated by the fact that by the end of the 1920s there was hardly a church to go to for the solemnisation of marriage, and hardly a priest left to bless it. As in the first centuries of Christianity, children were secretly baptised at home by their family members. After this successful "social engineering", the risk that, as soon as the requirement of State registration of marriage was relaxed, the population would resort to Church ceremonies, had disappeared. The communists proudly announced their victory over the "religious superstition of the population". This opened the gates for further experiments, and in 1926 informal marriage was given the status of legal marriage.[60] This innovation soon turned into a custom; in the 1920s and 1930s it became the fashion of the day not to go through a marriage ceremony. Marrying was considered something for backward peasants; the communist establishment lived in free unions.

3.3. EVALUATION OF REFORMS: "EXCESSES OF THE REVOLUTIONARY PERIOD" OR PAVING THE WAY TO THE FUTURE?

This rather peculiar combination of progressive family legislation and dictatorial methods of its implementation made it difficult to properly appreciate the place of the Soviet radical reforms in the overall development of family law in Europe. Some scholars, such as for instance Max Rheinstein, consider these reforms merely excesses of the revolutionary period with rather limited importance.[61] Others, like Roderick Phillips, are of the view that the Soviet reforms had "an immediate and enduring impact in social and political thought in Western Europe".[62] This is because these reforms were "the first translations into law of the ideas of the Western socialists on marriage, divorce, women, and the family".[63] In my view, the Soviet reforms were indeed of enduring significance for European family law, not so much because they "translated" socialist ideology into positive law, but rather because they implemented the ideas of the broad

59 NETCHAEVA, A., *Semeinoe prevo (Semeinoe pravo)* (Jurist, 1998), p. 74.

60 RAEVICH, *supra* note 48, p. 426.

61 RHEINSTEIN, M., *Marriage Stability, Divorce, and the Law* (University of Chicago Press, 1972), pp. 231–243.

62 PHILLIPS, R., *Putting Asunder: A history of divorcé in Western Society* (Cambridge University Press, 1988), p. 534.

63 *Ibid.*, p. 514.

Western progressive movement as a whole.[64] It is possible to delineate three distinctive components of the ideological background of the reforms: radical secularism,[65] liberal individualism[66] and the idea of the "withering away" of the "bourgeois" family. Only the latter element was of purely socialist origin.[67] As I have argued elsewhere,[68] although some of the Soviet innovations could rightly be called excessive,[69] the essence of the reforms was exactly in line with the general evolution of family law in Europe. Because of these reforms, Soviet family law had already, in the 1920s, attained a level of modernity that several European countries have not yet reached today. In my view, the Soviet reforms of the 1920s could best be appreciated as the same kind of radical modernisation breakthrough as the French revolutionary legislation of 1792. The reforms of the 1920s, even after their partial repeal by Stalin in 1944, were of lasting influence on the development of family law, not only in Eastern Europe but also in the West.[70]

---

64 Phillips acknowledges this: "Soviet family policy [...] found support – qualified and unqualified – across the liberal and socialist spectrum in Europe and America. It responded to liberal and socialist hostility to the oppressive character of bourgeois marriage, and complemented the socialist feminist critiques of Western family institutions and practices. In this sense the Soviet experiments [...] reinforced the individualistic tendencies of the Lefts' analysis of the family", *ibid.*, p. 538.

65 The secularisation of family law as such was broadly desired across the socialist and liberal spectrum. Of course, the Bolsheviks turned it into an excessive and bloody exercise that few would have stood for.

66 Liberal individualism was generally alien to Bolshevist ideology. It was, however, temporarily borrowed from liberal thought and employed in the reform of family law.

67 Some young communists from the first "romantic" generation, led by prominent feminists such as Inesse Armand and Alexandra Kollontay, who held important positions in the Bolsheviks' government, believed that under communism marriage would completely die out and make place for free sexual relationships (KOLLONTAY, A., *Sem'ia i kommunisticheskoe gosudarstvo* (N. Novgorod, Communist, 1918), p. 9 and ELWOOD, R., *Inesse Armand: Revolutionary and Feminist* (Cambridge University Press, 1992). A more moderate group, which was supported by Lenin, suggested, in accordance with the writings of Engels, that only "bourgeois" marriage and family would die out in order to be replaced by a "higher form of the family," freed from financial considerations and male dominance. See: LENIN, V., *Letter to I.F. Armand of 24 January 1915, Polnoe sobranie sochineniy*, V., 46 (Institut marksizma-leninizma, 1958–1965), p. 56. For a synopsis of this discussion see: MATWEEV, G., *Semeinoe pravo* (Juriducheskaia lliteratura, 1985), pp. 25–29.

68 ANTOKOLSKAIA, M., "De ontwikkeling van het Russische familierecht vanaf de Bolsjewistische revolutie: een poging tot verklaring", *70 Tijdschrift voor Rechtsgeschiedenis*, 2002, pp. 137–171.

69 For instance, the judicial establishment of paternity that offered the putative father no realistic opportunity to deny his fatherhood.

70 According to Sundberg, the early Soviet reforms served as one of the models for the Swedish law of 1973 that introduced divorce on demand: SUNDBERG, J., "Marriage or no Marriage. The Directives for the Revision of Swedish Family Law", *20 International and Comparative Law Quarterly* (1971), p. 233.

3.4. STALIN'S COUNTER REFORM

On the eve of the great terror unleashed in 1937, Stalin's Constitution of 1936 hypocritically proclaimed that "citizens enjoy the freedom of performing religious rituals and carry out anti-religious propaganda". During the great terror almost all of the remaining clergy was massacred and professing religion openly put one's life in grave danger.

Stalin's regime substantially turned back the liberal family law reforms of the 1920s. Homosexual acts between consenting adults were made a criminal offence in 1934.[71] Abortion was forbidden in 1936 and also became a criminal offence for both the performer and the woman in question. Marriage and divorce law became less permissive[72] in 1944.[73] Obligatory civil registration of marriage was restored in importance, and informal marriage lost its legal standing. Church celebration was still formally allowed, but those who resorted to it risked their life and freedom. The easy administrative divorce procedure was replaced by a cumbersome judicial procedure in which courts of two instances were involved. The court of first instance could merely act as a conciliator. Only the court of second instance was entitled to grant a divorce, after a thorough inquiry as to whether the marriage had indeed irretrievably broken down. The position of illegitimate children deteriorated dramatically. The acknowledgement of children, born outside wedlock, as well as the judicial establishment of paternity, were altogether forbidden. Even maintenance claims on behalf of natural children were no longer possible.[74]

Thus, the libertarian spirit of the 1920s gave way to unlimited State interference, justified by the official propaganda of the day as "strengthening the socialist family as a basic cell of socialist society". The spirit of the Soviet family law of those days is perhaps best epitomised by the following statement of Sverdlov, one of the most influential scholars of that time:

> "the Socialist State rejects the interpretation of the relationships between the sexes as individualistic, personal and neutral for society and the State. The State dictates the rules and determines these relationships in order to safeguard the interests of the society and to enforce the fulfilment of the duties in regard of society."[75]

---

71 ALEKSEEV, N., *Pravovoe regulirovanie polozgenia sexual'nikh men'shinstv* (2002), p. 198.

72 This was a step back in relation to the Law of 1926, but compared to the average European standard of those days, what remained was still a very liberal divorce law.

73 Ukase of 8 July 1944.

74 ANTOKOLSKAIA, M., *Family Law* (*Semeinoe pravo*) (3rd ed.) (Norma, 2010), pp. 114–115.

75 SVERDLOV, G., *O predmete i sisteme sotsialisticheskogo semeinogo prava (O predmete i sisteme sotsialisticheskogo semeinogo prava)*, Sovjetskoe gosudarstvo i pravo, 1 (1941), p. 58.

In the same period of interbellum, in Portugal, Spain, Italy, Austria and France, restrictive family policy was related to the right wing governments' aspirations to conform to the doctrines of the Catholic Church. In the Soviet Union, by contrast, the conservative backlash had nothing to do with religion. The association of conservative family policy with religion is so strong that Max Rheinstein was inclined to search for the roots of Stalin's counter-reform in the "survival of Christian tradition".[76] In fact, this was not the case at all. Stalin's conservative policy can be explained perfectly in terms of "purely secular statism", the second underlying motive suggested by Rheinstein.[77] Even the prohibition of abortion had nothing to do with restoration of the religious value of the sanctity of unborn human life, but was rather grounded in demographic concerns about supply of canon fodder on the eve of the pending war. The communists' brief flirtation with individual freedom in family matters was over. As the desire of the totalitarian regime grew to bring all corners of society under its control, "the socialist family" had to submit to the needs of society as defined by the State.[78] Thus, the focal point of family law policy shifted from individualism to communitarian.

3.5. FROM STALIN TO PERESTROIKA

After the death of Stalin the terror was over. The country still knew neither democracy nor religious freedom. Persons professing religion openly were no longer threatened by imprisonment or death, but rather faced total impossibility of studying and having a decent job. Family law was made more liberal again in 1969 with the adoption of the Code on Marriage and Family.[79] However, the level of permissiveness of the law of the 1920s has never been equalled. The attitude toward religion did not change: militant atheism remained the state policy of the Soviet State and any influence of religion on family law was unthinkable.

The 1969 Family Code gave informal marriage no legal standing. Divorce law was made more permissive again. The general ground for divorce remained the irretrievable breakdown of marriage. In the administrative procedure, spouses were not obliged to present any proof of it. Irretrievable breakdown was presupposed. In the court procedure, however, irretrievable breakdown of marriage still had to be proven.[80] The Code of 1969 restored both the possibility

76 RHEINSTEIN, *supra* note 61, p. 236.
77 *Ibid.*
78 See ANTOKOLSKAIA, *supra* note 68, pp. 137–151.
79 "Kodex Zakonov o Brake i Sem'ie RSFSR" 30 July 1969, *Ved. RSFSR*, 1969, No. 32, item 1086.
80 ANTOKOLSKAIA, *supra* note 74, pp. 115–118.

of voluntary acknowledgment of paternity and of establishing paternity against the will of the father. Thereby a certain balance between the interests of children born out of wedlock and those of putative fathers was achieved.

4. THE PERIOD OF SECULAR FAMILY LAW IN A RELIGION-FRIENDLY ENVIRONMENT

After the collapse of the Soviet System, religion was restored in all its rights and standing. All religions were granted equal status. Freedom of religion became a reality. The Russian population has made rapid use of the newly obtained freedom and religious life is now experiencing a general revival. Many religious buildings regained their function and the numbers of believers have grown explosively. By far the most influential religions are Russian Orthodoxy and Islam. Approximately 129 millions (90 per cent) traditionally adhere to Christianity, mostly Russian Orthodoxy; 14.5 millions (10 per cent) – to Islam.[81]

The Church is still separated from the State. Family law remains secular. Due to the particularity of Russian history and the prevalence of an Orthodox population, the interactions of Orthodox canon law rules related to family and the secular family law are the most interesting subject of enquiry.

Secular family law is now incorporated in the 1995 Family Code.[82] Canon law of the Russian Orthodox Church, on the family, is not codified and consists of ancient canons, acts of the Church Counsels, the *Sinod* and of the head of the Church – the Patriarch. Only one part of this law, related to the ground for divorce, is more or less codified.[83] At present there is no evidence of influence of religion on family law. The correlation between those two sets of rules could be depicted as benevolent co-existence.

Secular law of marriage has not changed much since the previous period. Only civil marriage has legal effect. Thus, Russia did not follow the path of some

81 ALESHIN, O., "Influence of the Orthodox customs on family relationships" 5 *Semeinoe I zgilishnoe zakobodatel'stvo* (2009), p. 8.

82 Russian Family Code of 8 December 1995, in force since 1 March 1996.

83 GARVISH, I., "Correlation between the rules of Family Code of Russian Federation and the matrimonial law of the Russian Orthodox Church", *2 Semeinoe I zgilishnoe zakobodatel'stvo* (2010), p. 22.

post-socialist countries such as Latvia,[84] Lithuania,[85] Poland,[86] the Czech Republic[87] and Croatia[88] which, after the fall of the Socialist system, have introduced a dual system of civil and religious celebration of marriage. Neither secular nor canon law contains any rules precluding Church celebration of marriage prior to civil registration. However, the current practice of the Church is not to celebrate a Church wedding before a civil registration.[89] In this way, church ministers can be sure that all the requirements of secular law concerning age, consent and impediments are fulfilled.

The list of impediments to marriage in canon law is far more extensive than in secular family law. The only requirements of the Family Code are: full legal capacity; absence of another marriage; having reached the age of 18, or having obtained dispensation; and not being related to one another by blood or adoption as ascendants of descendants or as brother or sister. One more unwritten requirement is the different sex of the parties. The predominantly negative attitude to the introduction of a same-sex marriage or partnership into the secular law is sometimes related to the influence of the negative attitude of the Church towards same-sex relationships. The canon law list of impediments goes much further. In the first place, both parties should at least be Christians. Admissibility of marriages of Orthodox Christians with members of other Christian confessions is currently a matter of controversy. Some render them possible, referring to the Act enacted in 1721 on the initiative of Peter the Great in order to enable Swedish prisoners of war to settle in Russia and take a Russian wife. Others believe this rule to be an act of impermissible indulgence and adhere to the strict old canons requiring the unity of faith. In addition, the canon law age of majority is attained by girls at 13 and by boys at 15, even though the law of the Russian Empire set the age of marriage at 16 for girls and 18 for boys.[90] Currently the Church sticks to the rules of the Family Code, which provides for

---

84 Introduced in 1993 by the restored Latvian *Civil Code* of 1937. VEBERS, J., "Family Law in Latvia: From Establishment of the Independent State of Latvia in 1918 to Restoration of Independence in 1993" in BAINHAM, A. (ed.), *The International Survey of Family Law* (Martinus Nijhoff Publishers, 1997), p. 212.

85 By the 1992 Constitution. KASERAUSKAS, Š., "Moving in the Same Direction? Presentation of Family Law Reforms in Lithuania" in BAINHAM, *ibid.*, p. 322.

86 Introduced in 1998 in line with the Concordat with the Holy See of 1993, ratified in 1998. SMYCZYNSKI, T., "Das Polnische Familienrecht im Reformprozeß der staatlichen Ordnung", *Deutsches und Europäisches Familien Recht* (1999), p. 38.

87 Introduced in 1992. HADERKA, J., "A Half-Hearted Family Law Reform of 1998" in BAINHAM, A. (ed.), *The International Survey of Family Law* (Jordan Publishing, 2000), p. 122.

88 Introduced by the Croatian *Family Act* of 1999. TOMLIJENOVIC, V., "The Canonic Marriage – Revision of Croatian Family Law and Its Conflict of Laws Implication" in BAINHAM, A. (ed.), *The International Survey of Family Law* (Jordan Publishing, 2003), p. 109.

89 ALESHIN, *supra* note 21, p. 10.

90 GARVISH, *supra* note 83, p. 24.

the equal age of marriage of 18 for both sexes with a possibility of dispensation. In contrast to secular law, canon law also upholds the maximum age of marriage: 60 years old for women and 80 years old for men.[91] Also in contrast with secular law, canon law allows no more than three marriages. The prohibited degrees of relationships are more extensive in canon than in secular law and include not only relations by blood and adoption but also by marriage – affinity and baptism; spiritual kinship.[92]

Secular family law allows for an easy divorce by mutual consent and, in contested cases, on the ground of the irretrievable breakdown of marriage. Canon law does not recognise divorce by mutual consent. Christian marriage is rendered indissoluble, except in cases of adultery. The Church, however, by way of indulgence, allows divorce upon a limited number of other serious grounds.[93] The divorce suits are dealt with by bishops after civil divorce has been acquired.

Many Russians make use of both systems of marriage law. Charmed by the beauty of the Church wedding ceremony, they celebrate marriage in the Church and are satisfied with obtaining only civil divorce in case the marriage breaks down.

5. CONCLUDING REMARKS

During the last two millennia, Russia has experienced various periods of interaction between family law and religion: from the exclusive competence of the Church in family matters in the Middle Ages to strictly secular family law grounded in the militant, atheistic attitude. Russian developments generally follow the same pattern as those of other European countries.[94] The difference lies in the radicalism of the break with religion in the 1920s and the unprecedented level of secularisation of family law throughout the Soviet period. Analysis of these radical reforms allows a conclusion that, after some delay, the new secular rules became entrenched in Russian society. After the Soviet anti-religious pressure was removed in the 1990s, no general urge to adapt secular family law to religious standards has been felt. At present, the secular and the religious family law rules co-exist, without much interaction, in fairly perfect harmony.

91 ALESHIN, *supra* note 21, p. 10.
92 GARVISH, *supra* note 83, p. 24.
93 *Ibid.*
94 For a more extensive comparison see ANTOKOLSKAIA, *supra* note 4.

HOW FAR CAN RELIGION BE ACCOMMODATED IN THE LAIC FAMILY LAW OF TURKEY?

Esin Örücü

1. INTRODUCTORY OVERVIEW

The Turkish Republic came into existence following the collapse of the Ottoman Empire in 1923. The *élite dirigeante* of the Republic, with a vision for modernity, created a brand new legal framework between 1926 and 1930 by the adoption and adaptation of Codes of foreign origin from Switzerland, Italy, Germany and France, and passed a series of social reform laws (*inkilap kanunları*)[1] to supplement these Codes, aimed at "changing the people" and forging a new identity to fulfil the requirements of the vision, and to appease the Western powers. Thereby the new Turkish Republic went through a process of total modernisation, westernisation, laicism (secularisation), democratisation and constitutionalism.[2]

For the purposes of the inquiry here, it must be pointed out at the outset that the official family Law in Turkey today, derived from the Swiss model, is entirely secular. As will be seen below, however, in some respects there is some accommodation of the religious mores of the people, 98 percent of whom are of the Islamic faith.

An overview of the state of affairs in the Ottoman Empire shows us that this was a multi-ethnic state, culturally and legally pluralist and decentralised. Although the official law of the Empire was Islamic, until the second half of the fifteenth

1 The social reforms were introduced by the eight reform laws (*İnkilap Kanunları*), establishing secular education and civil marriage, adopting the Latin alphabet, introducing the hat, closing the dervish convents, abolishing certain titles and prohibiting the wearing of certain garments. Their constitutionality cannot be challenged even today (Article 174 of the Constitution of 1982), nor can their amendment be proposed.

2 The Turkish radical reforms aimed at the basics: language reform, a new system of law, a new sense of national identity based on a newly created culture excluding the Ottoman heritage (the Islamic and Arabic elements).

century, the Ottoman Empire had a Christian majority under the rule of a Muslim minority. Eclecticism and pragmatism prevailed in the running of the Empire, and the principle of tolerance of diversity, inherent in the Muslim governmental tradition, meant that there was no one language, no single distinct culture, no one religion and therefore no one law.[3] Muslims lived under Islamic law and the other religious groups were allowed to abide by their own personal laws.[4] This meant that the system was culturally and legally pluralistic and the primary connecting factor in choice of law was religion. Cultural and religious differences functioned as structuring elements in the law. The different groups were identified by religion: Muslim, Orthodox, Christian (Catholic and Protestant), Armenian (Gregorian) and Jewish. Any Ottoman subject could become a Muslim.[5] Obviously this arrangement was reflected strongly in family laws of the Empire.

Pluralism was both as to substantive law to be applied and the courts which had jurisdiction to apply the law. Some non-Muslims, the *zımmis* (mostly Armenian, Greek and Jewish communities and Christian groups given asylum), lived in and around İstanbul. In personal status and private law, their own religious laws and customs applied and their disputes were settled in their own community (*cemaat*) courts. The people of the conquered lands in Europe were the second group of non-Muslims and their own local indigenous laws applied in existing local courts. The third group were non-Muslim foreigners (mainly French, Dutch and the British), who were traders residing in İstanbul and İzmir with special status. Their disputes were settled in consular courts.

Until 1917, for the Muslims, family law in the Ottoman Empire was based on the *Şeriat* (*shari'a*) reflecting *Sunni* beliefs and the *Hanafi* School's interpretation.[6] In fact it grew as an outcome of interpretations of the Muslim jurists over the

---

3 It can be said that here lay a paradox: the Ottoman Empire had the richness of multiculturalism and yet this multiculturalism prevented her from becoming a unity which led initially to her rise and ultimately to her demise.

4 By the fourteenth century, the Ottomans ruled the Balkans and by the early seventeenth century, the Empire, which was set up in the thirteenth century, had expanded as far as Vienna. In Europe it extended to embrace the Balkans, Greece, Albania, Serbia, and the greater part of Hungary and Austria. They controlled the Black Sea and in the north included Crimea. The Ottomans controlled most of the Mediterranean, and in Africa, included Egypt, Libra, Tripoli, Tunisia and Algeria. In Asia Minor they took Syria, Iraq, Palestine and the western shores of the Persian Gulf.

5 The system applied was the *millet* system, a term first used for Muslims and later also for non-Muslim religious communities.

6 See ESPOSITO, J.L., *Women in Muslim Family Law* (Syracuse University Press, 1982), pp. 26–39 for family law in Islam and specifically divorce = *talak* or *talaq* (divorce proper, delegated divorce, mutual divorce, divorce by judicial process and divorce by apostasy), its consequences and maintenance. Also see for general information, AYDIN, M.A., "Family Law in Turkey: The Journey from Islamic Law to Secular Law" in SINGER, A., JANTERA-JAREBORG, M. and SCHLYTTER, A. (eds.), *Familj – religion – ratt* (Iustus Förlag, 2010), pp. 163–183.

centuries. The provisions were applied not by the clergy however, but by the (*kadı*) *qadis*, or judges (and sometimes with *qadis*' permission, by the *imams*, the clerics), who were appointed by the state authorities. There were no independent religious courts. The Sultans at times intervened if social circumstances justified this interference. Islamic law recognised the equal worth of human beings, but stressed different roles and rights for men and women within the framework of marriage, and therefore was not based on the equality of the spouses.

In 1916 two imperial edicts (*İrade*) were promulgated granting wives the right to sue for divorce in cases of desertion and a husband's contagious disease making conjugal life dangerous. These were followed in 1917 by the first ever officially adopted codification of Muslim family law in the Islamic world: the *Aile Hukuku Kararnamesi*. This codification again sought to establish grounds that would enable wives to sue for judicial divorce: contagious disease of a husband, his mental illness, him not providing support for the family and incompatibility (section 122); and also to limit a husband's exercising repudiation by putting marriage and divorce under state control. The Law had two books, nine chapters, 21 sections and 157 articles. It included separate articles that applied to non-Muslims.

Although used by many Middle Eastern states as a model for their own family law codes well into the twentieth century, at home the effects of this codification spread only to urban areas and remained controversial, since both the conservatives and minority religious groups resisted it, and nationalists and westernisers found it inadequate. For conservative Islamists, as women occupied a secondary position in social life, there was no need to depart from classical Islamic law. They were also concerned that some of the rules reflected not only the teachings of the *Hanafi* school but other schools of Islamic law and this eclecticism was not welcomed. The modernists insisted that women should be given more rights with regard to divorce, that polygamy should be outlawed completely and that underage marriage of girls should be prohibited. The nationalists adopted a middle position, claiming that there was a need for a new understanding of family and women; yet, though the society needed to be westernised, not all that was western should be taken on board. They believed that the Sultan should be more actively involved in this departure from Islamic law. In spite of the fact that the Jewish and Christian legal rules related to family law were preserved in the law, the non-Muslim minority groups were not keen to be subjected to this law. Especially the Chief Rabbi and the Patriarchs were against judicial unity brought in by the law, and the Western powers were not happy with these developments either.

It must be pointed out however, that although religion is in the essence of this law, that is, it is not a secular law by any means, it introduced new regulations for marriage and divorce contracts so as to subject them completely to state control. Thus, though Islamic law is religious law, it was controlled and applied by the state; a development reflected today in the existence of the Directorate of Religious Affairs, to be seen below.

Mehmet Akif Aydın is of the opinion that unification of the judicial system in the realm of family law "is possible in religiously and culturally homogeneous societies, whereas attempts at unification [...] in heterogeneous and cosmopolitan societies like the Ottoman society of the time, seem non practical although they may appear applicable in theory."[7] This opinion should be tested against the realities of our day, especially facing vast movements of immigration in Europe.

After less than two years, in 1919, the 1917 codification was unexpectedly abrogated in the Ottoman state by another Decree.[8] The 1917 codification was indeed a transitional law (*kanunu muvakkat*), paving the way to efforts based on it in 1923 and 1924 to regulate family law, and finally to the 1926 Civil Code, adapted and adopted from the Swiss Civil Code. It is important to note, however, that during the first few years of the Republic, the Turkish government had the intention to preserve the legacy of Islamic law in the field of civil law, and specifically in family law.[9] This was mostly to appease the conservative camp among the elite and in the country at large. Although various efforts were made to produce home-grown codes, in the end, under internal and external pressures, the Turkish Republic embraced secular Western Codes and abandoned Islamic law, which had applied for eight centuries in Anatolia.

The ideology underlying the Turkish Republic drew on "some of the more extreme concepts of 'modern' nationalism which were current in late-nineteenth- and early-twentieth-century Europe. Homogeneity – one language, one religion, one Volk – was considered to be the prerequisite of a strong and independent

7 AYDIN, *supra* note 6, p. 170.

8 Though abrogated in the Ottoman state, it remained in effect in Palestine, Syria, Lebanon, Jordan, Israel and Iraq for much longer. See for an evaluation KURNAZ, Ş., *II.Meşrutiyet Döneminde Türk Kadını* (Turkish Women in the II Meşrutiyet Period) (Istanbul, 1996), pp. 107–114, and KURNAZ, Ş., *Cumhuriyet Öncesinde Türk Kadını (Turkish Women before the Republic)* (Istanbul, 1997), pp. 89–91. Also see AYDIN, *supra* note 6.

9 For interesting information of the trends and their analysis, the role of the sociologist Ziya Gökalp and the Lausanne Peace Conference, see AYDIN, *supra* note 6, pp. 173–179.

state."[10] Obviously, the multi-ethnic, decentralised and, in many ways, tolerant Ottoman Empire was offensive to this scientific spirit of the Republic.

Effie Voutira observes that the unreformed Ottoman State "looked like a Kokoschka painting where the plurality and diversity of the different points of colour is such that there is no clearly discernible pattern, though the picture as a whole does have one [...]", especially when one stands back. "By contrast, the modern world map looks more like a Modigliani painting, where all shapes and colours have clearly circumscribed boundaries and well defined surfaces with no ambiguity or overlap [...]."[11] Ascherson says that, in Effie Voutira's sense, the Turkish legal revolutions of the early twentieth century were the overthrow of Kokoschka in favour of Modigliani, since the reformers wanted those single, well-circumscribed blocks of primary colours.[12]

Turkey of today, is a country of paradoxes, an example of a centralist monolithic system in which the cultures and customs that the law meets are indigenous. But as noted earlier, by choice, desire and design, the legal system was constructed by borrowing from Western sources and reflects those other cultures. The legal system is laic and yet the vast majority of the people are Muslims. The legal system has the aspiration to erase certain cultures and create a new culture, thereby assimilating people into a chosen image;[13] yet, when law meets local indigenous cultures and religion which it does not cater for, the judges either try to eradicate or ignore them in keeping with the vision of the founding legislator, or, where they can, to accommodate them within the official framework.[14] At the present time new inside and outside forces also are exerting pressure for change in two different directions. On the one hand, there are attempts at reform seen at the level of the Constitution and the Civil and Penal Codes in a westwardly direction. Here the effort is directed to prospective membership of the European Union. On the other hand, there is an attempt at the level of the civil courts to accommodate religious sentiments and tradition, to be seen below. Here the effort is directed to meeting the needs and expectations of the people.

---

10 Quoted in ASCHERSON, N., *Black Sea: The Birthplace of Civilisation and Barbarism* (Vintage, 1996), p. 197.

11 *Ibid.*

12 *Ibid.*

13 Western, laic, contemporary, following Atatürk nationalism, the democratic state, human rights, the rule of law and the social state.

14 See for analysis and examples, ÖRÜCÜ, E., "Judicial navigation as official law meets culture in Turkey", 4:1 *International Journal of Law in Context* (2008), 35, and ÖRÜCÜ, E., "Turkey's Synthetic Legal System and her Indigenous Socio-culture(s) in a 'Covert' Mix" in ÖRÜCÜ, E. (ed.), *Mixed Legal Systems at New Frontiers*, JCL Studies in Comparative Law No: 1 (Wildy, Simmonds and Hill Publishing, 2010), pp. 150–203.

2. TURKISH LAICISM AND FAMILY LAW

2.1. TURKISH LAICISM

Laicism (laicity), as a concept of a secular society, was implicitly introduced into the Turkish legal system with the amendment to the 1924 Constitution in 1928, by removing the provision "The Religion of the State is Islam". With the Constitution of 1924 coming into effect, the Caliphate, a position held by the Ottoman Sultans since 1517, was already abolished. In 1937 laicism was explicitly stated as a fundamental principle in article 2 of the same Constitution, hence constitutionalised.[15] This can be seen as the final act in the project of instituting complete separation between governmental and religious affairs in Turkey.

The original version of the ideological message of the Republic, sometimes referred to as the tenets of "Kemalism", was symbolised by "Six Arrows": nationalism, laicism, republicanism, populism, statism and reformism. These, all interlocked, constitute the official world-view. Parts of this vision have found their way into the preambles of Constitutions.[16] Of the tenets of Kemalism, the one that is crucial for the purposes of this inquiry is laicism, as this essay looks at the possible place for religion in family law in Turkey.

In the Preamble of the 1982 Constitution, laicism is somewhat defined: "As demanded by the principle of laicism, sacred religious feelings being in no way permitted to interfere with State affairs and politics." As can be observed, this is a one sided definition which indicates that religion and the state are to be kept separate, but, though the interference of religion into state affairs and politics is not permitted, the interference of the state into religious affairs is. Turkey's laicism does not call for a strict separation of religion and the state. There may be no strong normative theory here, but the State is definitely defended from the

---

15 This is still the case in the 1982 Constitution (see Articles 2,13, 14, 24 and 174). It seems that Temperman does not cite Turkey among the countries whose constitutions declare the State to be secular. This is erroneous. TEMPERMAN, J., "State-Religion Relations and Human Rights Law", unpublished manuscript, March 2009, p. 125 ff. cited by BADER, V., "Constitutionalizing secularism, alternative secularism or liberal-democratic constitutionalism? A Critical reading of some Turkish, ECtHR and Indian Supreme Court cases on secularism", 6:3 *Utrecht Law Review* (2010), p. 9, footnote 5.

16 At present they are in the Preamble of the 1982 Constitution. Furthermore, Articles 1–3 of the Constitution, which are immutable, pose the characteristics of the Republic and reiterate that the State is a Republic, that it is democratic, laic and social, governed by the rule of law, respecting human rights within the concepts of public peace, national solidarity and justice, loyal to the nationalism of Kemal Atatürk, and based on the fundamental tenets set forth in the Preamble; the Republic is an indivisible whole comprising its territory and the nation; and its official language is Turkish. These articles and their immutable character are of the utmost importance for our purposes as they limit the manoeuvrability of the courts to adjust the law to the needs and mores of the people, including religious beliefs.

perceived threats of religion and there is practice of constitutional laicism. Veit Bader finds Turkish laicism, similar to the French one:

> "aggressively secular in all regards when it comes to 'strict separation' of state and public institutions from religion [...] but does not respect the relative autonomy of religion (particularly Islam) from the state, so defending a rather myopic variety of the 'two autonomies' [...]."[17]

He further finds this type of laicism "clearly incompatible with liberal constitutionalism".[18]

Turkish laicism can be described as "an active neutrality", or as "assertive laicism", since religion is under the control of the Directorate of Religious Affairs (*Diyanet*), a constitutional institution.[19] The Presidency of this institution keeps an eye on the beliefs, worship and ethics of Islam, enlightens the public about their *Sunni* religion and administers the sacred worshipping venues. When the *Demokratik Barış Hareketi Partisi* (the Democratic Peace Movement Party), criticised the placing of the *Diyanet* in the State's administrative system, as the provider of a social service, and suggested the transfer of its functions to the religious communities, the Public Prosecutor of the Republic demanded the dissolution of this political party. The claim was that their proposal, which appeared in their programme, was a violation of the Constitutional principle of laicism, although the Party's defence was that this would strengthen laicism. The *Anayasa Mahkemesi* (the Constitutional Court),[20] however, did not dissolve the Party.[21]

---

17 BADER, *supra* note 15, p. 16.

18 *Ibid.*, p. 19.

19 This, together with mandatory religious education in state schools for children deemed to be Muslims, can be interpreted as a *de facto* violation of the principle of laicism and the state neutrality in religious practices by the State, which supports and regulates *Sunni* religious institutions. Article 136 of the 1982 Constitution is also telling: "The Directorate of Religious Affairs, which is within the general administration, shall exercise its duties prescribed in its laws, in accordance with the principles of laicism, removed from all political views and ideas, and aiming at national solidarity and integrity." For the story of Islam and laicism in the Ottoman Empire and the Republic, and covering a vast range of topics, including the Directorate of Religious Affairs, see KOÇAK, M., "Islam and national law in Turkey" in OTTO, J.M. (ed.), *Sharia Incorporated: A Comparative Overview of the Legal Systems of Twelve Muslim Countries in Past and Present* (Leiden University Press, 2010), pp. 231–272.

20 It must be noted here that the decisions of the Constitutional Court (*Anayasa Mahkemesi*) are binding for all, but apart from the "unification of judgments" of the Court of Cassation (*Yargıtay*), judicial decisions do not form binding precedents in the Turkish legal system.

21 1996/3; 1997/3; 22.5.1997, 36 *Anayasa Mahkemesi Kararlar Dergisi* (2001), pp. 978–1033. However, this political party was only questioning the "placing" and the "status" of the *Diyanet*. Another political party, the *Özgürlük ve Demokrasi Partisi- ÖZDEP* (the Freedom and Democracy Party) advocating its abolishment was dissolved, in accordance with section 89 of the Law on Political Parties: "Political parties shall not have an aim that runs counter to Article 136 of the Constitution, which provides that the Directorate of Religious Affairs is

Article 24 of the 1982 Constitution on freedom of religion and conscience, states that,

> "Everyone has the right to freedom of conscience, religious belief and conviction. / Acts of worship, religious services, and ceremonies shall be conducted freely, provided they do not violate the provisions of Article 14.[22] / No one shall be compelled to worship, or to participate in religious ceremonies and rites, to reveal religious beliefs and convictions, or be blamed or accused because of his religious beliefs and convictions. / Education and instruction in religion and ethics shall be conducted under state supervision and control. Instruction in religious culture and moral education shall be compulsory in the curricula of primary and secondary schools. Other religious education and instruction shall be subject to the individual's own desire, and in the case of minors, to the request of their legal representatives. / No one shall be allowed to exploit or abuse religion or religious feelings, or things held sacred by religion, in any manner whatsoever, for the purposes of personal or political influence, or for even partially basing the fundamental, social, economic, political and legal order of the state on religious tenets."

Laicism in fact connotes the absence of religious involvement in government as well as the absence of governmental involvement in religious affairs. In our day it has also come to mean equal treatment of all religions by the State rather than interference of the State in religion, as it seems to be in Turkey; it implies for the state to be equidistant from all religions.

According to the *Anayasa Mahkemesi*, which has discussed and used this concept over the years on innumerable occasions:[23]

> "Laicism, as it appears on articles 2, 14 and 24 of the Constitution, hails from respect for freedom of conscience and leaves religion to the confines of this freedom. The principle of laicism requires the State to be equidistant to individuals with different beliefs and not to differentiate between them."[24]

---

bound to carry out the duties assigned to it in accordance with the principle of laicism." (1993/1; 1993/2; 23.11.1993, 30 *Anayasa Mahkemesi Kararlar Dergisi* (1995), pp. 845–935).

22 Article 14 on the abuse of fundamental rights and freedoms states that, "None of the rights and freedoms embodied in the Constitution shall be exercised with the aim of violating the indivisible integrity of the state with its territory and nation and to destroy the democratic and laic Republic based on human rights. [...] No provision of the Constitution shall be interpreted in a manner that would grant the right to destroy the rights and freedoms embodied in the Constitution or to enable an activity aimed at wider limitation than foreseen by the Constitution."

23 For example, see 1997/62; 1998/52; 16.9.1998, 36 *Anayasa Mahkemesi Kararlar Dergisi* (2001), pp. 198–314; 1999/27; 1999/42; 24.11.1999, 1992/2; 2001/2; 22.6.2001, 37 *Anayasa Mahkemesi Kararlar Dergisi* (2002), pp. 922–1552; 38 *Anayasa Mahkemesi Kararlar Dergisi* (2003), pp. 160–170.

24 38 *Anayasa Mahkemesi Kararlar Dergisi* (2003), p. 169.

Considering the presence of the Directorate of Religious Affairs in Turkey, this does not seem to be the stance the State takes, however.

The Court on many occasions stipulated that laicism accepts that religion cannot be effective and sovereign over the affairs of the State; it gives constitutional guarantee to religions irrespective of differences in belief which are related to the moral existence of the individual; it accepts that limitations can be imposed on religion for the purposes of public order, security and public interest when religion crosses over from individual moral existence to acts and actions of the individual; and prohibits abuse or exploitation of religion. That the State, as the protector of public order and rights, has the power to regulate religious rights and freedoms, is also to be understood as a requirement of laicism. In this context, the *Anayasa Mahkemesi* sees a connection between laicism and the State, democracy, law, freedom of conscience and religion and the right to education.

The proponents of laicism assert that it is based on respect for freedom of thought and freedom of religion, which culminates in the absence of a State religion. Laicism relies on the separation between private life and the public sphere. Religion belongs in the private sphere. In the public sphere, the individual is a citizen equal to all other citizens regardless of ethnic, religious or other particularities. Religious laws are of specific communities whereas the secular law is of the State. In this understanding the government should refrain from taking positions on religious doctrine. In fact, suggestions of contextualising laicism in normative theory have led to theories of alternative secularism(s): "inclusive", "passive", "moderate", "evolutionary", "weak", "tolerant", "liberal", "benevolent", "ameliorative", and so on.[25]

Critics of laicism however, see it as a disguised form of anti-individual right to religious expression, preventing the believer from observing his or her religion and therefore not promoting freedom of thought and freedom of religion as its proponents claim. Especially in countries historically dominated by one religious tradition, such as in Turkey – by the *Sunni* tradition – governments avoiding taking any position on religious matters are seen by some critics of laicism as favouring the dominant religious tradition of the relevant country. For them, laicism must in fact limit the State, by telling it how not to act. A laic State should not impose a world-view, such as laicity, upon its citizens, instead, it should guarantee freedom of religion and conscience. Any other action by a State leads to its losing its neutrality. Indeed, "too many controversies have already been stated" on laicism (secularism).[26]

---

25 See BADER, *supra* note 15, p. 9.

26 See TAYLOR, C., "Foreword: What is secularism?" in LEVEY, G.B., MODOOD, T. and TAYLOR, C. (eds.), *Secularism, Religion and Multicultural Citizenship* (Cambridge University

In a more extreme approach, Veit Bader finds the concept "contested", "fuzzy", "chameleonic", and instead of juxtaposing "secular" versus "religious", suggests "liberal" versus "non-liberal" and "democratic" versus "non-democratic", and the concept "secularism" to be replaced by "liberal-democratic constitutionalism".[27] Bader also points specifically to "Turkish '*laiklik*', as French predominant *laicité*, is not pluralist, inclusive or moderate and defenders of alternative secularisms might say it is a badly distorted (Kemalist) interpretation of a good principle."[28]

The European Court of Human Rights (ECtHR) showed where its sympathies lay regarding laicism, as practised in Turkey, in the *Refah Partisi* (the Welfare Party) judgment,[29] where the Court indicated that it saw religion on the whole as a threat to human rights, specifically to the principle of equality, and to democracy:

> "[...] the principle of secularism is certainly one of the fundamental principles of the State [Turkey] which are in harmony with the rule of law and respect for human rights and democracy. An attitude which fails to respect that principle will not necessarily be accepted as being covered by the freedom to manifest one's religion and will not enjoy the protection of Article 9 of the Convention."[30]

The ECtHR also stated that "plurality of legal systems, as proposed by *Refah*, cannot be considered to be compatible with the Convention system".[31] Such a plurality would also "infringe the principle of non-discrimination between the individuals."[32] Most importantly, the Court then went on to say, "[...] that *sharia* is incompatible with the fundamental principles of democracy, as set forth in the Convention [...]"[33] Thus, the Court favours the laic approach which limits the scope of freedom of religion, which it sees to be "primarily a matter of individual conscience."[34]

Laicism in the official form accepted in Turkey does seem to disregard autonomy and liberty of the individual, clashing with religious family affiliation, and projecting a fairness symbol of gender. Of the three characterisations within the

---

Press,2009), p. xi. See also KURU, A.T., *Secularism and state policies toward religion: The United States, France, and Turkey* (Cambridge University Press, 2009).

27 *Ibid.*, pp. 9–10.

28 *Ibid.*, p. 13.

29 ECtHR 13 February 2003, *Refah Partisi (Welfare Party) and others v Turkey* (GC), ECHR 2003–11. For a critical and harsh assessment of this case see *ibid.*, pp. 29–32.

30 *Ibid.*, para. 93.

31 Para. 119.

32 *Ibid.*

33 Para. 123.

34 Para. 128. For an analysis of this case, see KOÇAK, M. and ÖRÜCÜ, E., "Dissolution of Political Parties in the Name of Democracy: Cases from Turkey and the European Court of Human Rights", 9 *European Public Law* (2003), p. 399.

wider expression of liberalism, "Liberal-Legal Pluralist Approach, Liberal-Formal Equality Approach, and Liberal-Substantive Equality Approach",[35] Turkey can be said to be closer to the second, though paying lip service to the third. Turkish laicism would also qualify as statist, exclusive, assertive and strong.[36]

2.2. FAMILY LAW

Both the 1961 Constitution and the present 1982 Constitution contain articles that make sex equality a constitutional principle, but in family law most provisions of the Civil Code remained unchanged well into late 1980s. Then, slowly but surely things started to change in an effort to further modernise and westernise Turkish family law and bring it in line with the developments in Europe. For instance, a few of the Code articles were amended by the legislator: divorce by mutual consent for irretrievable breakdown was introduced (1988), legitimate and illegitimate children gained equal status (1990); the wife could retain her own surname as well as gaining her husband's (1997). In 1990, by annulling the relevant article of the Code, the Constitutional Court (*Anayasa Mahkemesi*) enabled the wife to work outside the home without her husband's permission. These developments however, did not do much for the social deficit, in fact, at times widened the gap between law and society.

In October 2001, a package of Constitutional amendments was introduced in an effort to further harmonise Turkish laws with the European Union *acquis,* the European Convention on Human Rights and the laws of the European Union member states. In addition to the already existing provision in Article 10 on "equality before the law", which stated that: "All individuals are equal before the law without any discrimination, irrespective of language, race, colour, sex, political opinion, philosophical belief, religion, sect, or any such consideration", an additional clause was introduced into the framework: "Women and men have equal rights and the State is under an obligation to ensure that equality between women and men is implemented in actuality." Article 41 on "the protection of the family" originally read: "The state shall take the necessary measures and establish the necessary organisation to ensure the peace and welfare of the family, the protection of the mother and the children in particular, and for family planning education and practical application." Article 41 gained a first paragraph,

35 FOURNIER, P., *Muslim Marriage in Western Culture: Lost in Transplantation* (Ashgate, 2010), p. 3.

36 Veit Bader finds Turkish laicism an assertive secularism, "a strong and state-centric model that, eventually, is too secular for the Islamists, too Sunni for the Alevis, too Muslim for the non-Muslims, and too Turkish for the Kurds". BADER, *supra* note 15, footnote 22. Also KURU, *supra* note 26.

which reads: "The family is the foundation of Turkish society and is based on equality between the spouses."

A number of articles of the 1982 Constitution were amended again in 2010. Among these, there are two that concern us. The first is an addition to the second clause of article 10, introducing positive discrimination into Turkish law. It states that measures to be taken to implement equality between men and women cannot be interpreted contrary to the principle of equality. A further clause is added to article 10, so that measures to be taken for children, the elderly, the disabled, the widows and orphans of persons who have died while serving the State, and for war veterans cannot be regarded as contrary to the principle of equality. The second is a change of the title of article 41, adding "and children" to "Protection of the family". Then the following has been added to this article: "Every child has the right to be protected and nurtured and to establish personal and direct contact with his/her parents, unless openly contrary to his/her high interests. The State takes measures to protect children from all kinds of abuse and violence." Though very welcome additions they await internalisation and implementation.

Efforts to update the Civil Code had been made over a number of decades unsuccessfully, but with the added impetus for change, the Civil Code was extensively revised on 22 November 2001 and the new Civil Code came into force on 1 January 2002. This is not a brand new Civil Code, and many of the old provisions are the same apart from their numbering and modernising of the language. The fundamental tenets have remained unchanged. Nevertheless, in the field of family law, there are extensive amendments, the most important being related to equality between the spouses in the case of family law, and strengthening the position of the spouse (in this case to be understood as the wife) in law of succession. Family law is regulated in the Second Book of the Code, now between sections 118 and 494 (previously sections 82–438) and Succession in the Third Book, now between sections 495 and 682 (previously sections 439–617).

This Code is still not home-grown as it follows mostly the changes in the Swiss Civil Code, though by now partially internalised by the populace. The social deficit however, is still there.

We will look at four areas in family law: religious marriages, children, adultery and the position of the wife as an equal spouse.

2.2.1. *Religious marriages*

As laicism is in the essence of Turkish family law, it follows that only a civil marriage is legally recognised.[37] For the valid conclusion of a marriage contract, certain conditions have to be fulfilled: the capacity to marry and the absence of certain degrees of consanguinity and affinity, of an already existing marriage, of an adoptive relationship, and of certain diseases.[38]

Following the civil marriage ceremony, a marriage certificate (family record book) is given without which a religious ceremony, *imam nikahı*,[39] cannot take place, and it is a criminal offence to undertake or perform such a ceremony without this certificate.[40] A religious ceremony is not needed for the marriage to be binding. Today this is explicitly reiterated in section 143 of the new 2002 Civil Code to indicate the secular nature of marriage in Turkey.

Nevertheless, it is a fact that a large number of Muslim couples perform a religious marriage ceremony, a verbal contract of partners in the presence of an *imam*, in accordance with the classical Islamic law, along with a civil marriage contract. Again, a big majority of those who have adhered to religious marriage, even though only subsequent to a civil marriage, would also like to obey the rules of religion on divorce. This can create a serious problem for such couples. Since marriage in Islamic law can be dissolved by repudiation (*talak, talaq*), the unilateral or bilateral decision of the spouses without going to court, if the spouses pronounce the specific statements that result in divorce in Islamic law, they would be considered divorced in Islamic law. Yet, they would be still married according to the laic legal system under which they married in the first place, unless they also go to court to obtain a civil divorce. If they do not, and they continue to live together, which they are not permitted to do under Islamic law,

---

37 There are obviously exceptions to the rule that religious practices in family law are not legally acceptable in a laic legal system: Islamic family law can penetrate the system either in accordance with international private law rules, which may incorporate Islamic family law, or through the interpretation of secular domestic laws. For instance, foreign marriages concluded abroad will in principle be recognised *ex lege* if they meet the requirements of the *lex loci celebrationis*, that is, the validity of religious marriages validly concluded abroad are recognised.

38 Mehmet Akif Aydın bemoans the fact that during laicisation of marriage one very important impediment to marriage in Islamic law was left out: fosterage (*süt kardeşliği* = milk sibling). This is a relationship between a man and a woman who were breastfed by the same woman during their infancy, which is an impediment to marriage between these two in Islamic Law and still in Turkish Islamic tradition. See AYDIN, *supra* note 6, pp. 181–182. This was not and is not mentioned in the Civil Code as an impediment, though most people do adhere to this rule.

39 *İmam nikahı* is a consensual marriage performed by an *imam* as a religious ceremony, permissible in Turkey only after a civil marriage ceremony.

40 This is today regulated by the 2005 Penal Code in section 230.

this would amount to the sin of "fornication". Another result would be that any child conceived after this time would be considered illegitimate by their religious beliefs. Obviously, this is not a concern of the laic official family law, but has religious consequences for the couples.[41] In fact, there should be no problem here, since the solution is indeed quite straightforward: they should immediately seek a proper civil divorce.

Section 237/4 of the 1926 Penal Code was amended in 1936 to criminalise religious unofficial unions (*imam nikahı*) entered into without prior civil marriage, and imposed a prison sentence of from two to six months on the man and the woman. This amendment also imposed a prison sentence on persons performing such religious ceremonies without seeing the official certificate of marriage.[42] In addition, such informal marriages have no civil legal status in the formal legal order, though they are generally justified by certain sections of society, by existing tradition.[43] The constitutionality of section 237/4 was challenged in 1998 as violating several Articles of the 1982 Constitution: Article 2 (the principle of laicism), Article 10 (equality), Article 12 (the character and the scope of fundamental rights and freedoms) and Article 24 (freedom to conduct religious services and ceremonies).

The *Anayasa Mahkemesi* stated that section 237 was inserted into the Penal Code in 1936 to give support to civil marriage, that without this section, polygamous unions would become possible and that, though such unions have no legal consequence, they pose a threat to the concept of family, being detrimental to the social order. The Court opined that if couples enter such illegal unions, women cannot use their rights arising from marriage, children are illegitimate and lose their inheritance rights and such marriages cannot be invoked against third parties, and thus have no legal protection. Therefore, civil marriage must be strengthened in order to protect the family and the rights of women and children. The Court then added that there is no violation, as was claimed, of the principle of equality here between those who live together with no marriage of

---

41 See AYDIN, *supra* note 6, pp. 181–182. In fact, this situation can be assessed as the reverse of the Jewish *get*, where the woman who is not given the *get* is chained to her husband in the religious sense but not in the civil sense. Here, however, for the Muslim couple there is no religious marriage any longer, but they are tied in a civil marriage.

42 It must be pointed out however, that there are indeed very few cases where a sanction is applied, since it is an offence that needs to be brought to the knowledge of the authorities and when it is, it often results on acquittal. Though, recently, the Fourth Division of the *Yargıtay* in a judgment of 6 June 2000 (2000/3127; 2000/4891) overturned a criminal court ruling acquitting an *imam* who had performed a religious marriage ceremony without first checking the document proving that a civil marriage had taken place. This case was alluded to in the *Şerife Yiğit* case in the ECtHR Grand Chamber judgment of 2 November 2010, application no. 3976/05, para. 31, to be discussed below.

43 For a comparative assessment of such informal unions see RUTTEN, S., "Protection of spouses in informal marriages by human rights", 6:2 *Utrecht Law Review* (2010), 77.

any kind and those with only a religious "marriage", since the first group do not wish their unions to be regarded as marriage. This means that what distinguishes spouses in the religious "marriage" from persons living in non-marital relationships, is that in the former case the spouses are considered to be in fact, married. Equality before the law does not mean that everyone must be treated alike; differentiation based on Article 13 on limitation of rights and freedoms,[44] is not unconstitutional. The Court further pointed out that, "the Civil Code is a fundamental building block in the structure of the bridge to a contemporary and laic legal system for the Turkish Republic", and civil marriage, "being in the essence of that block, is also specifically protected by Article 174 of the Constitution."[45] The Court said that to keep law and religion separate is the most important function of laicism.[46]

This decision, by providing an authoritative answer to any question that might arise related to the acceptability of religious marriage as an alternative to civil marriage, sets the scene for Turkish laic family law. This scene did not change after the introduction of the New Penal Code in 2005. The new Penal Code covers this issue in section 230 under the rubric "offences against the family".

Yet, in 2005 the *Anayasa Mahkemesi*, by annulling section 104/2 of the 2005 Turkish Penal Code, has added a controversy to the debate on the possibilities of encouraging religious unions.[47] Section 140/1 states that a person who enters a sexual relationship with a child of 15, without pressure, threats or deceit, shall be imprisoned for from six months to two years, upon complaint. The annulled section 140/2 stipulated that, if the perpetrator is older by five years than the injured, the punishment shall be doubled, without seeking the condition of complaint. The Court based its decision on the principle of equality before the law. Yet, as pointed out in one of the dissenting opinions, this provision did not violate the principle of equality, was not contrary to the principle of protection of the family, the principle of privacy of private life or proportionality in criminal

44 Article 13: "Fundamental rights and freedoms may be restricted, without touching their core, only for specific reasons set forth in the relevant articles of the Constitution and only by law. These restrictions cannot be contrary to the letter and the spirit of the Constitution, democratic social order, requirements of the laic Republic and the principle of proportionality."

45 Article 174: "No provision of the Constitution shall be construed or interpreted as rendering unconstitutional the Reform Laws indicated below, which aim to raise Turkish society above the level of contemporary civilisation and to safeguard the laic character of the Republic, and which were in force on the date of the adoption by referendum of the Constitution of Turkey: [...} 4. The principle of civil marriage according to which the marriage act shall be concluded in the presence of the competent official, adopted by the Turkish Civil Code No: 743 of 17 February 1926, and Article 110 of the same Code."

46 1999/27; 1999/42; 24.11.1999; 2.5.2002; *Resmi Gazete:* 24743; 38 *Anayasa Mahkemesi Kararlar Dergisi* (2003), pp. 160–170.

47 2005/103; 2005/89; 23.11.2005, (2006) 42 *Anayasa Mahkemesi Kararlar Dergisi*, pp. 437–454.

sanctions; and the Court should have considered the meaning, the purpose and the context of the provision. This annulment could encourage illegal unions entered into without official marriage, or at the very least, send a signal to the traditional sectors of the society, that such relationships will be tolerated from now on. This also creates a discrepancy with the new arrangements in the Civil Code, where majority is reached at 18, which is also the normal age for marriage. Both sexes can get married at 17 and the judge can reduce this to 16 for exceptional circumstances. This decision is a retrograde step.

Quite a different signal was sent though, through the Law on the Protection of the Family, passed in 1998,[48] pursuant to the amendment to Article 41 of the Constitution, seen above. This law states that when a spouse, a child or any other member of the family living under the same roof as the violent spouse, informs the Justice of the Peace that she/he has been a subject of domestic violence, the judge can decide on any number of sanctions.[49] Though this law uses the word "spouse" throughout, it was passed as affirmation by the legislator that it is women and children who are subjected to violence in this male dominated society, that society should not tolerate this kind of behaviour and that women and children should have an official power to turn to when unprotected.[50] Because the wording used covers "spouse" and "family", the woman who may be married off by her family at a very early age to a man through religious marriage alone (that is the unofficial spouse living together with the other as if married), or cohabiting partners, get no protection whatsoever. This law is in keeping with the laic approach and strengthens civil marriage by introducing measures in addition to the Civil and the Penal Codes to protect the wife and children, and yet does not cater for the realities of the Turkish families or offer any protection for such "families", which is a persistent social issue in Turkey.

In fact, neither the legal framework nor the *Yargıtay* (the Court of Cassation) accept in essence the fact that couples living out of wedlock can be regarded as in a relationship to be protected by law. For instance while the *Yargıtay* was

48 Law No. 4320; 14.1.1998; *Resmi Gazete*, 1.17.1998; No. 23233.

49 The offending spouse will be cautioned that he or she must not behave in such a way as to frighten other members of the family; must leave the family home and not return to it which will then be allocated to the other spouse and the children, and must not visit their place of work; must not damage the belongings of the other spouse or the children; must surrender any firearms to the security forces; must not come to the family home drunk or having used drugs and must not use such materials there.

50 There was very heated debate in Parliament while this law was discussed, a very powerful view being that the law should not interfere with family relationships and family violence as the father of the family should be able to use his discretion on how to treat and chastise his wife and children, such intrusion not being law's business – a view especially upheld by religious right-wing politicians. The day was won by the strong feminist lobby and the progressive camp in Parliament.

determining what is an "engagement" in order to decide on whether gifts beyond the ordinary should be returned upon the breaking up of the relationship, it was careful to differentiate between the breaking up of an "engagement", that is a promise to marry, in which case gifts beyond the ordinary would be returned, and of "living together without a valid marriage act", in which case they need not be returned.[51] In this second instance, the law protects the possessor, since both parties act outside legality.

Another consequence of being in such a relationship is related to losing the maintenance or destitution alimony. Section 176/3 of the 2002 Civil Code (the old section 145 of the 1926 Civil Code) refers to couples living together without a civil marriage, in that, a former husband is not required to pay such maintenance or destitution alimony to his ex-wife if the latter (among other reasons) is living in a *de facto* marital relationship with another man. The Third Division of the *Yargıtay*, set aside a judgment of a lower court on the grounds that a former husband was no longer required to pay such alimony to his ex-wife who was living with another, albeit without a marriage certificate, and the couple had a child together.[52]

Here it is most worthwhile to look at a recent and significant case against Turkey that went to the ECtHR: *Şerife Yiğit v Turkey: Family life and the prohibition of discrimination (Article 8 in conjunction with 14 ECHR)*.[53] ECtHR decided on 20 January 2009 on rights that can be derived from a religious marriage.[54] The case was referred to the Grand Chamber on 14 September 2009. The original Chamber decision was reached by a narrow majority of four to three. The case is related to a couple with an *imam nikahı* union entered into in 1976. They had six children. The husband died in 2002 and the wife, Şerife Yiğit, asked for registration of their marriage and of the children and also requested the dead husband's pension and health benefits. Only the registration of the children was accepted, and all other claims were refused. She argued that the refusal was a violation of her right to family life. According to the ECtHR, there was indeed a *de facto* family life, but, since Turkey did not recognise other stable relationships alongside the civil marriage, Turkey could not be obliged to do so. The Court concluded that Turkey's aim is legitimate, that there is an objective and reasonable justification and therefore the distinction drawn between married and non-married persons is justified in this context. The principle of equality

---

51 1998/10173; 1998/12105; 24.11.1998; 25 *Yargıtay Kararlar Dergisi* 1999, p. 170.

52 2003/14484; 2003/14212; 11.12.2003, cited in the Grand Chamber judgment of *Şerife Yiğit*, *supra* note 42.

53 Application no. 3976/05.

54 Already a similar decision was reached in 1975 in *X v Germany* (Application no. 6167/73), where the refusal to register a religious marriage was seen as not violating Articles 9 and 12 ECHR. See for a thorough discussion of a number of such cases in RUTTEN, *supra* note 43.

cannot be invoked successfully so as to acquire a civil legal status for a religious union.

The conclusion of the ECtHR judgment, finding for Turkey, indicates that States (in this case Turkey) are not obliged to recognise other relationships alongside marriage, neither are they obliged to protect unofficial marriages as they would formally valid marriages. They are not obliged to attribute legal status to religious marriages. The separation of religion and the state allows States, in order to attribute legal status to a marriage, to require a civil marriage or a civil registration. The judgment, reminiscent of the decision in the *Refah* case,[55] also implies that the exercise of freedom of religion can be restricted in favour of other rights and interests.

After a year, the Grand Chamber has finally reached a unanimous decision with two separate concurrent opinions, on 2 November 2010.[56] The Grand Chamber considered the case under article 1 of Protocol 1 in combination with article 14 of the Convention and under article 8. On the question of whether there was discrimination on the basis of the nature of the marriage, the Court accepted that the difference in treatment between civil and non-civil marriages pursued the legitimate aims of protecting public order and the rights and freedoms of women.[57] On the question of proportionality, the Court opined that Şerife Yiğit could not argue that she had a legitimate expectation of obtaining a pension and that she was well aware of the fact that she had to regularise her relationship in accordance with the Civil Code, therefore she could not be considered to be in good faith. In addition, being religiously married for 26 years she had ample time to contract a civil marriage. Although Mrs Yiğit argued that "religious marriage was a social reality in Turkey" and that "religious marriage was a feature of Turkish life",[58] the Court took into account "the importance of the principle of secularism in Turkey" and that "Turkey requires a civil marriage from all its citizens", and concluded that the difference in treatment was proportionate. There was also no violation of article 8, as the applicant was not prevented from enjoying peaceful family life. The Grand Chamber thus followed the Turkish authorities in its assessment of the legitimate aims. The Court was keen to state that, "Turkey aimed to put an end to a marriage tradition which places women at a clear disadvantage, not to say in a situation of dependence and inferiority to men."[59]

---

55 See *supra* note 29.

56 Application no. 3976/05; 2.11.2010.

57 This does leave the women unprotected however. The situation can be considered to be indirect discrimination on the basis of gender, since in the existing gender patterns the man works and the woman stays at home and takes care of the children, and would fall into destitution upon the death of her spouse.

58 *Ibid.*, para. 65.

59 *Ibid.*, para. 81.

Though both Judge Rozakis and Judge Kovler agree with the Court's argument that States have a certain margin of appreciation to treat differently those couples who have contracted a civil marriage and those who have not, they also have misgivings. In his concurring opinion, Judge Rozakis is of the view that religious marriage is actually the backdrop here. He believes that the real issue to be considered should have been a comparison of "long-standing and stable family relationships outside marriage," that is, cohabitation, and "marriage, as understood by domestic law". He opines that the Court should have decided "in view of new social realities which are gradually emerging in today's Europe, manifested in a gradual increase in the number of stable relationships outside marriage, which are replacing the traditional institution of marriage without necessarily undermining the fabric of family life".[60] Judge Kovler on the other hand, believes that the Court demonstrated "ideological activism" and "committed a serious error of judgment on the Islamic system of values", and would like to see the Court take "a more anthropological approach in the position it adopts, by 'not just exploring difference, but exploring it differently'." Otherwise, he thinks that "the Court is in danger of becoming entrenched in 'eurocentric' attitudes."[61]

It is clear that the ECtHR does not support legal pluralism and considers that human rights law cannot be applied in different ways depending on the differing beliefs of the individuals. The judgments of the ECtHR also show that laicism in Western modern society is not a myth. Nevertheless, this may be far from resolving the contradictions of modern existence, as legal systems cannot be successful if they are not linked to social values and moral sensibilities which in their turn are not universal and apolitical. Laicism as a western legal concept has a cultural specificity, which may have to be re-considered.[62]

2.2.2. Children

2.2.2.1. The problem of legitimacy of children born into religious marriages

One of the most pressing problems of the early years of the Republic was the status of children born to parents who had religious marriage alone. Religious conviction, long established tradition, remoteness of villages, strict formalities attached to civil marriages, the long time involved in getting documents sorted out, the embarrassment of medical examination and the like, are among the causes that lead spouses and their families to opt for religious marriage alone.

---

60 *Ibid.*, pp. 17–18.

61 *Ibid.*, p. 19.

62 See the suggestion by Veit Bader, to replace the word secularism once and for all with "liberal-democratic constitutionalism". See BADER, *supra* note 15.

This type of cohabitation is illegal in Turkey, as we have seen above. Therefore, children born into these relationships are illegitimate in the eyes of the legal system. At intervals, the legislature feels under pressure to legislate on the status of children born into such illicit relationships. These Acts, cited as "Amnesty Acts" or "Legitimacy Laws" allow the registration of consensual marriages in the civil status register for those without a civil marriage contract who are living together as husband and wife and who have children, as long as no marriage impediment exists between the parties. Although there is no legal recognition of cohabitation in the 1926 and the 2002 Civil Codes, such enactments as Amnesty Acts create legal consequences for such relationships.

These Amnesty Acts, by which the legitimacy of a child born into cohabitation not tied to a secular marriage contract is administratively corrected, make possible the legitimisation of thousands of this special category of illegitimate children, that is, illegitimate in the eyes of the Civil Code, and validate their status. These children are registered as legitimate if they are born to parents who were living together continuously as husband and wife, and not born from an occasional relationship. Even the children of fathers who are legally married to women other than the mother can be registered as legitimate, as long as the mother is not married to another man.

Prior to the first Amnesty Act of 1933,[63] the *Yargıtay*, attempted to resolve this problem by way of interpretation: children of such consensual informal marriages were considered as legitimate by the Court when one of the parents died, by an analogous application of section 249 of the 1926 Civil Code, which said that children of couples who have made promises to marry each other, but were then unable to marry owing to the death or incapacity of one of them, could be declared legitimate by a court upon the application of the other party or of the child himself.

Turkey passed the most recent Amnesty Act in 1991, creating yet another possibility to legitimise the status of children born out of official wedlock.[64] In the 2002 amendments to the Civil Code, we now see a partial accommodation of such realities: the concepts of legitimate and illegitimate have been erased for inheritance purposes. Nonetheless, from the point of view of family ties, a legitimate child is the one born into a secular marriage. A child born out of marriage to an unmarried woman is a natural child and belongs to the mother by the act of birth, though she does not have automatic parental authority. Family

[63] These Acts were introduced in 1933, 1945, 1950, 1956, 1965, 1975, 1981 and 1991. For more information on this "innovation" see ÖRÜCÜ, E., "Turkey: Reconciling Traditional Society and Secular Demands", 26 *Journal of Family Law* (1987–88), 221.

[64] Law no. 3716 of 8 May 1991 on the correct recording of the parentage of children born within or outside marriage and those born of a relationship not based on a marriage certificate.

ties can be established between this child and the natural father by the subsequent official civil marriage of the parents (section 292), by acknowledgement by the natural father (section 295),[65] or the recognition of the natural father's paternity by a court decision upon a claim brought to court either by the mother or the child (section 301).

A few developments prior to the new Civil Code coming into effect in 2002 are worth mentioning here. First, in 1981 the *Anayasa Mahkemesi* found unconstitutional and annulled section 310 of the 1926 Civil Code which stated that a judge could not declare paternity for a child whose father was already married to a woman other than the child's mother at the time of sexual intercourse.[66]

Then in 1987, the *Anayasa Mahkemesi* annulled section 443/1/2, thus removing the distinction between legitimate and illegitimate children as far as succession is concerned; the position up to then being that succession rights of an illegitimate child were only one half of a legitimate child.[67] This section was then reworded in 1990 by the legislator thus equating legitimate and illegitimate relatives for the purposes of inheritance rights.[68] In 1991, the then section 292, which stated that a married man could not acknowledge his child from an adulterous or an incestual relationship, was also found to be unconstitutional by the *Anayasa Mahkemesi* and annulled.[69]

Following upon these developments, in 1993 the *Yargıtay* reiterated that the existence of blood ties alone is not sufficient to create rights of succession and that the existence of such ties must be established by law, that is, by birth within marriage, marriage of parents after birth, correction of legitimacy by a judge or through Amnesty Acts.[70] There are no other means to establish this relationship. This is so even when the tie between the father and the child is well known to everyone or the father admits to this through means other than those foreseen by law. Thus all children born out of wedlock are natural as to their father.

65 The natural father must make a formal unilateral acknowledgement by a written application either to the official in charge of the civil status register or to a court, or by an official deed or by declaration in a will (section 295). A child with prior family ties to another man cannot be acknowledged, unless disowned by that other. The mother and the child, or upon the death of the child, his/her descendants, the Public Prosecutor for the Republic or the Treasury can sue against such acknowledgement (section 298). The man who acknowledged a child can also sue for the annulment of that acknowledgement on the grounds of mistake, deceit or intimidation (section 297).

66 1981/29; 1981/22; 21.5.1981.

67 1/18; 11.9.1987, published in 1988.

68 Law no. 3678; 14.11.1990.

69 1990/15; 1991/5; 28.2.1991.

70 1993/603; 1993/4179; 26.4.1993.

Finally in 1997 the *Yargıtay* reached a Unification Decision in view of the contradictory decisions emanating from its Divisions, and declared that an illegitimate child is one born out of wedlock, and has either been acknowledged by the father or whose paternity, with whichever consequence,[71] has been determined by a court decision. This child has equal status to a legitimate child for inheritance purposes.

This gradual change has now been distilled in the 2002 Civil Code. The natural father can acknowledge any child of his born out of wedlock by following the procedure laid down in section 295, without any additional conditions attached. There is no distinction left between legitimate and illegitimate children or between cases that determine paternity in the 2002 Civil Code. So now, in keeping with developments in other European states, a child born into wedlock and a child born out of wedlock but whose family ties have been established by the acknowledgement of the natural father or a court decision, have equal rights as far as inheritance is concerned (section 498).[72]

These are intriguing developments. Although they have all been in the interest of the child, and in keeping with modern developments, they can also be construed to mean that the legal system is condoning relationships outside secular marriage rather than being concerned solely with the interests of the child. On the one hand it accords with the values upheld by the ECHR and on the other with those of some at home who want to have children born out of *imam nikahı* relationships to be equated to those born in wedlock. In fact, in some quarters, this has even been hailed as a covert acceptance of *imam nikahı* unions. Thus it has a paradoxical consequence, which gives the judges a freer hand to uphold indirectly a religious culture which otherwise clashes with one of the values of the official framework: laicism.

2.2.2.2. Religious instruction

As for religious instruction to be given to children, we see that section 341/1 of the 2002 Civil Code deals with religious instruction and education, the

---

71 The section at that time made a distinction between "paternity with all its consequences" and "paternity for financial support", which distinction had given rise to a line of varying interpretations by different Sections of the *Yargıtay*. "Paternity for financial support" was important at a time when a child born to persons prohibited from marrying or into an adulterous relationship could not be acknowledged. Neither could a court declare "paternity with all its consequences" for such a child. See for a thorough discussion, ÖRÜCÜ, E., "Improving the Lot of Women and Children" in BAINHAM, A. (ed.), *The International Survey of Family Law 1997*, (1999) 465, at pp. 473–479. Now there are no longer two types of paternity suits.

72 Also see for a comprehensive discussion of various decisions by this Court, the *Yargıtay* and the doctrine on this issue ÖRÜCÜ, *ibid*.

determination of which is the absolute right of the parents. All agreements limiting this right are void. Thus, if parents are not of the same religion and if dispute arises as to which religion the child should be brought up in, it is for the judge to resolve this dispute since neither parent is superior to the other.[73]

Article 174 of the Constitution under item 1 protects the unification of the educational system.[74] Though, according to Article 24/4 of the Constitution, religious and moral education and learning are under the supervision of the State, the fact that custody is an absolute right of the parents has some serious consequences in Turkish society. The parents have the sole right to decide on the religious education of the child. Recently children as young as five are being sent to *Quran* courses by their parents, where they are told for instance, that not to cover the head is a sin. Such children would lose their capacity to think freely and would not be in a position to make an independent choice when they reach majority, choice of religion at majority being recognised as a right by section 341/3 of the Civil Code. In this regard, a view expressed by some academics is quite worrying. It is said that the parents should not be bringing up a child without religion or instil in the child anti-religious feelings.[75] In a laic society everyone should be free to believe or not to believe, and instruct their children, over whom they have custody, accordingly.

The rights of the child to develop his/her potential to the full should trump the parents' unfettered right to give religious instruction to the child; and this unfettered right too can be limited by the constitutional principle of laicism. In the present political climate in Turkey however, this would not happen.

2.2.3. Adultery

Until 1915, in the Ottoman Empire, there were no specific grounds for divorce, since the husband did not have to show cause when he pronounced divorce (*talaq*). In Islam, adultery was a criminal offence for both men and women (the *Quran* 24:2): "Flog the adulteress and the adulterer [...] with a hundred stripes", was the punishment. During the rule of Caliph Ömer (634–644) "stoning to death" of the woman was added as a punishment for adultery, but was rarely used in the Ottoman Empire, the last time being the 17th century when it was banned by the Sultan. The 1858 Ottoman Penal Code was based on the 1810 French Code. An adulterous woman was to be punished by imprisonment for from three months to two years, and so would her accomplice. However, a

---

73 In the 1926 Civil Code (section 263), in cases of dispute the decision of the father prevailed.

74 Law no. 430 of 2 March 1340 (1924). For the wording of article 174 see, *supra* note 45.

75 See AKINTÜRK, T., *Türk Medeni Hukuku: Aile Hukuku* (Turkish Civil Law: Family Law), 11th ed. (Beta, 2008), p. 414, and BERKİ, Ş., *Medeni Hukuk, Umumi Esaslar – Şahıs ve Aile Hukuku* (Civil Law: General Principles: Law of Persons and Family) (1961), p. 228.

husband would only be considered adulterous if he lived with another woman in the house he shared with his wife. This accorded with the traditional mores and religious beliefs of the people. This Code remained in force until 1926.

The 1926 Penal Code of the Turkish Republic, based on the Italian Code, also regarded adultery as a punishable offence. Though the punishment for adultery was for from six months to three years in all cases, a husband's adultery was defined as living with an unmarried woman as man and wife in his house of residence with his lawful wife, or in another place known to the public (section 441). For the wife however, any sexual intercourse with a man other than her husband constituted adultery; one voluntary sexual act being enough for punishment (section 440). This again satisfied the mores and the religious feelings of the populace and was not challenged as unconstitutional after 1962, when the *Anayasa Mahkemesi* was created,[76] until 1996.

In 1996, the *Anayasa Mahkemesi* annulled section 441, without going into a discussion of the meaning and place of adultery in society, finding the difference between the adultery of the husband and of the wife to be in violation of article 10 of the Constitution on equality.[77] The Court suggested that the legislature could either remove adultery from among punishable offences for both spouses or keep it with new conditions without creating distinction between them, this being the preferred option of the majority of the population and the government. The legislature however, took no steps to regulate this area. So, it was again for the *Anayasa Mahkemesi* to take action: in 1999, section 440, dealing with the wife's adultery, was also annulled.[78] Again, the issue was dealt with within the context of equality of the sexes, the Court pointing out that there was now a new inequality as the husband had acquired a privileged position.

This now left section 442 dealing with the adultery of the spouses who were legally separated, but still married, and living separately. The sanction was imprisonment for from three months to one year. Finally, in 1999 section 442 was also annulled.[79]

During the deliberations of the 2005 Penal Code, the issue of adultery became a hotly debated topic. Though in the original Draft there was no mention of

---

76 It must be remembered that the *Anayasa Mahkemesi* was set up to protect the territorial integrity of the State, the institutions of the legal system above all else, rather than offer personal protection to the individuals' human rights. See, for an analysis ÖRÜCÜ, E., "The Constitutional Court of Turkey: The *Anayasa Mahkemesi* as the Protector of the System", 3:2 *Journal of Comparative Law* (2009), 254.

77 1996/15; 1996/34; 23.9.1996; *Resmi Gazete* No. 22860; 27.12.1996. Most such annulments by the *Anayasa Mahkemesi* rely on Article 10 on equality.

78 1998/3; 1998/28; 23.6.1998; *Resmi Gazete* No. 23638; 13.3.1999.

79 1999/24; 1999/30; 13.7.1999, 36 *Anayasa Mahkemesi Kararlar Dergisi* (2001), p. 545.

adultery, there were last minute efforts by some members of the government to put adultery back into the Code. This attracted immediate attention at home and abroad.

The anti-adultery camp relied on arguments of modernity and current developments in the civilised world. This camp argued that to regard adultery as a punishable offence was a conservative or even a religious step. Their concern was also related to the prospective membership of the European Union and they saw such a move as an obstruction in the way of Turkey's EU membership.[80] They relied on domestic facts and said that there had been no increase in the number of adulterous relationships since 1999 when adultery became no longer a criminal offence. In addition they pointed out that since adultery was still a divorce ground, this should suffice to satisfy the moral position that was taken in this field.

The pro-adultery camp relied on the decisions of the *Anayasa Mahkemesi*, saying that in the three decisions of 1996 and 1999 annulling adultery solely on the grounds of equality, there was at no stage any value-judgement, and that the Court showed the way on how to legislate in this field constitutionally. This camp's immediate concern was the mores and religious beliefs of Turkish society. The proponents of the proposal to re-introduce adultery into the Penal Code were mostly members of the pro-Islamic and conservative ruling Party, the *Adalet ve Kalkınma Partisi* (Justice and Development Party).

However, a bizarre argument was put forward by the anti-adultery camp, which had an immediate impact on the others. The argument ran thus: If adultery is to be re-introduced into the Penal Code, a man, who has a wife to whom he is officially married – and this is a secular marriage – but then has one or two other "wives" with whom he only has a religious marriage, would be deemed to be in an adulterous relationship and might end up in prison; as would the other women! This obviously had always been a possibility but had not come to light in open discussion. At this point the proposal was dropped. In the New Penal Code of June 1, 2005, there is no mention of adultery.[81]

Unless one day Turkey opts to accept law reform in the field of family law along the lines of the Principles of European Family Law as proposed by the

80 This may very well be a valid concern, considering the EU's attitude to European public order and the prerequisites for membership. See, McCREA, R., *Religion and the Public Order of the European Union,* Oxford Studies in European Law (Oxford University Press, 2010).

81 For the full story on adultery, see ÖRÜCÜ, E., "The Story of Adultery in Turkey" in BAINHAM, A. (ed.), *The International Survey of Family Law* (Jordan Publishing, 2006), p. 489.

Commission on European Family Law[82] and goes for the sole ground "divorce by mutual consent" or "divorce without consent", the conditions of which are that "the divorce should be permitted without consent of one of the spouses if they have been factually separated for one year", adultery will remain as a ground for divorce in Turkey. However, it will not re-enter the Penal Code.

In Turkey today, adultery is a rather frequently used ground for divorce (section 161 of the 2002 Civil Code), though viewed within the principle of equality of the spouses. In addition, adultery has consequences in the granting of moral damages, in alimony, upon death and related to matrimonial property. As seen earlier, since 1991 however, when the *Anayasa Mahkemesi* annulled the provision of the Civil Code banning the acknowledgement of a child born into an adulterous relationship, and stated that all children should be treated equally,[83] a father can acknowledge such a child, which is seen by the conservative camp, as indirectly giving recognition to unofficial religious unions.

2.2.4. *The position of the wife as an equal spouse*

2.2.4.1. The wife-as-guarantor

Section 169 of the 1926 Civil Code on "legal transactions between the spouses and transactions to the benefit of the husband" stipulated that transactions on the wife's personal property or on goods subject to community property could not be valid unless certified by a justice of the peace. This rule applied also to obligations undertaken by the wife towards third parties for the benefit of the husband. This was an exception to the wife's capacity to act.

The issue reached the *Anayasa Mahkemesi* with the claim of a violation of the principle of equality of the spouses, contrary to articles 10 and 12 of the Constitution. The claim was that this provision, which appears at first sight to be protecting the rights of a wife, actually treats her as a minor since the husband in the same position does not need permission; the insinuation being that she is a second class citizen. The lower court opted for the rhetoric of equality.

Treating the realities of Turkish society as paramount, the *Anayasa Mahkemesi* opined that:

---

82 *Principles of European Family Law Regarding Divorce and Maintenance Between Former Spouses* (prepared by BOELE-WOELKI, K., FERRAND, F., GONZALEZ BEILFUSS, C., JANTERA-JAREBORG, M., LOWE, N., MARTINY, D. and PINTENS, W.) (Intersentia, 2004).

83 1990/15; 1991/5; 28.2.1991.

> "The aim of this provision is to protect the wife from entering under obligations unwittingly as she may not know the consequences, the scope and the aim of this debt. She may enter such an obligation under the husband's influence. This limitation is to protect the unity of the family and is in the public interest and therefore not unconstitutional."[84]

We see that the *Anayasa Mahkemesi* took a traditional view of the family relationships and held other values above that of formal equality. Three dissenting judges however, observed that this unequal treatment of the woman violates the Convention on the Elimination of All Forms of Discrimination Against Women to the effect that any discrimination based on sex is illegal; national provisions should be viewed in the light of this Convention, not just the Turkish Constitution. For them, modernity, westernisation and becoming a member of the European Union were more important than facing the realities of the country, so they upheld the rhetoric rather than the family realities.

The decision of the *Anayasa Mahkemesi*, though it reflects the family realities in most Turkish marriages, has no bearing on the present situation since this section of the 1926 Civil Code has been changed, equalised and modernised in the 2002 Civil Code. Now section 189 dealing with liability lays down a brief principle: "liability to the third parties is joint and several".[85] Section 193 dealing with legal transactions of the spouses states that unless the law determines otherwise, "each spouse can enter every kind of legal transaction with the other and the third parties". These could be regarded as welcome developments, which put men and women on an equal footing not only with each other but also in view of European developments. However, it could also be easily claimed that the development is unfortunate in a society where most wives live under the pressure of their husbands and are not financially independent; a sacrifice of family reality to the rhetoric of equality. This development is detrimental to an illiterate woman who would sign any piece of paper under the threat of her husband, and therefore, the law does not accord with Turkish realities as they stand at present. The social deficit is thereby widened with these changes.

The question is, why has the 2002 Civil Code exposed the wife to the economic perils awaiting her in the precarious free-market of our times, at the mercy of the husband and his creditor? Is it just because the rhetoric of equality has to be

84 1997/27; 1998/43; 30.6.1998 (*Resmi Gazete*: 23934; 15.1.2000). When the *Anayasa Mahkemesi* had another bite at the cherry, it decided in exactly the same way. 1999/47; 1999/46; 28.12.1999 (*Resmi Gazete* 23989; 10.3.2000).

85 Section 189: "When representing the family unit, the spouses are liable to third parties jointly and severally. A spouse who enters into a transaction without the capacity to represent the union will be personally liable. However, if the capacity to represent has been exceeded to a degree not to be understood by third parties, the spouses are liable jointly and severally."

adhered to absolutely in the name of modernity? All that could be available to a wife-as-guarantor now is a defence against the enforcement of the contract, which would have to rely on other provisions of the law of contract based on the claim that there was no true consent since the agreement was obtained either under undue influence or by misrepresentation.[86]

2.2.4.2. The woman's surname

It is true that, today, there is total equality between the sexes in law and yet in fact, this is not so. The general attitude to equality between the spouses in Turkey can be illustrated by another decision of the *Anayasa Mahkemesi*. In this decision, delivered in 1998 and only published in 2002, the Court did not find the then section 153 (now section 187) of the Civil Code to be unconstitutional.[87] The case arose when a married woman who wanted to use her maiden name only, objected to section 153. In Turkish law, a woman acquires the surname of her husband upon marriage; but, she can add her surname before that of her husband's upon written request to the marriage registrar at the time of marriage, or subsequently to the administration for civil status (section 187). The challenge was that this provision violated articles 10, 12, and 17 of the Constitution related to equality, fundamental rights and freedoms, personality rights and rights to development of personality. The *Anayasa Mahkemesi* saw no violation of any of the articles mentioned. The Court followed a very conservative interpretation of the family and the place of the woman in it. The reasons put forth by the Court were that when surnames entered Turkish law in 1934, the right to choose this name was given to the husband as the head of the family, that this was a necessity stemming from a social reality, the consequence of 'long established traditions', that women have been created different to men, and that this arrangement

---

86 Sections 21, 23, 24, 28, 29 and 30. See for further analysis, ÖRÜCÜ, E., "The Rhetoric of Equality Juxtaposed to Family Realities: The Wife – an Equal Partner or a Protégé?" in SINGER, A., JANTERA-JAREBORG, M. and SCHLYTTER, A. (eds.), *Familj – religion – ratt* (Iustus Förlag, 2010), pp. 295–317.

87 1997/61; 1998/59; 29.9.1998; 15.11.2002, *Resmi Gazete*: 24937; 38 *Anayasa Mahkemesi Kararlar Dergisi* (2003), pp. 124–134. In fact this decision is as relevant today as it was then. This is so in spite of the ECtHR judgment *Ünal Tekeli v Turkey* (Application no. 29865/96, 16.11.2004) against Turkey. Ünal Tekeli objected to only being able to add her maiden name in front of her husband's, as she wanted to use her maiden name alone. Her demand was refused in Turkish courts. She applied to the ECtHR basing her case on violation of Articles 14 and 8 of the ECHR, saying that there was discrimination in Turkish law since her husband could carry his surname, a 'difference in treatment' on grounds of sex between persons in an analogous situation. Turkish government's defence was that giving the husband's surname to the family stemmed from a tradition designed to reflect family unity by having the same name. The ECtHRt opined that family unity could also result from the choice of the wife's surname or a joint surname. The Court found that the Turkish position had no objective and reasonable justification and this was an obligation imposed on married women, which contravened Article 14, amounting to adequate just satisfaction for the non-pecuniary damages, costs and expenses.

protected women, strengthened family ties and created harmony within the marriage union.[88] Obviously, the fact that it took four years before the decision was published indicates how the *Anayasa Mahkemesi* finds it extremely difficult to pass judgement in cases related to equality of the sexes in Turkey, which for years was not part of the law and definitely not part of religious tradition. Traditions formed as a consequence of religion appear to have a strong hold on the people and on the judiciary, who are torn between modernity and the forces of traditionality, religion and conservatism. In fact, the 2002 Civil Code preserves this stance in section 187.[89]

2.2.4.3. The wife's right to work

Section 159 of the 1926 Civil Code stated that a wife needed her husband's explicit or implicit permission to work outside the home. The publication of the decision of the *Anayasa Mahkemesi* annulling this section was also delayed for two years; the decision reached in 1990 was only published in 1992.[90] The delay must have been due to the difficulty in composing the reasoning through which the Court tried to satisfy all sides, and perhaps to hold back the introduction of the change. What is worthy of note in relation to our study here is that the *Anayasa Mahkemesi*, having found this section unconstitutional and drawn Parliament's attention to other such sections in the Civil Code in need of removal, has tried hard not to be misunderstood by its traditionalist target audience at home. After a very thorough and progressive comparative survey and with full reference to contemporary foreign and international developments, the *Anayasa Mahkemesi* nevertheless felt that it should end its opinion upon an apologetic note with a statement reflecting a very traditional view. It said that this decision should not be taken to mean that the Court condoned a new life style for the family in which a working wife could neglect her family duties towards her husband and children. If she intended to work, the Court would like to see her making arrangements for these domestic duties to be performed by another person. Thus, it was reiterated by a court decision that the working wife

88 We see a very similar approach when the *Anayasa Mahkemesi* rejected a claim that "the husband's abode is also the wife's" in the 1926 Civil Code was unconstitutional (1993/23; 1993/55; 2.12.1993, 35 *Anayasa Mahkemesi Kararlar Dergisi* (2000), pp. 82–88). This decision has no binding force anymore, since the 2002 Civil Code, having abolished the position of the husband as the head of the family, does not have such a section.

89 A draft amending Bill has been on the agenda of the Parliament for a while. When and if it becomes law the section 187 will read: "A woman acquires the surname of her husband upon marriage; however, in addition to being able to add her own surname before that of her husband's upon a written application to the marriage registrar or the administration of personal status, she can continue to use her own surname alone. A woman who was using two surnames already can benefit from this right for only one of the surnames."

90 90/93; 29.11.1990. This case was reported in ÖRÜCÜ, E., "Turkish Family Law: A New Phase", 30 *Journal of Family Law* (1991–1992), 431.

has a mission in life, that of family duties as home-maker for her husband and her children.

Although the legislator has opted for the extremes of modernity in the case of the wife-as-guarantor, it has preferred to reflect social realities and traditional sentiments of the people in the case of the surname of the wife. And, it has done a remarkable thing by inserting into the 2002 Civil Code a new section 192 "the profession and job of spouses", replacing the annulled section 159: "Each spouse is free to choose a profession or a job without seeking permission of the other. However, in the choice and performance of a profession or a job, the peace and interest of the marriage union must be considered". This can only be aiming at wives. It would be interesting to observe how the judges will navigate round this point, and balance the inside religious and traditional forces with the outside westernising ones. The legislator is surely sending mixed messages.

3. FAMILY LAW IN THE EARLY YEARS OF THE TURKISH REPUBLIC

As noted above, in 1926, with the adoption of a Civil Code, adapted from the Swiss, Turkish family law was entirely reshaped and laicised. The desire of the "*élite dirigeante*" of the Turkish Republic to westernise and modernise Turkish society, and to embrace laicism, transformed family law totally.[91] Although the concept of equality between the spouses was a fundamental principle of the 1926 Civil Code, "some were more equal than others" as could be seen in some of the Code provisions, such as those stating that the husband was the head of the family and chose the abode, and that the wife carried his surname and had no say in decisions concerning the home and the children. She needed his permission to work outside the home. In case of divorce, she was only entitled to property legally registered under her name.[92] Nevertheless, the 1926 Code was considered revolutionary both in Turkey and abroad when it was adopted in a country of Muslims. Yet it failed to keep up with the times, thus keeping closer to traditions. Moreover, until the 1961 Constitution there was no higher law demanding total equality between the sexes.

In earlier years, the *Yargıtay*, tried a number of ways to navigate round the fact that some couples were only interested in the religious marriage and felt the

91 For further general information on Family Law in the Republic see, ÖRÜCÜ, *supra* note 63; and on the then divorce law in particular see pp. 27–34 of ÖRÜCÜ, E., "Turkish Divorce Law", 2(96) *Migrantenrecht*.

92 In fact, none of the inequalities were challenged until well into the 1990s, though they could have been after the 1961 Constitution and the setting up of the *Anayasa Mahkemesi* in 1962.

arrangements of the Civil Code to be alien to them. One way was to stress the acceptability of the civil marriage, especially for those with religious objections to it. The Court stated:

> "The fact that the marriage contract is formed by the accord of the consent of the parties is in keeping with both Islamic and Canonical laws. In these laws also, the marriage contract is not completed by an act of the religious man but by the declaration of the wills of the parties."[93]

Thus, in the early years of the Republic, there was a total rejection of religion as a factor in family law, except for the case of protecting illegitimate children and encouraging registration of unofficial marriages by passing Amnesty Acts, seen above. This was considered a lesser evil for the laic legal system, which preferred to give amnesties rather than recognise religious marriage as an alternative to civil marriage.

There was one concession given to religious and traditional practices where there had been no age limit for marriage. When the 1926 Civil Code was adopted, the ages for marriage were kept rather low. As the principle of equality between the spouses had not been translated into the 1926 Civil Code, boys could marry at 17 and girls at 15, though the age of majority was still 18. Furthermore these ages were reducible to 15 for boys and 14 for girls by a judicial decision in exceptional circumstances, such as abductions, pregnancy or terminal illness. It can be said that the 1926 arrangement reflected Turkish realities, especially among the rural population. This was also considered a measure to combat abductions and elopements at these early ages.

Today, persons gain majority at 18 and that is the norm for when individuals should marry. However, section 124 of the 2002 Civil Code states that persons can marry at the age of 17. In addition, with a decision of a judge, couples can marry at 16. Section 124 is a fundamental amendment and will have considerable impact on Turkish society.[94] Upon divorce, both spouses retain the age of the majority acquired by marriage. We shall have to wait and see the impact of the new approach, which brings Turkish law more in keeping with developments in Europe.

---

93 1965/3; 14.6.1965.

94 However, we know from figures from 2006 that 24.6% of girls in rural areas and 16.9% of girls in urban areas marry before the age of 18. See AKPINAR, A., "Family and Social Change in Turkey" in SINGER *et al.*, *supra* note 86, p. 22.

4. FAMILY LAW IN THE LATER YEARS OF THE TURKISH REPUBLIC

The judgment of the *Anayasa Mahkemesi* published in 2002 discussed earlier, gives an authoritative answer to any question that might arise related to the acceptability of religious marriage as an alternative to civil marriage. The Civil Code was seen by the Court as "a fundamental building block of the bridge to a contemporary and laic legal system for the Turkish Republic", and civil marriage as being in the essence of that block. The most important function of laicism, said the Court, is to keep law and religion apart. In addition, as a religious marriage after the civil marriage is not banned, the Court decided unanimously that there was no violation of the Constitution.

It is worth remembering that in the Turkish legal system, "the source of law is determined by the formal legal framework", and cultural values, "custom and tradition become a source of law only when recognised by courts."[95] Claims based on traditional relationships not in keeping with the official law always create major problems for the courts.

Yet, it is also worth reminding ourselves that, from the very beginning, the *Yargıtay*, was able to make adjustments to the law by using the flexible rules present in the 1926 Civil Code and now the 2002 Civil Code sections 1, 2 and 4. These sections correspond *verbatim* to sections 1, 2 and 4 of the Swiss Civil Code. They are rules on justice and equity, objective good faith and judges' discretion. The flexibility afforded to the judges by section 1 has been invaluable in the development of the Turkish law and legal system:

> "The law must be applied in all cases that come within the letter and the spirit of its provisions. If no relevant provision can be found in the statute, the judge must decide in accordance with the customary law and, in its absence, in accordance with the rule, which he would lay down were he the legislator. In so doing, he must be guided by accepted legal doctrine and case law."

Although religious marriage prior to or instead of civil marriage, still clashes with the officially protected vision and the courts cannot pronounce such marriages as legally binding or with legal consequences, in the last couple of decades, we see that the *Yargıtay* can accommodate such "marriages" not accepted by the official system, when the matter at hand is not related to giving effect to the marriage, but for instance, to the law of obligations. In such cases,

[95] ÖRÜCÜ, E., "Turkey: Change Under Pressure" in ÖRÜCÜ, E., ATTWOOLL, E. and COYLE, S. (eds.), *Studies in Legal Systems: Mixed and Mixing* (Kluwer Law International, 1996), p. 106.

the Court does not have to go into the issue of marriage, which is related to laicism, protected by the Constitution, as seen earlier. Thus in a case related to the return of jewellery given at the religious "wedding" the Court referred to the female partner as the "unofficial partner" (*gayri resmi eş*) and accepted the claim for compensation as the jewellery was no longer available for return, under the law of obligations.[96]

In fact, the *Yargıtay*, in its effort to tune the law to the needs of society, and obviously with considerations of "justice" in mind, has in recent years taken a much milder position when the claims are based on private law but not on rights arising out of public law. For instance, compensation can be awarded to a woman whose partner in a religious marriage dies. This could either be compensation for pecuniary or non-pecuniary damages (*maddi ve manevi tazminat*) on the basis of sections 43 and 44 of the Code of Obligations, or, compensation for lack of financial support following a death (*destekten yoksun kalma tazminatı*), on the basis of section 45 of the Code of Obligations.[97] This means that courts can award a surviving partner compensation on the general principles of civil liability, but never grant such partners survivor's pension or social security benefits, arising from public law, based on the deceased partner's entitlements.[98]

The *Yargıtay* has extended the right to compensation arising out of private law, for death in work-related accidents to the unmarried cohabiting woman (*nikahsız eş*), though be it on a different basis from the married woman. Decisions of courts in this area, converting illegality into legality, are of the utmost importance for such couples. For instance, in one case,[99] the childless surviving partner of an *imam nikahı* union asked for material and moral compensation after the death of her partner in a work-related accident. The private insurance company

96 2002/1153; 2003/2380; 6.3.2003; 29 *Yargıtay Kararları Dergisi* (2003), p. 1044.

97 In 1997, the General Assembly of the *Danıştay* (Supreme Administrative Court) upheld a first instance judgment, thereby overturning the judgment of its own Tenth Division, on the ground that the four children and the surviving partner from a religious marriage should be awarded compensation after the father and partner was accidentally killed by police bullets. The children and the partner were deprived of his financial support. The Court pointed out that, while domestic law did not afford protection to or validate such a union, the couple had had children together whose births had been recorded under the parents' names in the civil status register and the deceased had supported the family financially (1998/79; 1997/479; 17.10.1997). This case was cited in the *Şerife Yiğit* judgment, *supra* note 42.

98 For instance in 1990, the Tenth Division of the *Yargıtay*, set aside a first instance judgment awarding such compensation in a work-related accident, because section 23 of the Social Security Act (Law no. 506) was involved, which only guarantees compensation to the children born of a marriage or a union other than marriage and not to the partner. The Court held that in the absence of legislation on the subject, the Social Security Agency (a public body) could require the woman in question to repay the sums wrongly paid to her after her partner's death. 1990/4010; 1990/6972; 11.9.1990. This case was cited in the *Şerife Yiğit* judgment, *supra* note 42.

99 1996/1606; 1996/1661; 21.3.1996; 22 *Yargıtay Kararları Dergisi* (1996), p. 1291.

objected, though the lower court agreed. The *Yargıtay* decided on a percentage lower than the one that would be the due of the married wife. In a later case,[100] again, the insured died in a work-related accident and the partner, who was this time referred to by the *Yargıtay* as the "cohabiting partner", was 18, had a child, and according to the Court, had more than a 35 per cent chance of re-marriage, which is the accepted percentage for an official widow. The Court was of the opinion that:

> "[H]er age, social status, position and family ties mean that she is not in the same position as a married woman who expects to live in the family home for an indefinite period and can expect support throughout her life. The compensation arising out of section 43 of the Code of Obligations therefore should be reduced in keeping with fairness and equity."

A telling dissenting opinion by a female judge attached to this decision, demanded further recognition of social facts, and a change in the law. Critical of the differentiation drawn between the two women, she said:

> "Here 'cohabiting couple' (*nikahsız eş*) refers to a traditional Anatolian relationship where couples live together as husband and wife, with close family ties and children. Therefore, the presence or absence of official wedlock should not be the criterion on which to treat the two women differently. The Social Security Agency will give a pension only to the officially married wife and this for life. This should be the only extra gain for the married woman. An Anatolian village woman is already oppressed and faces the risk of being officially unmarried owing to tradition. She should not be further weakened when facing the law. This situation would only lead to mistrust of justice. The present circumstance is the outcome of the social structure. She should be given equal compensation."[101]

In 2007 the *Yargıtay* quashed a first instance judgment on the ground that a woman married in accordance with religious rites should be paid compensation under sections 43 and 44 of the Code of Obligations following the death of her partner in a work-related accident. We can say that now this is the established approach of the *Yargıtay*.[102]

Now, empirical research informs us[103] that there are seven types of traditional marriage in Turkey: *berdel* (two families agree and sons and daughters are exchanged in a double marriage), *beşik kertmesi* (two families agree upon the

---

100 1997/3331; 1997/4819; 8.7.1997; 23 *Yargıtay Kararları Dergisi* (1997), p. 1785.

101 *Ibid.* In this connection, it is intriguing to re-read the ECtHR Grand Chamber judgment *Şerife Yiğit v Turkey* of 2 November 2010, discussed above.

102 2007/289; 2007/8718; 28.5.2007. This case was cited in the *Şerife Yiğit* judgment, *supra* note 42.

103 From a piece of empirical research carried out by the CEDAW Committee on Turkey in 81 cities and interviewing 453 women cited by *Milliyet* Newspaper.

birth of two babies on their future marriage), *kan bedelli evlilik* (made in order to put an end to blood feuds, one of the daughters of the family whose turn it is to carry out the next killing is given as a wife to the other family), *kayın evliliği* (a woman is married off to one of the brothers of her deceased husband upon the decision of the "family council"), *başlık paralı evlilik* (marriage takes place upon the payment of monies by the father of the prospective bride to the prospective husband),[104] *kuma evliliği* (a woman is married off to a man with more than one wife),[105] and *akraba evliliği* (marriage of a woman to a first degree relative).[106]

We know that, the official framework accepts only one type of marriage regulated in the Civil Code. Marriage is concluded upon the oral response of the two parties.[107] Most of the above types, apart form *kuma evliliği* and *akraba evliliği* (if violating the degrees enumerated in the Civil Code), would not create a problem if formally concluded as civil marriages.

İlhan Yılmaz tells us that the realities of marriage in Turkey are quite outside the formally regulated one.[108] So does Ayla Akpınar, who points to the existence of traditional collective values that have survived, "such as the code of honour and shame, and the practice of arranged marriages and cousin marriages," as part of "generally widespread patrilineal values".[109] In addition, Sema Erder states that there exist in Turkey a "rich and colourful variety of family types", although public discourse represents "the typical Turkish family as uniform [...]".[110] All these may very well be the case. In this inquiry, I am not looking into "narratives" related to cultural pluralism, but into what the courts (part of the official framework) are doing to fit some of this alternative behaviour into the legal framework. We may be dealing in Turkey today, at best, with a very weak version

104 This was banned but now is regarded as a gift and seems acceptable, to be seen below.

105 This would not be acceptable, as being polygamous.

106 This would form an impediment to marriage. Nevertheless, we know that marriage with the kin, especially cross-cousin marriage, has not decreased over the years and it was found to be 20.9% in 2006. This type of marriage comes from tribal tradition, stemming from religious practice legitimised by the fact that Prophet Mohammad gave his daughter in marriage to her cousin Prophet Ali. See AKPINAR, *supra* note 94, pp. 22–23.

107 Although, it is still a fact that most marriages are arranged by parents. For instance figures from 2006 show that 36.2% of women were given away in arranged marriages as a result of parental decision. In 39.9% of arranged marriages however, women made their own final decision. *Ibid.*, p. 21.

108 See YILMAZ, İ., "Non-recognition of Post-modern Turkish Socio-legal Reality and the Predicament of Women", 30(1) *British Journal of Middle Eastern Studies* (2003), 25 and YILMAZ, İ., *Muslim Laws, Politics and Society in Modern Nation States: Dynamic Legal Pluralism in England, Turkey and Pakistan* (Ashgate, 2005). See also ÇETİNER, S., BOZKURT YÜKSEL, A.E., "Fellow-wife and the Law" in ATKIN, B. (ed.), *The International Survey of Family Law* (Jordan Publishing, 2008), p. 475.

109 AKPINAR, *supra* note 94, pp. 20–21.

110 ERDER, S., "Urban Migration and Reconstruction of Kinship Networks: The Case of Istanbul" in SINGER *et al.*, *supra* note 86, pp. 40–41.

of legal pluralism, which accommodates some religious practices, though under the name of tradition.

Although laicism is reiterated in a number of *Anayasa Mahkemesi* decisions, in the later years of the Republic, and especially in the last 15 years or so, inroads for religion have been made, by presenting religion as tradition.[111] We have seen the softening approach of the *Yargıtay* here. As observed above, in some of the *Yargıtay* decisions, there is a certain willingness on the part of the Court to provide protection, though be it weak, to informal relationships, although never to any form of opposite-sex or same-sex cohabitation, and "allow the attribution of rights to be disconnected from the status of marriage in certain circumstances, therefore also granting legal consequences to a marriage which is in itself invalid".[112]

5. CONCLUDING REMARKS

From its inception the Turkish legal system tried to transform the social, political, ideological, religious and economic systems it encountered. Historians and comparatists may hail the Turkish experience as unique, representing the passage of a legal system from one legal culture to another. The interlocking of these systems however, may never be completed since the entire legal system has been imported from foreign sources, which are often referred to by courts and academics in developing the law, and yet the indigenous socio-culture is not related to the socio-cultures of the source laws (*kaynak kanunlar*).

In Turkey, alongside an assumed similarity of culture with Europe, there is an assumed similarity of culture with the Turkic and Islamic States; as indicated by the statement of the then Prime Minister, Bülent Ecevit in December 1999 on the occasion of Turkey's becoming a candidate to the European Union. He said that this official recognition was a landmark event not only for Europe, but also for the world and that full membership was "Turkey's birthright by virtue of Turkey's historical development, its geography, and its present day attributes as well as the provisions of the 1963 Association Agreement". Pointing out that "the Turks have been Europeans for 600 years", he then added that Turks are not only European; they are Asian, Caucasian and Middle Eastern and European all at

---

111 One needs to ask the question though, whether or not Islamic religion can be regarded as a tradition. See for a discussion and illustrations, MENSKI, W., "Ethnic minority studies in English law" in JONES, R. and GNANAPALA, W. (eds.), *Ethnic Minorities in English Law* (Ashgate, 2000), pp. i-xvii.

112 RUTTEN, *supra* note 43, p. 81. Although this did not happen in the *Şerife Yiğit* case discussed above.

once.[113] This statement should be assessed in relation to the particular world-view the Turkish Republic is based on, even more than 85 years after its inception. Yet, it is also important to note that besides the European element, the other cultural input was also being alluded to here.

There is clear affinity of culture and outlook with West Europe and the Western way of life at the level of the educated, urbanised and elite. Yet, a much larger part of the Turkish population is rural in essence and has a traditional outlook. This outlook is maintained even when this population moves into the cities.[114] Some of these poorly educated, rural Anatolians have become wealthy. Today they are also politically effective. Then there are those who, having started with a traditional rural lifestyle in Turkey, have worked in other countries, as close communities. In addition, in Turkish cities, the gap between the rich and the poor is wide and the middle class has shrunk. Ninety-eight percent of the population of Turkey is of the Islamic faith, but not all of them of the same sect. As would be expected, there are inherent problems in such a complex society where traditional values still dominate to a large extent. For years, the courts, the legislature and the executive tried to mould this socio-cultural diversity into a whole in the chosen direction. However, with the emergence of democratic ideals and principles, and values of human rights, it seems more and more difficult to achieve and maintain standardisation, even when supported by the ECtHR.[115] This monolithic centralist legal system faces problems to accommodate the Turkish socio-cultural fabric.[116] Laicism should be understood as a process but has been treated as an instant in time. It is a delicate path that requires tolerance

---

113 Available at www.infa.gov.tr/grupa/ad/adc/candidacy.html.

114 In fact, it is pointed out that as migrant families have difficulty in integrating into the urban environment, they are easily captured by fundamentalist Islamic groups and more migrant families send their daughters to religious schools rather than to public mixed-gender schools. See AKPINAR, *supra* note 94, p. 17.

115 Apart from the ones seen above, it is worth thinking of a few other cases here. For instance, ECtHR (*Hasan and Eylem Zengin v. Turkey*, Application no. 1448/04; 9.10.2007), and subsequently the *Danıştay* (2006/4107; 2007/7481; 28.12.2007 and 2007/679; 2008/1461; 29.2.2008), found the content of the obligatory nature of religious and ethical studies to be unacceptable. ECtHR in *Leyla Şahin v. Turkey* (Application no. 44774/98, 29.6.2004) upheld the ban on wearing g the Islamic headscarf in higher-education institutions. Recently, the legality of including religious information on identification cards was also addressed by the ECtHR (*Sinan Işık v. Turkey*, Application no. 21924/05, 2.2.2010).

116 For instance, as late as in 1997, an acting minister of the State said: "We could not watch over the family. The ills that the Turkish-Islamic family is confronted with are feminism, unmarried cohabitation, effects of social change on society through mass communication, tourism and industrialisation, which some call cultural change, but which have caused cultural deterioration", quoted by ARAT, N., "Yeni bir kimlik üretiliyor" (A new identity is under construction) in *Susmayan Yazılar* (Non-silent Writings) (Istanbul, 1997), cited in AKPINAR, *supra* note 94, p. 15.

and compromise. "Harmony in diversity" may have to be accepted.[117] The crucial question is: How far, and where should the line be drawn?

When elements from two interpretive models meet each other, one drawing its understanding from official law and the other from culture, tradition and religion, they are, on the whole, able to tap into each other and mesh, bringing "cultural conversation" and creating a "fit" in a wider narrative. The cases considered above show that in Turkey the official legal framework does not permit this, and at times there is contradiction. Officially, there can be no competition between the rules of the legal system and the rules of religion. It is the courts that try to create harmony. In the Turkish experience the concepts and values introduced in the early years of the Republic were to a large extent incompatible with those of the indigenous system, and the deeper values and purposes of the two were not commensurable. One way out was to establish a global purpose and hope that a bridge could be built between traditional culture and western style expression of the norms and standards, by the courts. Over the years however, we see that on the one hand the western link is strengthened, for instance with the amendments to the Constitution and to Family Law in the 2002 Civil Code; on the other, by treating religious claims as traditional or customary ones, the courts are trying to meet the demands of the people, which may have stemmed from their religious beliefs and yet can be fitted within the official framework. Considerations of the equality principle, freedom of religion, prohibition of discrimination and protection of the family life are being balanced by the legislature and the judiciary.[118]

A telling example of the evolution from religion to tradition and therefore from unacceptability to acceptability is the *başlık*[119] (bride price) cases, once banned but now regarded as gifts by the *Yargıtay*. For instance, some *Yargıtay* decisions up to the 1980's regarded moneys paid by the groom to the father of the girl to be against morality and therefore not to be returned upon the breaking up of the engagement.[120] Only gifts given by the two parties to the engagement to each

---

117 For the fundamentalist Islamic sector however, all that is Western represents unwanted cultural elements and therefore there has always been reaction from that quarter. Today, there are also those who challenge the lack of democratic consultation by the elite in deciding on the models.

118 Would these developments, I wonder, go some way to meet the demands of "embedded impartiality", "relational neutrality" and "fairness as even-handedness in matters of culture"? See BADER, *supra* note 15.

119 *Başlık* is money given by the man to the father of the girl to secure the engagement and thereby the marriage. *Ağırlık* is the goods given for the same purpose.

120 See, judgments of the 2nd and the 11th Divisions of the *Yargıtay*: for instance, in a judgment 2771/1858; 7.7.1949, the 2nd Division held: "to give moneys and goods under the name of *başlık* is against public policy and morality. The claim for repayment of such, given to secure an illegal cause cannot be upheld." Again, in the judgment 1980 – 620/620; 11.2.1980, the 11th Division held: "the moneys and goods taken by the father of the girl, under the name of *başlık*,

other were to be returned. Today, when the engagement comes to an end, among the gifts to be returned – either given to the parties or their families or those acting as such – are those whose value is out of the ordinary,[121] that is, things of great value. As moneys and goods, given under the name of *kalın*,[122] *ağırlık* or *başlık*, are now consistently considered by the courts as gifts, their return can also be demanded. The practice of these payments continues, especially in rural areas, and "is considered a compensation for the loss of unpaid labour in the household. Children in general and daughters in particular may be used as unpaid workers in the fields and in gardens and in households for domestic chores."[123]

These institutions are reminiscent of *mahr*, an Islamic legal conception, a Muslim custom, whereby the bridegroom has to give a gift to the bride in consideration of the marriage, which becomes the property of the wife.[124] As shown by Pascale Fournier, *mahr* is interpreted by western courts according to hugely varied legal constructs and concepts such as multiculturalism, fairness, public policy and gender equality, with Western law mediating the various voices of Islamic law.[125] Thus the Turkish courts appear to have taken very similar attitudes to this one time banned practice in the name of "politics of recognition",[126] in the name of equality and fairness, and are in fact accommodating an Islamic practice within the laic legal framework, navigating within the legal limits, by giving it a neutral name: *hediye* (gift).

It appears that in the area of family law and law of succession, the 2002 Civil Code and recent developments in the Constitution and the Penal Code, send mixed messages, at times adhering strictly to the principle of equality and laicism leading to results which are at times to the detriment of women and the family and at times protecting the family to the detriment of the principle of equality and laicism. We might be forgiven for thinking that the present situation in

---

in order to agree to the engagement, ... is illegal and therefore any such undertaking is not binding". However, some judgments regarded the repayment of *başlık* possible, relying on 'unjustified enrichment' of the Code of Obligations (section 61).

121 Section 122 of the 2002 Civil Code.

122 *Kalın* is money or goods given by the man to the girl to enable her to prepare her dowry.

123 AKPINAR, *supra* note 94, p. 22.

124 For a thorough analysis and comparative account of the "legal life" of this institution see FOURNIER, *supra* note 35. Fournier also demonstrates that there is an internal plurality of *mahr*, used as a tool of relative bargaining power, by looking at examples from Egypt, Tunisia and Malaysia.

125 *Ibid.*

126 Although proponents of "politics of recognition" in Turkey would claim that the liberal state has betrayed its commitment to neutrality by privileging the way of life of the hitherto dominant, laic elite minority group.

Turkish family law is ambivalent and suffers from conceptual incoherence.[127] The gap between what is in law and what is in fact is as wide as ever. The social deficit may even be widening.

In fact, many have been complaining that manifestation of religious sentiments are being encouraged and such sentiments are becoming more prominent in daily life, children are being harassed, alcoholic drinks have become expensive, religion has become a criterion of promotions in public sector jobs, more and more couples are preferring to have religious ceremonies following the civil marriage contract, and many areas of İstanbul look more like the Middle East, with girls and boys sitting separately in many places and an increasing number of covered women in the streets.

Nevertheless, in November 2006, the Turkish Economic and Social Studies Foundation (TESEV) published the results of their survey,[128] which showed quite a different picture. Respondents perceived as the five most important problems in Turkey: unemployment (38.2 per cent), terrorism/national security/the Southeast problem/the Kurdish problem (13.8 per cent), the high cost of living/inflation (12.1 per cent), education (10.2 per cent), and economic instability (6.5 per cent). Only 3.7 per cent of people saw the *türban* (religious headgear) issue as an important problem.[129] This might of course have two explanations. Either religion, being part of societal mores, does not appear as a problem since the majority of respondents were religious, or indeed, it is not perceived as a threat to laicism by those who are proponents of laicism.

Another finding, contrary to the general belief, was that there had been a fall in the number of "covered" women in 2006 compared to 1999. The percentage of women who said they did not "cover up" in public was 27.3 per cent in 1999, but 36.5 per cent in 2006. The percentage of those wearing a headscarf, stole and head-handkerchief (*yemeni*) was 53.4 per cent in 1999 but 48.8 per cent in 2006; the percentage of those wearing the over-garment (*çarşaf*) was 3.4 per cent in

---

127 It may be of interest to point out here that there are certain additional issues, now part of the laws of most of the member states of the EU, that have not found a place in Turkish family law: the recognition of cohabitation as equal to marriage (for historical and social reasons), joint custody after divorce (for social reasons), the acceptance of alternative marriage forms such as the religious (legal, constitutional and political reasons), surrogacy (for religious and social reasons), the acceptance of same-sex partnerships and same-sex marriages (for religious and social reasons), and adoption by gay couples (for religious and social reasons). It is interesting to note that the legal rights of transsexuals (in spite of being against social and religious mores) have been accepted, though be they worsened in the 2002 Civil Code compared to the 1926 one (because of social and religious mores).

128 ÇARKOĞLU, A. and TOPRAK, B., *Değişen Türkiye'de Din, Toplum, Siyaset* (Religion, Society and Politics in a Changing Turkey) (TESEV Yayınları, 2006), p. 30. Cited and discussed in KOÇAK, *supra* note 19, pp. 251–253.

129 ÇARKOĞLU *et al.*, pp. 23, 45.

1999 but 1.1 per cent in 2006; those wearing the *türban* went down from 15.7 per cent in 1999 to 11.4 per cent in 2006. The conclusions of the survey indicate that contrary to the claims of both the "laic" and the "Islamist" sectors, the "*türban* question" is not on the agenda of Turkish people.[130]

The survey however, also brought to light that pietism is on the increase in Turkey. The percentage of those who answered the question "How would you define yourself?" as "a Turk", did not change much in the intervening seven years and was constant at around 19–20 per cent. But the percentage of those who answered "a Muslim", which was 36 per cent in 1999, went up to 45 per cent in 2006. While 73 per cent of those surveyed said that laicism was not under threat, when they were asked whether they would like to see a *shari'a* state, the percentage of positive responses that was 21 per cent in 1999 fell to 8.9 per cent in 2006.[131] The survey also showed that, as the social status of the individual moved higher, religious tendencies were replaced by liberalism and laic law was preferred.[132]

There must be a Coda to this piece. Should laic Turkish family law accommodate religion? If yes, how far can it accommodate it? If not, how will law and society cope with the ever-widening social deficit? Is the answer for Turkey to effectively promote modernisation and yet reach out to more traditional and religious elements in the society? How far can this be done without upsetting the course taken thus far? Can a good synthesis be achieved between the positive aspects of traditional cultures and religion and demands of laicism? What can the proper place for religion be in laic Turkish family law? What can the different outcomes be, if we were to substitute the word "accommodate" by "tolerate" or "reconcile"?

130 *Ibid.*, p. 23.
131 *Ibid.*, p. 30.
132 *Ibid.*, pp. 39–43.

PART THREE

SUPPORTING A PLACE FOR RELIGION?

RELIGION AND FAMILY LAW IN IRELAND: FROM A CATHOLIC PROTECTION OF MARRIAGE TO A "CATHOLIC" APPROACH TO NULLITY

Maebh Harding

1. INTRODUCTION

In works about comparative family law Ireland is often portrayed as having a very conservative approach to the family, particularly in its attitude to divorce.[1] This approach has been attributed to the influence of the Irish constitution of 1937 which heralded an age of highly restrictive family law, in contrast to more liberal trends in the rest of Europe at that time.[2] Catholicism was an important part of the Irish national identity[3] and the articles of the Irish constitution relevant to family matters are influenced by Catholic values.

In this essay it will be argued that far from being an entirely conservative influence, Catholic doctrines were used by some of the judiciary to create a functioning alternative to divorce and circumvent the prohibiting provisions of the Irish Constitution.[4] This "catholic" approach to Church doctrines shows that in family law the courts will find a way to reflect a prevailing liberal morality even if they must use the tools of an inherently conservative framework. This aligns with Stone's findings in England that lawyers and judges will attempt to narrow a widening gap between the law and human practice by imaginative reinterpretation.[5]

---

1 ANTOKOLSKAIA, M., *Harmonisation of Family Law in Europe: A Historical Perspective* (European Family Law Series, Intersentia, 2006).

2 *Ibid.*, p. 253.

3 *Ibid.*, p. 252.

4 Found in the original Article 41.3.2° of the Irish Constitution.

5 STONE, L., *Road to Divorce* (Oxford University Press, 1995), p. 19.

2. PRE 1937: TWO SEPARATE FUNCTIONING SYSTEMS

Before the founding of the Irish Free State and the express legal recognition of Catholic values in the Irish constitution, the doctrines of the Catholic Church had a huge influence on the average Irish marriage. Although English rule had extended many English Marriage Acts to Ireland,[6] most left Catholic marriages outside their scope. The regulation of Catholic marriages was left to the devices of the Catholic Church. The grant of a Church annulment allowed a Catholic to remarry within the Catholic Church according to Catholic formalities and there was little reason for Catholics to turn to the secular courts.

The Marriages (Ireland) Act 1844 left most of the formalities of a Catholic marriage entirely up to the Catholic Church. This disinterest in the marital affairs of Roman Catholics tied in very well with the position taken by the Roman Catholic Church, that the regulation of marriage within the community of Roman Catholics was a matter in its exclusive competence.[7]

Judicial divorce was introduced to England and Wales in 1857, but no such facility was given to the Irish courts.[8] The possibility of a parliamentary divorce[9] continued until 1922 but was rarely exercised. The Matrimonial Causes and Marriage Law (Ireland) Amendment Act 1870 transferred matrimonial jurisdiction from the ecclesiastical courts to a new civil court. This ultimately gave the Irish High Court the right to grant decrees of nullity based on the same grounds as previously used by the English ecclesiastical courts.

Although, the Irish secular courts now had the power to grant nullity decrees they were not used by the vast majority of the Irish population. The civil courts were used far less than the Regional Matrimonial Tribunals of the Roman Catholic Church. Between 1901 and 1909 for example, there were only 36 decrees

---

6 These included prohibitions on marriage within the prohibited degrees (32 Henry VIII c6); Prohibitions on a Catholic priest celebrating a mixed marriage or a Protestant marriage (6 Anne c16; 12 Geo 1 c3; 19 Geo II c13: 23 Geo II c 10; 32 Geo III c21 ss.9 10; 33 Geo III c21 s. 12) and some legislation prohibiting clandestine marriage.

7 *Report of the Royal Commission on Divorce and Matrimonial Causes* 1868, appendix, Letter 13 from Archbishop Leahy suggests that any state regulation would be superfluous as the sanctity of marriage was held in high regard by all Irish Catholics; DUNCAN, W., "Supporting the Institution of Marriage in Ireland" [1978] *The Irish Jurist* 215, p. 217.

8 The 1857 Act implemented the recommendations of the *First Report of the Commissioners appointed by Her Majesty to enquire into the law of divorce, and more particularly into the mode of obtaining divorces a vinculo matrimonii* [1604], 1852–53i which only had a remit to look at the laws of England and Wales.

9 In the *Report of the Royal Commission on Divorce and Matrimonial Causes* [Cd.6478–9], 1912–13, xviii, 143, 18. Mr James Roberts, an Irish solicitor, noted that since 1857 there had been a total of 39 Irish Private Divorce Acts.

granted by the secular courts in total (including divorce *a mensa et thoro*, nullity and restitution of conjugal rights).[10] Most reported cases before the 1940s involve the marriages of the Protestant gentry in Ireland.[11] Without the benefit of establishment, the Roman Catholic Church became the focal point of marriage regulation for Roman Catholics.

Before the framing of the Irish Constitution, the judiciary tread a careful line when dealing with the secular invalidity of Catholic marriages. The judges were deferential to the religious scruples of Catholic parties and they often backed up their decisions with contemporary Catholic canon law to give their decisions public legitimacy. As a result, where the technically applicable law was in opposition to the position of contemporary Catholic teaching or the rulings of the Matrimonial Tribunals of the Catholic Church, a compromise to give effect to the Catholic teachings could usually be found.

In *A v A (Sued as B)*[12] where a Roman Catholic couple already had a decree of nullity from the Catholic courts, the court developed a sort of estoppel doctrine to give validity to Catholic rulings. Where the marriage had been declared invalid by the Catholic Matrimonial courts and this was accepted by the respondent, the respondent could not raise objections to a decree of nullity in the secular courts.

Hanna J. outlined the extent of the secular law applicable to Catholic marriages in *McM v McM* & *McK v McK*.[13] Under the Matrimonial Causes and Marriage Law (Ireland) Amendment Act 1870, the jurisdiction of the Irish High Court was the same as that enjoyed by the English ecclesiastical courts.[14] The Irish courts thus applied English ecclesiastical law which was made up of Catholic canon law as it existed in the reign of Henry VIII, subject to amendments made by the Bishops and Archbishops of the Church of England and by English secular legislation.

The creation of the myth, that medieval canon law formed part of the English ecclesiastical law,[15] opened the door for the import of contemporary canon law principles into Irish law. If medieval canon law was part of the secular law, then contemporary canon law merely showed the development of medieval canon law

10 *Report of the Royal Commission on Divorce and Matrimonial Causes* [Cd.6478–9], 1912–13, xviii, 143.

11 DUNCAN, *supra* note 7, p. 216.

12 (1887)19 LR (Ir) 403.

13 *McK v McK* [1936] IR 177.

14 *Ibid.*, p. 187.

15 Hanna J. relied heavily on *R v Millis* (1844) 10 CI & F 534; 8 ER 844: a case that was quickly distinguished and is now largely discredited.

principles and could be used as a persuasive source of authority. This fitted conveniently with the political dilemma faced by the judiciary of holding Catholic couples to rules that were not in harmony with the Catholic values held by the majority of the Irish people.

Although *McM* reached the secular courts, it is clear from the report that the parties involved gave first importance to the ruling of the Catholic Church courts. *McM* involved the nullity of a marriage entered into in 1927. The marriage had never been consummated and the parties were living apart after permission to do so had been granted by the Archbishop of Tuam. The husband sought to have the marriage annulled on the basis of his own impotence. The wife refused to repudiate the marriage, for reasons of conscience until set aside by the Catholic courts. Hanna J. noted that unlike in England and Scotland there was a strong public policy in Ireland to preserve marriages and nullity should not be granted lightly. Otherwise the law would create a way for petitioners to circumvent the law and established public opinion and "make their marriage vows as false as dicers' oaths."[16] He looked to a variety of sources to support his ruling that a petitioner could not rely on his or her own impotence including the 1917 Code of Canon Law, judgments from the English and Scottish Matrimonial courts, the *Codex Juris Ecclesiastici Anglicani*, the ecclesiastical law of the Church of Ireland and Pothier's *Traité du Contrat de Mariage*. Thankfully, all sources were consistent on the point giving his judgment both Catholic and secular legitimacy.

The case does little to clarify the principles applicable to nullity in Irish law. However, Hanna J.'s reliance on contemporary canon law source shows an understanding by the court that Catholicism was the most legitimate source of law in the eyes of most Catholic couples. His judgment is diplomatic, supported by secular authorities and canon law. This mixing of authorities was to continue in Irish nullity jurisprudence up until the late 1990s. However, the policy reasons for doing so were to change radically.

3. THE IRISH CONSTITUTIONAL PROTECTION OF MARRIAGE: A PROTECTION OF CATHOLIC VALUES?

Irish law is currently subject to *Bunreacht na h-Éireann*, a constitution brought into force in 1937. Although the Constitution has been subject to many

16 *McK v McK* [1936] IR 177, p. 185.

amendments since 1937, the family related Article 41 retains most of its original wording.

Many of the framers of the Irish constitution were devout Catholics with a good knowledge of canon law.[17] From the beginning of the drafting process, marriage and the family were subject to express constitutional protection. The original draft of the 1937 Constitution showed a desire to define marriage and the ways in which a marriage could be dissolved at a constitutional level. To give a flavour of the initial approach to family and marriage the Article is reproduced in full:

> "1. The State guarantees the constitution and protection of the family as the basis of moral education and social discipline and harmony, and the sure foundation of ordered society.
> 2. (1) The constitution of the family depends on valid marriage.
> (2) Marriage, as the basis of family life, is under the special protection of the State; attacks on the sanctity of marriage or of family life are prohibited.
> (3) Contraception and advocacy of the practice of contraception are prohibited and the possession, use, sale and distribution of contraceptives shall be punishable.
> (4) No law shall be enacted authorising the dissolution of a valid consummated marriage of baptised persons. No law shall be enacted authorising the annulment of marriage save on the following grounds, namely, that either or both of the parties did not agree to enter into the marriage contract, or was or were not free to enter, or did not freely enter into the marriage contract, or that the marriage was under the law for the time being in force invalid in form. Subject to the forgoing, the contract of marriage shall be regulated by law.
> (5) The State shall encourage early marriage and foster the production of large families by appropriate grants of remission of taxation in respect of children, by the promotion of saving and thrift schemes and by facilitating the provision of housing accommodation on reasonable terms."[18]

Under this Article, the constitutional family was based, not only on marriage, but on a valid marriage, and the grounds for nullity were spelt out. It is possible that under such a constitution the courts could have continued with all the previous common law grounds. The constitution technically only prohibited the *enactment* of law allowing nullity for other reasons, not the retention of the grounds in use. There is a strong prohibition on divorce that seems to apply only

[17] For example, John Hearne was part of the original committee set up to review the 1922 constitution in 1934. He had trained for the priesthood before becoming a barrister. See further: KEOGH, D. and McCARTHY, A., *The Making of the Irish Constitution 1937* (Mercier Press, 2007).

[18] UCDA P150/2373 October draft; reproduced in KEOGH *et al.*, *ibid.*, p. 113.

to Christians, being limited to "baptised persons."[19] This coincides with the idea of the sacramental nature of marriage between Catholics at the time.[20]

Further Catholic influences on the framing of the articles protecting the family are abundant. McQuaid[21] forwarded no less than two copies of the 1917 *Codex Iuris Canonicis* to the drafting team. In September 1936, Cahill[22] wrote to de Valera[23] arguing that the new Constitution must mark "a definite break with the Liberal and non-Christian type of State." He went on to suggest that, "A Constitution for Ireland should be, if not confessedly Catholic (which may at present be not feasible) at least definitely and *confessedly Christian*."[24] At De Valera's suggestion, Cahill put his submissions into the form of draft articles and with the input of a committee of Jesuits.[25] These draft articles suggested that Irish marriage law, as far as Catholics were concerned, should be given over to the competences of the Church and governed by canon law. In the alternative, they suggested that the nullity laws of Ireland should be identical to those of the Catholic Church.

The final version of Article 41 (before amendment by the 1995 referendum) read as follows:

> "1. 1° The State recognises the Family as the natural primary and fundamental unit group of Society, and as a moral institution possessing inalienable and imprescriptible rights, antecedent and superior to all positive law.
> 2° The State, therefore, guarantees to protect the Family in its constitution and authority as the necessary basis of social order and as indispensable to the welfare of the Nation and the State.
>
> 2. 1° In particular, the State recognises that by her life within the home, woman gives to the State a support without which the common good cannot be achieved.
> 2° The State shall, therefore, endeavour to ensure that mothers shall not be obliged by economic necessity to engage in labour to the neglect of their duties in the home.
>
> 3. 1° The State pledges itself to guard with special care the institution of Marriage, on which the Family is founded, and to protect it against attack.

---

19 This would include anyone baptised "in the name of the Holy Trinity" in canon law.

20 PETERS, E.N., *The 1917 Pio-Benedictine Code of Canon Law* (Ignatius, 2001) p. 351, Canon 1012.

21 John Charles McQuaid, Archbishop of Dublin (1940–1972).

22 Fr Cahill was de Valera's main link with the Jesuit order. See further: KEOGH *et al.*, *supra* note 17, p. 94.

23 Éamon de Valera, President of the Executive Council (1932–1937) later Taoiseach and President of Ireland and Head of the Constitutional Drafting Committee.

24 UCDA P150/2393 Letter from Fr Cahill with suggestions for the drafting of the new constitution: 4 September 1936.

25 The annotations ground this submission in paplical encyclicals: Leo XIII *Quod Apostolici Muneris, On Socialism,* 28 December 1878 and Leo XIII *Arcanum Divinici (On Marriage),* 10 February 1880.

> 2° No law shall be enacted providing for the grant of a dissolution of marriage.
> 3° No person whose marriage has been dissolved under the civil law of any other State but is a subsisting valid marriage under the law for the time being in force within the jurisdiction of the Government and Parliament established by this Constitution shall be capable of contracting a valid marriage within that jurisdiction during the lifetime of the other party to the marriage so dissolved."

Whether the institution of marriage envisaged by the framers was predominately Catholic or whether it was a more Christian notion is not possible to answer definitively.[26] Providing for the minority Protestant population was a concern for the framers. It is clear that the understanding of marriage in the Constitution was not based on the common law in force at the time. The evidence available suggests that the Irish framers had direct recourse to the current canon law and papal encyclicals.[27]

By using the language of *Casti Connubii*, the Irish framers rooted the constitutional understanding of marriage in sacrament rather than a civil institution of marriage or the rather confused jurisprudence of the common law. This understanding of marriage as inviolable and sacramental was underlined by the blanket ban on divorce. There was no real understanding of secular ideas of marriage in law that transcended all religious communities.

When introducing the draft of the present Constitution to the Dáil,[28] de Valera mentioned both the religious and social objections to divorce and emphasised the latter:

> "From the social point of view, without considering any other point of view, the obvious evil would be so great, and it has been proved to be so great in other countries, that I do not think that any person would have any difficulty... in making a choice in this matter."[29]

The framers believed in the evils of divorce and felt that the Catholic majority took precedence over the concerns of the Protestant minority. It was not that the

---

26 McQuaid had no doubts on this point: "Of course, once the State acknowledges God's right to public worship, it cannot be secular, even if be not Catholic...And when the State legislates according to natural law, of necessity, it legislates according to Catholicity, because the latter is the guardian of the natural law." McQuaid to de Valera, undated, UCDA P150/2395.

27 For example, Keogh suggests that the McQuaid article was heavily influenced by Leo XIII's Encyclical, *Rerum Novarum (On Capital and Labor)* May 15 1891. KEOGH *et al.*, *supra* note 17, p. 133. The encyclical is cited by McQuaid in UCDA P250/2408. In addition McQuaid refers to *Casti Connubii* and Pius XI, *Quadragesino Anno (On Reconstruction of the Social Order)* May 15 1931, UCDA P150/2395.

28 The Dáil is the main chamber of the Irish bicameral parliament or Oireachtas.

29 *Dáil Debates*, vol. 67, col. 1886.

framers of the Constitution saw themselves as enforcing the doctrine of the Catholic Church *per se* but they honestly believed that divorce was a great evil; a view that was bolstered by their Catholic beliefs.[30]

Some commentators have attempted to minimise the influence of Catholic teachings on the drafting of Articles 41 and 42. Sheehy, for example, argues that the influences of the canon law on Articles 41 and 42 were not due to "religious belief but rather … the law itself."[31] He dismisses any suggestion that Article 41 amounts to the importation of Roman Catholicism into the Constitution as "singularly unfortunate and misleading".[32] His argument is based on the latent content of medieval canon law that was part of the ecclesiastical laws of England and in turn inherited by the 1937 framers as part of the secular law. Thus, he argues, they had no choice but to include a canon law influence at a constitutional level.

However, as seen in *McM v McM*,[33] the only canon law that could be supposed to have legal force in Ireland was that passed before the Henrician Reformation.[34] Yet, the framers of the Constitution had greater recourse to the canon law than a mere glance at medieval canon law principles. Certain draft articles actually reproduced the 1917 Code of Canon Law.[35] This seems to contradict Sheehy's assertion that the only influence of canon law on Articles 41 and 42 was that mandated by the King's ecclesiastical law.

Articles 41 and 42 were in fact, subject to three religious influences: the latent influence of medieval canon law that remained in the civil law, the direct influence of the 1917 Code of Canon law and the papal encyclicals to which the framers made reference, and the Catholic influences of the personal beliefs of the framers: a form of cultural Catholicism. This means that the ideology behind the constitutional protection of marriage is based on the religious and social importance of marriage rather than the legal recognition of the institution by the common law at that time.

30 DUNCAN, *supra* note 7, p. 215.

31 SHEEHY, G., "The Right to Marry in the Irish Tradition of the Common Law" in O'REILLY, J. (ed.), *Human Rights and Constitutional* Law: *Essays in Honour of Brian Walsh* (The Round Hall Press, 1992), p. 21.

32 *Ibid.*, p. 13.

33 *Supra* note 13.

34 The Henrican Reformation occurred in the 16th century. During the reign of Henry VIII the Church of England broke away from the Catholic Church. The Church of England created its own Ecclesiastical Law which took the place of medieval canon law.

35 For example the emphasis in the October draft to baptised persons and the references in the X draft to the "essential properties of unity and indissolubility".

Although the 1937 Constitution did not create an Established Church, the secular idea of marriage that was to apply to all communities was inherently linked to Catholic doctrines.

4. JUDICIAL DEFERENCE TO CATHOLIC VALUES IN THE IMMEDIATE AFTERMATH OF THE 1937 CONSTITUTION

The express terms of Article 41.3.2° seemed to preclude the creation of new grounds for nullity. However, it took many years for the full effect of the constitutional protection of marriage to take hold in nullity jurisprudence. There was little case law until the 1970s due to the continuing reliance by most of the population on the Catholic Matrimonial Tribunals. Duncan suggests that this stagnation of the civil law was probably not the product of a conscious policy of deference by the State to the Church but resulted from the slowness of the legislators to recognise the social need to develop civil law remedies.[36] Litigation in the secular courts was also expensive and legal aid for family matters was not introduced until 1979.

In the absence of legislation, conflicts between Church law and State law continued to occur in family cases. In general, most conflicts were resolved in favour of Catholic teachings and where the secular law differed to the canon law the judiciary tried to bring the two regimes into compliance.

In *Griffith v Griffith*[37] Haugh J. brought the secular law and canon law together. This case concerned a nullity petition on the basis of duress. The husband petitioned for nullity as he had only married to prevent criminal conviction when his fiancée was found to be pregnant. The child turned out not to be his. Haugh J. based his ruling on the law as outlined in *McK v McK* and cited several authorities from the English ecclesiastical courts. He ruled that consent in this case was not real and that no marriage had been entered into. However, he also made reference to canon 1087 of the 1917 Code of Canon Law[38] and was influenced by the fact that the parties had secured a Church annulment. Haugh J. noted that canon 1087 applied to the facts and was similar to the test in the common law and held that in order for duress to erode the consent to marriage it had to come from a grave, external fear that is unjust.[39]

36 DUNCAN, *supra* note 7, p. 227.
37 *Griffith v Griffith* [1944] IR 35.
38 *Ibid.*, p. 52.
39 *Ibid.*

The report reflects Haugh's delight in bringing the parties into a legal situation that reflected canon law, "... I am glad that I can justly relieve the petitioner from the anomalous and unhappy position of being unmarried in the eyes of his Church and married according to the law of the land".[40]

Similarly, in *Tilson v Tilson*,[41] a child care dispute, the court gave effect to the *Ne Temere* decree by allowing the agreement that children be raised as Catholics to be enforced. In this case the husband and wife were married in a Roman Catholic church. The husband signed an undertaking that any issue of the marriage would be brought up as Roman Catholics. When difference arose between the husband and wife, the three elder children were removed by the husband and placed in a Protestant institution. In the High Court, Gavan Duffy P ordered that the children be returned to their mother on welfare grounds. However, his judgment was also motivated by Catholic values:

> "In my opinion, an order of the court designed to secure the fulfilment of an agreement peremptorily required before a mixed marriage by the Church, whose special position in Ireland is officially recognised as the guardian of the faith of the Catholic spouse, cannot be withheld on any ground of public policy by the very State which pays homage to that Church."[42]

Both *Griffith* and *Tilson* show that while courts were not in the habit of directly applying canon law, some judges did refer to it as an influencing factor and were delighted when the common law could be develop in a manner consistent with Catholic teachings.

Public confusion existed as to the laws applicable to marriage. In general, the public were much more familiar with Catholic teachings than the state of the common law. This created a two way problem between the Church and the courts in the area of bigamy cases. The grounds under which nullity could be granted by courts were narrower than those in contemporary Catholic teachings. Thus the courts were sometimes forced to declare valid a marriage that had been declared void by the Church courts. On the other hand, the Church was prepared to sanction re-marriage in the Church of a party to such a marriage in defiance of civil law.

This situation forced Ó Briain J. in *The People v Ballins*,[43] to convict the defendant of bigamy even though in canon law he had committed no crime. He made a plea that the law should be changed to comply with the canon law:

---

40 *Ibid.*

41 *Tilson v Tilson* [1951] IR 1.

42 *Ibid.*, p. 19.

43 *People (Attorney General) v Ballins* [1964] Ir Jur Rep 14 (IRCC).

"... after forty years of independence, it should be possible to amend the law here which for historical reasons now raises a grave problem of conscience for the majority of Irish citizens."[44]

The Catholic nature of the State continued to be stressed by the judiciary. In *Ryan v Attorney General*[45] Kenny J. expressly based the right to marry on the "Christian and democratic nature of the State" and backed up his argument by reading from papal encyclicals. This view, that, where possible, the common law should be developed to reflect Catholic values was not limited to the judiciary. At the end of the 1960s Walsh argued that Irish civil law still preserved the old canon law bequeathed to it through the common law.[46] In his thesis he argued that where possible the two laws should be made compatible and even called for the recognition of the exclusive matrimonial jurisdiction of the Catholic Church over Catholic marriages.[47] The idea that marriage law should reflect different religious values for different religious groups was also reflected in proposals for constitutional reform.

5. CONSTITUTIONAL REVIEW 1967: A CATHOLIC MARRIAGE LAW FOR CATHOLIC PEOPLE?

The only comprehensive review of Article 41 before the introduction of divorce in 1995 was the Report of the Committee on the Constitution, December 1967.[48] The main criticism of Article 41.3.2° at that time was that it took no heed of the wishes of the Protestant minority of the population, who wished to have divorce facilities and this was not prevented by the tenets of their religious denomination. As the Constitution was originally intended for the whole of Ireland[49] the prohibition was a source of embarrassment to those seeking to bring about better relations with the North. It was also argued that other predominately Catholic countries did not expressly ban the dissolution of marriage in their constitutions and that there was a more liberal attitude prevailing in Catholic circles since the Second Vatican Council.

44 *Ibid.*, p. 15.
45 *Ryan v Attorney General* [1965] IR 294 (IESC).
46 WALSH, J.A., *The Law of Marriage in Ireland* (UCD, 1969), p. 59.
47 *Ibid.*, p. 69.
48 Committee on the Constitution, *Report of the Committee on the Constitution* (Stationery Office PR 9817, Dublin 1967).
49 Articles 2 & 3 originally referred to the territory of Ireland as including Northern Ireland until the Nineteenth Amendment of the Constitution Act, 1998 changed these articles to allow Ireland to consent to be bound by the British-Irish Agreement done at Belfast on 10 April 1998.

The 1967 Committee on the Constitution suggested that a different wording of the Article 41.3.2° would be appropriate so as not to cause offence to the religious minorities:

> "In the case of a person who was married in accordance with the rites of a religion, no law shall be enacted providing for the grant of a dissolution of that marriage on grounds other than those acceptable to that religion."[50]

This amendment would mean that the applicable marriage law would be different for each religion. No enthusiasm for the idea of a single notion of civil marriage, applicable to all, can be seen. The Committee acknowledged that the proposed amendment might breach the constitutional prohibition on religious discrimination but suggested that a clause be introduced to make this Article a special exception. The proposal demonstrates that divorce is no longer seen primarily as a factual social evil. Instead, the focus is on not offending the religious beliefs of citizens by offering them a legal option that was contrary to their faith.

The Committee pointed out that Article 41 denied Catholics the right of dissolution of marriage in situations allowed by the Vatican. The canon law had moved on since 1937,[51] but the nullity law of Ireland based on pre-Reformation canon law had not. Many thousands of such cases were dealt with by diocesan and metropolitan courts every year. The absolute prohibition in the Constitution had the effect of imposing more rigid regulations on Catholics than those required by the law of the Church. The Committee declared that the original Article was unnecessarily harsh and rigid and they unanimously declared that it should be changed and some form of divorce introduced. The proposal of different marriage laws for different religions opened up the possibility that people would convert to Protestantism to obtain a divorce. The Committee thus outlined a need for laws to prevent people changing to another religion to avail of more liberal divorce laws.

The proposals of the 1967 Committee were never implemented. Nullity law continued to develop subject to the original wording of Article 41.3.2° until the introduction of divorce in 1995. However, the proposals of the 1967 Committee do provide a snapshot of policy concerns at the time and the desire for marriage law to reflect Catholic values, at least for Catholic people.

---

50 *Supra* note 48.

51 The interpretation of the nullity grounds of the 1917 Code of Canon Law had become more liberal by 1967. This was later reflected in the extension of many grounds under the 1983 Code of Canon Law.

6. AN EXPLOSION OF NULLITY GROUNDS: THE HIGH TIDE MARK OF CANON LAW

By the 1970s, a general tendency had developed in case law to give effect to Catholic values when appropriate. However, the express terms of Article 41 seemed to preclude the development of nullity grounds that would make it easier to end a marriage. The problem was that Catholic canon law had moved on and become more flexible since 1937. Should the judiciary give effect to these new developments in Catholic values that were contrary to the values that the original framers of Article 41 were trying to preserve? How was such a conflict to be resolved?

The constitutional ban on divorce did little to prevent marital instability actually occurring. In the 1970s, marital breakdown continued to persist. The applications for Church annulments increased and a demand for "postal divorces" from England[52] developed in the 1970s and 1980s.[53] In contrast to England and Wales,[54] no statutory reforms on nullity were adopted in Ireland and the area remained predominately one of common law doctrine.

In the 1970s, the judiciary continued to borrow principles from canon law.[55] Unlike the judiciary of the 1940s and 1950s these principles were borrowed, not to ensure the survival of orthodox Catholic values, but to respond to the increasing reality of marriage breakdown.

The old objective test for duress laid down in *Griffith v Griffith*,[56] and considered to be consistent with canon law in the 1940s, was rejected by several High Court judgments in the 70s and 80s in favour of a subjective approach to consent. Some of these decisions were rooted in canon law.

In *S v S*,[57] a nullity petition based on impotence, Kenny J. was influenced by the fact that the parties had already successfully obtained a decree of nullity from the Catholic Marriage Tribunal. He dealt with the case not on the basis of impotence but on intention and introduced the canon law doctrine of

52 Divorces granted by the English courts on the basis that the parties involved were resident in England. These divorces were not legally valid in Ireland contrary to the understanding of the applicants.

53 DUNCAN, W., *The Case for Divorce in the Irish Republic* (2nd ed.) (Irish Council for Civil Liberties, 1982).

54 The Nullity of Marriage Act 1971.

55 O'CONNOR, P., *Key Issues in Irish Family Law* (The Round Hall Press, 1988), p. 49.

56 *Supra* note 37.

57 *S v S*, Unreported judgment, Supreme Court July 1976 Kenny J.

simulation[58] into Irish secular law. He ruled that at the time of the marriage, the husband had decided not to engage in sexual intercourse. As this decision was not known to the wife, no true consent to the marriage had been given. This decision was to have an impact on the move away from set grounds for nullity towards a general subjective ground of proper consent.

In *MK (otherwise McC) v McC*[59] O'Hanlon J. referred to the fact that a Roman Catholic Tribunal had granted a decree of nullity on the basis of duress which included merely moral pressure. He took this as evidence that the canon law embraced a broader view of duress which should now be used by the Irish secular courts.

In the Supreme Court decision of *N (otherwise K) v K*,[60] the broad subjective approach to duress taken by O'Hanlon J. in *MK v F McC* was approved. However, it was held that the fact that a decree of nullity could be awarded by a Roman Catholic Court on the facts should not influence the court *per se*. Seeking a decree of nullity soon after a purported marriage, and some time before the petition for nullity in the civil courts, could, in certain cases, be accepted as evidence corroborating the allegation of an absence of real consent.[61]

Finlay C.J. limited the use of contemporary canon law principles, stating:

> "the principles and rules which the ecclesiastical courts of Ireland have heretofore acted on and given relief' must, in my view, be taken to refer to the ecclesiastical courts in Ireland established and in operation prior to 1870 and cannot be taken to refer to the current decisions of ecclesiastical courts of the Roman Catholic Church in Ireland."[62]

In Finlay C.J.'s judgment, canon law is replaced with Article 41.3.2°. He notes that because of the bar on divorce: "Consent to the taking of such a step must, therefore, if the marriage is to be valid, be a fully free exercise of the independent will of the parties."[63]

Henchy J.[64] called for the end of a system where the court went back to the principles of medieval canon law and worked forward. "Such a jurisdiction, defined by reference to what is now an obscure and outdated system of canon

58 Although he did not specifically point to canon law in his judgment.
59 *MK (otherwise McC) v McC* [1982] ILRM 277.
60 *N (otherwise K) v K* [1985] IR 733 (IESC).
61 *Ibid.*, p. 741.
62 *Ibid.*
63 *Ibid.*
64 *Ibid.*, p. 749.

law, can hardly be said to be suited to the needs of today." This movement away from canon law and towards Article 41 is also seen in Griffin J.'s judgment.[65] McCarthy J. also noted that the level of consent required for marriage should be commensurate with the constitutional status accorded to marriage.[66] This is an important step forward in judicial reasoning. The authority initially gleaned from canon law being part of the secular law of Ireland is now found in the wording of Article 41 itself.

Finlay C.J. stated that in order to rebut the presumption of validity of consent it was not necessary to prove a defined legal concept such as duress. Instead, such concepts were subservient to the ultimate objective which was to ascertain whether the consent of the party was real or apparent.[67] The standard of consent required to form a marriage was set at "free exercise of the independent will of the parties".[68] The consequence of this development was that consent could be rebutted by evidence of any flaw that rendered the consent less than perfect. By not limiting the grounds for which consent could be invalidated, the courts paved the way for a purely subjective approach to the level of consent required for marriage.

By the end of the 1980s, commentators recognised that the expansion of the civil law of nullity owed much to the canon law.[69] O'Connor suggested that there should be no objection to the courts taking note of the scientific advances that had shaped canonical jurisprudence and suggested that as the civil law and the Church law came to resemble each other, conflicts between the two would become less frequent.[70] In other words, both systems stemmed from medieval canon law. The Catholic courts had more case law and thus more experience of fitting the rules to modern facts and this should be considered as persuasive authority.

However, it would seem that by *N v K*[71] the use of canon law had been rejected in favour of the use of Article 41.3 itself. Because marriage was to be protected, a value based on Catholic teachings, it must be ensured that every marriage was properly formed. Instead of appealing to the minutiae of canon law rulings, the judiciary could now take a broad brush approach, justifying their liberal approach to nullity with the Catholic values embodied in Article 41.

65 *Ibid.*, p. 751.
66 *Ibid.*, p. 754.
67 *Ibid.*
68 *Ibid.*, p. 742.
69 O'CONNOR, *supra* note 55, p. 51.
70 *Ibid.*, p. 54.
71 *Supra* note 60.

For example in *O'R v B*[72] Kinlen J. seemed to suggest that the presumption of consent was very easy to rebut:

> "The institution of marriage is recognised and supported by common law and by the Constitution. In taking and conferring of a status the Courts must examine as to whether on both sides there was a full, free exercise of the respective independent will of the parties."[73]

The problem with the subjective test developed in *N v K* was that it did not seem to matter what sort of pressure caused the flaw in consent. It was only a matter of time before the courts dispensed with the need for duress altogether and focused merely on the consent itself. In *M O'M (orse O'C) v B O'C*[74] the Supreme Court unanimously decided that even in the absence of any form of duress, consent could be invalid where it was inadequately informed. The test laid down was whether: "this spouse, marrying this particular man, could be said to have had adequate knowledge of every circumstance relevant to the decision she was making, so that her consent could truly be said to be an informed one."[75]

According to *M O'M v B O'C*, in order to establish that consent is invalid it must be shown that the petitioner was ignorant of some material fact. The assessment of whether or not a fact is material was up to the retrospective judgment of the petitioner.[76] In *M O'M v B O'C*[77] itself, Blayney J. granted a decree of nullity on the grounds that the wife had not given informed consent where the husband had not disclosed that he had previously seen a psychiatrist. No intention to deceive was required. It became difficult to fix a limit on defective knowledge when the court began to accept the subjective, personal and retroactive opinion of the petitioner.[78]

So although leading constitutional lawyers had argued that the original Article 41.3 barred widely-framed nullity legislation or "back-door divorce" as well as divorce,[79] it would seem that the constitutional bar on divorce liberated rather than curtailed judicial imagination in according nullity decrees.

---

72 *O'R v B* [1995] 2 ILRM 57 (IEHC).
73 *Ibid.*, pp. 69–70.
74 *M O'M (orse O'C) v B O'C* [1996] 1 IR 208 (IESC).
75 *Ibid.*
76 WARD, P., "Defective Knowledge: A New Ground for Nullity?" in BAINHAM, A. (ed.) *The International Survey of Family Law* (Martinus Nijhoff, 1996), p. 223.
77 *Supra* note 74.
78 WARD, *supra* note 76, p. 225.
79 CASEY, J., *Constitutional Law in Ireland* (3rd ed.) (Round Hall Sweet & Maxwell, 2000), p. 621.

The respect accorded to the marital institution in the Constitution, stemming from the Catholic value of marriage as a permanent institution, meant that it could not be entered lightly, as to do so would fragilise marriage. This development reflects a changing value of marriage. No longer was the semblance of stability enough for the court. To merit protection, the marriage had to have a chance of being successful. It is argued that the judiciary went further than modernising the law by reflecting current Catholic values and in fact hijacked the rhetoric of canon law to create a nullity doctrine that was effectively nullity on demand. This development was undoubtedly inspired by a pragmatic need to respond to marital breakdown in a country with no divorce.

In *N v K*,[80] Finlay J. put this judicial pragmatism on more solid ground by confining canon law to its place as a medieval foundation for the system and using Article 41.3 on which to base a liberal nullity regime. The use of canon law as an intermediate step had softened the impact of circular reasoning whereby, in the 1940s, Article 41.3 was interpreted as preventing a liberal nullity doctrine, while in 1985 it was interpreted as mandating one. *M O'M v B O'C*[81] signalled the high tide mark for subjective nullity. After the introduction of divorce in 1995, judicial activism in this area retreated.

7. A NEW SECULAR AGE OF DIVORCE

The first serious attempt to change the constitutional ban on divorce occurred in 1986. The tenth Amendment of the Constitution Bill 1986 would have provided for divorce where the marriage had broken down and the failure had existed for five years. The proposal to amend the Constitution was rejected at the polls by 63.50% to 36.50%.[82] Instead a new regime for judicial separation was introduced.

In 1989, the Judicial Separation and Family Reform Act made it possible to get a judicial separation where the spouses had lived apart for three years or where the marriage had broken down for at least a year, as well as on fault grounds. A decree of judicial separation abolished the duty to cohabit which had up until this point been part of the legal obligations of marriage.[83] This radical change was challenged in *TF v Ireland*.[84] The plaintiff contended that, in order to fulfil the State's obligation in Article 41, the State must oblige parties to make an

80 *Supra* note 60.
81 *Supra* note 74.
82 SHATTER, A., *Shatter's Family Law* (4th ed.) (Butterworths, 1997), p. 383.
83 Section 8.
84 *TF v Ireland* [1995] 1 IR 321, [1995] 2 ILRM 321 (IESC).

attempt to save their marriage and that the Judicial Separation and Family Law Reform Act 1989[85] set too low a threshold for the protection of the institution of marriage against attack.

In the High Court, Murphy J. held[86] that the abolition of the restitution of conjugal rights was a clear and proper recognition that the institution of marriage could not be invoked in modern times to compel one party to live with another.[87] In this case Murphy J. declined to hear the evidence of Catholic moral theologians as to the obligations of marriage.[88]In the Supreme Court, Hamilton C.J. held that the protection accorded to marriage:

> "is given in recognition of the contribution made by the institution of marriage to the welfare of the nation and the State, and the pledge must be seen in this light. It is not concerned solely with marriage itself, or with the spouses in a marriage, but was also in the common good."[89]

In many cases, it was in the common good that spouses should be separated, and this action merely recognised the breakdown in the marriage and did not constitute an attack on the institution of marriage or a failure to treat it with special care.

In *TF* the constitutional duty to protect marriage became a duty not to reduce the appeal of marriage. If people could be forced to live together against their will after marrying, they would be unwilling to enter the institution. This reflects a change in social morality. In 1937, the idea of living apart when married would have been socially unacceptable. By 1989 it was more tolerated. In taking the purposive approach, Hamilton C.J.'s understanding of the protection of marriage was that the State must protect the aspects of marriage that contribute to the good of the society. This is a changeable standard that moves away from traditional Catholic values. By the standards of Irish modern society, forcible cohabitation served no good purpose and thus could not be retained solely on the basis that the State must protect marriage against attack. However, Hamilton C.J. was careful not to sever the Catholic heritage of Article 41 completely. He recognised that civil marriage was not limited by its traditional roots, although it was derived from Christian notions of partnership. This was the first clear judicial recognition of marriage as a secular concept, albeit with religious roots.

85 In particular, section 2(1)(1).
86 *Supra* note 84, p. 337.
87 He relied on *State (Healy) v Donoghue* [1976] IR 325.
88 *Supra* note 84, p. 333.
89 *Supra* note 84, p. 372.

The second effort to introduce divorce followed shortly after *TF.* The fifteenth Amendment to the Constitution Bill 1995 was supported at the polls by 50.28 per cent to 49.72 per cent.[90]

Article 41.3 now reads:

> "1° The State pledges itself to guard with special care the institution of Marriage, on which the Family is founded, and to protect it against attack.
>
> 2° A court designated by law may grant a dissolution of marriage where, but only where, it is satisfied that:
>
> i. at the date of the institution of the proceedings, the spouses have lived apart from one another for a period of, or periods amounting to at least four years during the previous five,
> ii. there is no reasonable prospect of a reconciliation between the spouses,
> iii. such provision as the court considers proper having regard to the circumstances exists or will be made for the spouses, any children or either or both of them and any other person prescribed by law, and
> iv. any further conditions prescribed by law are complied with."

The Family Law (Divorce) Act 1996 gave civil marriage a new existence separate from its original inception as an alternative to religious marriage. Divorce ended all marriages in the eyes of the State. The response of the individual churches was a matter for individual faith. At the same time, section 32 of the Family Law Act 1995 brought in standard preliminaries applicable to all marriages carried out in the State. Finally, in the 1990s, Irish law had conclusively moved to the idea of marriage as a legal concept applicable to all couples regardless of religion.

However, the importance of marriage as a value in Irish society was still so high that divorce could not be left to the regulation of mere statute. While Ireland has adopted a modern no-fault divorce regime, it is quite strict compared with many other European systems. Moreover, those conditions are written directly into the Constitution and cannot easily be changed. It is argued that the necessity to do this reflects the reality that Irish morality was changing. While a bare majority were in favour of divorce, some were more enthusiastic than others. In 1937 it was enough to promise to protect marriage against attack; in 1995 the conservative population needed the reassurance at constitutional level of when divorce would and would not be permitted.

One of the peculiarities of divorce law in Ireland is the total absence of fault grounds. This is partly due to the lateness of the introduction of divorce which

---

90 SHATTER, *supra* note 82, p. 390.

meant that Victorian ideas of matrimonial offence were unpopular.[91] It is more directly attributable to the decision by the Government that the grounds for divorce should be simple and judgmentally neutral.[92] The period of living apart is constitutionally set at a minimum of four years.

Divorce in Ireland cannot be obtained unless financial provision for a dependent spouse and children has been settled and deemed "proper" by a court of law. Section 20 of the Divorce Act 1996 allows the court to have great discretion in deciding what constitutes "proper provision" in any particular case. In addition, section 22 allows the court to review the orders made at any later stage, if it considers it proper to do so having regard to any change in circumstances or any new evidence.

Irish statute does not provide for "clean-break" divorce and so divorce does not completely sever the financial duties of the parties in regard to each other. The courts have no power to order that no further application for a lump sum or a property adjustment order can be made in the original divorce proceeding. It is therefore possible to apply for an adjustment order up until the death of your spouse,[93] although there is no guarantee that such an adjustment will be granted.

The Supreme Court has indicated that finality in financial adjustment is desirable after marital breakdown.[94] However, it is not ready to admit that marriage is no longer a lifelong commitment. In *DT v CT,* Murray J. reiterated that marriage is entered into in principle for life. Furthermore Murray J. interpreted the "proper provision" principle, as being linked to the nature of marriage as a lifelong commitment:

> "Even where a marriage is dissolved by judicial decree, the laws of many if not most states require that the divorced spouses continue to respect and fulfil certain obligations deriving from their dissolved marriage for their mutual protection and welfare, usually of a financial nature. This reflects the fact that marriage is in principle intended to be a lifetime commitment and that each spouse has fashioned his or her life on that premise. If the law permitted a spouse to cut himself or herself adrift of a marriage on divorce without any continuing obligation to the former spouse, it would undermine the very nature of the marriage contract itself and fail to protect the value

---

91 Although the *Government White Paper* PL 9104 (Dublin Stationery Office 1992) did give an option (5) suggesting that irretrievable breakdown be established by proof of adultery, desertion and unreasonable behaviour.

92 *Ibid.*

93 And indeed, after the death of one's spouse, in the case of secured maintenance.

94 *DT v CT (Divorce: Ample resources)* [2002] IESC 68.

which society has placed on it as an institution .... Hence the constitutional imperative of proper provision for spouses."[95]

The 2006 Constitutional Review took a more pragmatic view and concluded that the introduction of divorce had changed the nature of marriage and that the family in the Constitution had in turn been redefined as being based on a potentially temporary arrangement.[96]

The introduction of divorce in the 1996 brought an end to what Duncan described as "a policy which tries to counter the stresses which modern life imposes on the marriage relationship by strapping it into an institutional strait-jacket."[97] However, as can be seen by the decisions in *TF*[98] and *N(K) v K*,[99] the judiciary had already moved away from a policy of protecting all marriages to one where the potential functionality of the protected marriage was paramount. The courts ensured the stability of marriage, by making it easier for unstable couples to resolve their differences or to walk away from a failed relationship to form a new and, hopefully, more stable unit. The approach had been to favour the common good that the marital unit has brought to society, rather than to fossilise the letter of the 1937 protection of marriage as an irrevocable commitment based on Catholic teachings. It is argued that, in this way, the protection of marriage has developed to give greater respect to the private sphere of family relationships.

8. THE END OF SUBJECTIVE NULLITY

The introduction of no fault divorce meant that there was no longer any pragmatic need for a liberal nullity regime. However, the absence of financial certainty when a divorce was granted, led to one final hurrah for the subjective doctrine of nullity. In Irish law, if a decree of nullity was granted, the marriage was deemed never to have existed and the court had no powers for financial distribution.

Unsurprisingly the courts were unreceptive to this attempt to evade the "proper provision" requirement for divorce. *M O'M v B O'C*[100] signalled the high tide mark of subjectivism in Irish nullity law and from 1999 onwards the courts

95 *Ibid.*
96 The All-Party Oireachtas Committee on the Constitution, *Tenth Progress Report: The Family* (Stationery Office, Dublin 2006), 39.
97 DUNCAN, *supra* note 7, p. 227.
98 *Supra* note 84.
99 *Supra* note 60.
100 *Supra* note 74.

swung back to the 1940s standpoint that the Irish constitutional protection of marriage meant that nullity should be very difficult to prove and rarely granted.

In *O'B v R*[101] Kinlen J. reverted to the approach to Article 41 seen in *Griffith v Griffith*.[102] He held that the constitutional protection of marriage meant that:

> "There is undoubtedly a heavy burden of proof on a petitioner to establish that a marriage is null and void. It is for the trial judge to determine whether the parties' marriage is a nullity. As marriage is protected by the Constitution, it is important that the courts must exercise particular caution and scepticism in scrutinising the evidence proffered."[103]

Limitations were placed on the doctrine of defective knowledge in *PF v G O'M*.[104] In the Supreme Court, McGuinness J. stated that *M O'M v B O'C* had left the requirement for informed consent so wide as to cover almost any situation where a petitioner gave evidence that he or she would not have married the respondent had the information been available before the marriage. She held that this was incompatible with the Irish constitutional protection of marriage:

> "The introduction of a ground for nullity which, taken to its logical conclusion, could bring uncertainty into a wide variety of marriages is not only undesirable as a matter of public policy but is contrary to the clear intention of Article 41.3.1°."[105]

The Supreme Court limited the ruling in *MO'M v BO'C* to its facts.

The 2009 Supreme Court case of *LB v T MacC*[106] ends all further possibilities for a subjective approach to nullity. This case involved a financially successful woman who had married a man who had held himself out to be successful. He was in fact a financial drain on his wife, debt-ridden and did not contribute financially to the relationship. In the High Court, O'Higgins J. concluded that the respondent's lack of full disclosure about his financial affairs, family and social circumstances, were not grounds upon which one could base a claim for nullity.[107]

In the Supreme Court, Kearns J. clearly approved a return to the original understanding of the effect of Article 41 on nullity jurisprudence:

---

101 *O'B v R* [1999] 4 IR 168.
102 *Supra* note 37.
103 *O'B v R* [1999] 4 IR 168, p. 176.
104 *PF v GO'M* [2001] 3 IR 1 (IESC), p. 23.
105 *PF v GO'M* [2001] 3 IR 1 (IESC), p. 24.
106 *LB v T MacC* [2009] IESC 21.
107 *Ibid.*, p. 14.

> "The Constitution imposes a clear obligation on the courts to uphold the marriage contract and it would require far stronger evidence than has been adduced in this case to satisfy me that the respondent lacked the requisite capacity to enter a valid contract of marriage."[108]

The Supreme Court called for legislative action in the area of nullity in both *PF v GOM* and *LB v T MacC*. It is clear that after the introduction of no fault divorce, the door has shut on subjective nullity.

9. CONCLUSIONS

The approach of the Irish courts to the doctrine of nullity has come full circle. The interaction between canon law and Catholic values, and the secular doctrine of nullity, was instrumental in the development of a flexible nullity doctrine that filled the gap before the introduction of divorce in 1995.

The relationship between canon law and secular law in Ireland has always been uneasy and the extent to which one influences the other has depended largely on the politics and social morality of the time. Before 1937, Catholics remained largely outside the secular system. When cases did make it to the Irish secular courts, the mainly Protestant judiciary were eager not to rule in a way that was contrary to the morals of Catholic couples and the prevailing ideology at the time. The myth created in *McK v McK*,[109] that canon law is at the root of Irish secular nullity law proved an excellent tool for the judiciary to use in order to make their judgments publically acceptable. The development of a liberal nullity law through the rhetoric of canon law was merely an extension of this tendency.

Until 1970, the prevailing Irish morality was strictly against the breakdown of marriage and the possibility of divorce by nullity. The framing of Article 41 shows that the framers originally intended for the Article to hold people to their marriage vows and reflect 1940s Catholic values. Clearly, by design, Article 41 was supposed to prevent the creation of a liberal approach to nullity. For a time, the secular law was interpreted as being as close as possible to Catholic teachings and this reflected a clear national identity and homogeneous interpretation of Catholic teachings. However, the problem quickly appeared that the medieval canon law values on which secular nullity law was supposedly based, were not the same as contemporary Catholic values. Thus in the cases of *Griffith*,[110]

---

108 *Ibid.*, p. 22.
109 *Supra* note 13.
110 *Supra* note 37.

Tilson[111] and *Ballins*[112] there was a clear attempt by the judiciary to develop the law in line with contemporary Catholic values and where they could not, this was something that the legislature was implored to remedy. Until 1970, strict Catholic values, as represented by the constitutional protection of marriage, were used to justify a conservative law and this was acceptable to a largely conservative Catholic population.

After 1970 these strict Catholic values were used to create a stepping stone to the development of a flexible nullity doctrine that took the place of much needed divorce. The rhetoric of canon law was used in cases such as *S v S*[113] and *MK (Otherwise McC) v McC*[114] to legitimise what the judiciary were doing but many other cases from the time cited no authority whatsoever for the creation of a subjective approach to nullity.[115] The underpinning goal of the judiciary must be interpreted as responding to a changing social morality. The judiciary took a "catholic" approach to canon law, taking the bits that were useful to respond to the growing societal need for divorce.

Canon law provided a legitimacy which was replaced in *N v K*[116] by recourse to the wording of Article 41.3 itself. The logic of *N v K* left the doctrines of canon law behind, merely taking from Catholic values the idea that marriage is sacred; an idea embodied in Article 41. This protection meant that marriage was such a serious commitment that it must be very difficult to make. This interpretation ignored the original intention of the framers and the contemporary canon law yet the basis for its legitimacy was Catholic values.

After the introduction of divorce, this interpretation of Article 41.3 had served its purpose. The courts reverted to using Article 41 to limit the doctrine of nullity and the justifications found in *Griffith*[117] and *McK,*[118] used to legitimise a conservative Catholic law, resurfaced. The judiciary no longer used canon law to justify their "catholic" approach to nullity grounds. Marriage law became a more secular concept merely rooted in Christianity.

Although the constitutional protection of marriage remains, in the absence of homogenous religious values, it is having an increasingly inconsistent effect. The

111 *Supra* note 41.
112 *Supra* note 42.
113 *Supra* note 57.
114 *Supra* note 59.
115 *B v D* High Court Unreported Judgment 20 June 1973 Murnaghan J.; *S v S* Unreported High Court Judgment, 10 November 1978, Finlay P.
116 *Supra* note 60.
117 *Supra* note 37.
118 *Supra* note 13.

protection no longer ensures that marriage is protected from modern influences. The courts have established that the institutional protection of marriage is subject to the common good.[119] Other constitutional rights will take priority over the constitutional protection of marriage. Thus the institutional protection of marriage did not prevent marriage by transsexuals or those related by the prohibited degrees.[120] These cases have shown that when unremunerated personal rights under Article 40.3 of the Irish constitution come into conflict with the constitutional protection of marriage the personal rights take priority.

Neither does Article 41.3 grant very many rights to married couples as a unit. In *Malsheva v Minister for Justice Equality and Law Reform*[121] Article 41.3 did not grant a spouse a right to the company of his wife. However, in *Metock & Ors v Minister for Justice Equality and Law Reform*[122] such a right was granted by EU law.

It would seem, contrary to the intentions of the constitutional framers, that the institutional protection of marriage under Article 41 now has little effect in modern Ireland. Judicial interpretation on the priority of competing rights has eroded much of Article 41.3's power to preserve marriage as a conservative institution. The advent of EU law accords spouses more rights as EU citizens than they ever enjoyed under the Article 41 protection. Divorce has been introduced following the evolution of a nullity-on-demand system, apparently mandated by Article 41.3 itself. As Stone observed in his examination of English divorce, the common law lends itself easily to manipulation and reinterpretation.[123] Through the common law doctrine of nullity based on medieval canon law, Article 41.3 has become a mere fiction, inadequate to meet the needs of human behaviour.

119 *TF v Ireland* [1995] 1 IR 321, [1995] 2 ILRM 321 (IESC).

120 *Foy v An t-Ard Chlaraitheoir & Ors (No. 2)* Unapproved judgment, McKechnie J. 19 October 2007 (IEHC); *O'Shea v Ireland*, Unreported judgment of Laffoy J. delivered on 17 October 2006.

121 *Malsheva v Minister for Justice*, Unreported Judgment, (25 July 2003) Finlay Geoghegan J. (IEHC).

122 *Metock & Ors v Minister for Justice Equality and Law Reform* [2008] IEHC 77.

123 *Supra* note 5.

THE INFLUENCE OF THE ROMAN CATHOLIC CHURCH IN MALTESE FAMILY LAW AND POLICY

Ruth Farrugia

1. INTRODUCTION

This work examines the influence of the Roman Catholic Church in Maltese family law and policy. It looks at the historical and legal basis for the status of the Roman Catholic faith in Malta and reviews the impact this has had on legislation and its interpretation.

In a country where the Constitution proclaims the Roman Catholic Apostolic Religion as the religion of Malta, the ethos of legislation, at least in the field of family law, is unsurprisingly faithful to the teachings of the Church. It is submitted that Roman Catholicism has shaped Maltese law pertaining to intimate relationships, particularly in relation to the concept of marriage and responses to marital breakdown,[1] but also with reference to all caring relationships markedly in a show of solidarity with the more vulnerable members of society.

It is therefore not only marriage which has been influenced by religious mores, but also the legal relationship between care givers and dependants. More fundamentally, the Roman Catholic Church in Malta has influenced the understanding and interpretation of basic definitions of "family" and the well-defined responsibilities still applicable between family members. The law itself gives no single definition of family and seems to rely on the interpretation of various laws and policies which decreasingly reflect the position of the Roman Catholic Church.

For those persons whose family structure falls outside the definitions of the Catechism, access to rights may not be as straight forward. However, this is not

1 This is particularly pertinent in view of Malta's prevailing situation as the only European State without legislation on divorce. On 28 May 2011 a consultative referendum delivered a vote in favour of the introduction of divorce. Information in this paper is correct up to 1 June 2011.

to say that State response is unmitigated by humanitarian considerations when determining particular social support such as housing allocation and access to social assistance. Even where no specific legislation provides for formal recognition, policy enables access to benefits and (limited) rights.[2]

2. BACKGROUND

2.1. RELIGION IN MALTA

Malta is made up of three islands and is just 316 square metres in total area with a population of 400,000.[3] Approximately 98 per cent of the population[4] is estimated to be Roman Catholic with a total of 360 Catholic churches in Malta.[5] Today there are growing numbers of people who profess other religions, both Christian and non-Christian.[6]

Religion has always been important in Malta. Hagar Qim, Ggantija and Mnajdra are the oldest known temples in the world. They are in an excellent state of preservation and have been standing over 5,600 years,[7] drawing pilgrims to worship initially from Sicily and North Africa and now tourists from all over the world who come to visit these World Heritage Sites.

Roman Catholicism has been Malta's religion since St Paul was shipwrecked on the island in the year 60 AD.[8] In the centuries that followed, Malta was occupied by a number of powers, including a spell under Arab rule starting in 870 and terminating in 1090 when Count Roger the Norman captured Malta. When the Knights of St John were banished from Rhodes in 1530, they made Malta their

---

2 For instance, cohabiting partners and same-sex couples remain unrecognised at law but policy enables them to access housing and benefits.

3 National Statistics Office (NSO).

4 This estimate is based on a number of popular sources available on the Internet and probably refers to the number of persons baptised Catholic. Discern, the Malta Church Research Institute estimated that "There has been a significant fall in Sunday Mass attendance from 81.9% in 1967 to 51.0% in 2005", SAVONA VENTURA, C., Catholic Family Values, (rev)2007, www.discern-malta.org/research_pdfs/marriage.pdf.

5 There are 313 churches on Malta (in 64 parishes), 46 churches on the smaller sister island Gozo (in 15 parishes) and one small church on the tiny island of Comino. See www.carnaval.com/malta/ (accessed on 03.01.2011).

6 Malta has a Scottish Methodist Church, a Bible Baptist Church, a mosque and a Greek Orthodox Church among others.

7 TRUMP, D., PACE, A. *et al.*, *Malta Before History* (Miranda publication, 2004). Hagar Qim (literally translates to Stones of Worship) dates from the Neolithic Era 3,600–3,200 B.C.

8 "Once safely on shore, we found out that the island was called Malta. The islanders showed us an unusual kindness. They built a fire and welcomed us all because it was raining and cold": (The Bible, Acts of the Apostles 28:1–2 NIV).

headquarters and stayed for over 250 years.[9] Napoleon seized the Island for just two years[10] and faced uncharacteristic resistance to his anti clerical activity, leading the Maltese to request the British to offer protection which they did until 1964.

The 1964 Constitution[11] declared the Roman Catholic Religion to be the religion of Malta and in 2011 the text continues to read:

> "**Article 2.** (1) The religion of Malta is the Roman Catholic Apostolic Religion.
> (2) The authorities of the Roman Catholic Apostolic Church have the duty and the right to teach which principles are right and which are wrong.
> (3) Religious teaching of the Roman Catholic Apostolic Faith shall be provided in all State schools as part of compulsory education."

2.2. CHURCH-STATE RELATIONSHIP

Malta has a long history of close relations between Church and State. This is relevant to the issue under review because the introduction of legislation and changes to existing law and policy owe much to this relationship. While under British rule, Malta's first Self Government Constitution in 1921 made no reference to a state religion but the first Act of the Maltese Legislative Assembly was to declare the Catholic faith as the religion of Malta. Following the Second World War, the Church opposed the introduction of suffrage for women with the Labour Party backing its introduction.[12] Maltese politics have been fraught with Church intervention including the threat of the interdict[13] on two occasions.[14]

---

9 1530–1798. BLOUET, B., *The Story of Malta* (Malta Progress Press, 1993) and LUTTRELL, A.T. in MEDIEVAL MALTA (ed.), *Studies On Malta Before the Knights* (The British School at Rome, 1975).

10 June 1798 – September 1800. FRENDO, H. & FRIGGIERI, O. (eds.), *Malta: Culture and Identity* (Ministry of Youth and the Arts, 1994).

11 CREMONA, J.J., *The Maltese Constitution and Constitutional History Since 1813* (Publishers Enterprises Group Ltd (PEG), 1994).

12 The strongest opposition to the request of the Women of Malta Association, leading the lobby, came from the Church, primarily through its newspaper *Lehen is-Sewwa* (Voice of Truth), "on the grounds that they did not represent anyone except a few women whose heads were filled with these blessed 'equal rights'". *Lehen is-Sewwa*, 21 February 1945 in FARRUGIA, R., "Female Suffrage in Malta" in RODRÍGUEZ-RUIZ, B. and RUBIO MARIN, R. (eds.), *The History of Female Suffrage in Europe* (Brill publishing, 2011) (forthcoming).

13 In the Roman Catholic Church, the term interdict usually refers to an ecclesiastical penalty. It is similar to excommunication in that the person is barred from receiving the sacraments and participating in public worship. For instance, children of interdicted persons may not be baptised, the interdicted may not marry in church and the dead are refused burial in consecrated ground.

14 Between 8 April 1961 and 4 April 1969, the leadership of the Malta Labour Party, readers, advertisers and distributors of Party papers as well as its voters were interdicted. Previously, between 1930 and 1933, interdiction was imposed on the Constitutional Party and Labour

During the 1970s,[15] the Faculty of Theology was removed from the University Campus[16] and the continued existence of Catholic schools was threatened. The Labour government also introduced legislation to bring about the devolution of Church property[17] although this was successfully challenged in court.[18] Relations between Church and State, and therefore the legislature, may be said to have been affected by these past events although changing society and changing values may no longer weight Church opinion as strongly as in the past. That said, the current divorce debate continues to be hinged on principles of religion and has made repeated appeal to the "common good" with the leader of the Labour Party openly in favour and the Prime Minister and his Party formally declaring itself against.[19]

2.3. SOURCES OF MALTESE FAMILY LAW

The sources of Maltese family law are to be found in the Civil Code,[20] particularly in the part dealing with persons where the law treats issues including the rights and duties between married persons, the legal relationship between parents and children, adoption and separation. There are also other parts of the same Code which deal with matrimonial regimes and succession law, both of which impact directly on the family. Family law also finds its sources in other separate legislation such as the Marriage Act,[21] the Children and Young Persons (Care Orders) Act,[22] the Child Abduction Act[23] and legislation setting up the Family Court.[24]

Party. While the Constitutional Party no longer exists *per se*, the Malta Labour Party does and is currently led by the Leader of the Opposition.

15 Under a Labour government.

16 The Faculty is one of the oldest of the University of Malta and dates back to 1592. It was reincorporated in the University of Malta by an agreement signed by the University of Malta and the Holy See on 25 September 1988.

17 Devolution of Certain Church Property Act 1983 and Act XI of 1983.

18 First Hall Civil Court, *Mons Giuseppe Mercieca proprio et al v The Hon Prime Minister nomine et al.*, 24 September 1984. The Court declared that the Roman Catholic Church has a right to invoke a breach of Article 40 of the Constitution – freedom of conscience and religion.

19 Internally, Members of Parliament from both sides of the House have declared themselves for or against and both parties promised their members a free vote. As a matter of interest, the divorce proposal was introduced through a private members bill by a Government member backed by a member from the Opposition party.

20 Laws of Malta, Chapter 16.

21 *Ibid.*, Chapter 255.

22 *Ibid.*, Chapter 285.

23 *Ibid.*, Chapter 410.

24 This court treats all contentious issues relating to family while the court of voluntary jurisdiction continues to hear cases relating to adoption, absentees and succession.

However, it is readily evident that legislation relating to family draws its influence from the Catholic tradition and legal system. In general terms, in keeping with changes throughout most of Europe, the development of canon law in the Middle Ages revived and revamped the Code of Justinian and (re)established Roman law precepts within domestic law. Berman states that "it was the emergence of ecclesiastical courts after Pope Gregory VII that prompted civil courts to imitate and eventually supersede them."[25] Marriage itself was totally reliant on canon law until the Marriage Act in 1973 separated Church and State (only to be partially reunited through amendments in 1995).[26]

However, Malta has long been looking towards the rest of Europe by following selected developments in the field of family law. Malta has been a member of the Council of Europe since 1965[27] and has permitted the right of individual petition to its citizens before the European Court of Human Rights since 1987.[28] An interesting selection of judgments interpreting Article 8 of the European Convention on Human Rights which is incorporated into Maltese law, highlights changes in the definition of family and the rights accorded to its members which no longer tally precisely with Roman Catholic doctrine.

3. DEFINITION OF FAMILY

Perhaps one of the most substantial changes, therefore, has come about in the interpretation of the term family. While the Church in Malta is clear and steadfast in its definition of a family, Maltese law offers no set definition and the courts have increasingly been affected by decisions from the European Court of Human Rights in Strasbourg and have revised the interpretation over the last years.

For instance, under Maltese law, the definition in the context of the Refugees Act states, "dependent members of the family means the spouse of the refugee, provided the marriage is subsisting on the date of the refugee's application and such children of the refugee who on the date of the refugee's application are under the age of eighteen years and are not married."[29] In the Burials Ordinance,[30]

25 BERMAN, H.J., "Religious Foundations of Law in the West: An Historical Perspective" (1983), *The Journal of Law and Religion* 1:1, pp. 5–11.

26 Further elaboration on this point is to be found in the section on annulment, below.

27 29 April 1965 (www.coe.int/t/dc/files/themes/pays_membres/malte/default_en.asp).

28 1 May 1987 (http://conventions.coe.int/treaty/en/treaties/html/005-1-bis.htm). In November 1998, Malta also ratified Protocol Number 11 and in so doing, accepted the need for a stronger Court.

29 Laws of Malta, Chapter 420, Article 2.

30 *Ibid.*, Chapter 13.

Article 3: "For the purposes of this subsection (deposit in application for ownership of grave) 'family' means the father, the mother, the husband or wife, any brother, sister, son or daughter of the applicant", while in the Land Acquisition (Public Purposes) Ordinance,[31] Article 21 relating to acquisition of rural land for public use states that: "In this article 'member of the family' means a lineal ascendant, a lineal descendent, a widow or a widower, a son-in-law, and a widowed daughter-in–law while not remarried of the tenant or occupier".

However the definition may be widened to include: "Family member in relation to an individual means (a) the parents; (b) the spouse; (c) a son, daughter, brother or sister aged eighteen years or over; and (d) a legal guardian or curator of such individual", as in the case of the Equal Opportunities Act.[32] Other laws prefer the use of the term "household" when they are referring to family members or attempt to identify what constitutes a "family relationship".[33]

Notwithstanding this situation, the Maltese courts seem to imply that there exists a "legal definition of family" in Maltese family law.[34] The Catholic interpretation of "family" defines it as "that fundamental social group formed by the permanent union of one man with one woman and their children".[35] A series of judgments have displaced some of these criteria in keeping with Strasbourg's rulings in relation to cases brought under Article 8.

For instance in *Alexia Portelli and Wessam Mohammed Elsrmani v Minister for Justice*[36] the Maltese court decided that:

> "In order to see whether there is family life, the court must look to the de facto situation rather than to the legal definition of family. The fact that the applicants lived together as husband and wife and had children from this relationship is sufficient for the court to conclude that together they had a family life."

---

31 *Ibid.*, Chapter 88.

32 Laws of Malta, Chapter 413 (Equal Opportunities (Persons with Disability) Act).

33 Laws of Malta, Chapter 363, Local Councils Act, Article 20(4) and Laws of Malta, Chapter 481 (Domestic Violence Act), interpretation article.

34 *Alexia Portelli u Wessam Mohammed Elsrmani v Il-Ministru tal-Gustizzja u l-Intern u l-Ufficcjal Principali ta' l-Immigrazzjoni* Qorti Civili Prim'Awla (Gurisdizzjoni Kostituzzjonali) Onor.G.Caruana Demajo 16 Awwissu 2005 Rikors Numru 43/2004/1. My informal translation: *Alexia Portelli and Wessam Mohammed Erslmani v Minister for Justice and the Interior and the Principal Immigration Officer,* First Hall Civil Court (Constitutional Jurisdiction), G. Caruana Demajo J., 16 August 2005, Application Number 43/2004/1.

35 Www.newadvent.org.

36 My informal translation from the original: "Biex tara jekk hemmx hajja tal-familja, il-qorti ghandha aktar thares lejn is-sitwazzjoni *de facto* milli lejn id-definizzjoni legali tal-familja. Il-fatt illi r-rikorrenti ghexu flimkien *more uxorio* u minn din ir-relazzjoni kellhom l-ulied huma bizzejjed biex din il-qorti tghid illi flimkien ghandhom hajja ta' familja."

The European Court of Human Rights has further held that the concept of family does not necessarily require that a father and child live under the same roof and explained that it:

> "does not see cohabitation as a sine qua non of family life between parents and minor children. ... It follows from this concept of family on which Article 8 is based that a child born of such a union is ipso iure part of that relationship: hence, from the moment of the child's birth and by the very fact of it, there exists between him and his parents a bond amounting to "family life", even if the parents are not then living together ..."[37]

This is echoed in another local decision taken by the Constitutional Court in the case of *Lanouar Bounab v Attorney General*[38] where the court held that "Article 8 of the Convention protects the special relationship between father and son because this falls under the concept of 'family'".[39]

In delivering this judgment, it is relevant to note that the court also made reference to the European Court decision in the case of *Abdulaziz, Cabales and Balkandah v UK* (1985) citing: "Whatever else the word 'family' may mean, it must at any rate include the relationship that arises from a lawful and genuine marriage ..." It went on to hold that the European Court of Human Rights has said that the concept of family does not require that a father and son must necessarily live under the same roof:

> "... does not see cohabitation as a sine qua non of family life between parents and minor children. ... It follows from this concept of family on which Article 8 is based that a child born of such a union is ipso iure part of that relationship: hence, from the moment of the child's birth and by the very fact of it, there exists between him and his parents a bond amounting to 'family life', even if the parents are not then living together..."

However,

> "the mere existence of a family relationship is not sufficient for the applicability of Article 8; only in the case of a sufficiently close factual tie is there a question of family life. In fact, if the relationship does not imply genuine ties, an interference is not possible. Whether such genuine ties exist is determined, inter alia, by the nature of the family relationship invoked by the applicant; for married couples and children

---

37 ECtHR *Berrehab v The Netherlands* (1989) 11 EHRR 322.

38 *Lanouar Bounab f'ismu proprju u in rappresentanza ta' ibnu minuri Yousef Bounab v Avukat Generali u Karen Bounab*, Constitutional Court, decision of 27 February 2004, Appell Civili Numru 20/2003/1.

39 My informal translation from the original: "L-artikolu 8 tal-Konvenzjoni jhares ir-relazzjoni specjali bejn missier u ibnu ghax dan jidhol fil-kuncett ta' 'familja'."

born out of that marriage, and for other close family relationships they are assumed unless their absence is evident or proven."[40]

In *Samir El Yeferni v The Prime Minister*[41] the court held that:

"The European Court, in relation to the concept of family, has pronounced itself as follows. That the issue of the existence of family life is one of fact 'depending upon the real existence in practice of close personal ties.' In the exercise to determine this state of fact as a precondition to the application of Article 8, the European Court has adopted a notion of 'family' which is far wider than the meaning normally attributed to this term, in the sense that the situation should be considered in its reality rather than in its legality."[42]

Similarly in *Sen v The Netherlands*, the European Court of Human Rights had decided that:

"it follows from the concept of family on which art. 8 is based that a child born out of such a union is ipso iure part of that relationship; hence from the moment of the child's birth and by the very fact of it, there exists between him and his parents a bond amounting to family life, even if the parents are then not living together."[43]

This case led the Maltese courts[44] to conclude that appropriate measures be taken "to ensure that family life between parents and children can continue after divorce, and to refrain from measures which cause family ties to rupture".[45]

It is an accepted fact in the academic world that the notions of family (Article 8) and marriage (Article 12) have been widened by the Court in Strasbourg: "It has

---

40 VAN DIJK, P. and VAN HOOF, G.J.H., *Theory and Practice of the European Convention on Human Rights* (Kluwer Law International, 1998), pp. 506–507.

41 *Samir El Yeferni v L-Onorevoli Prim Ministru, l-Avukat Generali tar-Repubblika, il-Ministru tal-Gustizzja u l-Intern, il-Kummissarju tal-Pulizija u l-Ufficjal Principali ta' l-Immigrazzjoni*, First Hall Civil Court (Constitutional Jurisdiction) decision of 28 June 2005, Rikors Numru. 9/2004/1.

42 My informal translation from the original: "Illi l-Qorti Ewropea, dwar il-kuncett ta' familja, pronuncjat ruhha f'dan is-sens. Illi l-kwistjoni dwar l-ezistenza o meno ta' hajja familjari hija wahda ta' fatt 'depending upon the real existence in practice of close personal ties.'
Fl-esercizju ghad-determinazzjoni ta' dan l-istat ta' fatt, bhala presuppost ghall-applikazzjoni tal-Artikolu 8, il-Qorti Ewropea adoperat kuncett tan-nozzjoni ta' 'familja' aktar wiesgha mis-sinifikat ordinarju nomalment moghti lil dan it-termini, fis-sens li ghandha tigi kunsidrata s-sitwazzjoni fir-realta' taghha milli fil-legalita' taghha."

43 ECtHR *Sen v Netherlands* (2003) 36 EHRR 81.

44 *Mohannid Sogr Garzadin v L-Onorevoli Prim'Ministru, l-Avukat Generali tar- Repubblika, il-Kummissarju tal-Pulizija u l-Ufficcjal Ewlieni ta' l-Immigrazzjoni*, First Hall (Constitutional Jurisdiction), decision of 31 January, 2006, Rikors Numru. 35/2005.

45 "Fost l-obbligi pozittivi u negattivi ta' l-istat hemm id-dmir illi l-istat ghandu" (free translation: Amongst the positive and negative obligations of the state there exists the obligation).

established a whole set of family law rules from Article 8 of the Convention which initially contained no more than a negative obligation on the part of the state to refrain from arbitrary interference with the family."[46] Whether such interpretation has impacted on popular culture is another issue and it remains open to debate whether there has been any sign of the influence of the Catholic Church in the public mentality and in the local decision making process.

4. INTIMATE RELATIONSHIPS

4.1. MARRIAGE

The Maltese concept of marriage is directly influenced by classical Roman and canon law concepts. Under canon law, "a marriage which is ratified and consummated cannot be dissolved by any human power or by any cause other than death"[47] and the Maltese Courts have repeatedly emphasised the sacramental nature of marriage and the importance of monogamy and indissolubility.[48]

The Marriage Act of 1975[49] gives no definition of marriage but jurisprudence has constantly declared itself on the characteristics of a valid marriage: "the marriage contract on this Island remains always indissoluble for whatever class of person, catholic or non catholic ... the law in Malta, prior to the Council of Trent, has always retained the marriage bond as indissoluble outside the death of one of the spouses."[50] Furthermore, the Marriage Act confirms the principal characteristics of marriage echoing the understanding of marriage under the Roman Catholic religion, that is, the voluntary union for life of a man and a woman,[51] and leading to the conclusion that the concept of marriage under Maltese law reflects the classical Roman and canon law concepts.

The notions of monogamy and indissolubility remained unchanged by the advent of the Marriage Act of 1975. Article 6 provides that "a marriage contracted between persons either of whom is bound by a previous marriage shall be void."

46 SCHERPE, J.M., http://cels.law.cam.ac.uk/File/events/Laura%20Gyeney%20commentary.pdf.

47 Code of Canon Law, Canon 1141.

48 A marriage is deemed to be ratified when the spouses are baptised and the Maltese population is said to be made up of 98% baptised persons who are subject to Canon Law simply by virtue of their being baptised. *Emilia Wolgeshaffen noe. v S. Lanzon et al.*, Collected Cases, Volume XXXIX-281 (16/02/1928).

49 Laws of Malta, Chapter 255.

50 *David James Low v Marianna Micallef Low*, Collected Cases, Volume XIII-243 (27/06/1892).

51 The classical definition of marriage which forms the basis of the definition under canon law is "*nuptiae sunt coniunctio maris et foeminae et consortium omnis vitae divini et humani unis communication*". Therefore the essential properties of a canon law marriage are unity and indissolubility, subject to consent.

Also, although a marriage may be annulled in a number of circumstances akin to those listed in canon law, the Act does not provide for divorce. A decree of divorce would however be recognised in Malta, provided that it satisfies the requirements listed under Article 21 of the Marriage Act.

To date, marriage may only take place between a man and a woman, although the gay rights lobby has made efforts for recognition – if only of same-sex cohabitation – for a number of years. As cohabitation itself remains absent from Maltese law,[52] this is still a concern which requires attention. The issue recently came to a head in a much publicised judgment regarding the right of a transsexual to marry.[53] Maltese law permits the complete change of documentation for a person who has irrevocably changed sex,[54] provided that person is not married. A woman who had been born a man requested the publication of banns to marry a man and was refused by the Registrar of Marriages. The Court found that such a request should be upheld, but, on appeal, the decision was reversed. A case was then instituted on the grounds of discrimination where the court decided against her on the grounds of public policy. She appealed and won the case, but the Attorney General lodged another appeal and on 23 May 2011 the Constitutional Court upheld the Attorney General's appeal impeding Ms Cassar's right to marry. Ms Cassar's legal counsel have given notice of final recourse to Strasbourg.

The court's interpretation of marriage keeps well within the parameters of the ethos of the Catholic Church. A sample from the recent *Cassar* case just mentioned illustrates the pertaining interpretation of marriage:[55]

> "Regarding marriage, our law gives no definition of 'marriage' but gives a definition of 'Catholic Marriage'. Not every marriage recognised by law is a catholic marriage

52 The introduction of cohabitation formed part of the electoral manifesto of the present Nationalist government in 2008.

53 *Id-Direttur Registru Pubbliku fil-kwalita' tiegħu ta' Reġistratur taż-Żwiġijiet v Joanne Cassar (Director of Public Registry in his capacity as Registrar of Marriages v Joanne Cassar)*, First Hall, Civil Court, Citazzjoni Numru (Writ of Summons Number) 202/2007, decided on 21 May 2008.

54 In keeping with Strasbourg judgments on the issue.

55 My informal translation from the original text in Maltese:
"Illi dwar żwieġ il-liġi tagħna (li, minbarra d-dispożizzjonijiet ta' liġi ġenerali fil-Kapitolu 16 tal-Liġijiet ta' Malta, hi regolata wkoll b'liġi speċjali Att XXXVII tal-1975 dwar iż-Żwieġ (Kap 255 tal-Liġijiet ta' Malta) kif mibdul) ma tagħtix tifsira ta' 'żwieġ' imma tagħti tifsira ta' 'Żwieġ Kattoliku'. Mhux kull żwieġ li l-liġi tagħtih għarfien huwa żwieġ kattoliku, għaliex il-liġi tagħraf żwieġ kemm fil-forma reliġjuża u kif ukoll fil-forma ċivili biss. Art. 2(2) tal-Kap 255 ... Iżda, għall-kuntrarju ta' dak li jaħsbu xi wħud, l-liġi tagħti għarfien għal żwieġ biss jekk kemm-il darba dan isir minn raġel u mara bejniethom. Dan joħroġ minn kliem l-artikolu 15(2) tal-Kap 255 li jitkellem dwar 'martu jew żewġha rispettivament' li jidher li jiġbru fihom il-kunċett ta' 'coniunctio maris et feminae' u 'viri et mulieris coniunctio' kif imfissra fid-Dritt Ruman sa minn żmien Modestinu u Ulpjanu. Dawk huma s-sisien ġuridiċi li fuqhom inbnew u tħarsu l-prinċipji ġuridiċi tal-istitut taż-żwieġ fis-sistema legali tagħna f'Malta."

> because the law recognizes marriage in a religious form as well as only in a civil form. However contrary to what is thought by some, the law only recognises marriage if concluded between a man and a woman. This results from the words of Article 15(2) … which speaks of 'a wife or husband respectively' which appear to gather the concept of 'coniunctio maris et feminae' or 'viri et mulieris coniunctio' as understood by Roman Law since the times of Modestino and Ulpian. These are the juridical bases on which the institute of marriage in the Maltese legal system is based and protected."

4.2. ANNULMENT[56]

In a country which has no divorce legislation, annulment obviously takes on considerable importance.[57] Most Maltese couples marry both civilly and according to Catholic Church rites in one ceremony which affirms both aspects. An annulment presupposes a marriage which was void *ab initio.*[58] For a Maltese court to annul a marriage celebrated in Malta, the court must examine whether the formalities prescribed by Maltese law have been observed and where the marriage has been celebrated. A civil action is then brought before the courts and is a contested case decided by a judge. Where the marriage is declared null, section 20 of the Marriage Act lists the effects of this declaration in terms of Maltese law.

The Catholic Church teaches[59] that the word "annulment" can be rather misleading since the Church has no authority whatsoever to *annul* a valid marriage. It holds that it is more exact to speak of a *declaration of nullity.*[60] The canonical trial establishes a state of fact, stating that the marriage never existed in the first place and makes a declaration of nullity. In the words of the official website of the Ecclesiastical Tribunal:

> "'Annulments' ARE NOT Catholic divorces. A divorce is a civil legal action whereby the contract of marriage is dissolved, division of property and custody of children are

---

56 In 1980 there were three annulment cases as compared with 174 in 2003.

57 "The Census Report for 2005 suggests that in the total population, individuals with a history of a failed marriage [separated/annulled/divorced – and not remarried] amount to 4.0% of the population aged 16 years or more [i.e. 1 in 25 of the population in Malta today aged 16 years or more has had a failed marriage]. The proportion reported in the previous Census in 1995 was 1.7% [i.e. 1 in 59]": SAVONA VENTURA, *supra* note 4.

58 If the marriage was celebrated abroad, the foreign law will govern the issue of whether the marriage was void or merely voidable.

59 Explanation cited from the Metropolitan Ecclesiastical Tribunal of Malta site: www.maltachurchtribunals.org.

60 "Such a declaration … declar(es) that after a careful examination of all the facts, it has resulted that such a particular union, which so far appeared to be a marriage, was indeed never a true marriage; …" *ibid.* Available at www.maltachurchtribunals.org/faqs.

settled, and a husband and wife are declared free to enter new unions with different partners. A Catholic Declaration of Nullity states that, in the eyes of the Church, a true bond was never established."

The criteria for civil annulment follow those listed under canon law, from which they are derived, affirming the continued influence of the Catholic Church on the effects of such proceedings.[61] In 1995, an additional amendment directly influenced by canon law was introduced, specifying the ground of non-consummation in keeping with canon law legislation.[62] As a matter of interest – and in isolation from the canon law text – the Article includes a three month period before the parties may institute the action. This has been explained as providing a deterrent to any marriage of convenience. However, it seems to go directly against the very notion the Article seeks to promote.

---

61 Marriage Act, Article 19:
"A marriage shall be void:
(a) if the consent of either of the parties is extorted by violence, whether physical or moral, or fear;
(b) if the consent of either of the parties is excluded by error on the identity of the other paty;
(c) if the consent of either of the parties is extorted by fraud about some quality of the other party which could of its nature seriously disrupt matrimonial life;
(d) if the consent of either of the parties is vitiated by a serious defect of discretion of judgment on the matrimonial life, or on its essential rights and duties, or by a serious psychological anomaly which makes it impossible for that party to fulfil the essential obligations of marriage;
(e) if either of the parties is impotent, whether such impotence is absolute or relative, but only if such impotence is antecedent to the marriage;
(f) if the consent of either of the parties is vitiated by the positive exclusion of marriage itself, or of any one or more of the essential elements of matrimonial life, or of the right to the conjugal act;
(g) if either of the parties subjects his or her consent to a condition referring to the future;
(h) if either of the parties, although not interdicted or infirm of mind, did not have at the time of contracting marriage, even on account of a transient cause, sufficient powers of intellect or volition to elicit matrimonial consent.
(2) Subject to the provisions of this Act, an action for the annulment of a marriage may only be commenced by one of the parties to that marriage, and this provision shall apply even where such party is, under any provision of law, incapable of suing or being sued, and in any such case the action may be commenced by such party notwithstanding such incapacity, saving any assistance or other condition the court may deem appropriate to order. Where an action has been commenced by a party to a marriage, the action may be continued by any of the heirs."

62 Article 19A:
"(1) A valid marriage may be annulled at the request of one of the spouses on the grounds that the other party has refused to consummate the same.
(2) The provisions of article 19(2) shall apply to an action for the annulment of a marriage referred to in sub-article (1) as it applies to an action for the annulment of a marriage therein referred to.
(3) An action for the annulment of a marriage under this article may not be instituted before the lapse of three months from the date of the celebration of the marriage."

The 1995 amendments also brought about recognition of canonical annulment by the civil courts so that according to Article 25:

> "A decree given by the Roman Pontiff 'super matrimonio rato et non consummato', when one of the spouses is domiciled in or is a citizen of Malta, shall, subject to the provisions of article 26, be recognised and, upon its registration in accordance with the said article 26, shall have effect as if it were a decision given by a court and which has become *res judicata*, annulling a marriage on the grounds of non-consummation, in accordance with article 19A."

Furthermore, administrative steps were introduced to enable the registration of an annulment obtained before the Ecclesiastical Tribunal by its presentation in the Civil Marriage Registry following a decree of the Court of Appeal relating to its enforceability. It is restricted to persons who can prove their domicile in Malta or Maltese nationality.[63]

The law actually prohibits the Court of Appeal from entering into the merits of the case and makes it a requisite for the judicial authority to ascertain which court was first seized of a petition for annulment. In this way, a party who is anxious to have a case heard before the Ecclesiastical Tribunal can pre-empt the other party by filing proceedings before the chosen court, or vice versa. The raison d'être of this provision seems to have been the elimination of dual proceedings with accompanying financial, psychological and logistical strain for the parties. It also aims at relieving the burden of additional cases from already overburdened civil courts. The final effect seems to veer towards giving primacy to the Catholic Church in matters of annulment procedures.[64]

---

63 Article 26:

"(1) Registration of a decree as is referred to in article 25 shall be effected by the Court of Appeal.

(2) A request for such registration shall be made by application accompanied by an authentic copy of the pontifical decree filed in the registry of the said court, and which shall be served on the Director of the Public Registry and where it is presented by one only of the spouses, on the other spouse.

(3) The respondents shall have a right to file a reply within twelve working days of service upon them of the application.

(4) (a) Registration shall be effected by an order of the Court of Appeal declaring the decree of the Roman Pontiff enforceable in Malta.

(b) The Court of Appeal shall register the decree if it is satisfied that it refers to a catholic marriage which was celebrated after the coming into force of this article and either of the spouses is domiciled in or is a citizen of Malta.

(5) Notwithstanding the provisions of sub-article (4) hereof, the Court of Appeal shall give a decree which refers to a catholic marriage celebrated before the coming into force of this article where the application therefore is filed by both spouses, or where it is filed by one only of the spouses, the other spouse does not oppose the registration."

64 Article 28:

"(1) In the course of an application under articles 24 and 26 the Court of Appeal shall not go into the merits of the case leading to the decision or the decree the registration of which

Having said this, the law then enters this proviso:

> "Article 35: Without prejudice to articles 21 to 31, Canon Law shall, in so far as it had effect as part of the law of Malta on marriage, cease to have such effect, and all jurisdiction in relation to marriage shall vest in the courts of Malta in accordance with the relevant provisions of the Code of Organization and Civil Procedure."

It is also pertinent, however, to point out that the influence of the Catholic religion in relation to the annulment of marriage was further affected by formal agreements entered into between the State of Malta and the Holy See. In 1993, the Republic of Malta entered into an agreement with the Holy See,

> "granting civil recognition to canonical marriages and decisions delivered by Ecclesiastical Authorities and Tribunals regarding these marriages. An additional Protocol giving recognition also to Negative decisions delivered by the same Ecclesiastical Authorities and Tribunals was also signed on the 3rd February 1993 and a Bill amending the 1975 Marriage Act passed through all the stages of Parliament on the 31st January 1995. The Agreement was then ratified by the Holy See and the Republic of Malta on the 25th March 1995, and the Marriage Act as amended became law on the 15th May 1995."[65]

---

is demanded in the application but shall limit itself to ascertain if the requirements of this Act for the registration requested exist.

In the case of a conflict between the two jurisdictions the 1995 amendments clarify that a petition whereby a case for the declaration of nullity of a catholic marriage celebrated after the coming into force of this article, is initiated before such Tribunal, the Chancellor of the Tribunal or his substitute shall deliver a certificate of such acceptance, duly authenticated, to the Registrar of Courts who shall keep the same in an appropriate register.

(2) Upon the registration as is referred to in sub-article (1), the court shall cease to be competent to deal with the matter; and where an action is pending before the court for the declaration of nullity of a marriage in relation to which a certificate has been delivered to the Registrar in accordance with sub-article (1), the court shall suspend the hearing of the case before it, and may not resume hearing the case and, in any case, shall not again be competent until the said case has, in accordance with the procedures of the Tribunal, been withdrawn from before the Tribunal or been declared abandoned.

(3) It shall be the duty of the Registrar to bring to the notice of the court any certificate which refers to that case, delivered to him in accordance with sub-article (1), as well as any decision relative thereto, registered in terms of article 24.

(4) There an action for the declaration of nullity of a catholic marriage is brought before a court, the court shall ascertain its competence in terms of this Act."

65 FORUM n. 1, vol. 6, 1995.

Text of Agreement:

"The Holy See and the Republic of Malta,

- considering, on the part of the Holy See, Catholic doctrine on marriage, as also expressed in the Code of Canon Law, as well as the teaching of the Second Vatican Ecumenical Council on relations between the Church and the State, and, on the part of the Republic of Malta, the principles enforced by the Constitution of Malta;
- wanting to ensure, in line with fundamental human rights and the values of the family based on marriage, a free choice in matters of marriage; have recognized that it is opportune to reach an agreement on the recognition of civil effects to canonical marriages and to the decisions of the ecclesiastical Authorities and tribunals about the same marriages."

4.3. DIVORCE

Malta remains the only country in Europe[66] not to have a divorce law and one of the countries which has not introduced any regulation of cohabitation, whether of heterosexual or homosexual couples, or civil partnerships. The only acknowledged couple relationship exists in marriage and therefore the term "spouses" can only be understood in the context of the Marriage Act[67] as a man and a woman who are married to one another in terms of civil law.

Prior to 1975, the Maltese Courts categorically refused to recognise foreign divorces on the ground of public policy. Following the enactment of the Marriage Act in 1975, foreign divorces are recognised, provided they conform to the requirements established under the Marriage Act. Article 21 provides that the decision of a foreign court on the status of a married person, or affecting such status, shall be recognised for all purposes of law in Malta if the

---

Article 3:
"The Republic of Malta recognizes for all civil effects, in terms of this Agreement, the judgments of nullity and the decrees of ratification of nullity of marriage given by the ecclesiastical tribunals and which have become executive."
Article 5:
"The judgments of nullity and the decrees of ratification of nullity of marriage given by the ecclesiastical tribunals are recognized as producing civil effects, provided that:
a) a request is presented, by the parties or either of them, to the Court of Appeal together with an authentic copy of the judgment or decree, as well as a declaration of its executivity according to canon law issued by the tribunal that has given the executive decision;
b) the Court of Appeal ascertains that:
   (i) the ecclesiastical tribunal was competent to judge the case of nullity of the marriage insofar as the marriage was celebrated according to the canonical form of the Catholic Church or with a dispensation therefrom;
   (ii) during the canonical judicial proceedings there was assured to the parties the right of action and defense, in a manner substantially not dissimilar to the principles of the Constitution of Malta;
   (iii) in the case of a marriage celebrated in Malta after the 11 August 1975, there has been delivered or transmitted to the Public Registry the act of marriage laid down by the civil law;
   (iv) there does not exist a contrary judgment pronounced by the civil tribunals and which has become res judicata, based on the same grounds of nullity.
The Protocol of application sets out:
With reference to article 1,2:
For the purpose of putting into effect article 1,2 the following are understood to be impediments considered mandatory or not dispensable by the civil law:
a) the lack of age, which is sixteen years completed for both parties;
b) the infirmity of mind of at least one of the parties which renders it incapable of contracting marriage;
c) consanguinity in the direct line and up to the second degree in the collateral line;
d) the subsistence of a previous marriage, valid in civil law, of at least one of the parties."

66 The other countries without divorce are Andorra and The Vatican City, which both have a religious "leader" as head of State, and the Philippines.

67 Laws of Malta, Chapter 255.

decision is given by a competent court of the country in which either of the parties to the proceedings is domiciled or of which either of such parties is a citizen.[68]

The first months of 2011[69] saw renewed debate on the introduction of divorce with members from both sides of the House of Representatives having disparate views. The Prime Minister declared himself against divorce, while the Leader of the Opposition expressed himself in favour. Both parties declared that they would give a free vote to their members, although internal discussions at party level make this "freedom" questionable. There were two movements for and against the introduction of divorce: Iva Ghaz-Zwieg, Iva Ghad-Divorzju (Yes to Marriage, Yes to Divorce) in favour of the introduction of divorce legislation and Zwieg Bla Divorzju (Marriage without Divorce) against. Following agreement to put the matter to a national referendum, a series of marathon debates in Parliament were held to determine the wording of the question to be put to the vote.[70] On 16 March 2011 the debate was concluded and a referendum was held on 28 May 2011 when the electorate decided in favour of the introduction of divorce.[71]

The Roman Catholic Church also entered into the argument with the Archbishop of Malta cautioning against the weakening of family values and the responsibility

---

68 Article 21:
"(1) A marriage celebrated in Malta after the coming into force of this article, in accordance with the norms and formalities established by Canon Law shall as from the moment of its celebration, be recognised and have the same civil effects as a marriage celebrated in accordance with the norms and formalities of this Act."
(2) The provisions of sub-article (1) shall apply only where:
(a) the banns required by this Act have been either published or dispensed with in accordance with articles 7 to 10 and the Registrar has issued a certificate attesting such publication or dispensation;
(b) the parish priest who in accordance with Canon Law has jurisdiction in the place where the marriage was celebrated transmits to the Director of the Public Registry an act of marriage in the form as may be prescribed duly signed by such authority as is provided for in the Agreement; and
(c) no impediment to the marriage as is referred to in articles 3, 4, 5 and 6, subsists. So however that the competent organs of the Catholic Church may for the purpose of catholic marriages under this Act grant authorisations or dispense from the restrictions in article 3(2) and article 5(1)(*c*) and (*d*).
(3) The certificate referred to in sub-article (2)(*a*) hereof shall constitute definite and conclusive proof of its contents."

69 As at 1 February 2011.

70 The question read: "Do you agree with having the option of having divorce for married couples who have been separated for four years when there is no reasonable hope for reconciliation and when adequate maintenance is guaranteed and the children are cared for." A majority voted Yes. The next step will be the introduction of legislation to be debated in Parliament.

71 *Sunday Times of Malta* 29 May 2011: "52.67 per cent of the 230,518 valid votes cast were for divorce."

of the Parliament to uphold the common good.[72] The Bishop of Gozo went so far as to liken those who supported the entry of divorce to "wolves in sheep's clothing"[73] and the clergy presented a fragmented position with some expressing sympathy for the faithful struggling with their conscience[74] and others declaring a vote in favour of divorce a sin.[75] The clear majority vote in favour of the introduction of divorce has undermined the authority of the Church and, although it is early days, public sentiment seems to be increasingly veering towards more distance between Church and State.

4.4. COHABITATION

Recognition of heterosexual cohabitation is an issue both for persons with no intention of marriage, but more so, for a number of the population who cannot marry post-separation.[76] Legislation to regulate cohabitation has been mentioned in various pre-electoral manifestos over the years and, while no direct legislation has been introduced, a number of measures in the social sector have been taken

72 The Archbishop of Malta 3 April 2011: "The whole question is about choosing what we prefer: the difficulties of the present situation, which would result eventually in an increased incidence on marriages today and for future generations, or to consolidate and protect this value. Countries that have introduced divorce are now perhaps reflecting that this kind of reasoning on (*sic*) favour of the 'common good' would have been an act of love for those who are seeing their marriages break down, or for the great number of children suffering from an increased number of marriage breakdowns" (http://maltadiocese.org/lang/en/marriage-and-familyzwieg-u-familja/the-archbishop-on-the-divorce-question and *Times of Malta* 17 April 2011: "Any legal measure that threatens the permanency of marriage is an action that goes against the common good, according to Gozo Bishop Mario Grech. A society that really wants to promote the common good cannot neglect the ethical responsibilities of protecting the family that hinges on marriage.").

73 *Times of Malta* 17 May 2011.

74 *Times of Malta* 14 October 2010: Theologian Fr Charlò Camilleri: "If research showed divorce was beneficial for the common good mentioned also in the Catechism, a Catholic politician can, according to his conscience, vote in favour of divorce" and Fr Joe Borg: "I think it could be morally legitimate for Catholic politicians to decide in conscience to vote for a law introducing divorce if they judge that within a particular circumstance it's a lesser evil."

75 *The Times* 14 October 2010: Judicial Vicar Mgr Arthur Said Pullicino: "Whoever cooperates in any way in the introduction of divorce, even those who apply the law, would be breaking God's law and so would be committing a grave sin" and *The Times* 13 August 2010: "A convinced Catholic who voted in favour of divorce would be going against Christ's teachings and this was a sin, the Curia's Pro-Vicar said during an interview on church radio RTK" and *Malta Today* 8 May 2011: "The Malta Independent on Sunday reports today that a number of people were denied the absolution of sins in Lija and Birkirkara. One individual said they were told that a vote for divorce goes against the teachings of the Church, and that the intention alone of voting 'yes' is already a sin in itself."

76 According to the 2005 census, 62.8% of the population is married, 29.3% are single, 5.9% are widowed and not remarried and just 1.4% are separated. However it has been questioned whether a proportion of the self-proclaimed 'single' people are in fact cohabiting and choose not to admit to this because of financial implications (such as cuts in social assistance allocation). Data from the Central Office of Statistics, 2008: www.nso.gov.mt.

to address the position of cohabiting couples, particularly where there are children of the relationship. With regard to same-sex partnerships, the Malta Gay Rights Movement has unsuccessfully been lobbying for the recognition of same-sex partnerships and in the present climate, the introduction of such legislation does not seem imminent.[77]

Although the law makes no explicit reference to cohabitation, the courts have consistently interpreted the right to respect for family life in the context of including cohabitees, particularly where there are children. For instance, under the regulations to the Refugees Act, protection is extended to spouses or unmarried partners in a stable relationship.[78] State policy as to allocation of housing is provided for under the allocation of housing units which must include persons with children (even if unmarried). Following the enactment of Act XI of 2009, an amendment has been made to the Criminal Code so that criminal sanctions against those who fail to pay maintenance are not restricted to spouses but may be extended to any person bound by law to pay such maintenance.[79]

5. THE INFLUENCE OF THE CATHOLIC CHURCH IN MALTA TODAY

The Catholic Church continues to exercise substantial influence on public opinion, policy, and indirectly on the law itself although the recent loss of the

77 A current focus in the courts is directed towards the right of a person post gender reassignment surgery to marry. Act XVIII.2006 amended the law so as to permit automatic recognition of status on sex change but the Registrar of Marriages contends that this does not include transsexuals. Notwithstanding the European Court of Human Rights judgment in *Goodwin v UK*, ECtHR judgment of 11 July 2002, application no. 28957/9, a recent case (*Joanne Cassar v Director of Public Registry, supra* note 49) has been affirmed in the Constitutional Court but the Attorney General has given notice of appeal.

78 Laws of Malta Chapter 420, Refugees Act, Temporary Protection for Displaced Persons (Minimum Standards) Regulations, 2005:

"(1) For the purposes of this regulation, in cases wherefamilies already existed in the country of origin and were separated due to circumstances surrounding the mass influx, the following persons shall be considered to be part of a family:

(a) the spouse of the sponsor or his or her unmarried partner in a stable relationship, *in so far as Maltese legislation or practice in force treats unmarried couples in a way comparable to married couples under Maltese law relating to aliens*; the minor unmarried children of the sponsor or of his or her spouse, without distinction as to whether they were born in or out of wedlock or adopted;".

79 Laws of Malta, Chapter 9, Criminal Code Article 338(*z*):

"... when so ordered by a court or so bound by contract fails to give to a person the sum fixed by that court or laid down in the contract as maintenance for that person, within fifteen days from the day on which, according to such order or contract, such sum should be paid."

referendum on divorce is a significant blow.[80] It runs a radio station and a weekly newspaper. Half the population still go to Mass on Sunday and practically the whole population follows the liturgical calendar of the Catholic Church on a weekly and annual basis, with a number of religious feasts declared public holidays.[81] Approximately 25 per cent of school children attend one of the 60 schools run by the Catholic Church.[82]

A number of provisions listed under regulations to family legislation rely heavily on service delivery by Church institutions. For instance, provision of child care, residential care for the disabled and domestic violence support would be seriously affected were the Church to stop giving its services. The Church in Malta has a long history of philanthropic service towards the vulnerable, including children, victims of domestic violence, refugees and asylum seekers, and the elderly.

A number of orphanages were built, administered and managed by religious congregations who responded to the social needs of the country at specific periods in time. These have decreased over the years, following dwindling numbers of vocations and changing social requirements, but continue to make a significant contribution. The Church also set up a number of homes to provide for the needs of the elderly who can no longer be cared for by their family or who have no family. The Church was also in the forefront to render support to victims of domestic violence, setting up the first shelter, and has developed services providing additional support in conjunction with State agencies.

Refugees and asylum seekers are also protected and supported by Church institutions, which take on their care and advocacy and provide assistance to reuniting families. The Church has a number of hostels for young people who have no family to care for them, while transitioning to adulthood, and also makes provision for the homeless. It provides residential homes for the care of disabled persons who cannot remain in their home environment, including day care and respite care, as well as rehabilitation programmes for substance abusers, support for unmarried mothers and a number of services in preparation for marriage, in support on widowhood, separation, childlessness and the loss of a child. The most recent venture is to strengthen the assistance to families by providing day care for children whose parents require support. Throughout its service, the

80 *Times of Malta* 31 May 2011: "The Church has to carry out a soul-searching exercise to understand why people voted for divorce, the Church's Pro-Vicar Mgr Anton Gouder, has told *The Times* … Mgr Gouder admitted that he was surprised by the margin of the Yes victory … He said more Maltese were distancing themselves from the Church's moral teachings while at the same time feeling they may remain Catholics."

81 Eight public holidays per annum observe religious feast days.

82 It may also be relevant to note that the Church owns the third biggest bank in Malta, the APS Bank.

Catholic Church in Malta has consistently striven to impart values of solidarity and an ethic of care, replicated in the Roman law tradition of the Civil Code which still requires maintenance to the extended family as a matter of right.[83]

The brief review of court judgments also reveals that judicial interpretation, while at times in keeping with the tenets of the Catholic faith, is increasingly bringing about changes in the application of the law and in the application of policy which no longer necessarily reflect the terms of the Roman Catholic Church. This may be the result of a number of factors but certainly owes a debt to the impact of judgments of the European Court of Human Rights and their observance in Maltese law.

The Roman Catholic religion has had a significant effect on family law in Malta and, I would argue, continues to do so, although to a decreasing extent, mainly because its policies in promoting a family model are still protected and endorsed by a substantial representation of Maltese society. The Diocesan Synod published a document on Marriage and the Family, identifying the family as a special area of concern,[84] and the Church continues to promote solidarity and support structures to assist the family according to its values. Although practising Roman Catholics of Maltese nationality may be slowly dwindling, and while increasing numbers of persons from other, both Christian and non-Christian, faiths continue to visit Malta, the impact of Roman Catholicism on policy and law retains significance.[85]

83 Laws of Malta, Chapter 16, Civil Code, Articles 7–25. Although enforcement of these Articles has dwindled and is increasingly replaced by recourse to the Welfare State structures in place.

84 Arcidjocesi ta' Malta, Zwieg u Familja, 2003, available on line (in Maltese) at www.maltachurch.org.mt/Dokument%Sinodu/ZwiegUFamilja.pdf.

85 This influence is apparent in the current debate following the divorce referendum where members of both sides of the House of Representatives have expressed their dilemma in choosing whether to respect the will of the electorate or follow their own conscience formed according to the Roman Catholic faith. *Times of Malta* 1 June 2011: "Labour MP Marie-Louise Coleiro Preca said today that after assuring herself that the Divorce Bill will be approved in Parliament, she would abstain from the vote … Another MP who had spoken against divorce, Carmelo Abela, said on Monday he would respect the will of the people and vote in favour. MP Adrian Vassallo declared before the referendum result that whatever the outcome, he would vote against." And the Chairman of the Social Affairs Committee MP Edwin Vassallo said "the referendum result had to be expected. It had been a test on religious belief. The choice was a moral one. The result showed that Christian values did not seem to be as popular as in the past … The divorce debate had started in Parliament with a free vote to MPs but now the argument shifted in a yes vote or an abstention on the Bill. While accepting that to abstain was a right, Mr Vassallo argued that parliamentarians should not do so because the issue was a question of faith. He encouraged MPs to vote according to their conscience. He said he was not embarrassed to form part of a minority on the divorce issue because it was a matter of faith and he would not mind losing his electoral seat because of this."

JEWISH FAMILY LAW AND SECULAR LEGAL ORDERS: THE EXAMPLE OF *GET* REFUSAL

Matthijs De Blois

1. INTRODUCTION

The Canadian couple Stephanie Brenda Bruker and Jessel (Jason) Benjamin Marcovitz got married in 1969. Their marriage broke down and a civil divorce was granted in 1981. Both spouses belonged to the orthodox Jewish community in Canada. The provisional decision on the divorce, the *decree nisi,* ordered the parties to comply with a previously negotiated "*Consent to Corollary Relief*" which included arrangements with respect to the custody of their children and financial support. They had also agreed to appear before a rabbinical tribunal, a *Beth Din,* in order to obtain a *get*, which is a religious bill of divorce, immediately after the granting of the *decree nisi.* To be valid the *get* should be provided by the husband voluntarily. Without a *get* the religious marriage is not dissolved and as a consequence the wife cannot remarry under religious law. The husband, Marcovitz, refused to provide the *get* for 15 years. After nine years, the wife, Bruker, started civil proceedings for breach of contract by Marcovitz. Eventually, in 1995, Marcovitz appeared before the *Bet Din* to give the *get*. Bruker continued the proceedings to receive the payment of damages, which were awarded after long proceedings ending in the Supreme Court of Canada. This case, to which we will return later, is illustrative of a collision between two law systems: the venerable Jewish law, with a history of several thousands of years and the very modern secular law of Canada.

Not only in Canada but in many other countries there appears to be a tension between the Jewish religious law and the secular law of the state in this field. It can be imagined that the coexistence of religious and secular law may lead to tensions. This becomes all the more clear when not only the origin of the law – God-given or man-made – is mutually exclusive but also the content may be diametrically opposed. The hierarchical idea of family relations collides with the egalitarian equality principle. Next to that we should realise that religious law, as well as secular law, may have a multi-faceted character. We are sometimes confronted with different interpretations, as to the precise meaning of its concepts. For many modern states and religious communities the question is how to cope with the tensions between the religious law of a specific community and the secular law of the state. In this connection the perspective of human rights is a rather obvious one. It shows, however, not an unequivocal direction. It is evident that a community may invoke the freedom of religion. But is that also a guarantee against interferences by state law motivated by other rights, such as the right to equal treatment?

Legislators and judges in different states, all adhering to the rule of law and the protection of human rights, are approaching the relationship between religious law and secular law in diverse ways.

The purpose of this contribution is first to analyse the Jewish law of divorce and more specifically the issue of *get* refusal.[1] Next to that we will discuss the various approaches to this issue in legal systems. It is worthwhile to start with the special case of the incorporation of the Jewish law on marriage and divorce as such in the legal system of Israel. Next to that we discuss examples of secular legislation on divorce, which include provisions to cope with the problem of *get*-refusal. A third category consists of examples of ways and means developed by courts to address this problem. Some courts appear to be inclined to take the religious law into account when deciding in a conflict on the *get* refusal; other courts prefer to ignore the religious law, while stressing their own exclusively secular role. Finally some evaluative reflections on the relationship between religious law and secular law and on the relevance of human rights in this respect will be undertaken.

2. JEWISH LAW

Jewish law is religious law, more specifically God-given or theonomous. That follows directly from the description of the revelation of the *Torah* on Mount Sinai as described in the book of Exodus: "And God spoke all these words…".[2] The law is binding *ipso facto,* independent of the consent of the governed. It may be a living instrument, but is not subject to adaptation, to changing opinions or practices among those who are bound by it. It is in that sense unchangeable, although it has to be interpreted by the members of the religious community or more specifically by those endowed with the task of interpreting the law. As far

1 See also my "Religious law versus secular law. The example of *get* refusal in Dutch, English and Israeli law" (2010), *Utrecht Law Review,* Vol. 6, Issue 2 (June).

2 Exodus 20:1. Translation from The Koren Jerusalem Bible (2008).

as the content of the law is concerned, religious law tends to stress *inter alia* communal values and submission to authority within hierarchical structures. It should also be underlined that in religious law there is no "public" and "private" distinction, which is so common to an Enlightenment approach to the law. It is not even possible to separate the relationship between God and man from relationships among men themselves. Violation of our obligations to other persons implies a violation of God's law and has therefore its effect on the relationship with God. The religious is not a separate sphere next to the secular. There is no secular sphere. This is especially true for Judaism, which, in Asher Maoz's words "encompasses all aspects of society and of an individual's life".[3]

Jewish law (*Halakha*) is based on the *Torah*, the first five books of the Bible (in Greek: Genesis, Exodus, Leviticus, Deuteronomy), given to the people of Israel by God at Mount Sinai. It is, in the most literal sense, God-given law, although transmitted through mediation of Moses. In the Jewish tradition this is called the *written Torah*. It includes 613 commandments (*mitzvoth*). The written Torah is accompanied by the *oral Torah*, based on the oral tradition as from Moses, which was codified in the second century (Common Era) as the *Mishnah*. It explains the written Torah and is itself commented upon in the *Talmud* written in the 5th (Jerusalem) and 6th (Babylon) centuries. On this foundation, the Jewish or Talmudic legal tradition has been developed ever since up to our times.[4]

2.1. JEWISH LAW ON MARRIAGE AND DIVORCE

Marriage is a central concern of both ethical doctrines and legal rules within the Bible and the Talmud.[5]

In Jewish law, marriage is seen not as an ordinary contract, but as a covenant with a holy character, in principle to be honoured until the death of one of the parties.[6] It is regarded as "the most important and sacred of all domestic relations" and as a "divine institution".[7] In the conclusion of a Jewish marriage

3 MAOZ, A., "Can Judaism Serve as a Source of Human Rights?", *ZaöRV (Zeitschrift für ausländisches öffentliches Recht und Völkerrecht)* 64 (2004), pp. 677–721, at p. 678.

4 See for a general overview: GLENN, H.P., *Legal Traditions of the World* (Oxford University Press, 2004), pp. 92–124. See further, AL, J.C., *Overzicht van het Joodse Huwelijks- en Echtscheidingsrecht* (Wolf Legal Productions, 2002) and VESTDIJK-VAN DER HOEVEN, A.C.M., *Religieus recht en minderheden* (Gouda Quint, 1991), pp. 127–161.

5 MIELZINER, B., *The Jewish Law Of Marriage And Divorce In Ancient And Modern Times* (Bloch publishing and printing company, 1884), Reprint Bibliolife, p. 13.

6 NOVAK, D., "Jewish Marriage and Civil Law: A Two Way Street?" in LAQUER ESTEIN, A., *The Multicultural Family* (Ashgate Publishing Group, 2008), pp. 209–228 at pp. 213–214. See also MIELZINER, *ibid. passim*.

7 MIELZINER, *supra* note 5, pp. 13 and 15.

two separate legal acts can be distinguished. In the first place an agreement, the *kiddushin* or betrothal (symbolised by the exchange of rings) and, secondly, the *nisu'in*, leading the bride under the *chuppah* (wedding canopy). They are performed in the presence of two witnesses.[8]

While the ethical ideal of the Torah is against the dissolution of marriage, Jewish law, taking into consideration the circumstances of life, knows the possibility of divorce.[9] This is based on Deuteronomy (*Dewarim*) 24:1:

> "When a man has taken a wife, and married her, and it come to pass that she find no favour in his eyes, because he has found some unseemliness in her: then let him write her a bill of divorce, and give it in her hand and send her out of his house."[10]

The divorce document, the *sepher kerithoth,* is referred to in the *Talmud* as *get,* which is now a common expression. The text quoted endows the husband with discretionary power to divorce from his wife by giving her a *get.*

This discretionary power is restricted in the *Torah,*[11] the *Mishnah,* the *Talmud* and in later rabbinical ordinances, both as to the substance of the law (grounds for divorce) and concerning the procedure. Later developments have introduced the requirement of the approval of the wife for the divorce (Rabbenu Gershom, 11th century), except in certain specific cases.[12] It is also assumed that the husband may sometimes be obliged to divorce: his wife may ask a rabbinical court (*Beth Din*) to order her husband to divorce. Some important reasons are the lack of material support, the refusal of sexual intercourse or frequent instances of adultery.[13] The *get* should be given voluntarily in order to be valid.[14] Otherwise it is a *get me'useh,* a coerced get, which is void.[15] However, it is assumed that in some cases a husband may be compelled by a rabbinical court, depending on the grounds for the divorce. It has to be added that there are controversies among the experts as to which grounds qualify for the use of compulsory measures. Coercion to provoke an action that should be voluntary, is defended by the assumption that every Jew wants to submit to religious law

8 See AL, *supra* note 4, pp. 39–42.

9 MIELZINER, *supra* note 5, pp. 15–19 and 115–129.

10 Translation from The Koren Jerusalem Bible (2008).

11 Compare Deuteronomy 22:13–19 and 28–29. See, for the tradition followed in the New Testament, Matthew 19: 3–9.

12 MIELZINER, *supra* note 5, p. 120.

13 *Ibid.*, pp. 123–124; AL, *supra* note 4, pp. 146–154 and WOLF, D.A., "Het joodse echtscheidingsrecht in Nederland en de New York Get laws', *Familie- en Jeugdrecht* 1995–8, pp. 178–183 at p. 178.

14 WOLF, *ibid.*, pp. 178–179.

15 See *inter alia* ZORNBERG, L., "Beyond the Constitution: is the New York Get legislation Good Law?" (1995), *Pace Law Review* Vol. 15, pp. 703–784, at p. 709.

and that each refusal to do so is the consequence of his free will having been temporarily affected by bad inclinations. The coercion restores the free exercise of the will.[16] The procedure is nowadays that the spouses appear before a rabbinical court, where the husband gives the *get*, prepared by a specially appointed writer, to his wife, who accepts it. That act constitutes the divorce. A rabbinical court is required because, according to Jewish law, only a Jewish religious court is competent to decide on issues of religious law. Decisions of secular courts applying religious law are therefore not acceptable. It is, however, not excluded that secular courts are used to enforce the decisions of religious courts.[17]

2.2. THE PROBLEMS OF *GET* REFUSAL

We have seen that, in general, divorce under Jewish law is dependent on the will of both parties. The husband should deliver the *get* and the wife should accept it. If either of them refuses, the marriage cannot be dissolved. Also, only in exceptional cases, the *Beth Din* may interfere either to force the husband to give the *get* or to grant the divorce, notwithstanding the wife's refusal to accept it.[18] It is appropriate to add here that many assume that, at least in our days, frequently the refusal to grant or to accept a *get* is motivated by other than religious concerns. It is sometimes used as a means to put pressure on the other party to agree to less favourable arrangements in, for example, the financial field.[19] Therefore, the *get* refusal is also seen as a problem in the circles of the experts of religious laws. They have perused the sources of the tradition to cope with this problem.

If the husband refuses to give the *get* to his wife, she cannot remarry according to Jewish law because, in religious terms, she remains married to her husband. She becomes an *agunah*, a "chained wife". If she enters into a new relationship, she commits adultery. The children born from this new relationship are regarded as *mamzerim*, a term referring to those born of incest or adultery.[20] This entails social stigma as well as restrictions under Jewish law as to marriage. According to Jewish law, they may only marry other *mamzerim*.[21] As we have seen, the wife's approval is also required for a divorce. However, if she refuses the

16 See for this reasoning from Maimonides (1135–1204), AL, *supra* note 4, p. 155; WOLF, *supra* note 13, p. 179 and ZORNBERG, *ibid.*, pp. 709–710.

17 NOVAK, *supra* note 6, p. 217 and WOLF, *supra* note 13, p. 179.

18 MIELZINER, *supra* note 5, pp. 120–121.

19 See FREEMAN, M., "Is the Jewish *Get* any Business of the State?" in O'DAIR, R. and LEWIS, A. (eds.), *Law and Religion* (Oxford University Press, 2001), pp. 365–383 at p. 380.

20 MIELZINER, *supra* note 5, p. 43.

21 *Ibid.*, pp. 43–44.

consequences for her husband are less serious. Remarriage is not completely excluded, and the children born from a new relationship are not regarded as *mamzerim*.[22]

Not infrequently, interested parties have invoked secular law to solve the problems created by the *get* refusal. That, of course, brings the relationship between religious law and secular law to the fore. There are a wide variety of approaches to this problem in Western legal orders which share the principles of religious freedom, equality and the rule of law. We will start with the specific case of Israel.

3. LEGISLATIVE INCORPORATION: ISRAEL; RELIGIOUS LAW AS LAW OF THE STATE

3.1. GENERAL

Israel, both a Jewish and a democratic state,[23] is not a theocracy in the Biblical sense. Its legal system shows influences of several legal traditions, reflecting its complex history. For the greater part Israeli law has a secular character. Religious law plays a role in a limited field.[24] Several aspects of family law are governed by religious law, while religious courts have jurisdiction in these matters. In these fields Israel recognises legal pluralism, not unlike the situation under the Ottoman Empire and during the Mandate period before 1948 (the *Millet*-system). The pluralism concerns both the substantive law to be applied and the courts which have jurisdiction to apply the law. Different religious communities have their own religious law and their own courts. In that connection Israel recognises 14 religious communities: Jewish, Muslim, Druze and Christian (various denominations).[25] The members of their religious courts are appointed by the President of Israel. There are variations as to the jurisdiction of these courts. Jewish rabbinical courts have exclusive jurisdiction in matters of marriage and divorce for Jews. As to other aspects of the law of personal status and family law the jurisdiction of religious courts and state courts is concurrent. In these cases religious law may only be applied with the consent of the (adult) parties. State (family) courts have jurisdiction in areas that are not exclusively within the jurisdiction of religious courts. To make the situation even more complex it has

---

22 FREEMAN, *supra* note 19, p. 371.

23 See its Declaration of Independence of 14 May 1948 and Basic Law: Human Dignity and Liberty of 17 March 1992.

24 See, e.g., SINCLAIR, D., "Jewish Law in the State of Israel" in HECHT, N.S. *et al.*, *An Introduction to the History and Sources of Jewish Law* (Clarendon Press, 1996), pp. 397–419.

25 SEZGIN, Y., *A New Theory of Legal Pluralism: The Case of Israeli Religious Courts*, Association for Israel Studies, 19th Annual Meeting, 27–29 April 2003, San Diego, CA.

to be underlined that religious courts are to a certain extent subject to (secular) Israeli law, while state courts may have to apply religious law in questions of personal status, family law and inheritance law.

3.2. THE LAW OF MARRIAGE AND DIVORCE

This area of family law is governed by the religious law of the parties. Therefore their religious affiliation is decisive for the law applicable. Recently the Israeli Parliament, the Knesset, adopted a Civil Union Bill, which provides for the possibility of civil marriage in case both parties have no legal affiliation with a recognised religion.[26] It is assumed that the effect of this legislation will be limited. It is not applicable in cases of religious intermarriage or where one of the parties has a recognised religious affiliation. Israelis without a religious affiliation (or a religious affiliation not recognised for the purposes of family law) traditionally have the possibility to conclude their marriage elsewhere (e.g. in Cyprus). Such a marriage is recognised under Israeli law.

The law concerning Jewish marriage is determined by the Rabbinical Courts Jurisdiction (Marriage and Divorce) Law 1953. It holds that:

> "(1) Matters of marriage and divorce of Jews who are Israeli citizens or residents will be under the exclusive jurisdiction of the rabbinical courts.
> (2) Marriage and divorce of Jews will be carried out in Israel according to the law of the Torah."

What the Torah entails in the field of marriage and divorce has already been summarised above. It is worthwhile to underline in addition that in Israeli legal practice there is an officiating rabbi present at the solemnising of a marriage. He is responsible for registration of the marriage.[27] It is ensured that only orthodox rabbis will conduct marriages.[28] A marriage solemnised by a non-orthodox rabbi is not recognised.

It has to be remarked in this connection that the religious nature of the law of marriage and divorce has led the state of Israel to make a reservation upon ratifying the International Covenant on Civil and Political Rights (ICCPR) with the following text:

---

26 *Haaretz*, 4 November 2010.
27 ROSEN-ZVI, A., "Family and Inheritance Law" in SHAPIRA, A. and DEWITT-ARAR, K.C. (eds.), *Introduction to the Law of Israel* (Kluwer, 1995), pp. 75–109 at p. 88.
28 EDELMAN, M., *Courts, Politics and Culture in Israel* (University Press of Virginia, 1994), p. 61.

> "With reference to Article 23 of the Covenant, and any other provision thereof to which the present reservation may be relevant, matters of personal status are governed in Israel by the religious law of the parties concerned. To the extent that such law is inconsistent with its obligations under the Covenant, Israel reserves the right to apply that law."

Article 23 protects *inter alia* the right to marriage. The formulation of this reservation, which refers next to Article 23 to "any other provision" is interpreted by Margit Cohn to extend also to Article 18 (freedom of religion) and Article 26 (Prohibition of discrimination).[29]

When ratifying the Convention on the Elimination of All Forms of Discrimination against Women (CEDAW) Israel made several reservations. The first is in connection with article 7 (b) on the participation of women in the political and public life of a country:

> "The State of Israel hereby expresses its reservation with regard to article 7 (b) of the Convention concerning the appointment of women to serve as judges of religious courts where this is prohibited by the laws of any of the religious communities in Israel. Otherwise, the said article is fully implemented in Israel, in view of the fact that women take a prominent part in all aspects of public life."

The second reservation concerns the prohibition of discrimination against women in the field of family law:

> "The State of Israel hereby expresses its reservation with regard to article 16 of the Convention, insofar as the laws of personal status binding on the several religious communities in Israel do not conform with the provisions of that article."

3.3. THE ISRAELI APPROACH TO THE *GET* PROBLEM

As we have seen under Jewish law, it is impossible for a court to decree a divorce. It is up to the husband to provide his wife with a *get*. It has been accepted that the wife herself may request the court to order the husband to provide one, in cases where there are good reasons to do so. The *get* must not, however, be provided under pressure which has the effect of precluding the free will of the husband. In order to see how courts in Israel have coped with the problem of *get* refusal it is necessary to make a distinction between religious courts and secular courts.

---

[29] COHN, M., "*Women*, Religious law and Religious Courts in Israel – The Jewish case" (2004), *Retfaerd (Scandinavian Journal of Social Sciences)* Vol. 107, pp. 57–76, at p. 67.

So far the rabbinical courts have developed several ways to coerce a husband to grant a *get* in cases where they think he should do so. Similarly they can coerce the wife to accept a *get*. Rabbinical courts are however rather reluctant to impose such sanctions. If they do not, the husband may continue his refusal to provide a *get* or, in the case of a non-cooperative wife, she may persist in the refusal to accept one. It is nevertheless important to specify the several instruments at the disposal of the rabbinical courts to apply degrees of pressure and coercion in the case of *get* refusal.

The first option is that a court *recommends* the parties to divorce. The strength of such a *recommendation decree* is primarily of a moral nature. It assumes that there are reasons for a divorce under Jewish law. The second possibility is that the court issues a decree stating that there is an *obligation* (for the man) to give or (for the woman) to accept the *get*. Noncompliance with this *obligation decree* may lead to the imposition of a larger sum of spousal support for the wife. Next to that, pressure from the community may play a role. This type of decree is not often imposed. The most serious intervention of the court is the order of a *compulsion decree* imposed on a party to give or accept a *get*. Such an order may be accompanied by sanctions such as fines or imprisonment, without consequences for the validity of the *get*. These orders are even rarer than the previous category.[30]

Although divorce as such is exclusively within the jurisdiction of the religious courts, secular courts in Israel also have dealt with issues related to divorce. They have, since 2004, introduced a device to enforce rulings of rabbinical courts on *get* refusal by accepting a tortious liability for *get* refusal. In 2004, the Family Court of Jerusalem awarded damages because it considered a husband to be negligent by not complying with a rabbinical *obligation decree*. It held that,

> "refusal to grant a get constitutes a severe infringement on her [the wife's] ability to lead a normal life, and can be considered emotional abuse lasting several years. (...) [T]his is not another sanction against someone refusing to give a get, intended to speed up the process of granting a get, and this court is not involving itself in any future arrangements for the granting of a get, but rather, it is a direct response to the consequences that stem from not granting a get, and the right of the woman to receive punitive damages."[31]

---

30 BLECHER-PRIGAT, A. and SHMEULI, B., "The Interplay between Tort Law and Religious Family Law: the Israeli Case" (2009) *Arizona Journal of International & Comparative law* Vol. 26, No. 2, pp. 280–301, at pp. 282–283.

31 Quoted by SPALTER, N.D., "Gevangen in het huwelijk" (2007), *Familie- en Jeugdrecht* 29, no. 2, pp. 37–43, at pp. 41–42.

The Family Court in Kfar Sava did the same in 2006. It concerned also an obligation decree. The judge stated in an *obiter dictum* that he would also have awarded the damages in harsh cases that only had led to a *recommendation decree*. This was used in a subsequent case decided by the Tel Aviv Family Court in 2008. The development did not stop there. In the same year the Jerusalem Family Court assumed the principle of liability for negligence irrespective of a decree by a rabbinical court, although there was in that case an obligation decree issued by the High Rabbinical Court. The husband's refusal to give a *get* was regarded as negligent in this case as from the time of one year after the woman started her divorce action.[32]

The question is whether the secular courts have not overplayed their hands by using the means of secular law to induce parties to perform an action governed by religious law. It is in any case clear that the rabbinical courts do not accept the use of tort law to cope with the problem of *get* refusal. On March 11, 2008, the Supreme Rabbinical Court held:

> "All petitions filed outside the rabbinic court – like petitions to civil courts for damages – that relate to *get* refusal, whose practical consequence is to accelerate the delivery of the *get*, are an interference with the laws of the Torah regarding divorce, and effectively preclude the possibility of the execution of a [kosher] *get*..." (J. Algrabli).[33]

Apparently, in the view of the Supreme Rabbinical Court, it is within the exclusive powers of the religious courts to cope with the problem of *get* refusal. The intervention of secular courts in the realm of religious courts has led to a stalemate. It illustrates the clash between religious and secular law and, as a consequence, the unresolved competition between secular and rabbinical courts when it comes to efforts to solve the problem, for the parties concerned, that the *get* refusal creates.

4. THE APPROACH TO THE *GET* PROBLEM IN WESTERN SECULAR JURISDICTIONS

4.1. GENERAL

The legal order of Israel is, as compared to (other) Western states, unique for the integral incorporation of Jewish law in its legislation in the field of family law.

---

32 BLECHER-PRIGAT and SHMEULI, *supra* note 30, pp. 286–287.

33 File 7042-21-1. See WEISS, S., *From religious "Right" to Civil "Wrong": Using Israeli Tort Law to Unravel the Knots of gender, Equality and Jewish Divorce*, www.brandeis.edu/hbi/pubs/SusanWeiss.doc.

Most Western states have, however, a complete, or almost complete, secular family law. I say almost complete because many systems give civil effect to marriages solemnised in a religious context, although many other systems do not (for example Dutch law). An example of integration of religious law as to the conclusion of marriages is the English system which knows both religious and non-religious marriages. The first category is even subdivided into three sub-categories: In the first, there are marriages solemnised in the Church of England, in the second, are so called non-Church of England marriages and, in the third sub-category, both Quaker and Jewish marriages; the latter defined in section 26 of the Marriage Act 1949 as follows: "a marriage between two persons professing the Jewish religion according to the usages of the Jews". Also, in for example the United States, civil marriages may be solemnised in religious communities, in front of an officiating religious functionary. On the other hand, there are many Western countries where only a marriage solemnised by a state official has effect in civil law. It is up to the parties themselves if they afterwards will enter a religious marriage as well or if they want to receive a blessing in a religious service. While marriages may be solemnised according to religious rites, divorce is now – in England as well as in other Western countries – exclusively a matter for the civil courts.

Many Western countries do have communities that live in accordance with their own religious law, *inter alia* Jewish communities. As in Israel, they have to cope with the problem of *get* refusal. They are facing the question whether the law should, in one way or the other, address this problem, in order to accommodate their Jewish citizens who will otherwise be affected by the consequences in religious law of the failure of one of the parties to cooperate in the religious divorce proceedings. Without any pretension to completeness we will try to give an impression of the great diversity in approaches in various Western countries: England, the United States, Canada, France, the Netherlands and Germany. A general subdivision can be made in legislative and judicial approaches.

4.2. LEGISLATIVE APPROACHES TO RELIGIOUS DIVORCE LAW

Recently the legislation on divorce of some countries has taken religious law into account, specifically to cope with the problem of *get*-refusal. We will not give an exhaustive overview, but restrict ourselves to some striking examples.

First of all we see instances of legislation, which makes the granting of a divorce dependent on cooperation in religious divorce proceedings. The State of New York in the US has enacted legislation which, although drafted in neutral terms, was adopted primarily in respect of the *get* problem.[34] Section 253 of the Domestic Relations Laws of New York State provides that a claimant can only obtain a divorce if he or she has done everything to remove any barrier to the defendant's remarriage after the divorce. It is specified that the concept of barrier includes:

> "any religious or conscientious restraint or inhibition, of which the party ... is aware, that is imposed on a party to a marriage, under the principles held by the clergyman or minister who has solemnized the marriage, by reason of the other party's commission or withholding of any voluntary act."

The legislation is restricted to marriages solemnised in a religious ceremony. In its 1983 version (which was amended slightly in 1984), it only addressed the problem created by a claimant who refuses to be cooperative in obtaining a religious divorce. If the problem is the result of a refusal by the defendant there is no remedy.

In 1990 a similar provision was introduced in the Canadian Divorce Act, in section 21.1, which empowers the court to withhold the granting of a divorce if it has not been made clear that the claimant has removed the barriers to remarriage based on religious law. The Canadian Federal Law differs from its New York equivalent in that it allows the court to refuse to exercise its power in a case where the refusing spouse has genuine grounds of religious or conscientious nature for refusing to remove the barrier (section 21.1(4)(b)).[35] That addition underlines the complexity of the issue and illustrates that, in addition to concerns in the field of equality, privacy and the right to marriage, freedom of conscience and religion is also involved.

More recently a similar legislative approach was taken in England. Where the previous examples of legislation only referred to religious law in general terms, the English law refers explicitly to Jewish law. The Divorce (Religious Marriages) Act 2002 amends the 1973 Matrimonial Causes Act to the extent that the grant of the final decision on the divorce (*decree absolute*) can be made dependent on the cooperation in the procedure that leads to a divorce under religious law. In terms of section 10A of the amended legislation it is applicable where parties:

> "were married in accordance with – (i) the usages of the Jews, or (ii) any other prescribed religious usages; and (b) must co-operate if the marriage is to be dissolved in accordance with those usages. (2) On the application of either party, the court may order that a decree of divorce is not to be made absolute until a declaration made by

34 See for an excellent analysis, ZORNBERG, *supra* note 15.

35 See also KLEEFELD, J.C. and KENNEDY, A., "'A Delicate Necessity': *Bruker v Marcovitz* and the Problem of Jewish Divorce" (2008), 24 *Canadian Journal of Family Law*, pp. 206–282.

both parties that they have taken such steps as are required to dissolve the marriage in accordance with those usages is produced to the court."

The Act implies that a relevant religious authority confirms the compliance with the religious usages concerned.[36] That may be a rabbinical court of the various Jewish 'denominations': Orthodox, Masorti (Conservative) or Reform, as well as the Rabbinic Board of the Union of Liberal and Progressive Synagogues. It should however be realised that only a *get* granted under the auspices of an Orthodox *Beth Din* is recognised universally.[37] Finally, the court *may* suspend the *decree absolute* in case of *get* refusal, but it is not obliged to do so. It has discretionary powers. It will also be possible for the English judge to take into account religious concerns similar to those included in the Canadian legislation. The Act received support from representatives of the various branches of the Jewish community, among them the British Chief Rabbi, Dr Jonathan Sacks and the presidents of the most important religious courts.[38] The other examples given so far of legislative interventions have also been welcomed by experts on Jewish law and representatives of the Jewish community.[39] These solutions apparently do not create problems from the perspective of religious law. While there is of course an incentive for the refusing spouse to cooperate in the divorce proceedings, there seems to be no improper coercion. The legislation does not interfere with the freedom of the husband to grant or not to grant a *get*. He is not obliged to do so. The only consequence is that there will not be a civil divorce.[40]

Next to the legislation that makes the civil divorce conditional on cooperation in the religious divorce there are other legislative approaches that have met more opposition from the side of the experts in Jewish law. An example is the legislation adopted in 1992 in New York to adapt the Domestic Relations Laws in order to cope with the limitations of the previous amendment of this Law in 1983 already discussed. The 1992 law introduced section 236B(5)(h) and (6)(d), which concerns the equitable distribution of marital assets and alimony after the dissolution of marriage. It is provided that, in taking decisions in this field, the court shall, where appropriate, consider the effect of a barrier to remarriage as defined in the 1983 legislation. This provision is applicable to both the claimant

36 This follows from Rule 3 of The Family Proceedings (Amendment) Rules 2003. See on this FAITH, S. and LEVINE, D., "Religious Divorce" (2003), *Family Law Journal* (May), pp. 11–14 at pp. 13–14.

37 LEVINE, D. and FAITH, S., "Divorce, religion and the law", *Family Law Journal*, December 2002/January 2003, pp. 18–20.

38 See Divorce (Religious Marriages) Bill. House of Lords debates, 10 May 2002, www.theyworkfor you.com/lords/?id=2002-05-10a.1401.3, p. 3.

39 ZORNBERG, *supra* note 15, p. 749; see also the majority opinion in the case of *Bruker v Markovitz*, Supreme Court of Canada, 14 December 2001. http://scc.lexum.unmontreal.ca/en/2007/2007scc54/2007scc54.html.

40 WOLF, *supra* note 13, pp. 180–181.

and the defendant and to both religious and non-religious marriages. This second piece of legislation has been criticised because the procurement of a *get,* due to the financial pressure resulting from the legislation, would amount to a nullification of the free will of the husband.[41] That would make the *get* involuntary and as a consequence void. Of course there are also other voices.[42] The disagreement on this issue will lead to insecurity as to position of the spouses and their children in religious law.

4.3. JUDICIAL APPROACHES

In global terms, the legislative adaptations to cope with the problem of *get* refusal are exceptional. We find more examples of the various ways courts have addressed the problem of *get* refusal. The examples from different legal systems display a great variety of approaches. There are examples of decisions where courts without specific legislation used their judicial powers to make the granting of a civil divorce dependent on cooperation in the religious divorce proceedings. In other cases, the refusal to provide or accept the *get* has been approached as a breach of contractual obligation. Next to that, *get* refusal is accepted as a tortious act, as is the case in Israeli law, as we have seen. In these contract and tort cases, the question arises as to which remedies may be imposed: specific performance, *astreinte* or damages. Finally, there are instances where national courts simply reject the possibility of a remedy for the failure to cooperate in the religious divorce procedure. Their argument is that they, as secular courts, may not impose the performance of religious duties.

4.3.1. Civil divorce proceedings

In English law, before the amendment of the Matrimonial Causes Act 1973 by the Divorce (Religious Marriages) Act 2002, courts used the application of the civil law on divorce to address the problem of *get* refusal in various ways. Courts tried to find ways and means to make the refusing spouse cooperate in the religious divorce. In the case of *Brett v Brett,* where a husband refused the *get* as a weapon in the struggle with his wife on her maintenance demands, the Court of Appeal increased the sum payable as a strong incentive for the former husband to grant a *get.*[43] Another judgment concerned the consent required for a divorce after two years of separation. In that case the wife had made her consent subject to the grant of a *get*; this was approved by the court.[44] A third approach was

41 ZORNBERG, *supra* note 15, p. 757.
42 *Ibid.*, pp. 758–759.
43 Court of Appeal, *Brett v Brett* [1969] 1 All ER 1007.
44 *Beales v Beales* [1972] 2 All ER 667.

followed in a decision of the Watford County Court. It refused to grant a *decree absolute* (the final decision on the divorce) in a case where the husband refused to give a *get*.[45] Michael Freeman, commenting on this decision, assumed that it would be seen, in terms of Jewish law, as unjustified coercion resulting in the *get* being invalid.[46] This can be doubted, however, having regard to the high degree of acceptance also from the side of orthodox experts on Jewish law of the amendment of the Matrimonial Causes Act in 2002, which basically accepts the direction chosen by the County Court.

4.3.2. Breach of contract

There is a rather old French judgment which qualified the refusal to deliver a *get* as a breach of contract.[47] The reasoning is that, once you enter into a religious marriage in accordance with Jewish law, you accept at the same time the obligation to comply with the rules for the dissolution of the marriage in Jewish law. It is very doubtful whether this reasoning is taking sufficiently seriously the, in principle, voluntary nature of the deliverance of the *get*. It has in any case not been followed by more recent French case law.

Some American courts have derived an obligation to cooperate in the dissolution of the religious marriage from the *ketubah*; the religious marriage contract entered into before solemnisation of the marriage.[48] In that contract there is a reference to "the law of Moses and Israel" and the idea is that this reference to Jewish law implies cooperation in the divorce proceedings prescribed by that law. A very clear example is the judgment of the New Jersey Superior Court of July 22, 1981 in the case of *Minkin v Minkin*. The Court held that:

> "The parties were married in a Jewish ceremony where they entered into a contract, called a 'ketuba' in which they agreed to conform to the provisions of the laws of Moses and Israel. These laws require the husband to give his wife a get when he alleges an act of adultery on his wife's part. In the instant case the husband counterclaimed for divorce on the ground of adultery, giving rise to the wife's claim to require her husband to secure a get."[49]

45 Judge Viljoen of the Watford County Court, *O v O* (Jurisdiction: Jewish Divorce) [2000] 2 FLR 147, referred to by FREEMAN, *supra* note 19, p. 373.

46 FREEMAN, *ibid.*, p. 373.

47 Tribunal civil de Metz, 27 April 1955, referred to by RENUCCI, F., "Les solutions aux conflits en matière de divorce religieux du XIXe siecle a nos jours. Le cas de refus de deliverance du *gueth* en droit interne" in DAUCHY, S. *et al.*, *La résolution des conflits*, Le Centre d'Historique Judiciaire, Lille, September 2008, pp. 152–161, at p. 153.

48 MIELZINER, *supra* note 5, pp. 85–89.

49 Http://nj.findacase.com/research/wrfmDocViewer.aspx/xq.fac.%5CNJ%5CNJ2%5C198.

Subsequently the Court examined the claim of the husband that such an order would violate the Establishment of Religion Clause of the First Amendment. That was, according to the Court, not the case, while the specific performance of the obligation to provide a *get* simply required the defendant to do what he had agreed voluntarily to do. Basing its decision on the testimony of several rabbis, the Court held that the acquisition of a *get* is not a religious act: it did not require participation in a religious ceremony nor action contrary to religious beliefs. Especially in America, it has become a practice to add a clause to the traditional *ketubah* including the obligation of the parties to appear before a *Beth Din* and accept its orders when it comes to abiding by the standards of Jewish law, including in the case of a dissolution of marriage. This device was developed in the circles of Conservative Jewish community and met initially with opposition from the Orthodox side. However, in 1993, the orthodox Rabbinical Council of America advised couples to sign such a prenuptial agreement.[50]

The contractual approach is of course also likely where parties, in the framework of their civil divorce proceedings, have accepted an obligation to appear before a *Beth Din* in order to provide or accept a *get*. An example of this is the Canadian case of *Bruker v Markovitz*, already referred to in the introduction.[51] In this case the parties agreed to a Consent of Corollary Relief to settle their matrimonial disputes, including the obligation to appear before the rabbinical authorities to obtain a *get*, immediately after the granting of the *decree nisi* (the provisional decision on the divorce). As we have already noted, the husband refused and the wife started (after nine years) proceedings claiming damages. Eventually, after 15 years, the husband appeared before the rabbinical Court at Montreal to deliver the *get*. The court of first instance awarded a considerable amount of damages This decision was quashed by the Quebec Court of Appeal, holding that a religious obligation could not be enforced by a secular court. The Supreme Court of Canada, in its turn, allowed the appeal in a majority judgment and found that in such cases damages should be awarded. Madam Justice Abella, who gave reasons for the majority, held:

> "I do not see the religious aspect of the obligation in Paragraph 12 of the Consent as a barrier to its civil validity. It is true that a party cannot be compelled to execute a moral duty, but there is nothing in the *Civil Code* preventing someone from transforming his or her moral obligations into legally valid and binding ones."[52]

---

50 See ZORNBERG, *supra* note 34, pp. 767–768.

51 Supreme Court of Canada 14 December 2007 http://scc.lexum.unmontreal.ca/en/2007/2007scc54/2007scc54.html. The majority opinion was written by Abella J.

52 *Ibid.* at para. 51.

A minority of two Justices in the court, however, agreed with the Court of Appeal.[53]

4.3.3. *Tort*

In several countries we find judgments qualifying the refusal to deliver a *get* as a tort. This is the common approach in French law.[54] The *délit* or *quasi-délit*, sometimes appears in the shape of an abuse of right (*abus de droit)*: the husband abused his right under religious law to withhold the *get*. To prove such an abuse, an intention to harm has to be established. The judgments have sometimes been enforced by the imposition of partly conditional damages: the defendant has to pay an amount, which would be reduced considerably if he delivered the *get*. The use of an *astreinte* (a judicially imposed penalty) to enforce the judgment, of which we find examples in decisions of lower courts, was ruled out by the *Cour de Cassation* in 1982.[55] It held that deliverance of a *get* falls within the scope of freedom of conscience. Therefore, the use of the *astreinte,* as a means of enforcement, was apparently excluded. This decision was confirmed in a later decision.[56] This approach seems to be in line with Jewish law which excludes in principle a forced *get*. It may be doubted whether that is also the case with the acceptance by the *Cour de cassation* of the imposition of an obligation to pay damages.

In Dutch civil law, which traditionally has been close to the French system, we find a similar approach. The judgment of January 22, 1982 of the Dutch *Hoge Raad* (Supreme Court) is looked upon as the leading authority on the issue of *get* refusal.[57] In a divorce request a woman *inter alia* claimed that her husband should be ordered by the court to cooperate in a procedure before a rabbinical court in order to procure a divorce, in accordance with Jewish law. The District Court, in its decision of 4 December 1979, declared this claim to be inadmissible. It observed that, according to Article 1:30 of the then Civil Code, marriage should only be considered in its civil aspects. The court could therefore not decide on the consequences of the divorce which have a religious nature. The Court of Appeal at Amsterdam upheld, on 4 March 1981, the decision of the court of first instance. It observed in an *obiter dictum* on the question at issue

53 See for a discussion of this case, CARTER, T.S. and MIX-ROSS, D.B., "Supreme Court of Canada Decision Permits Judicial Interference in Religious Disputes", *Church Law Bulletin* No. 21, 20 December 2007 (revised 8 January 2008); KLEEFELD and KENNEDY, *supra* note 35 and DE BLOIS, M., "Respect of neutraliteit? Over de omgang met religieus recht in een seculiere staat" in DOORNBOS, N., HULS, N. and VAN ROSSUM, W., *Rechtspraak van buiten* (Kluwer, 2010), pp. 237–242.

54 See RENUCCI, *supra* note 47.

55 Cour de cassation (chambre civile), 21 April 1982, *GP*, 1983, p. 590.

56 Cour de cassation, 21 November 1990, No. 89-17.659.

57 HR 22 January 1982, *NJ* 1982, 489, annotated by WHH.

that, having regard to a letter of the Supreme Rabbinate of Utrecht, it had no means to force the husband to procure a *get*. According to the Court of Appeal, it is unacceptable to assume that a civil court possesses powers in the field of a religious marriage that are lacking to the religious court concerned. The claimant submitted a cassation request against this judgment before the Supreme Court. This court chose a completely different approach. On the point at issue, it observed that the fact that the Supreme Rabbinate had no powers to force the husband to procure a *get*, did not exclude the possibility that such a refusal may be qualified as an unlawful act. It could be a violation of a rule of unwritten law pertaining to proper social conduct vis-à-vis his divorced wife. If that is the case, the Dutch court can order him to cooperate. Whether the refusal of a *get* is unlawful has to be determined, having regard to special features of the case concerned. The court mentioned, in that connection, the extent to which the wife is restricted in the free development of her life, the nature and seriousness of the objections of the man against cooperation in the procedure and the costs involved, having regard to the financial position of the parties and the preparedness of the woman to pay the costs. In other words, the Supreme Court tried to reduce the problem to a balancing of interests within the framework of the law on unlawful conduct (tort). The Supreme Court referred the case to the Court of Appeal at The Hague, which condemned the man to cooperate under threat of a judicially imposed penalty ('*dwangsom*'), in other words, an *astreinte*. The *Hoge Raad* apparently did not share the scruples of the *Cour de cassation* with respect to this remedy. The judgment has also been criticised in other respects. First of all, the Supreme Court did not, unlike the District Court and the Court of Appeal, respect the principle of Jewish law that is opposed to the application of this law by a non-Jewish court.[58] An expert in the field of Jewish law also remarked that the compliance of the man, with the order of the court to procure a *get* under the threat of the penalty imposed, will result in a forced *get (get me'useh')* which, according to Jewish law. is invalid. Therefore the *Beth Din* will not cooperate.[59]

The judgment of the Supreme Court has been followed in several decisions of district courts and a court of appeal.[60] In these cases, the courts referred to a letter of the Supreme Rabbinate, from which they inferred that it was prepared to cooperate in the divorce procedure based on an order of the civil court. Wolf underlines, in this connection, that in these cases the husbands could be coerced to cooperate also according to Jewish law. As we have seen, that is not always the case. It should be observed that the Supreme Court rather easily overstepped the requirements of Jewish divorce law in order to reach a result that was considered

58 See VAN DER PLAS, C.G., *De taak van de rechter en het IPR* (Kluwer, 2005), p. 161.

59 WOLF, *supra* note 13, pp. 178–183.

60 See Gerechtshof (Court of Appeal) Amsterdam, 31 August 1989, *NJ* 679.

to be in conformity with Dutch tort law. The Supreme Court's decision of 1982 has not always been followed, as is illustrated by a judgment of 28 May 1986 of the District Court of Middelburg.[61] It opted for a slightly different approach, maybe inspired by the criticism of the Supreme Court's ruling. It held that the refusal of a *get*, to which the (former) wife was entitled according to Jewish law, and which restricted her in her options in life, might lead to the conclusion that the (former) husband acted unlawfully. The court continued by stating that it was not competent to judge on this issue, apparently considering this to be within the competence of the religious courts. That was, however, not the end of it, because the court held that the refusal of the (former) husband to cooperate in a procedure before a rabbinical court was unlawful, having regard to the weighty interest of the wife. Her claim to order her (former) husband to cooperate in the religious divorce proceedings was granted.[62] In other words, the court made a subtle distinction between the provision of the *get* as such and the participation in the procedure which possibly could result in the provision of the *get*. This is a more cautious approach, which acknowledges both the value of religious law and the competence of the religious courts, while at the same time recognising the plight of the woman.

4.3.4. *Rejection of the claim*

There are also examples of courts which have rejected claims to force, by any means, a recalcitrant party to cooperate in the religious divorce procedure. In an old case from Pennsylvania, a court refused to impose an obligation to deliver a *get* because "civil tribunals are certainly without authority to order one to follow the practices of his faith".[63]

German courts have a long tradition of rejecting such claims on similar grounds. In 1904, the German *Reichsgericht* declared impossible the enforcement of agreements to cooperate in the religious divorce, having regard to the separation of Church and State. It held:

> "We must dismiss the Appellate Court's idea that the declarations and the acts prescribed by the Jewish religion for the ritual divorce are 'by and large or 'predominately' or even 'exclusively' of a legal nature. From that fact it immediately

---

61 There is no formal rule of binding precedent in Dutch law.

62 Rechtbank (District Court) Middelburg 28 May 1986, *Nederlands Internationaal Privaatrecht* (*NIPR*) 1986, nr. 413.

63 16 District and County Reports 290 (Pa. County Ct. 1932, quoted by Leo PFEFFER and Alan PFEFFER, "The Aguhnah in American Secular Law", *Journal of Church and State* 31 [1989], p. 487–525, at p. 496.

follows that the execution of such acts by way of coercion is not within the reach of the State."[64]

More recently, in 1973, the *Oberlandesgericht* of Cologne took the same approach. It rejected the claim for compulsory measures by a husband, who sought the cooperation of his wife to accept the *get*. The court held that this would mean enforced participation in a religious ceremony, which was held contrary to the freedom of religion.[65]

This approach was basically also behind the minority opinion of the two judges of the Canadian Supreme Court who dissented from the majority decision in the case of *Bruker v Markovitz*. They held: "contract law cannot be relied on to enforce religious undertakings" and stressed the neutrality of the state, which is "indispensable in a pluralistic and multicultural society."[66] The claim of the wife should be rejected. The secular judge should therefore not award damages as a consequence of the refusal to perform an act prescribed by religious law, provided that there was not any barrier to remarriage under the secular law of the state.

5. EVALUATIVE REFLECTIONS

5.1. GENERAL

It is an understatement that the preceding lines show the complexity of the relationship between religious law and secular law in general and of the issue of *get* refusal in particular. First of all, we have discussed the example of the integration of the religious law as such into the legal system – the case of Israel. But, as we have seen, only a limited part of the Israeli family law is religious in nature. Next to that, there exists secular private law relevant to family relations. Therefore, a clash between religious law and secular law could not be evaded, leading to a stalemate.

The legislative adaptations in some Western states, to a certain extent found ways and means to solve in some, but not all, cases the problems of the *get* refusal. There remains a tension between the requirements of religious law as to the validity of a divorce on the one hand and the interest of one of the spouses

64 RG 16 February 1904, *RGZ* 57, 250 at p. 257. Translation in TAGER, E., "The Chained Wife" (1999), *Netherlands Quarterly of Human Rights*, Vol. 17, No. 4, pp. 425–457 at p. 450.

65 See GLENN, H.P., "Where Heavens Meet: The Compelling of Religious Divorces" (1980), *The American Journal of Comparative Law*, Vol. 28, pp. 1–38, at p. 17.

66 See *supra* note 51, paras. 180 and 181 (dissenting opinion of DESCHAMPS, J., joined by CHARRON, J.).

concerned to be divorced in accordance with religious law on the other hand. Not all secular solutions seem to be compatible with the religious law concerned.

Furthermore, the judicial ways of tackling the problem of the get refusal display a spectrum of approaches. They vary from making a secular divorce dependent on complying with the requirements for a religious dissolution of the marriage, to the enforcement of contractual obligation and finally the establishment of tort liability. As we have seen, there are also examples of courts and judges refusing to enforce in any way an obligation which, in their view, is a religious one, referring to the separation of "Church and State". That may preserve the integrity of the religious law, but it is of no avail to parties faced with the reluctance of their partners to comply with religious law.

What we see are efforts to achieve partial solutions to the problem, which seems to be insoluble in a definitive way. That, to begin with, is related to the uneasy cohabitation of religious and secular law.

5.2. RELIGIOUS LAW AND SECULAR LAW

The integration of religious law and secular law appears to be complex. As we have seen, marriage and divorce are not only important concerns of Jewish law, but also of secular law. We can even say that the fact that the marital relationship became a matter of public concern in secular law in Western countries is a direct consequence of the long predominance of religion, more specifically Christianity in the West. On the Continent, until the French Revolution, marriage and divorce remained strongly determined by religious law. This was enforced by the state, by the church or, in the case of the Jews living in several countries, to a certain extent by their own authorities. The Enlightenment, however, inspired the development towards a secularised family law in many countries; although the contents of the law was or is (depending on the degree of secularisation of the society) to a certain extent influenced by religious morality, which is the consequence of the democratic process. It is remarkable that the whole idea of marriage as a legal concern is, in general, not questioned in even the most liberal of states, although its meaning and content is different from the original religious roots.

As a consequence of that, there may be tensions or a clash between the religious law and the secular law on these issues, as exemplified here by the problem of *get* refusal. Such a clash is, as such, not surprising. It is to a certain extent even inevitable.[67] Is there not in principle a fundamental incompatibility between the

67 See COHN, *supra* note 29, p. 68. She uses similar terms.

basic tenets of religious law on the one hand and Enlightenment inspired secular law on the other? Both the source of the law – divine or human – and its contents, are at issue. The principle of equality is crucial in that respect. Religious law, in many cases, while recognising the equal worth of human beings, tends to stress different roles for men and women in the framework of marriage. Against that background, the differences as to the rights of men and women in the Jewish law on divorce can be explained.

It should be added that what has been said applies to the orthodox interpretations of religious law. There are, of course, also more liberal approaches, which are inclined to incorporate more or less the values that dominate the secular law in the countries discussed. Often there are strong tensions within the religious communities and debates between factions of the same religions as to the correct interpretation of the divine prescriptions. The fact that some versions of religious law may be in conformity with the prevailing notions of equality does not, however, solve the problem of the clash with the orthodoxy, which sticks to the traditional approach. The only solution would be to impose on a religious community a specific interpretation of its sacred texts. But that will be at odds with other principles, such as religious freedom.

Human rights…

That brings me to a second reflection on the relevance of human rights. It is frequently submitted that the problem of the *get* refusal should be solved by application of human rights law, which almost by definition is presumed to prevail over conflicting religious or secular law.[68] The problem is that "human rights" does not refer to a fixed body of law; an unambiguous set of norms, with an unequivocal meaning. On the contrary: its meaning is floating and often controversial. Divergent and often competing approaches of human rights as such may also lead to different views as to the degree of acceptability of religious law.

… in favour of the recognition of religious law

There are strong human rights arguments for the prevalence of religious law, in the issue of *get* refusal, over secular law and, in that connection, for a reticent approach where the issue becomes controversial in terms of religious law (think of the financial "penalties" in the case of *get* refusal).

We should remember that traditionally human rights had strong religious connotations. Sometimes human rights are even seen as originating from religious sources. The central notion of human dignity is seen as the translation

68 See for example RADAY, F., "Culture, Religion and Gender", 1 *I.Con*, (2003), pp. 663–715, at p. 668.

of the biblical idea that man is created in the image of God, as stated in Genesis 1: 26–27: "And God said: 'Let us make Mankind in our image after our likeness ... So God created Mankind in his own image, in the image of God created he him; male and female he created them."[69] Already the biblical context makes clear that this approach to human dignity points in the direction of equal dignity of men and women, in terms of respect for them as human beings, but does not exclude different roles of the spouses in family law, as follows from the basic text on divorce in Deuteronomy discussed above.

This approach may lead in principle to a positive evaluation of the role of religious law, in general, and in the field of family law, in particular. The Jewish law on the issue of marriage and divorce, based on *Torah* and *Talmud*, has been developed over the centuries and its precise contents have been debated on this basis ever since. It plays an important role within the religious community and is accepted by its observant members as the law that should be followed. It is obvious that its enforcement should be entrusted to courts that are themselves not only versed in the law but also, from an internal perspective, convinced of its divine character. That is the case with the religious courts. Of course there is the issue of dissent within religious communities, as well as diverging views on the proper interpretation of the sources concerned. Also within religious communities, a more egalitarian interpretation of human dignity is defended.[70] Respect for religious law requires that these issues should in principle be solved within the community itself, by the authorities concerned. Secular authorities who want to intervene in favour of or against one of the opposing groups, will inevitably have to make a choice between diverging religious views. Should that not be in general outside the realm of the secular state? In addition, it should be noted that the membership of religious communities is not compulsory. It always remains possible to quit the religious community concerned.

Respect for religious law can be based on freedom of religion, if we take for granted that this freedom not only protects the right to have and to express a belief, but also the right to live in accordance with its tenets. That is especially relevant for religions which stress the unity of life, in the sense that acts of worship *per se* and obedience to religious rules are both indispensible parts of the manifestation of a religion. That is *inter alia* true for Judaism, as is illustrated by the words of Freiman: "Jewish religion and law are a single entity. The *Torah* makes no dogmatic distinction between religious teachings and legal

69 Translation from The Koren Jerusalem Bible (2008). See further MAOZ, *supra* note 3, pp. 691–692.

70 See *inter alia*, MAGID, S., "Is egalitarianism heresy? Rethinking gender on the margins of Judaism", *NASHIM: A Journal of Jewish Women's Studies and Gender Issues*, 2004, pp. 189–229 and LONGMAN, C., "Waar een rabbijnse wil is, is er een halachhische weg?", *RoSa. Uitgelezen*, Vol. 10, No. 4, 2004, pp. 1–9.

provisions."[71] It is important to realise this when interpreting the relevant human rights provisions, such as Article 9 of the European Convention of Human Rights (ECHR), which encompasses the protection of the manifestation of one's religion or belief in worship, teaching, practice and observance.[72] The precise scope of freedom of religion, as to activities motivated by one's religion or belief, is under debate.[73] That is also true for the more specific question of whether the application of religious law is protected by freedom of religion. There is a rather old decision of the (then existing) European Commission of Human Rights (6 December 1983) in which it held that a refusal of a Jewish husband to hand over the *get* was not to be recognised as a manifestation of his religion in observance. Therefore the Commission did not have to answer the question whether the decision of the French court in question, to order the refusing husband to pay damages, was justified by the second paragraph of Article 9.[74] The question may be asked whether this isolated admissibility decision still has to be regarded as the authoritative ruling on this issue. In a more recent judgment, the European Court of Human Rights accepted the observance of Jewish law in another field as a manifestation of a religion by observance, in terms of Article 9; namely in the case of *Cha'are Shalom ve Tsedek*, which concerned ritual slaughter according to Jewish law.[75] It should be noted that the case for religious law, as protected by freedom of religion, does not show the way to an easy solution of the problem of *get* refusal. Both the husband who refuses to deliver the *get* and the wife who needs the *get* in order to enter into a new religious marriage, have a claim to the application of religious law under freedom of religion.[76]

In addition to the individual aspect, freedom of religion has a collective aspect, which protects the rights of a religious group to uphold its religious principles. That is also illustrated by the *Cha'are Shalom ve Tsedek* case, which originated in an application not from an individual, but from a religious association. The Court held that "a religious body may, as such, exercise on behalf of its adherents the rights guaranteed by Article 9".[77] In this connection, Article 6 of the Declaration on the Elimination of All Forms of Intolerance and of Discrimination Based on Religion or Belief (1981) is also relevant. It includes in religious liberty, the freedom to establish and maintain charitable or humanitarian institutions,

71 Quoted by MAOZ, *supra* note 3, p. 678 (emphasis in the original).
72 Article 18 ICCPR uses similar terms.
73 See DE BLOIS, M., "Two Cities in Conflict" in LOENEN, M.L.P. and GOLDSCHMIDT, J.E. (eds.), *Religious Pluralism and Human Rights in Europe: Where to Draw the Line?* (Intersentia, 2007), pp. 167–183, at pp. 172–174.
74 Application 10180/82, *D v France*, *Decisions and Reports* 35, February 1984, p. 199.
75 ECHR 27 June 2000, *Jewish Liturgical Association Cha 'are Shalom ve Tsedek v France*, ECHR 2000-VII, paras. 73 and 74.
76 Compare the case of *Bruker v Markovitz*, *supra* note 51.
77 *Supra* note 75, para. 72.

thereby implying the right to provide services in this field based on the principles and tenets of the religion or belief involved. That is an argument for the respect of religious rules within the community concerned. This may also be applied to the recognition of religious law applied within a specific religious group.

In addition to freedom of religion, the rights of minorities should also be mentioned, in connection with states where religious minorities exist.[78] These rights entail the right of members of the minorities to profess and practise their religion with other members of their group. In this framework, the application of religious law is also relevant.

Finally, when it comes to the level of states, which provide for the application of religious law within the broader framework of their national legal system, even the right to self-determination is at stake.[79] This right includes the right of a people to determine its cultural identity. This includes fundamental issues like the relationship between "Church" and State or of secular and religious law in the state concerned. In the case of Israel, the Jewishness of the state is *inter alia* expressed by the fact that part of its law has a religious nature, especially the part we have been discussing. Like any other state it may in principle decide on the contents of its law.

... against the recognition of religious law

It should on the other hand not be overlooked that, from a human rights perspective, the application of religious law may also be very problematic. Is not the whole idea of religious law contrary to human rights? A religiously inspired view of human rights has since the first formulations of human rights been rivalled by a secular one, inspired by the Enlightenment. It appears that this view is now popular in both theory and practice of human rights law. Secularism, far from being a neutral stand towards religion in society, has been defined:

> "as an ideology [that] denotes a negative evaluation towards religion and might even be appropriately seen as a particular 'religious position' in the sense that secularism adopts certain premises *a priori* and canvasses a normative (albeit negative) position about supernaturalism."[80]

---

78 Article 27 ICCPR.

79 Article 1 of both ICCPR and ICESCR.

80 Quotation from WILSON, B., "Secularisation: Religion in the Modern World" in SUTHERLAND, S. and CLARKE, P. (eds.), *The World's Religions, the Study of Religion, Traditional and New Religion* (Routledge, 1991) at p. 196, in BOYLE, K., "Human Rights, Religion and Democracy: The Refah Party Case" (2004), *Essex Human Rights Review*, Vol. 1, No. 1, pp. 1–16, at p. 14.

It has even been submitted that "the fundamental tenets of monotheistic religions are at odds with the basis of human rights doctrine".[81] This secular approach is exemplified by the opinion of the Committee on the Elimination of Discrimination against Women (CEDAW), which gave expression to its strong feelings on the issue of religious law when it condemned, in unequivocal terms, Israel's reservations on Articles 7 and 16 of the Women's Convention. It held:

> "The Committee suggested that in order to guarantee the same rights in marriage and family relations in Israel and to comply fully with the Convention, the Government should complete *the secularization of the relevant legislation*, place it under the jurisdiction of the civil courts and withdraw its reservations to the Convention" (emphasis added).[82]

Religion, especially in its orthodox garbs, is seen as a threat to human rights, especially to the principle of equality.

One gets a similar impression of the approach of the Human Rights Committee (HRCttee), which held that the secular emancipatory ideal prevails over a religious interpretation of human rights: "Article 18 [ICCPR: freedom of religion] may not be relied upon to justify discrimination against women by reference to freedom of thought, conscience and religion."[83] From this it can be concluded that, in the opinion of the Committee, the prohibition of discrimination against women prevails over freedom of religion. That is of course only the case if we assume that this freedom protects the right to apply religious law, which does not comply with the secular equality principle.

In conclusion, the CEDAW and HRCttee tend towards a conclusion that international human rights law is opposed to religious law, especially when its requirements may interfere with the equal rights of women. These general remarks lead us to a brief discussion of specific human rights at issue.

To begin with, it is held that the Jewish law on *get* refusal is contrary to freedom of religion and conscience. At first sight, that is the case where the refusal of a *get* is a blockade for the spouse to remarry under Jewish law. There is, however, a paradoxical element in this reasoning. The recognition of a religious rule is criticised in order to be able to benefit from the application of other religious

---

81 RADAY, *supra* note 68, at p. 668.

82 Report of the Committee on the Elimination of Discrimination against Women 16–17 Sessions, 1997, at p. 91. See also HALPERIN-KADDARI, R., "Women, Religion and Multiculturalism in Israel" in LAQUER ESTEIN, A., *The Multicultural Family* (Ashgate Publishing Group, 2008), pp. 267–294, at p. 274.

83 Human Rights Committee, General Comment No. 28 Equality between men and women (Article 3) UN Doc. CCPR/C/21/Rev.1/Add.10 (2000), para. 21.

rules. It illustrates that there might be a friction between convictions of individual believers and the tenets upheld by other believers, or the representatives of the religious community, due to different interpretations of the sacred texts concerned.

In addition to that, the rights of (former) spouses, related to marriage and divorce, are protected as human rights in, for example, Article 12 ECHR, Article 23 ICCPR and Article 16 CEDAW. These treaty provisions all stress the equal rights of men and women in the field of marriage and divorce.[84] Where religious law interferes with the fundamental right to equal treatment, the latter should prevail according to several international supervisory organs in the field of human rights, as we have seen above. Finally, the right to family life and the rights of children may be relevant, in cases where their position is an issue: think of *mamzerin*. Article 2 of the Convention of the Rights of the Child provides that states parties have to ensure that children are not subjected to discrimination *inter alia* based on birth or other status.

Finally

The preceding reflections on the human rights aspects of the application of religious law in a secular state do not provide for an easy "solution" to the problems that result from the coexistence of the two spheres of law, as is illustrated by the problem of the *get* refusal. It was not my purpose to provide such a solution, but rather to explain the complexity of the issue. This complexity cannot be reduced by an easy reference to human rights law, having regard to the sometimes strongly diverging views on the meaning of human rights. What has been said may hopefully contribute to a critical reconsideration of the easiness of the common, human rights approach to the problems of collision between religious and secular law. The preference for secular law over religious law is the outcome of an interpretation of human rights law from a secularist perspective; which by no means is the only perspective possible. Perhaps that may inspire national courts and international supervisory bodies with some modesty, when it comes to the judgment of cases where religious law and secular law collide, as in the difficult case of *get* refusal.

---

84 See *inter alia* TAGER, *supra* note 64, pp. 425–457.

PRAYERS IN THE PLAYGROUND: RELIGION AND EDUCATION IN THE UNITED KINGDOM AND BEYOND

Frankie McCarthy

1. INTRODUCTION

The debate in the United Kingdom over the appropriate role for religion to play within the education system has generated many newspaper column inches over the past decade or longer.[1] Faith schools,[2] despite unequivocal support from successive Prime Ministers,[3] have been the subject of attack from high profile critics who consider them antiquated and divisive.[4] The impact of the religious lobby on curriculum content such as sex education has attracted comment,[5] and the prescriptions of religious dress have been at the centre of fierce disputes for both pupils[6] and teachers.[7] Unlike European neighbours such as France and Spain, the UK has never embraced a secular system of education. It might be said that religion is built into British schools from the foundations, with the earliest schools established by the Christian churches and teaching carried out by the clergy. When Irish immigrants flocked to the west coasts of Scotland and England in the mid-1800s, the Roman Catholic communities often built schools

1 A collection of recent news reports on the topic can be accessed here: www.guardian.co.uk/education/faithschools.

2 In the legislation, faith schools are referred to as "schools of a religious character" in England and "denominational schools" in Scotland.

3 For example, Tony Blair's interview on the BBC's *Newsnight* in 2002, transcribed here: http://news.bbc.co.uk/1/hi/programmes/newsnight/1988874.stm and "David Cameron calls for more faith schools," Daily Telegraph, 26 January 2010, available at www.telegraph.co.uk/education/educationnews/7073322/David-Cameron-calls-for-more-faith-schools.html.

4 A recent high profile example can be found in the documentary "Faith School Menace" by Richard Dawkins: www.channel4.com/programmes/faith-school-menace/episode-guide/series-1/episode-1.

5 "Faith schools free to preach against homosexuality", *The Guardian* 28 April 2009, available at www.guardian.co.uk/education/2009/apr/28/sex-education-faith-state-schools.

6 *R (on the application of Begum) v Denbigh High School* [2007] 1 AC 100.

7 *Azmi v Kirklees MBC* [2007] ICR 1154.

before they built churches.[8] The oldest universities in the United Kingdom, at Oxford and Cambridge, have long religious histories.[9] In a country which may now consider itself to be largely secular,[10] the religious roots of the education system continue to hold firm.

The rapid development of the law of human rights in the UK, and Europe more generally, has allowed for an examination of the intersections between religion and education to take place within a new framework. In this essay, the rights to freedom of religion and to provision of education will be considered in concert with domestic equalities legislation to offer an overview of actual and potential points of conflict in the current discourse. In addition to examining the position of faith schools, the interplay between religion and the curriculum, and the difficulties of recognising the right to religious dress in schools, the chapter will touch on the potential future conflict between parents and children which may arise through the increasing recognition of children's rights.

The examination of the case law will attempt to demonstrate a broader uncertainty around the appropriate role for religion in the modern educational context. The recent jurisprudence of the European Court of Human Rights at Strasbourg, which has traditionally allowed states a wide margin of appreciation in interfering with the right to religious belief, suggests a move towards more stringent control over religious influence in the classroom, with a focus on the state's positive duty of neutrality. This restrictive approach to religion may not sit entirely comfortably with recent UK equalities legislation, which has placed religious belief on a footing with race and sex, amongst other things, as a "protected characteristic" benefitting from anti-discrimination provisions. The interaction between the various political and legislative objectives of a government which seeks to support children of all faiths and none within a diverse, multi-faith society, when added to the complexities caused by courts at various levels considering similar problems from different legal angles, creates a picture of overall confusion about the "correct" approach to religion in schools and universities today. The text will consider some reasons for these underlying tensions and offer some thoughts on potential solutions.

---

8 A detailed history can be found in HANDLEY, J.E., *The Irish in Modern Scotland* (Cork University Press, 1947).

9 See www.ox.ac.uk/about_the_university/introducing_oxford/a_brief_history_of_the_university/index.html and www.cam.ac.uk/univ/history/records.html.

10 "UK among most secular nations", *BBC News*, 26 February 2004, available at: http://news.bbc.co.uk/1/hi/programmes/wtwtgod/3518375.stm.

2. THE LEGAL FRAMEWORK

2.1. HUMAN RIGHTS

The human rights obligations imposed on the United Kingdom by the European Convention on Human Rights ("ECHR") and the United Nations Convention on the Rights of the Child ("UNCRC") have been an important influence on current education legislation, and also form the basis of many of the legal challenges which have arisen in this area. Three rights emerge as critical to the discussion: the right to education, the right to freedom of thought, conscience and belief, and the prohibition on discrimination.

The right to education is set out in article two of the First Protocol ("P1–2") to the ECHR, which reads:

> "No person shall be denied the right to education. In the exercise of any functions which it assumes in relation to education and to teaching, the State shall respect the right of parents to ensure such education and teaching in conformity with their own religious and philosophical convictions."

This right was ratified by the UK, subject to the reservation that it would be adhered to only insofar as compatible with the provision of efficient instruction and training, and the avoidance of unreasonable expenditure. It is worth noting that this right is held by *parents* in respect of their children, rather than by the children themselves. However, articles 28 and 29 of the UNCRC set out detailed provision as to the nature and goals of the education to which children are recognised to be entitled. Children also have a right to express their views in all matters affecting them, following article 12 of the UNCRC, and their schooling would inevitably fall within this category.

Freedom of thought, conscience and religion is protected for both children and adults by article 9 of the ECHR, although children enjoy a further right with similar wording provided by article 14 of the UNCRC. In each case, although the right to *hold* such beliefs is absolute, the freedom to *manifest* those beliefs is qualified, and may be compromised where necessary to *inter alia* maintain public safety or protect the rights and freedoms of others. As will be discussed further below, it is the right to education itself which can sometimes give rise to a qualification of the right to manifest religious beliefs in relation to, for example, the sex education content of the curriculum.

The right to freedom from discrimination is contained within article 14 of the ECHR and article 2 of the UNCRC. In both cases, religion is specifically mentioned as a prohibited ground of discrimination, although neither article sets out a closed list, allowing for discrimination on the basis of "any other status" to be taken into account. The protections offered by these two articles are parasitic in the sense that they protect only against discrimination in relation to the enforcement of the other rights contained within their respective treaties. For example, an applicant would need to demonstrate that discrimination against them on the basis of their religion had interfered with their right to an education in accordance with their beliefs. Domestic equalities legislation augments this protection, however, as set out below.

It should be recalled that rights under the ECHR have been implemented into UK law through the Human Rights Act 1998[11] (and, in Scotland, the Scotland Act 1998). The UNCRC does not have the same direct effect, and its provisions cannot be founded on to raise court proceedings.

2.2. EDUCATION LAW

England and Scotland have separate systems of education. Responsibility for the former rests with the Westminster Parliament whilst authority for the latter has been devolved to Holyrood.

In outline, the schemes are not dissimilar. The principal obligations in respect of school education in England are set out in successive Education Acts, which place general responsibility for education[12] including provision of schools[13] on the local authority ("LA").[14] In line with P1-2, education must be provided on the basis of the principle that children are to be educated in accordance with their parents' wishes so far as compatible with the provision of efficient instruction and training and the avoidance of unreasonable expenditure.[15] In terms of faith schooling, as that term is used in the course of this discussion, it has been possible to apply for designation as a school of a religious character since the Education Act 1944. Application for this designation is now governed

---

11 The Human Rights Act 1998, s. 13 provides that where a court is asked to determine a question impacting on the exercise by a religious organisation (or its members collectively) of the right to freedom of thought, conscience and religion, it must have particular regard to the importance of that right. This section has played little part in the jurisprudence on religion and education to date.

12 Education Act 1996, s. 13.

13 *Ibid.*, s. 14.

14 LAs acting in this capacity had for some time been known as Local Education Authorities or LEAs, but subsequent to the Local Education Authorities and Children's Services Authorities (Integration of Functions) Order 2010, that title is no longer to be found in the legislation.

15 Education Act 1996, s. 9.

by the School Standards and Framework Act 1998 ("SSFA").[16] Special rules exist for the administration of such schools including the obligation to reserve up to one fifth of teaching posts for staff fit to provide religious instruction in the tenets of the relevant faith[17] and the power to give priority to applicants who are of the faith of the school.[18]

In Scotland, the key piece of legislation is the Education (Scotland) Act 1980,[19] as substantially amended. The local authority, acting as an Education Authority ("EA"), has an obligation to secure adequate and efficient provision of school education within its area.[20] In performance of this obligation, pupils are to be educated in accordance with the wishes of their parents insofar as compatible with the provision of suitable instruction and training and the avoidance of unreasonable public expenditure.[21] The EA has a duty to provide schools,[22] and it is lawful for the Authority to provide denominational schools where representations are made by members of the denomination to the effect that such a school is needed to accommodate their children.[23] The rules as to management of denominational schools are set out in section 21, providing amongst other things that the religious beliefs/character of a teacher must be approved by representatives of the denomination.

Since the introduction of the Standards in Scotland's Schools Act 2000,[24] Scottish children have also held a domestic right to an education on their own behalf, without need for resort to the rights of their parents. This provision has yet to be replicated in England.

2.3. EQUALITIES LEGISLATION

The complicated, piecemeal legislation through which protection from discrimination slowly developed in UK domestic law has now largely been consolidated by the Equality Act 2010 ("EqA"), the majority of which came into force in October 2010. The Act establishes nine protected characteristics,[25]

16 S. 69 and schedule 13, with the detailed procedure set out in the Religious Character of Schools (Designation Procedure) Regulations 1998 (SI 1998/2535).
17 SSFA, ss. 58–60.
18 *Ibid.*, s. 84 and the School Admissions Code (London: TSO, 2010).
19 Hereinafter referred to as the E(S)A.
20 E(S)A, s. 1(1).
21 *Ibid.*, s. 28.
22 *Ibid.*, s. 17(1).
23 *Ibid.*, s. 17(2).
24 S. 1.
25 *Ibid.*, s. 4.

including religion or belief,[26] and sets out prohibited conduct in relation to those characteristics[27] in various specific contexts, including education.[28] Public sector bodies, including LAs and EAs, have been subject for some time to statutory equality duties in relation to race,[29] sex[30] and disability.[31] The 2010 Act creates a single equality duty on public sector bodies in relation to all the protected characteristics,[32] requiring such bodies to have regard to the need to advance equality of opportunity and to foster good relations between persons who share a relevant characteristic and those who do not. This duty is due to be brought into force both north and south of the border in April 2011.

Part 6 of the Act sets out what will be unlawful conduct in the context of schools.[33] A key caveat is that none of the provisions apply to anything done in relation to the content of the curriculum.[34] Amongst other things, schools must not discriminate against or victimise a pupil in the way it provides education for the pupil,[35] by not providing education for the pupil[36] or by subjecting the pupil to any other detriment.[37] Schools must also not harass a pupil.[38]

Denominational schools are subject to special exemptions in relation to discrimination on the grounds of religion or belief.[39] The prohibition on religious discrimination in relation to admissions and provision of education, benefits, facilities and services does not apply, allowing denominational schools to conduct themselves in accordance with the tenets of their faith.

---

26 *Ibid.*, s. 10.

27 *Ibid.*, ss. 13–27. The forms of conduct prohibited are essentially direct discrimination, indirect discrimination, harassment and victimisation.

28 *Ibid.*, ss. 84–99.

29 Race Relations Act 1976, ss. 71, 71A and 71B.

30 Sex Discrimination Act 1975, ss. 76A-C.

31 Disability Discrimination Act 1995, ss. 49A-49D.

32 EqA, s. 149.

33 *Ibid.*, ss. 84–89.

34 *Ibid.*, s. 89(2).

35 *Ibid.*, s. 85(2)(a), s. 85(5)(a).

36 *Ibid.*, s. 85(2)(c), s. 85(5)(c).

37 *Ibid.*, s. 85(2)(f), s. 85(5)(f).

38 *Ibid.*, s. 85(3)(a).

39 *Ibid.*, schedule 11, paras. 5 and 6.

3. FAITH SCHOOLS AND THE PLACE OF SECULAR EDUCATION

3.1. (NON) FAITH SCHOOLS IN THE UK

The stated policy of the governments both at Westminster and Holyrood is to support education for children of all faiths and none.[40] In practice, this means providing state-funded faith schools where the available resources allow. In Scotland, there are currently 389 state-funded denominational schools, 385 of which are Roman Catholic, three Episcopalian and one Jewish.[41] In England, there are almost 7,000 faith schools, all but 58 of which are associated with major Christian denominations. There are also 38 Jewish schools, 11 Muslim schools, four Sikh schools and one school associated with each of the Greek Orthodox, Hindu, Quaker, Seventh Day Adventist and United Reform Church faiths.[42]

Education beyond specifically designated faith schools is not, however, entirely free of religious influence. For the historical reasons explored in the introduction to this essay, education and religion have always been closely connected in the United Kingdom, and the principle of secularism has never found favour in the UK. In England, the local authority has a duty to secure provision of religious education as part of the basic curriculum.[43] The syllabus should reflect the religious tradition of Christianity within the UK,[44] although not all classes need be concerned with Christian faiths and no catechism or formulary should be included in the lessons.[45] State school pupils are also required to take part in a daily act of collective worship,[46] which again should be of a broadly Christian character.[47] Parents have the right to withdraw their children both from religious education and from worship.[48] In Scotland, both the practice of religious observance and religious instruction should be made available,[49] unless a resolution to discontinue this has been passed by the EA and approved by electors in that local authority area.[50] Governmental policy guidance to EAs

40 See www.education.gov.uk/schools/leadership/typesofschools/b0066996/faith-schools/ for the position of the Westminster government and www.scotland.gov.uk/Topics/Education/Schools/FAQs for the position at Holyrood.

41 Www.scotland.gov.uk/Topics/Education/Schools/FAQs.

42 Www.teachernet.gov.uk/wholeschool/faithschools/.

43 SSFA, s. 69(1) and (2) and schedule 19.

44 Education Act 1996, s. 375(3).

45 SSFA, schedule 19, para. 2(5).

46 *Ibid.*, s. 70.

47 *Ibid.*, schedule 20, para. 3.

48 *Ibid.*, s. 71. Sixth form pupils may exercise the right to be excused from worship on their own behalf under s. 71(1B).

49 E(S)A, s. 8(1).

50 *Ibid.*, s. 8(2).

suggests again that the national Christian heritage should be reflected in the content of these activities.[51] Parents have the right to withdraw their children from both observance and instruction.[52]

3.2. FLAWS IN THE ACCOMMODATIONIST MODEL

The framework employed in UK schools, whereby the curriculum requirements of religious education and worship of a primarily Christian nature are tempered by the right of parents to withdraw their children from participation, can be described as an accommodationist approach to the right to freedom of thought, conscience and religion. The position of the Strasbourg court seemed to be that such an approach fell competently within the margin of appreciation available to states in determining how best to uphold article 9 and P1–2 within religiously pluralistic societies.[53] No positive right to a secular education was found to exist in *X v United Kingdom*,[54] where the applicant parents sought to establish a non-denominational school, and contended that the 15% contribution required of them by the state towards the capital costs of the building amounted to a breach of P1–2 since the existing state schools in Northern Ireland were essentially Protestant in character. The European Commission of Human Rights could find nothing in the wording of the article to suggest that states had a duty to provide schools in accordance with the convictions or beliefs of every group of parents. The right to education was subject to available resources, and since parents had the option to send their children to a state-funded school without making any financial contribution, and to exercise their right to withdraw their children from religious education that conflicted with their beliefs, it was reasonable for the state to demand a contribution for the alternative school the applicants sought to establish.

Other jurisdictions have, however, been less sanguine about the reality of the protection afforded to non-mainstream religious beliefs (or absence of belief) within an accommodationist system. One clear example is found in the jurisprudence of the Canadian Supreme Court, which was asked to consider whether the right of a parent to withdraw their child from the two half-hours per week of essentially Christian religious education prescribed by the Elgin County Board of Education was sufficient to uphold the parent's constitutional right to freedom of conscience and religion. The Court was not satisfied that removing

---

51 Provision of Religious Observance in Scottish Schools, Circular 1/2005, available at www.scotland.gov.uk/Publications/2005/03/20778/53820.

52 E(S)A, s. 9.

53 The keynote example of the Strasbourg position here is *Kjeldsen, Busk Madsen and Pedersen v Denmark* A-23, (1979–80) 1 EHRR 711, discussed further below in connection with curriculum content.

54 7782/77, (1978) 14 DR 179.

the child from the class was a meaningful solution to the difficulty of religious education weighted heavily in favour of one faith, since the effect of the withdrawal would be to single out the child within the classroom, potentially drawing the opprobrium of her classmates and alienating her from the rest of the group. Since no real protection was therefore offered in respect of the parent (and child)'s minority beliefs, the court found the curriculum to carry the risk of indoctrination, in breach of the parent's constitutional rights.[55]

The fears expressed by the Canadian Supreme Court have been supported by factual evidence in the context of the Irish school system, which again operates on the accommodationist principle. Alison Mawhinney analysed quantitative research in the form of questionnaire surveys of school authorities alongside interviews with parents and teachers in order to establish how the opt-out provisions were operating in practice. The reality of withdrawing a child from religious education and observance was fraught with difficulty, as summarised in her discussion of the results:

> "Parents may be reluctant to exercise [the right to opt out] for fear of isolating their child; opt-out provisions do not satisfy parental wishes and may simply mean that the child sits at the back of the class; children who opt out may suffer stigmatisation; and often it may be impossible for teachers to schedule the school day to facilitate children who wish to opt out."[56]

In the United States, it has been noted that the accommodationist approach creates particular difficulties for school-age education because children may not yet have developed the rational and critical faculties that might shield adults from indoctrination in similar circumstances. This was expressed succinctly in *McCollum v Board of Education*,[57] a case concerning time reserved in class for religious instruction where an opt-out was offered, in which Justice Hugo Black noted:

> "The law of imitation operates, and nonconformity is not an outstanding characteristic of children. The result is an obvious pressure on children to attend."[58]

Given the detailed list of educational rights set out for children in the UNCRC, including the state's duty to allow development of respect for the child's parents,[59]

55 *Canadian Civil Liberties Association v Ontario (Minister of Education)* (1990) 65 DLR (4th) 1. See also *Zylberberg v Sudbury Board of Education* (1988) 65 OR (2d) 641 (CA).

56 MAWHINNEY, A., "The Opt-out clause: imperfect protection for the right to freedom of religion in schools" [2006] 7(2) *Ed Law* 102.

57 333 US 203 (1948).

58 *Ibid.*, at p. 227.

59 UNCRC, article 29(1)(c).

for her own cultural identity and values,[60] and to prepare the child for responsible life in a free society in a spirit of understanding and tolerance among people of all religious groups,[61] this argument about the difficulty of an accommodationist approach is perhaps one to which particular attention should be given.

3.3. *FOLGERO* AND *LAUTSI*: TOWARDS STATE NEUTRALITY?

Recent jurisprudence of the European Court of Human Rights suggests that, in fact, these concerns may be carrying increasing weight in Strasbourg. A focus has been placed on state's positive duty of neutrality both as regards appropriate provision of religious education, and the more difficult question of what might be permissible in terms of religious observance or other forms of religious influence on daily school life.

The first indicator of the current position on these issues is *Folgero and Others v Norway*.[62] The Evangelical Lutheran strand of Christianity is the state religion in Norway, and Norwegian schools have traditionally provided religious education which reflected the importance of this faith within Norway's history and culture, with parents who held conflicting beliefs free to withdraw their children from such classes. However, in 2008, a new course on Christian Knowledge and Religious and Ethical Education, or KRL, was introduced into the school curriculum. One aim of the course was stated to be increasing tolerance and understanding of all faiths, and so an exemption from the course as a whole was not permissible, with parents obliged rather to write to the school advising which part of the course conflicted with their beliefs in order that their child might be withdrawn from that particular part of it. In determining whether this amounted to a breach of P1–2, the Court displayed a new willingness to look at the detail of the curriculum, noting that 55% of the content focused on Christianity and observing that certain aspects of the syllabus, such as singing hymns and learning the ten commandments, blurred the line between Christian education and Christian confession quite significantly. The requirement that parents write to request specific exemptions was considered unduly onerous and impractical, and by a slim majority of 9:8, the court ultimately found that a violation had occurred. It concluded:

> "The verb 'respect' [in P1–2] … in addition to a primarily negative undertaking … implies some positive obligation on the part of the state.[63] […] In fulfilling its

60 *Ibid.*

61 *Ibid.*, article 29(1)(d).

62 (2008) 46 EHRR 47.

63 *Ibid.*, at para. 84.

functions in respect of education and teaching, the respondent state had not taken adequate care to ensure that information or knowledge included in the curriculum for KRL be conveyed in an objective, critical and pluralistic manner sufficient to respect the limits implied by P1–2."[64]

The decision, although very close, has been followed in at least one subsequent case, where a breach was again found as a result of the failure of the Turkish school system to allow an exemption for minority Muslims from religious education classes in which only the Sunni perspective was put forward.[65] Taken together, these cases suggest a new stringency in the court's view of what can be appropriately characterised as "religious education", with an increased emphasis on the obligation of the state to ensure sufficient objectivity to guard against the risk of indoctrination. It seems the limits of what can acceptably be described as an accommodation will also be more tightly drawn: any right to opt out must be freely available, and no requirement for parents to explicitly divulge details of their own faith as a *quid pro quo* for the exemption can be imposed. It should be stressed that accommodationist approaches *can* still meet the required human rights standards in respect of religious education. The cases simply suggest that the form of the accommodation will be more stringently controlled than ever.

More difficult, however, is the question of religious influence bearing on schooling beyond the strict confines of religious education properly so called. *Lautsi v Italy*[66] dealt with an application by a parent who contended that the display of a crucifix in every classroom of her children's school violated the secular principles by which she wished them to be educated. In the domestic courts, it had been accepted that the crucifix was a symbol of Italian culture, history and Italian identity itself, and could no longer be considered as belonging strictly to the Roman Catholic faith. A Chamber of the Strasbourg court was not convinced that the association with Catholicism had been broken, or could even be said to be of secondary significance. A violation of P1–2 in conjunction with article 9 was found. In its deliberation, the court noted that:

"The schooling of children is a particularly sensitive area in which the compelling power of the state is imposed on minds which still lack (depending on the child's level of maturity) the critical capacity which would enable them to keep their distance from the message derived from a preference manifested by the state in religious matters."[67]

---

64 *Ibid.*, at para. 102.

65 *Zengin v Turkey* (2008) 46 EHRR 4.

66 (2010) 50 EHRR 2 (Chamber); 18 March 2011 (Grand Chamber) as yet unreported but available at http://cmiskp.echr.coe.int/tkp197/view.asp?item=1&portal=hbkm&action=html&highlight=lautsi&sessionid=68508341&skin=hudoc-en.

67 *Ibid.*, at para. 48.

It was also observed that:

> "The court does not see how display in classrooms of public schools of a symbol that it is reasonable to associate with Catholicism (the majority religion in Italy) could serve the educational pluralism that is essential to the preservation of a 'democratic society' as conceived by the Convention."[68]

This decision, with its underlying suggestion of a shift towards secularism as the appropriate mechanism by which to respect article 9, proved extremely controversial. It seems fair to say that the approach of the Chamber was somewhat removed from the view expressed by the court in, for example, *X v UK*,[69] although there was no acknowledgment of a change of position within the judgment itself. Was it the case, as Ian Leigh argued, that the court misdirected itself in applying dicta from judgments in which the respondent nation had a constitutional principle of separation of church and state to a case involving a state in which no such secularist principle applied?[70]

Unsurprisingly, the Italian government sought a referral to a Grand Chamber, which declined to equate the absence of religion with state neutrality in the way which the Chamber arguably did. The Grand Chamber disagreed with the Chamber's findings, holding by a majority of 15 votes to two that there had been no violation of P1–2, and unanimously that article 9 did not merit consideration as a separate issue. Although the positive duty on states to act neutrally and impartially in ensuring the exercise of various religions was once again emphasised, the court was not satisfied that the mere presence of a crucifix in a classroom could be enough to have a proselytising or indoctrinating effect, particularly not against a background where non-Catholic religious beliefs were allowed expression (for example, the wearing of headscarves by female Muslim students) and non-Catholic religious holidays were sometimes celebrated.

In giving their opinion, however, the Grand Chamber was quick to express the limited application the decision should have. It noted particularly:

> "A crucifix on a wall is an essentially passive symbol and this point is of importance in the Court's view, particularly having regard to the principle of neutrality ... It cannot be deemed to have an influence on pupils comparable to that of didactic speech or participation in religious activities."[71]

68 *Ibid.*, at para. 56.

69 7782/77, (1978) 14 DR 179, discussed above.

70 LEIGH, I., "New trends in religious liberty and the European Court of Human Rights", 2010 *Ecc LJ* 266.

71 Grand Chamber decision at para. 72.

Taken together with the reasoning developed in *Folgero*, the overall picture is still of a trend towards a more rigorous regulation of religious influence in state schools bearing to operate on the accommodationist principle. A question mark must exist as to whether the UK curriculum in its current form continues to meet with the standards expected by Strasbourg. The mixture of religious education and observance that is compulsory in all state-funded, non-faith schools may risk the kind of overlap that the court was unimpressed by in *Folgero*, and could raise similar issues around the practicability of the right for parents to opt out of the confessional elements of the curriculum. An additional concern may be familiar school activities, such as singing hymns at assembly or staging a nativity play, which clearly have roots in Christianity, no matter that the schools concerned might considered them to be merely traditional and essentially benign in religious terms. Such activities seem closer to the didactic speech and participation in religious activities that concerned the Grand Chamber in *Lautsi* than to the passive backdrop of a crucifix which could have no proselytising effect.

As recently as 2007, Westminster officials were of the view that an entirely secular education in England remained a "political impossibility".[72] Given the trend of the Strasbourg jurisprudence, that definition of impossible may have to be unpicked fairly rapidly.

3.4. CHALLENGES TO FAITH SCHOOLS

Against this background, the potential conflicts arising around the provision of faith schooling appear less pressing. As with secular education, P1–2 and article 9 are not considered to provide parents with a positive right to any particular type of religious education, as found in *R (on the application of R) v Leeds City Council.*[73] Here, parents sought judicial review of the local education authority's refusal to provide transport for their children to a Jewish school 45 miles away. The court was satisfied that the authority had acted reasonably in offering parents places in a local school which gave the option to take Hebrew as a modern language, and considered that the per capita cost of transport for each child would be sufficiently excessive that a compromise of the parents P1–2 rights was justified to avoid the cost. The importance of religious motivations underlying school placing requests should not, however, be understated, particularly in situations where there are no balancing concerns in connection with cost. This

72 "Crisis of faith in first secular school," *The Observer*, 23 September 2007, available at www.guardian.co.uk/uk/2007/sep/23/schools.faithschools.

73 [2006] ELR 25.

point was confirmed in *R (on the application of K) v Newham LBC*,[74] in which a Muslim father sought review of the education authority's refusal to grant his daughter a place in a local single-sex secondary school. The request for a place was motivated by religious convictions, in particular the applicant's belief that his daughter should not mix with boys or young men after the age of 11. In quashing the education authority's decision, the court emphasised that religious convictions had to be specifically taken into consideration by education authorities in determining the allocation of school places in line with P1–2. There was no evidence that the applicant's beliefs had been taken into account here.

One question that might be levelled at state-funded faith schools concerns the necessary discrimination in admissions policies in favour of students of the particular faith concerned. As mentioned above, the Equality Act 2010 provides faith schools with an exemption to the prohibition on discrimination on religious grounds in relation to admissions policies.[75] Schools are therefore free to prefer applicants of a particular faith. Is this compatible with the requirements of P1–2 and article 9 in conjunction with article 14? Philip Petchey discusses the issue[76] in the context of the Privy Council decision of *Bishop of Roman Catholic Diocese of Port Louis v Tengur*,[77] an appeal from the constitutional court of Mauritius. The appellants represented a group of Roman Catholic colleges who were found to operate an admissions policy which contravened the Mauritian constitutional requirement of freedom from discrimination on grounds of religion[78] by favouring Catholic applicants. Although the Privy Council noted that discrimination could be justified where it had a legitimate aim, no argument suggesting such an aim had been put forward by the appellants here.

Petchey speculates on a potential justification along the lines that a non-faith (or alternative faith) child who does not obtain a place at a faith school will nevertheless always have the opportunity to attend a different school where her religion (or scepticism) will not be a factor.[79] This could be seen as a variation on the "specific situation" rule accepted in Strasbourg as a justification for an interference with rights under article 9. The gist of this rule, which will be discussed further below in connection with the school uniform cases, is that where a person voluntarily places herself in a situation *knowing* that her ability to manifest her beliefs will be circumscribed thereby, this circumscription will

74 [2002] ELR 390.
75 Equality Act 2000, schedule 11, paras. 5 and 6.
76 PETCHEY, P., "Legal Issues for Faith Schools in England and Wales", 2008 *Ecc LJ* 174.
77 [2004] 16 BHRC 21.
78 Constitution of Mauritius, s. 16.
79 PETCHEY, *supra* note 76, pp. 188–189.

not violate article 9.[80] For example, if a student enrols at a university in which a headscarf ban is in operation, her rights will not be contravened provided that an alternative university where she could have worn her headscarf freely was available to her.[81] Could it follow that a non-faith child who misses out on a place at a faith school has no claim, since another school will necessarily be available to her? Petchey notes an immediate flaw in the argument, namely that schools are not a like-for-like comparison, and there is no guarantee that the alternative school will offer the same qualities, academic or otherwise, as the desired faith school. A more successful argument in justification of the discrimination may be that interference with the non-faith child's article 14 rights is necessary for the protection of the rights of the faith child and her parents under article 9 and P1–2. This argument relies on the fact that the non-faith child's educational needs can be met elsewhere more easily than the faith child's needs can be accommodated outwith the school in question. Given that faith schools are still very much in the minority, it seems that in almost all situations, this test will be met. Such a balancing of rights seems consistent with the Convention framework here.

One final point of interest in connection with faith school admission policies concerns the difficult overlap which can exist between membership of a particular religious group and identification as a particular race. The petitioner in *R (on the application of E) v JFS Governing Body*[82] was the father of a child who had been refused admission to a Jewish school on the grounds that, although the petitioner was Jewish by descent, the child's mother had converted to Judaism through a non-orthodox synagogue. Preference was given by the school to children whose status as Jews was recognised by the Office of the Chief Rabbi, which required that the child's mother be Jewish by matrilineal descent or by conversion under orthodox auspices. Before the Supreme Court, the argument focused on whether the admissions policy discriminated purely on religious grounds, thereby falling within the exception to the prohibition on discrimination in schools provided by the equalities legislation,[83] or whether it amounted to discrimination on the basis of race. The court noted that race, as defined in the Race Relations Act 1976, included a focus on ethnic or national descent,[84] and considered that the matrilineal test was therefore clearly one of

80 *Ahmad v UK* (1982) 4 EHRR 126, in which a teacher's contention that his article 9 rights had been breached by his employer-school's refusal to allow him time off to worship on a Friday afternoon was dismissed as manifestly ill-founded since he was free to resign the post at any time. See also *Stedman v UK* (1997) 23 EHRR CD 168.

81 *Karaduman v Turkey* (1993) 74 DR 93. See further discussion of religious dress in an educational setting below.

82 [2010] 2 WLR 153.

83 This exception was, at the time of the case, contained within s. 50 of the Equality Act 2006.

84 Race Relations Act 1976 (as amended), s. 3. This legislation has now been subsumed into the Equality Act 2010.

ethnic origin. The fact that the focus on this line of descent had been motivated by religious law was irrelevant – a racial group is a racial group irrespective of the fact it might overlap with or match entirely with an identified religious group. There was no exemption for racial discrimination in school admissions policies, and so the appeal by the school had to be rejected.

The overlap between religion and race is not restricted to the Jewish community: Sikhs are also protected under each of these designations.[85] Aileen McColgan has cogently argued that greater understanding is required of the concept of religion as an indicator of ethnicity, noting that identification as Catholic or Protestant in Northern Ireland has in many cases little to do with the tenets of Christianity, whilst the hostility experienced by Muslims in the UK occurs largely because they are Muslim rather than as a result of particular aspects of Islam.[86] The multifaceted nature of religious identification described here is a useful tool for analysing the tensions inherent in the EqA in an educational setting, to which this essay will now turn.

4. DELIVERING THE CURRICULUM

4.1. RELIGION AND THE SCHOOL SYLLABUS

Beyond the specific issues of religious education and observance, parental belief can have a broader influence on the content of the school curriculum and the way in which it is delivered. The legal requirements again vary on either side of the border. In England, schools are statutorily obliged to work within the parameters of the National Curriculum.[87] In Scotland, in addition to the requirement for religious observance and instruction[88] discussed above, the E(S)A requires the EA to provide adequate facilities for social, cultural and recreative activities and for physical education and training,[89] and school education must include the teaching of Gaelic in Gaelic-speaking areas.[90] Beyond that, curriculum content and delivery is subject to the guidelines set out in the Curriculum for Excellence,[91] which create no legal obligations.

---

85 *Mandla v Dowell Lee* [1983] 2 AC 548.

86 McCOLGAN, A., "Class wars? Religion and (in) equality in the workplace", 2009 *ILJ* 1 at p. 24.

87 Http://curriculum.qcda.gov.uk/index.aspx.

88 E(S)A, ss. 8(1) and (2).

89 *Ibid.*, s. 1(3)(b).

90 *Ibid.*, s. 1(5)(b)(iii).

91 Detailed information is available through the Learning and Teaching Scotland website here: www.ltscotland.org.uk/understandingthecurriculum/whatiscurriculumforexcellence/index.asp.

The parental beliefs which may be relevant to the curriculum obviously comprise the tenets of various faiths, but P1–2 is not limited to religious concepts. The Strasbourg court has emphasised that mere ideas will not be enough to attract the protection of the right to education, which will relate only to "views that attain a certain level of cogency, seriousness, cohesion and importance".[92] This clarification came from *Campbell and Cosans v United Kingdom*,[93] in which parental convictions about the undesirability of corporal punishment were held to meet the required standard as they concerned a "weighty and substantial aspect of human life and behaviour".[94] The issue has yet to receive much attention domestically, but in one useful example, *T v Special Educational Needs Tribunal and Wiltshire County Council*,[95] parental belief in a Lovaas programme[96] as the most appropriate educational provision for an autistic child was not considered sufficient to meet the Strasbourg test.

Europe has yet to see litigation on curriculum content on a scale such as that which surrounded the debate over teaching of creationism rather than evolution as a matter of religious freedom in the United States.[97] One important Strasbourg decision does exist in respect of sex education, however. In *Kjeldsen, Busk Madsen and Pedersen v Denmark*,[98] parents of state school pupils argued that the Danish law by which sex education became a compulsory part of the curriculum was in breach of their right to have their children educated in accordance with their beliefs. It is clear from the report of the case that the issue was not instruction in the biological facts of reproduction, but rather what the court referred to as "sex education proper" including information on contraception, termination of pregnancy, sexually transmitted diseases and the broader emotional and societal aspects of sexual relationships. The Court took the view that sex education could not be a breach of parents' rights simply by existing. A breach could arise if the type of sex education provided was seen as indoctrination, if it advocated a specific kind of sexual behaviour or "exalted sex", but there was no evidence of such an approach in Denmark. In line with the accommodationist approach to article 9 discussed above, the court also noted that parents were free to continue in their natural function as educators at home and to guide their children along a path in line with their own religious or philosophical convictions. Alternatively, parents could send their children to

92 *Campbell and Cosans v United Kingdom* (1982) 4 EHRR 293 at para. 33.

93 *Ibid.*

94 Para. 36.

95 [2002] ELR 704.

96 The Lovaas technique is an approach to the education of autistic children which focuses on intensive behavioural intervention during their early years. More information is available at www.lovaas.com/.

97 For an overview, see BROWNFIELD, E.Y., "The first amendment implications of teaching the theory of evolution and creationism in public schools" (2007) 36(1) *JL & Educ* 141.

98 A-23, (1979–80) 1 EHRR 711.

private schools, where sex education was not compulsory, or educate them entirely at home. Accordingly, the Court was satisfied that the parental beliefs had been respected and that there was no breach of the parents' rights.

4.2. DELIVERING THE CURRICULUM: EQUALITIES LAW IN CONFLICT?

The matter of delivery of the curriculum could, however, turn out to be more contentious, at least at the domestic level. As mentioned, a key caveat to the prohibition on discrimination contained within the Equality Act 2010 is that the provisions do not apply to anything done in relation to the content of the curriculum.[99] The way in which the material is delivered will, however, be subject to the prohibitions on discrimination, victimisation and harassment outlined earlier, regardless of whether the school is denominational or otherwise.

Detailed guidance on the implementation of the 2010 provisions in schools has been produced by the Equality and Human Rights Commission.[100] The guidance emphasises the absence of any restriction on curriculum content, so that even where ideas are taught which might cause offence to pupils with certain religious beliefs, this will not be unlawful provided that the teaching is not delivered in such a way as to amount to harassment or other detriment to the pupils. The following examples are provided:

> "A school curriculum includes teaching of evolution in science lessons. This would not be religious discrimination against a pupil whose religious beliefs include creationism.
>
> Although Jewish pupils may find studying the holocaust very upsetting it is not unlawful for a school to cover this topic."[101]

The EHRC notes the exemptions relating to faith schools, and clarifies that, although schools are entitled to convey their beliefs through the curriculum, they must not do so in a way that involves "haranguing or berating" a particular pupil or group of pupils as a result. This example is provided:

---

99 EqA, s. 89(2).

100 Www.equalityhumanrights.com/advice-and-guidance/equality-act-guidance-for-education-providers-schools/providing-education-and-access-to-any-benefit-service-or-facility/.

101 Www.equalityhumanrights.com/advice-and-guidance/equality-act-guidance-for-education-providers-schools/providing-education-and-access-to-any-benefit-service-or-facility/what-does-this-mean/.

> "A teacher at a Church of England school tells pupils that homosexuality is 'wrong' and that gay and lesbian people will 'burn in hell' unless they are 'cured of the disease'. A gay pupil in the class is deeply offended and intimidated by this hostile and degrading language. This may be unlawful direct discrimination on the grounds of sexual orientation."[102]

Further guidance is available on the government's Teachernet website.[103]

It is difficult to ignore the inherent tension between the aims of the equalities legislation and the tenets of certain faiths. At the most basic level, it seems impossible to imagine how the position of any belief system which considers homosexuality to be a moral wrong could be put across in a classroom without causing a gay or lesbian pupil to feel victimised. Presumably the absence of any acknowledgement of this tension within the legislation itself or the policy guidelines is the result of the volatility of the political situation surrounding these issues: the dispute as to whether Roman Catholic adoption agencies should have the right to refuse to place children with same-sex couples as a religious exemption to the general prohibition on sexual orientation discrimination is one recent high profile example of how such conflict can erupt.[104] Governmental diffidence, though perhaps understandable, nevertheless seems unlikely to prevent a legal challenge being made in due course.

Similar tensions were identified by McColgan writing in the employment context.[105] She suggests that designating religion as a protected characteristic goes further than is required by the ECHR, and suggests an attenuated protection for religion which recognises the particular difficulties experienced by religious individuals in particular settings without placing religion on a par with characteristics like sex and race. She describes a system of religious accommodations in respect of matters such as hours of worship, food and dress. Although such accommodations might create some inconvenience, she contends:

> "This inconvenience is quite a different cost from that associated with permitting religious individuals or collectives themselves to discriminate on grounds of sex, race etc., at least in the public sphere, involving as it does no assault on individuals' equality rights or dignity."[106]

---

102 Www.equalityhumanrights.com/advice-and-guidance/equality-act-guidance-for-education-providers-schools/providing-education-and-access-to-any-benefit-service-or-facility/exceptions/.

103 Www.teachernet.gov.uk/docbank/index.cfm?id=12504.

104 A brief overview is available here: http://news.bbc.co.uk/2/hi/uk_news/politics/6298477.stm.

105 McCOLGAN, *supra* note 86.

106 *Ibid.*, at p. 25.

The focus, she suggests, where religious discrimination is concerned, should be on disadvantage, exclusion and alienation from "mainstream" society, asking how best equality might be furthered.

It may be that McColgan's attenuated protection of religion would offer some solutions in the educational context also, although whether it would strike the balance of rights that would appear to be demanded in this situation is unclear. Certainly, in areas where sufficiently sized religious communities exist, the accommodation of religious worship would, in itself, appear to justify the existence of faith schools and the modified forms of religious education and instruction within the curriculum which these might entail. The attenuated model would also suggest that where religious teachings come up against other equalities objectives – for example, ending discrimination on grounds of sexual orientation – the equality objective should take precedence. This would, of course, apply only at school, and parents would remain free to educate their children at home as always. In Convention terms, the rights of faith parents under article 9 and P1–2 would be compromised in order to protect the rights of, for example, gay or lesbian pupils and their parents under P1–2 and article 9. Whether the Strasbourg court would accept this as an appropriate balance of rights is difficult to say. In the past, it would have been tempting to suggest that the issue would have fallen within the margin of appreciation available to the state in determining how best to meet the range of legitimate objectives in question here, but given the more interventionist approach taken recently by the court as discussed above, this may no longer be the case. A definitive answer is unlikely to be found without litigation either domestically or at the European level.

5. SCHOOL UNIFORM AND RELIGIOUS DRESS

5.1. RESTRICTIONS ON RELIGIOUS DRESS: THE STRASBOURG APPROACH

McColgan also argues that the designation of religion as a protected characteristic has, to some extent, skewed the interpretation of the equalities legislation by the courts, benefiting neither the protection of religious beliefs nor the other protected characteristics.[107] An attenuated approach to religious discrimination would help prevent this dilution of the overall strength of the equality provisions. An inverse difficulty seems to have come about through the domestic courts' interpretation of the Strasbourg jurisprudence on religious dress in an educational setting. Here, the equalities legislation on religion has been used to

107 *Ibid.*, at pp. 11–15.

bolster the much diluted protection under article 9 brought about by domestic misinterpretation of the European dicta. The result is a seemingly arbitrary divergence of decisions in cases on essentially the same issue, depending on the legal basis on which they have been argued.

Wearing religious dress is a manifestation of religious belief, and therefore protected under article 9. The Strasbourg court has been willing to allow compromise of this right for two main reasons. The first, as touched upon in the discussion of faith schools above, is where a specific situation exception could be said to apply. The second is where conflicting objectives, particularly protection of the rights of others, could be said to justify the compromise. In an educational setting, two keynote examples emerge in the form of cases raised by Turkish Muslim women, both of whom sought to wear headscarves in line with the Islamic prescription on modest dress for women. In *Karaduman v Turkey*,[108] the student was refused permission to graduate unless she was prepared to be photographed without her headscarf. The Commission did not accept that article 9 had been engaged at all by the prohibition on headscarves, pointing out that the student had chosen to comply with the rules of the institution when she chose to apply there. More recently, in *Şahin v Turkey*,[109] the University of Istanbul had instituted a complete ban on headscarves inside its buildings in line with the view of the Turkish courts that wearing Islamic headscarves inside higher education institutions offended against the principle of secularism enshrined within the Turkish constitution. Although it was accepted that article 9 was engaged here, it was again highlighted that the applicant could have exercised the option of attending University elsewhere. Additionally, the court noted, as a matter of principle, that the headscarf ban sought to protect the rights of women, and was necessary for the maintenance of public order. In all the circumstances, the court felt the ban represented a proportionate interference with the applicant's rights.

The focus on protection of the rights of others was also adopted in Strasbourg where the applicant, rather than being a student, was a classroom teacher of children aged four to eight. In *Dahlab v Switzerland*[110] the court determined that the ban on headscarves within the Swiss secular system of education engaged the applicant's article 9 rights. However, justification was found in the need to protect children from religious disharmony. It was said to be impossible to assess the potentially proselytising effect of a "powerful external symbol" such as the hijab on children as young as those taught by the applicant.

---

108 (1993) 74 DR 93.

109 (2005) 41 EHRR 8.

110 15 February 2001, 42393/98.

These decisions have not been without criticism.[111] Although the court in each case has made claims towards the promotion of equality for women and the protection of their rights as objectives of a ban on headscarves, it is notable that the circumstances of the individual claimants received little attention. For some Muslim women, the pursuit of higher education or employment is already a struggle against cultural norms which a ban on modest dress will do nothing to ameliorate. Additionally, the decision to wear religious dress has been expressed by some Muslim women as a positive, feminist choice in a patriarchal world where objectification of women is common. As in the discussion of faith schools above, the choice to attend another institution (or, in the case of Dahlab, to find another job) may not be as straightforward for various reasons as the jurisprudence of the court would seem to suggest. Nevertheless it may be true to say, as the court did on each occasion, that it falls within the margin of appreciation of individual states to determine how best the compromise should be struck between respect for religious freedom and the protection of the rights of others, and at least the cases have the benefit of consistency in their application of the law.

5.2. RESTRICTIONS ON RELIGIOUS DRESS: THE UK PERSPECTIVE

Unfortunately the jurisprudence of the UK courts on the same issue cannot be said to share that merit. The lead domestic case is the House of Lords decision in *R (on the application of Begum) v Denbigh High School.*[112] Shabina Begum sought judicial review of the decision to exclude her from school for her failure to adhere to the uniform policy. She believed that the Islamic dress code for women required her to wear a jilbab, a long, loose-fitting overgarment. The school uniform policy allowed only for the wearing of a shalwar kameez, a loose tunic and trousers, which the applicant did not believe to fulfil the requirements set by her religion. The school, situated in Luton, was a multi-faith community where 79% of students were Muslim. The uniform policy had been designed a few years earlier following consultation with parents and local religious leaders, including local Imams. The shalwar kameez had been adopted as it was felt to meet the needs of Muslim, Sikh and Hindu female students equally, thereby respecting the demands of each faith whilst minimising religious distinctions amongst the

111 See, for example, MARSHALL, J., "Freedom of religious expression and gender equality: Şahin v Turkey", (2006) 69(3) *MLR* 452; LEWIS, T., "What not to wear: religious rights, the European Court and the margin of appreciation", 2007 *ICLQ* 395; MARSHALL, J., "Women's right to autonomy and identity in European human rights law: manifesting one's religion", 2008 *Res Publica* 177; STUART, A., "Freedom of religion and gender equality: inclusive or exclusive?", (2010) 10(3) *HRL Rev* 429.

112 [2007] 1 AC 100.

student body. The applicant and her family had actively sought a place in the school, which was outside her catchment area, and were aware of the uniform policy in advance.

All five House of Lords judges were satisfied that no violation of the applicant's rights under article 9 had occurred, but the reasoning by which this decision was reached varied from judge to judge. By a 3:2 majority, it was determined that article 9 had not even been engaged by the uniform policy. The reasoning behind this seems to have been drawn from the reliance placed by Strasbourg on the specific situation rule in *Şahin*, amongst other cases. The applicant had chosen to attend the school in the first place, even though it was beyond her catchment area, and had chosen to cease attending during the dispute over uniform. At all times, the option was available to her, it was said, to attend another school. However, as Baroness Hale noted in her speech disagreeing with the majority on this point, the situations of Leyla Şahin and Shabina Begum are not analogous. Unlike Şahin, who had a free choice to attend university, a child under English law is compelled to go to school. Additionally, the choice of school is not made by the child, but rather by her parents. It might also have been expected that some consideration would have been given to the difficulties associated with changing schools partway through the year or even partway through the pupil's educational career before the blithe assertion that she had a free choice was made, although no reference is made to this concern in the speeches.

All five judges agreed that, had the article been engaged, any interference with the applicant's rights could be justified by the legitimate aims the uniform policy sought to achieve. The particular effort that had been made to design a policy that could meet the needs of all students whilst promoting harmony within the school was rightly highlighted, and the burden on the applicant was held to be proportionate.

Although the outcome of the case did not differ from what might be expected at Strasbourg, the divergence in opinions amongst the judges meant the ratio decidendi was not easy to discern. An opportunity to resolve the confusion arose not long afterwards in *R (on the application of X) v Headteachers and Governors of Y School*.[113] The applicant, again a female Muslim student, had been refused leave to wear the niqab (a veil which covers the entire face and head except for the eyes), which did not comply with the uniform policy. In following the *Begum* decision, the High Court's opinion in the case could unfortunately be said to complicate matters further. The court drew a somewhat subtle distinction in saying that the applicant's article 9 rights were *engaged*, but not *interfered with*, by the uniform policy since she had the option of attending another school

113 [2008] 1 All ER 249.

within her catchment area where the niqab would have been allowed. The judgment goes on to say that, even if there had been an interference with her rights, it could have been justified on the basis of the aims the uniform policy sought to achieve, such as creating harmony, minimising religious differentiation between students and additionally promoting school security by enabling pupils to be readily identifiable to members of staff.

Hill and Sandberg summarise the combined outcome of these two cases as follows:

> "Provided the right to manifest can be exercised elsewhere, it seems that the court will be entitled, or even obliged, to find that there had been no interference [with article 9.] Surely the better approach would have been to require schools to provide a balanced policy, judged against the factors in art 9(2)?"[114]

It does seem that a misapplication of the specific situation rule has left article 9 rights in this context considerably weaker in the United Kingdom than would be the case at the European level. This outcome is particularly frustrating given that the same result could have been achieved in each of the cases concerned by finding that an interference had existed and then finding it to be justified by the uniform policies which, in each case, were clearly well thought through and had significant justification underlying them. The generic rule which now seems to be in place must equally offer protection in a situation where a uniform policy has no legitimate basis at all.

The situation is an unhappy one. Unfortunately, the complications do not end there. Developing almost contemporaneously with the line of article 9 jurisprudence, a separate series of decisions has emerged in which similar disputes have been determined by reference to the equalities legislation. In *R (on the application of Watkins-Singh) v Aberdare Girls' High School,*[115] the applicant had been refused permission to wear the Kara, a steel bangle which has religious significance within the Sikh faith, on account of the school uniform policy. The school banned all jewellery with the exception of stud earrings and watches. The argument here was founded on the prohibitions on discrimination in respect of both race and religion,[116] to the effect that the school's refusal to grant an exception to the uniform policy amounted to indirect discrimination. The court accepted that the applicant had suffered discrimination to her detriment on both grounds, since it was clear the Kara held great importance for both her racial

114 HILL, M. and SANDBERG, R., "Is nothing sacred? Clashing symbols in a secular world", 2007 *PL* 488 at p. 499.

115 [2008] ELR 561.

116 These duties were, at that time, contained within s. 1 of the Race Relations Act 1976 and s. 45(3) of the Equality Act 2006 respectively.

identity and her religious beliefs.[117] In determining whether the discrimination could be justified, the court was, in fact, directed to the decisions in *Begum* and *X v Y School*, focusing solely on the arguments made in those cases as to justifications for restrictions on religious dress at school. The court took the view that both cases could be distinguished, since the need to promote religious harmony through minimising visible "difference" amongst students which applied to the jilbab or the niqab could not apply to a small bangle that was not even visible when long sleeves were worn. Accordingly no justification for the discrimination was established.

The second religious dress case decided under the equalities legislation was *Azmi v Kirklees MBC*,[118] in which the applicant was a teaching assistant in classes where children were learning English as a second language. The applicant sought to wear the full Islamic face veil and alleged that the local authority's refusal to permit this amounted to discrimination on grounds of religion. The justifications put forward by the local authority centred on the practical rather than the ideological reasons for the restrictions, explaining the difficulties caused to learners of English where non-verbal signals such as facial expressions could not be communicated as a result of the veil. There was evidence that the authority had observed the applicant's teaching on more than one occasion before concluding that the veil was impeding the efficacy of her work. There was no requirement for the applicant to remove her veil outside of the classroom, and the authority had looked for alternative ways to accommodate her religious dress within the classroom but had been unable to come up with a compromise acceptable to both itself and the applicant. In the circumstances, the Court did not accept that the applicant had been the victim of direct discrimination, since the dress code applied to all teachers regardless of their beliefs. Although the provisions were indirectly discriminatory given their detrimental impact on the applicant as a result of her religious convictions, this discrimination was justified by the importance of the aim of providing a high standard of education to the children concerned and the fact that the restriction was only in place at such times as the applicant was actually interacting with her pupils.

It may be that there is little to argue with in the outcomes of any of these cases, but the divergence in approaches cannot be ignored. If *Watkins-Singh* had been

---

117 There is a contrast here with *R (on the application of Playfoot) v Millais School Governing Body* [2007] ELR 484, in which wearing a "purity ring" to signal a commitment to chastity prior to marriage was not found to be a manifestation of Christian religious belief. The difficulty for schools in being required to act as an arbiter of religious doctrine in this way is beyond the scope of this essay, but an interesting discussion can be found at BACQUET, S., "School uniforms, religious symbols and the Human Rights Act 1998: the 'purity ring' case" (2008) 9(1) *Ed Law* 13.

118 [2007] ICR 1154.

determined on the same principles as *Begum*, the case would necessarily have failed, since the option of an alternative school that was presumably open to the applicant would have prevented any engagement with her rights in the first place. The same can be said of *Azmi*, where the local authority need not have explained the complications of teaching with a headscarf, since the fact the applicant could have resigned and sought employment elsewhere should have been the end of the question. It is perhaps a relief to see the equalities legislation providing to some extent the protection that should flow from article 9, but it is obviously difficult to reconcile the conflicting approaches taken by the courts. It surely cannot be correct that a ban on certain types of religious dress is discriminatory and yet does not engage article 9 (or, for that matter, article 14). The inherent tension between protection of religious beliefs and the objectives of the equality legislation in matters of curriculum content and delivery does not exist here. The irony is that the discrimination cases have been decided in a manner more clearly compliant with the article 9 jurisprudence than the article 9 cases themselves.

The confusion here is not beyond resolution, however. It seems likely that further religious dress cases will emerge. When they do, it is to be hoped that the domestic courts drag the domestic jurisprudence into line with the protection offered in Strasbourg, marrying neatly with the discrimination decisions already in place here.

6. CONFLICT OF RIGHTS: PARENTS VERSUS CHILDREN

One final issue which merits brief consideration is the potential for conflict between parental views on their child's education and the views of the child herself. Both parents and children are beneficiaries of human rights in respect of the provision of education for the child, and both have a right to respect for their religious beliefs. If the child's wishes should diverge at some stage from that of her parents, then whose rights would prevail?

This may be a matter of particular concern in Scotland.[119] Although the parental right to education contained in P1–2 has direct effect throughout the UK by virtue of the Human Rights Act 1998, Scotland alone has legislated for the protection set out in articles 28 and 29 of the UNCRC. The Standards in Scotland's Schools Act 2000 provides the child with a domestic right to

119 BARNES, L.A., "Education law" in CLELAND, A. and SUTHERLAND, E. (eds.), *Children's Rights in Scotland* (3rd ed.) (W. Green, 2009).

education[120] and makes specific provision for consultation with the child in respect of this.

The reported jurisprudence offers guidance in the form of an unusual case where, although the child's view was not directly represented, the case was determined through a balancing of the wishes of the parents with the rights of the child. The applicants in *R (on the application of Williamson) v Secretary of State for Education and Employment*[121] were teachers and parents at several independent schools which had been established to provide Christian education based on biblical observance. Corporal punishment was in line with the fundamental Christian beliefs of the applicants, based on biblical teaching that physical discipline was necessary in order to form a "godly character". They argued that the ban on corporal punishment in schools therefore amounted to a breach of article 9. The House of Lords accepted that their rights were engaged, but considered that the compromise created by the ban on corporal punishment was justified in order to protect the rights of others, in particular, the right of the child to be protected from abuse. Distress, pain and other harmful effects could result from the discipline sought by the applicants, and that was sufficient to override their right to manifest religious belief in this way.

The case offers some authority for the idea that the right of parents may be subordinated to the rights of children, although different rights were in conflict here. Whether such a sympathetic approach would be given to a child who wished to exercise her educational rights in defiance of her parents' wishes is less clear. More useful assistance may be obtained domestically through consideration of the minority medical consent cases in which under-16s have sought medical advice or treatment against the will of their parents. The position in England appears to be that a child under the age of 16 can consent to medical treatment where she is sufficiently mature to understand the nature of that treatment,[122] although questions remain about whether the treatment must also be objectively considered to be in the child's best interests, and whether the right to consent carries with it the right to refuse.[123] In Scotland, the position has been incorporated into the Age of Legal Capacity (Scotland) Act 1991, s. 2(4) of which provides that an under 16 may consent to surgical, medical or dental treatment where, in the opinion of the treating practitioner, the young person understands the nature and possible consequences of the treatment. Weak authority exists for the idea that the once the child has established such understanding, her parent will no longer have any veto in respect of medical decisions.[124]

120 S. 1.
121 [2005] 2 AC 246.
122 *Gillick v West Norfolk and Wisbech Area Health Authority* [1985] 3 All ER 402.
123 *Re R (A Minor) (Wardship: Consent to Treatment)* [1991] 4 All ER 177.
124 *Houston, Applicant* 1996 SCLR 943.

If this approach is correct in terms of physical health, it seems logically consistent to suggest a similar approach be employed for questions of spiritual well-being. If there comes a point at which a child is deemed sufficiently mature to have their own understanding of faith, there seems no reason why this should not be respected within her educational provision notwithstanding that it may be contrary to her parents' views. Indeed, it could be argued that the test of maturity should be less stringent in the religious context, since neither parent nor child has a huge amount of latitude to make decisions within the framework of compulsory school education, and the impact of any decision taken is less likely to be immediately life-threatening than in the medical context. The legal logic is perhaps unlikely, however, to be the determining factor in an issue of such political and emotional sensitivity.

7. CONCLUSION

In the introduction to this contribution, it was suggested that the case law demonstrated a broad uncertainty over the appropriate role for religion to play in an educational context in the modern day. Having reviewed the key areas of conflict, it seems that two strands of underlying tension can be identified.

The first strand concerns the complexities of the legal provision governing this area. Any topic which sits at the intersection between three equally significant human rights protections will be subject to constant small shifts in the law. Balancing and rebalancing is required by signatory states and the Strasbourg Court to ensure that each of the rights continues to be respected to the fullest extent possible, and the flexibility necessary to accommodate this ongoing exercise comes at the cost of a certainty that might otherwise be desired. Connected to this fact are the inevitable imperfections introduced where a number of courts at different levels are asked to look at the same issues. Interpretation and application of the dicta is a process of evolution, with occasional missteps and hiccups taking place along the way. The legal landscape here goes some way to explaining the seeming shifts in the Strasbourg position on state neutrality and particularly the difficult situation surrounding religious dress as a manifestation of belief in the UK. Over time, and as practitioners and the courts become more familiar with the newer legislation such as the Equalities Act 2010, it can be expected that some of these issues will be resolved, although the balancing exercise that lies at the heart of the human rights provisions here will always be in place.

The second, and undoubtedly more difficult, area of tension lies in the realm of the political and social. The goals we seek to achieve through education are complex, as the UNCRC rightly recognises in the protection it offers to children in articles 28 and 29. Education should instil knowledge, but it should also allow the child to develop into maturity with an ethical sensibility and a respect for herself and others. In the United Kingdom, and in Europe more broadly, there is a lack of consensus as to whether religion has a role to play in facilitating this development. The Chamber decision in *Lautsi* may have suggested an equation of state neutrality with educational secularism, but dispute remains as to whether these positions are truly equivalent, or whether secularism is just another faith-based position among the many options.[125] Neutrality is a difficult concept to apply meaningfully in a country where even the calendar year is arranged around Christian holidays and the national anthem references a (presumably Christian) deity. UK society may consider itself largely secular, but faith schools are more popular than ever.

The volatile state of the law here might simply be seen as a reflection of the underlying unease in society. Unless and until such tensions begin to resolve, it seems likely that jurisprudence in this area, plagued with the same ambiguities, will continue to grow. On this topic, it may be some time yet before class can be dismissed.

[125] An interesting discussion can be found in AHDAR, R. and LEIGH, I., *Religious Freedom in the Liberal State* (Oxford University Press, 2005) at chapter 8.

PART FOUR

REFLECTING A PLACE FOR RELIGION?

RELIGION IN THE HISTORY OF FAMILY LAW IN SCOTLAND

John FINLAY*

"No city, no not the least society, could subsist without law, more than a Body without a soul. 'Tis a Hedge and Fence to the Law of God, by punishing Atheists, blasphemers, Sabbath breakers, cursers of parents, thieves, murderers, adulterers, & other offenders against the Moral law."[1]

1. INTRODUCTION

These are the words of William Forbes, the first regius professor of civil law at the University of Glasgow (1714–1745). He wrote them in 1714. They suggest a legal system in which immorality, large or small, was not to be tolerated and where law existed to support biblical precepts. This was expressed nowhere more clearly than in the spheres of family relations and sexual conduct (although Forbes in this instance did not mention fornication). In his later classification of criminal law, however, Forbes in his more considered view chose to regard adultery not as a crime against God but as a crime against the person.[2]

Indeed during his lifetime there is evidence that attitudes towards the prosecution of some biblical crimes were beginning to change. It has recently been argued that 1709 saw the "de facto decriminalization of the secular crimes of fornication and adultery in Scotland".[3] This followed an act of indemnity which was used as

* The author would like to thank the Keeper of the Advocates Library for permission to quote from the session papers.

1 Glasgow University Library, Special Collections, MS Gen. 204/144, Professor William Forbes to Principal John Stirling, 6 April 1714.

2 See the discussion by CAIRNS, J.W., "John Millar's lectures on Scots criminal law" 8 (1988) *Oxford Journal of Legal Studies*, pp. 386–7. The "person" was the wronged husband, who enjoyed a claim for damages until this was abolished in 1977: Divorce (Scotland) Act 1976, s. 10(1).

3 LEVACK, B., "The prosecution of sexual crimes in the early eighteenth century (abstract)", 29 (2008) *Journal of Legal History* 148; *idem*, "Sexual crimes in early eighteenth-century Scotland", 89 (2010) *Scottish Historical Review* 172.

a justification for deserting the prosecution of, amongst others, adulterers, fornicators, cursers of parents and blasphemers.[4] These "offenders against the Moral law" provide an interesting mixture of those who transgressed Christian morality by committing crimes against God and crimes against the person. But the substance of these offences reflects an attitude to family life in Scotland which had been supported and fostered through legal reform and church organisation since the Protestant Reformation in Scotland in 1560. The content of "family law", or rather the contemporary equivalent of "family law", was heavily influenced by rules drawn from religious tradition and also from Roman law (in itself often identified with the rules of natural law).

This essay will investigate the rise and fall of religious influence from the late medieval period to modern times in the shaping of family law in Scotland. But this can be no more than a preliminary enquiry into a complex socio-historical subject given that historians are still engaged in the process of seeking to reconcile the disparate methodological approaches that have in the past been taken to the disciplines of legal history, family history, sociology and historical demography.[5] Any discussion of family law must always fully appreciate the prevailing social and economic context and this is particularly true when that law is treated historically. Isolating religion as a causal force is therefore potentially to misunderstand the fact that there were many causal forces, social, economic and psychological, which influenced the development of the idea of the family and also the law which regulated its place in the social structure of the community.

Scotland, as a mixed jurisdiction influenced by both the civilian tradition and the common law, was a small and geographically peripheral kingdom but an old one which was integrated fully into the western legal tradition.[6] The effect of this integration can be clearly seen in the statutes enacted in the Scottish parliament prior to the creation of the British parliament in 1707, as can the impact of the religious change which came with the Reformation. Judicial decisions and legal treatises were often fuller and more dynamic sources in the development of the law than acts of parliament and it was by these means that the law was shaped by advocates and judges (who had been practising lawyers) and, mainly from the eighteenth century, also by academic lawyers within Scotland such as Forbes. These lawyers were trained as civilian lawyers but increasingly grew familiar

4 National Archives of Scotland, Minutes of the criminal circuit at Perth, 20 May 1709, JC10/37.

5 See the comments of GROSSBERG, M., "Crossing boundaries: nineteenth-century domestic relations law and the merger of family and legal history", 10 (1985) *American Bar Foundation Research Journal* 799.

6 See generally SELLAR, W.D.H., "Scots Law: Mixed from the very beginning? A tale of two receptions", 4 (2000) *Edinburgh Law Review* 3.

with English law as well as *ius commune* ideas. Just as parliamentary legislation in pre-Union Scotland had religious contexts, the treatises and legal arguments which this class of men produced cannot be viewed in isolation from their individual religious faith, their own family upbringing and the religious and social experience of their country. All of these factors helped to determine their outlook, their expectations and their understanding of the role of law in society.

A demonstration of why such factors are important, and how elusive a proper understanding of them may be, can be seen in the debate that has surrounded the simple question of the extent to which social attitudes were changing in the later eighteenth century. The claim by some historians during the 1970s that morals became looser and there was something akin to a sexual revolution in the eighteenth century was made on the basis of the increasing rate of illegitimate births during the century.[7] Yet this has been largely repudiated by a more nuanced explanation of the same data from a different perspective. Rather than a sign of a new hedonism, social and feminist historians have tended to explain the apparent increase in illegitimacy in terms of class-exploitation and the economic vulnerability of women at a time of significant economic and social change.[8] The change in prosecutorial practice which Levack detects in Scotland in 1709, if further archival research were done to generate the relevant data, might provoke similar competing explanations based on the social, economic, legal, political, religious or psychological context. Even if solid data is buttressed with a range of anecdotal evidence, reliable general conclusions concerning social attitudes, particularly below the level of the social elite, can be difficult to discern.

The shaping of family law in Scotland is also not a straightforward issue since family law itself is a relatively novel concept. To those introduced to law through the Roman categories of persons, things and actions, much of the content of modern family law was taught within the law of persons but these terms are far from synonymous. Forbes, in his passing reference to "the law of God", was not discussing family law in the modern sense but he clearly regarded aspects of it as properly falling within the moral and legal sphere dominated by the influence of religious ideas. His words reflect the long-felt impact of the Reformation in Scotland and the predilection which it had for criminalising moral offences and

---

7 STONE, L., *The Family, Sex and Marriage in England 1500–1800* (revised ed., Penguin, 1979), pp. 395–398; SHORTER, E., "Illegitimacy, sexual revolution and social change in modern Europe", 2 (1971) *Journal of Interdisciplinary History*, pp. 237–272; SHORTER, E., *The Making of the Modern Family* (Collins, 1976), chapters 3–4; cf. TILLY, L.A. *et al.*, "Women's work and European family patterns", 6 (1976) *Journal of Interdisciplinary History*, pp. 447–476; ROGERS, N., "Carnal knowledge: illegitimacy in eighteenth-century Westminster", 23 (1989) *Journal of Social History*, pp. 355–375.

8 E.g. TILLY, *supra* note 7, pp. 463–75.

converting penitential discipline to capital and corporal punishments. The Scots reformers, in their hatred of sin, "turned canon law into an engine of death" to use David Sellar's memorable phrase.[9] Scotland's family law has been particularly susceptible to religious influence due to the impact and long-term influence of the Reformation. Before considering how and why this was so, it is important first to ascertain precisely what is meant in historical terms by our modern phrase "family law".

2. FAMILY LAW

Family law in Scotland emerged as an independent field of study at a time when the fundamental basis of the subject across Europe was undergoing what Harry Willekens has described as a "revolution".[10] Scotland fits a general pattern of western democracies over the last 35 years in removing discrimination between legitimate and illegitimate children, promoting strict formal equality between husband and wife and, at the same time, removing some of the civilian terminology that had been in use for centuries.[11] The decriminalisation of homosexuality (and, in some countries, of divorce), the development of civil partnerships, the introduction of the contraceptive pill and the technology of assisted reproduction have created, and reflect, a very different social landscape.

In Scotland, as elsewhere, the modern development of family law is based almost entirely on statute. Its context reflects the legislature's acceptance, in the last quarter of the twentieth century, of the language of equality and human rights. Over centuries Scottish judges had proved themselves to be conservative in their approach to matters of religion. When the central civil court was founded as a College of Justice in 1532, with money from the church, the first lord president and half of the senators were churchmen. A generation after the Reformation, when churchmen stood aloof from holding secular office, the judges were often prominent elders in the church, in some cases, were the sons or sons-in-law of

---

9 SELLAR, W.D.H., "Marriage, divorce and the forbidden degrees: canon law and Scots law" in OSBOROUGH, W.N. (ed.), *Explorations of Law and History* (Irish Academic Press, 1995), p. 82.

10 WILLEKENS, H., "Is Contemporary Western Family Law Historically Unique?", 28 (2003) *Journal of Family History*, pp. 70–107. The earliest English law textbook under the title *Family Law* seems to have been that of BROMLEY, P.M., published in 1957. The earliest Scottish textbook was the first edition in 1987 of J.M. Thomson's now standard introductory text on the subject, *Family Law in Scotland* (Butterworths, 1987). The traditional focus had been very much on branches of the law of persons. The subject division Part II of the *Introduction to Scottish Legal History* (Stair Society, 1958) very much reflects the tradition of writers up to the 1980s.

11 For historical background, see RONFANI, P., "Family Law in Europe" in KERTZER, D.I. and BARBAGLI, M. (eds.), *Family Life in the Twentieth Century* (Yale University Press, 2003), pp. 113–151.

prominent ministers of religion and, on formal occasions, collectively heard sermons while seated on pews specially reserved for them in the New Kirk in Edinburgh.[12] One of the longest-serving judges in eighteenth century Scotland, Lord Dun, advised his colleagues on the bench to be "frequent and fervent in prayer to God", and each of them to observe his duty to God through constant acts of worship "in secret, in his family, and in public attending upon all the public ordinances of divine worship and institution."[13] Another notable judge of the period, Lord Dreghorn, as a young advocate in 1750s wrote a tract investigating the Mosaic law which he no doubt hoped might bring him to public notice.[14]

Judicial conservatism is important in the story of Scottish family law because prior to the 1970s it was an area subject to relatively few statutes. Those which did exist remained on the statute books for centuries, even if they were not always enforced with full rigour. The Marriage Act 1567 was only repealed in 1977; the Incest Act of the same year was not repealed until 1986.[15] Irregular marriage, swept away by the Council of Trent in Catholic Europe, continued in Scotland until the twentieth century.[16] The significance of statute as a source of law in Scotland grew significantly under the reign of James VI (1567–1625) in the sixteenth century and, after the religious and political difficulties of the middle years of the seventeenth century, began to burgeon again in the 1680s only to receive a considerable check by the Union of parliaments in 1707.[17] According to one recent historian, in the period 1689 to 1707 the Scottish Estates passed 43

---

12 Under the influence of men such as Andrew Melville (1545–1622) in the 1580s, the Presbyterian kirk insisted on a compete separation of church and state with the theory of the "two kingdoms": SMITH, D.B., "The Reformers and divorce: a study on Consistorial Jurisdiction", 9 (1911/12) *Scottish Historical Review* 15; see also LYNCH, M., "Calvinism in Scotland, 1559–1638" in PRESTWICH, M. (ed.), *International Calvinism* (Oxford University Press, 1985), pp. 241–242.

13 ERSKINE OF DUN, *Lord Dun's Friendly and Familiar Advices adapted to the various stations and Conditions of Life, and the mutual Relations to be observed amongst them* (G. Hamilton and J. Balfour, 1754), pp. 8–9.

14 MACLAURIN, J., *Observations on Some Points of Law. With a System of the Judicial Law of Moses* (Sands, Donaldson, Murray & Cochrane, 1759).

15 SELLAR, W.D.H., "A historical perspective" in STYLES, S.C. (ed.), *The Scottish Legal Tradition* (enlarged edition, Salture Society, 1991), p. 41.

16 DEMPSEY, B., "Making the Gretna Blacksmith redundant: who worried, who spoke, who was heard on the abolition of irregular marriage in Scotland", (2009) *Journal of Legal History* 23. Marriage by cohabitation with habit and repute continued as a form of irregular marriage in Scotland beyond 1940 until recently abolished by statute. But this form of irregular marriage was, arguably, purely Scots law and not directly derived from canon law. Its historical status remains controversial: SELLAR, W.D.H., "Marriage by cohabitation with habit and repute: review and requiem" in CAREY MILLER, D.L. and MEYERS, D.W. (eds.), *Comparative and Historical Essays in Scots Law: A Tribute to Professor Sir Thomas Smith, QC* (Butterworths, 1992), p. 117.

17 GOODARE, J., "Scottish politics in the reign of James VI" in GOODARE, J. and LYNCH, M. (eds.), *The Reign of James VI* (Tuckwell Press, 2000), p. 38; CAIRNS, J.W., "Historical

acts concerning religion; in the year 1707–1829, the Westminster parliament passed only 15 such acts; a similar decline in legislative interest can be found in other categories including the sphere of private law generally.[18]

As suggested above, the idea of the family can mean different things to scholars in different disciplines and it is a concept that may be defined in terms of economic or social function. The focus of research varies from marriage patterns in different types of society (or the same society at different periods of development), to the "family cycle" (by which variables have been identified which governed the composition of the household, such as the tendency of children to leave the household when they marry, the organisation of labour, the nature of education and training and the effect of urbanisation all of which are included in the factors that might affect the pattern of inter-generational cohabitation).[19] The importance and longevity of ideas of kinship, and attitudes to "fictive" ties of kinship, have also interested scholars in recent years in a variety of wider contexts not simply that of the family itself.[20]

Historically, the concept of the family came to be linked to the definition and function of the household and there is a sense in which family law can be viewed largely in terms of the division, protection and transmission of household property. That is certainly the presupposition of many early Scottish legal writers, including the sixteenth century compiler of Balfour's *Practicks*.[21] Laurent Waelkens has recently discussed the development of the term *familia* from its Roman origins in the context of civil lawsuits – somewhat removed from the modern notion of the nuclear family – to medieval interpretations of Roman law.[22] Particularly from the twelfth century, under the influence of Judaeo-Christian teaching, jurists placed marriage and cohabiting spouses at the centre of the concept of *familia* and it was from then that the traditional law of persons developed on the basis of a new legal definition of matrimony which had been

Introduction" in REID, K.G.C. and ZIMMERMANN, R. (eds.), *The History of Private Law in Scotland* (2 vols., Oxford University Press, 2000), I, p. 131.

18 INNES, J., "Legislating for three kingdoms: how the Westminster parliament legislated for England, Scotland and Ireland, 1707–1830" in HOPPIT, J. (ed.), *Parliament, nations and identities in Britain and Ireland, 1600–1850* (Manchester University Press, 2003), pp. 24–25.

19 See e.g. DAVIDOFF, L. *et al.*, *The Family Story: Blood, Contract and Intimacy 1830–1960* (Longman, 1999), esp. chapter 2; HOULBROOKE, R.A., *The English Family 1450–1700* (Longman, 1984), chapter 1.

20 E.g. GAGER, K.E., *Blood Ties and Fictive Ties: Adoption and Family Life in Early Modern France* (Princeton University Press, 1996).

21 McNEILL, P.G.B. (ed.), *The Practicks of Sir Jame Balfour of Pittendreich* (2 vols., Stair Society, 1962–3), vol. I, pp. li-lii.

22 WAELKENS, L.J.M., "Medieval family and marriage law: from actions of *status* to legal doctrine" in CAIRNS, J.W. and DU PLESSIS, P.J. (eds.), *The Creation of the Ius Commune* (Edinburgh University Press, 2010), pp. 106–110.

accepted in the church courts.[23] This conception of family life linked to spousal cohabitation was the context within which lawyers developed particular rules regulating the relationships between husband and wife and between parent and child. Principles concerning the protection of individual reputation also developed that had a particular emphasis in respect of sexual morality.[24] Although underlying rules were often drawn directly from Roman law, canonists developed, modified and applied them within their understanding of Christian teaching. Thus they were able to direct with legal rules the development of relationships within the medieval household. But they said little or nothing about the "family" in the sense of the kin-group, household or extended family; their focus was overwhelmingly on the relationship of married partners.[25] While the modern notion of "family law" therefore seems like a perfectly natural construct, it is in fact an artificial and transient one. Not only does it not reflect the priorities or thinking of the past but it is free to develop in new directions in the future.[26]

3. THE HOUSEHOLD

The laws that related to the development of the family ultimately helped to regulate the household. But just as the family can mean different things at different times, so there is no uniform picture of the household, and it is worth pausing to consider what the early modern Scottish household actually looked like. The available evidence suggests that early modern Scotland followed the norm in north-west Europe in having on average about five persons per household, but it is clear that households often included more than simply parents and children.[27] More than a quarter of Edinburgh households in the

23 *Ibid.*, pp. 122–125. It is worth noting that the first thing Balfour has to say in his title on husband and wife is that the husband may answer for his wife in judgement: Balfour's *Practicks*, I, 93.

24 BLACKIE, J., "Unity in diversity: the history of personality rights in Scots Law" in WHITTY, N.R. and ZIMMERMANN, R. (eds.), *Rights of Personality in Scots Law* (Dundee University Press, 2009), p. 65.

25 SHEEHAN, M., *Marriage, Family, and Law in Medieval Europe* (University of Toronto Press, 1996), p. 261.

26 E.g. WILLEKENS, *supra* note 10, p. 92.

27 HOUSTON, R.A. and WHYTE, I.D., "Scottish society in perspective" in HOUSTON, R.A. and WHYTE, I.D. (eds.), *Scottish Society 1500–1800* (Cambridge University Press, 1989), p. 4. The general acceptance of the growth of the nuclear family and the diminution in the average size of the family therefore needs to be treated with caution: *The Family Story*, pp. 31–39; cf. ROTHENBACKER, F., "Social change in Europe and its impact on family structures" in EEKELAAR, J. and NHLAPO, T. (eds.), *The Changing Family* (Hart Publishing, 1998), pp. 12–14. For the importance of class divisions in the early twentieth century on the question of attitudes to child-bearing, see DEVINE, T.M., *The Scottish Nation 1700–2000* (Allen Lane, 1999), pp. 524–527.

1694 poll tax contained more than four persons and a small proportion contained more than 13.[28] The number of servants per household seems to have been similar in both Edinburgh and Perth, and Aberdeen seems to have been similar to Edinburgh in terms of household size at the end of the seventeenth century.[29]

Whether the picture in rural communities was similar is more difficult to determine. A case brought to the Court of Session in 1734 is interesting in this respect.[30] While the matter in dispute involved the authority of a constable to take a person into custody without a warrant from the local magistrate (the justice of the peace), the circumstances reveal what must have been a fairly typical circumstance in rural communities. A 16 year-old girl named Margaret Hamilton was removed from the house of her sister and brother-in-law by a constable on the basis that she was not in service. Constables had authority to round up known vagabonds and take them to the magistrate; but Margaret, according to her brother-in-law, Thomas Brown, was not "an idle girl lying out of Service". She had resided in their family for over a year and was contracted to go into service in the house of Brown's own brother-in-law. The clear inference from the pleading is that Brown did not regard Margaret to be part of his "family". He nonetheless asserted the liberty to keep her in his household, provided she was no burden to the parish, and he regarded himself as entitled to resist with reasonable force any attempt to remove her without a warrant.

Servants and apprentices sometimes had a family link to their masters. Whether they did or not, they were nonetheless included as part of the household (what has been called the "extended family household").[31] They made a productive contribution to the household structure and were subject to the discipline of their master and the normal standards of Christian moral behaviour. When Patrick (later Lord) Fraser wrote his classic text on the subject of the law of persons in Scotland, the title he selected reflected this tradition.[32] This aspect of domestic relations imposed upon servants customary, and sometimes contractual, duties which counterbalanced the obligation of their master to

28 DINGWALL, H.M., *Late Seventeenth-century Edinburgh: A Demographic Study* (Scolar Press, 1994), p. 35.

29 *Ibid.*, pp. 36, 47; FLINN, M. (ed.), *Scottish Population History from the seventeenth century to the 1930s* (Cambridge University Press, 1977), p. 194. For servants as part of the family, see FLANDRIN, J.L., *Families in Former Times* (trans. SOUTHERN, R.) (Cambridge University Press, 1979), pp. 140–145.

30 Advocates' Library Session Papers, *The Petition of Thomas Brown in Town-head of Auchlochan*, 21 February 1734, Drummore collection, vol. 3, no. 113.

31 LASLETT, P. and WALL, R., *Household and Family in Past Time* (Cambridge University Press, 1972), pp. 29–30.

32 FRASER, P., *A Treatise on the Law of Scotland as applicable to the Personal and Domestic relations: comprising Husband and Wife, Parent and Child, Guardian and Ward, Master and Servant, and Master and Apprentice: with an Appendix of Forms* (2 vols., T. & T. Clark, 1846).

maintain them within the house. There were also moral obligations. The head of a Scottish household was expected to ensure his servants attended church and if servants committed moral transgressions their masters regularly accepted the responsibility of paying any fines that were imposed.[33] The apprentices of legal writers normally boarded with their masters and indentures make it clear that if they behaved immorally their apprenticeship would be terminated and a financial penalty would be forfeit. Thus in 1630 the new legal apprentice Andrew Robertson promised not "to abuse his bodie be committing of fornicatioun adulterie or onie uthere & lyk abhominable act (as god forbid)".[34] In 1729 John Mackenzie gave a similar undertaking that, by then, had become almost a standard term in such indentures, by agreeing not to "defile his Body with fornication or adultery with no person or persons nor shall be a carder dicer night walker nor haunter or bearer of company with such vitious persons".[35] The behaviour of servants and apprentices often reflected on the head of the house to whose discipline they had voluntarily subjected themselves by written contract, just as his wife and children were subject to his discipline by both biblical tenet and natural law.

Mitchison and Lenemen have demonstrated from their study of the commissary court records that some eighteenth century landowners rejected the authority of the church locally (exercised by the kirk session) and thereby set an example which their servants occasionally followed.[36] But in most cases the authority of the Reformed kirk was firm and it tended to promote a system of household discipline which aimed at creating a "secular demonology" of certain categories of people and offence, particularly fornication and adultery.[37] This created the conformist view of morality to which so many generations of Scots were taught to subscribe. That conformist view was the long-term product of the influence of the church before and, in particular, after, the Reformation.

33 TODD, M., *The Culture of Protestantism in Early Modern Scotland* (Yale University Press, 2002), pp. 31, 175–176.

34 National Archives of Scotland [NAS], Henderson of Fordell family papers, GD 172/2398. Anglicised from the Scots, the text reads "not to abuse his body by committing fornication, adultery or any other similar abominable act (as God forbid)".

35 National Library of Scotland [NLS], Mackenzie of Delvine papers, MS 1173, fo. 3 v.

36 MITCHISON, R. and LENEMEN, L., *Girls in Trouble: Sexuality and Social Control in Rural Scotland 1660–1780* (Scottish Cultural Press, 1998), pp. 116–19. On the lay commissary courts, see note 60 *infra*.

37 The phrase is Lyndal Roper's, *The Holy Household: Women and Morals in Reformation Augsburg* (Oxford University Press, 1989), p. 57.

4. THE INFLUENCE OF CANON LAW

The Scots had a very long relationship with canon law. If canonists said little about "family law" as a concept, they were expert in developing legal principles from scripture, the various canons of church councils, the writings of the patristic fathers and papal legislation as well as Roman law. They did not ignore direct biblical example, drawing ideas about due process, for example, from the story of Adam and Eve and from Christ's attitude to the woman taken in adultery (the basis of the maxim *nemo punitur sine accusatore*).[38] The medieval church courts held an important place in Scottish society and it was through them that many rules from the Roman civil law entered medieval Scottish legal practice, albeit sometimes having undergone necessary modification.[39] Although canon law was universal, it is clear that it was not implemented in an identical way throughout Christendom and that there were local differences in practice and in emphasis. In his recent study of Franco-Belgian and English church courts, Charles Donahue has found a number of differences in terms of the prevalence of certain types of legal claims that were made and the way in which judges in the church courts disposed of them.[40] But fundamentally, the main rules and principles of canon law were respected everywhere and there was a basic uniformity which he ascribes to two things: the common academic training of the judges and lawyers and the availability of appeal to Rome.[41]

Scotland was a significant source of appeals to Rome, so much so that it has been stated authoritatively that between 1464 and 1560 there was no year in Rome without Scottish litigation.[42] There is also evidence of Scottish advocates being employed as lawyers in Rome during this period. Even before the foundation of the University of St Andrews, at some time around 1413, it is known that at least 200 Scottish students gained a university education in canon law and/or Roman law on the continent.[43] They brought home with them key texts, which are

---

38 Genesis 3.12; John 8.10–11. Examples of theological input can be found in HELMHOLZ, R.H., "The Privilege and the *Ius Commune*" in *ibid.* (ed.), *The Privilege against Self-Incrimination* (University of Chicago Press, 1997), pp. 21–2 and, generally, in PENNINGTON, K., "Due Process, Community, and the Prince in the Evolution of the *Ordo iudiciarius*", 9 (1998) *Revista Internazionale di Diritto commune* 9–47.

39 ROBERTSON, J.J., "The Canon Law Vehicle of Civilian Influence with Particular Reference to Scotland" in CAREY MILLER, D.L. and ZIMMERMANN, R. (eds.), *The Civilian Tradition and Scots Law* (Duncker & Humblot, 1997), p. 123.

40 DONAHUE jr, C., *Law, Marriage, and Society in the Later Middle Ages* (Cambridge University Press, 2007).

41 *Ibid.*, p. 600.

42 ROBERTSON, *supra* note 39, p. 123; also, DOLEZALEK, G., "The Court of Session as a *ius commune* court – witnessed by Sinclair's Practicks, 1540–1549" in MACQUEEN, H.L. (ed.), *Miscellany Four* (Stair Society, 2002), p. 51.

43 CAIRNS, J.W., "Historical Introduction" in REID, K. and ZIMMERMANN, R., *A History of Private Law in Scotland* (2 vols., Oxford University Press, 2000), I, p. 46.

found cited in surviving medieval cases and which suggest the availability in Scotland of considerable legal scholarship that might be brought into play by churchmen in both the secular and the church courts.[44] There is also evidence of Scots teaching canon law in Scotland and elsewhere. The lectures of the theologian William Hay on the subject of marriage, given in Aberdeen in the 1530s, make more than 500 references to the major texts of canon law.[45]

This body of supranational law provided the rules and opinions by which most matters of family law (in the modern sense) were determined, the church courts dealing principally with matrimonial matters (including actions to establish the validity of a marriage, or seeking its annulment or a separation of the parties); questions of personal status and also prosecution for sexual offences such as adultery, fornication and bigamy.[46] The reach of the Catholic church was long but not necessarily deep enough to shake off customary practices in the Scottish Highlands and Islands. There, thanks to long influence of Celtic traditions, such unorthodox practices as Celtic secular marriage persisted, whereby men might put away (i.e. divorce) one wife and take another in a manner not approved by the Roman church.[47] These practices eventually died out but they appear to have done so only after the sixteenth century.

5. THE SIGNIFICANCE OF THE REFORMATION

Despite the abolition of the authority of the Pope by the Scottish Estates on 24 September 1560, the Reformation, when it came, did not happen overnight.[48] It took a substantial time for its effects to be felt across the country.[49] In

44 STEIN, P. (ed.), *The Character and Influence of the Roman Civil Law* (Hambledon Press, 1988), pp. 292–293; 302–306. On the interaction of spiritual and temporal jurisdictions, see now MACQUEEN, H.L., "The king's council and church courts in later medieval Scotland" in DONDORP, H. *et al.* (eds.), *Ius Romanum, Ius Commune, Ius Hodiernum: Studies in Honour of Elto J.H. Schrage on the occasion of his 65th birthday* (Scientia Verlag, 2010), p. 277.

45 Barry (ed.), *Hay's Lectures*, p. xxv.

46 For details of how this operated in Scotland, see OLLIVANT, S., *The Court of the Official in pre-Reformation Scotland* (Stair Society, 1982) and MACFARLANE, L.J., *William Elphinstone and the Kingdom of Scotland, 1431–1514* (Aberdeen University Press, 1985), chapter 2. The literature on canon law is large. Useful overviews of the relevant aspects of canon law in English are BRUNDAGE, J.A., *Law, Sex and Christian Society in Medieval Europe* (University of Chicago Press, 1987); HELMHOLZ, R.H., *Marriage Litigation in Medieval England* (Cambridge University Press, 1974) and REID jr, C.J., *Power over the Body, Equality in the Family: Rights and Domestic Relations in Medieval Canon Law* (William B. Eerdmans Publishing Company, 2004).

47 SELLAR, W.D.H., "Marriage, divorce and concubinage in Gaelic Scotland", 51 (1978–80), *Transactions of the Gaelic Society of Inverness*, p. 464.

48 BROWN, K.M. *et al.* (eds.), *The Records of the Parliaments of Scotland to 1707* (University of St Andrews, 2007–2010), A1560/8/4.

49 LYNCH, *supra* note 12, esp. pp. 232–234; 247–250.

European terms it was a late reformation and Scotland therefore was able to receive a well-developed theological programme. Moreover, the Reformation was just in time to avoid the reforms of the Council of Trent being given effect. That is why, for example, irregular marriage in Scotland notoriously survived to such a late date. It is a clear reminder of the fact that although Calvinism replaced Roman Catholicism this did not mean that the rules of canon law were simply swept away.[50] Just as canon law itself had adopted, and sometimes adapted, rules from Roman law, at the Reformation no wholesale change in application of the rules of canon law was necessary or deemed desirable. A number of rules and principles simply continued to be used by lawyers in their arguments. The concept of cruelty or *saevitia*, for example, adopted by the pre-Reformation officials in the church courts in respect of the judicial separation of spouses continued to be used until the twentieth century.[51] As late as 1958, in preference to the scientific evidence derived from blood samples, Lord Clyde directly cited a decretal of Gregory IX to support a wider claim that Scots law had incorporated from canon law a reluctance to take evidence from a parent that their child was illegitimate where the parent had previously acknowledged the contrary.[52] The desire to support the social bond of matrimony, and to fight the scourge of illegitimacy, was shared by all Christians, Catholic and Protestant alike.

In the German states Lutheran theologians and jurists had already shown the acceptability of assimilating what was useful in canon law for the needs of the visible church.[53] This same process of absorption (and rejection) took place in Scotland. The jurist Thomas Craig, writing about 1600, said that "notwithstanding we have thrown off the papal yoke, the authority of the Canon Law endures"; the eighteenth century judge Lord Hailes observed that, although the two laws were not the same, Scots law contained much canon law and that cases were often unknowingly determined in accordance with it.[54] Craig had studied in Paris where the university, famed as a medieval centre of theology, was kept pristine from the baleful influence of Roman law; Hailes, on the other hand, had studied at Utrecht where he did not directly encounter canon law.[55] Yet both understood the essential continuity.

50 MACQUEEN, *supra* note 44, p. 278.

51 IRELAND, R.D., "Husband and wife: divorce, nullity of marriage and separation" in PATON, G.C.H. (ed.), *Introduction to Scottish Legal History* (Stair Society, 1958), p. 97.

52 *Imre v Mitchell* 1958 SC 439 at 463–4.

53 See WITTE jr, J., *Law and Protestantism* (Cambridge University Press, 2002), esp. pp. 70–85.

54 Cited by SELLAR, *supra* note 15, p. 41.

55 CAIRNS, J.W., "Legal study in Utrecht in the late 1740s: The education of Sir David Dalrymple, Lord Hailes" in VAN DEN BERGH, R. (ed.), *Summa Eloquentia: Essays in honour of Margaret Hewett* (University of South Africa, 2002), p. 30.

The experience of being taught canon law was something which, like Hailes, most Scots advocates and judges lacked after they turned to the Protestant universities of the Netherlands during the seventeenth century; its rules had nonetheless been woven into the fabric of Scots law. Nor did the fact that all of the most significant writers on Scots law in its most important formative period (from the advocate and judge Viscount Stair writing in the 1650s to the advocate and law professor David Hume in the 1790s) were Protestant mean that the canon law heritage became irrelevant.[56] In fact Stair, in particular, was highly influenced by some of the Spanish scholastic writers of the later sixteenth century.[57]

In the new Calvinist environment from the 1560s some rules, of course, had to change. But this was not necessarily brought about through legislation. The first major alteration was that divorce with the possibility of remarriage was recognised by the earliest kirk sessions (the minister and the elders who operated as disciplinarians at parish level) even before 1560.[58] The kirk session of St Andrews, for instance, handled a dozen cases of divorce in the period 1560–63 prior to the establishment of the civil commissary courts in 1564.[59] A major practical consequence of the Reformation, in Scotland and elsewhere, was the secularisation of most of the jurisdiction of the church courts. In Scotland lay commissary courts were introduced, the most important of which was in Edinburgh, which were established by royal charter and drew their authority from the crown and not the church.[60] With no formal link to the church, appeals from the commissary went straight to the central civil court, the Court of Session, even though the earliest commissaries drew their procedures and personnel from the old church courts.

Despite a clear break in Scotland between the church and the civil authorities in the years following the Reformation, some of the functions of the state continued to be strongly supported by the church. The kirk regarded itself, in the service of

---

56 I would not necessarily exclude George Joseph Bell from this "formative period" but this descriptor in itself is a dangerous one. It might be argued that much of the substance and character of Scots law was in place by 1800 but that the body of accepted doctrine looked much less impressive in the 1640s. It can well be argued, however, that the development and continuity of Scots law goes back to its medieval foundations.

57 HUTTON, G.M., "Stair's philosophic precursors" in *Stair Tercentenary Studies* (Stair Society, 1981), pp. 87–88. On canon law, see WALKER, D.M. (ed.), *Sir James Dalrymple of Stair, Institutions of the Law of Scotland* (University Presses of Edinburgh and Glasgow, 1981) I, I, 16.

58 "The Reformers and divorce: a study in consistorial jurisdiction", (1911/12) *Scottish Historical Review* pp. 22–23.

59 DAWSON, J.E.A., "The noble and the Bastard: the earl of Argyll and the law of divorce in Reformation Scotland" in GOODARE, J. and MACDONALD, A.A. (eds.), *Sixteenth-Century Scotland* (Brill, 2008), at p. 149.

60 SMITH, D.B., "The Spiritual Jurisdiction 1560–1564", xxv (1993) *Records of the Scottish Church History Society*, pp. 1–18.

a godly community, as having an interest not only in preserving individual souls but also having a licence to interfere directly in household life in the name of protecting the wider interests of the parish. This is found clearly in measures for the parochial support of the poor and in the sphere of education, but it also had a huge effect on family life, with the church taking measures to ensure adequate child support within families and, in particular, taking a close interest in the regulation of matters of morality and sexuality.[61] Marriage and baptism, for example, were occasions on which people's knowledge of the reformed faith were most readily tested. A condition commonly imposed prior to the baptism of a new child, for instance, was to require his or her father to promise to learn the Ten Commandments before the next communion.[62]

For its own part, the state reinforced the position of the church through passing appropriate legislation. After the forced abdication of the Roman Catholic Queen Mary, in 1567, Parliament enacted a significant programme of law reform which placed adherence to scripture at its centre. The legislation of 1560 removing the pope's authority was ratified; any older statutes which did not agree "with God's word, and [were] contrary to the Confession of Faith, [were] to be of no value, force nor effect" in future.[63] New acts were passed punishing fornication and incest while an act was passed restricting the forbidden degrees of relationship to those set out in chapter 18 of Leviticus.[64] In 1573, in line with Calvinist thought, divorce on the grounds of desertion was permitted by statute although wilful desertion and adultery remained the only grounds of divorce until legislation in 1938.[65] The earl of Argyll, as lord chancellor, was prominent in facilitating the 1573 Act. It allowed him to divorce his wife for desertion after the General Assembly had prevaricated over granting him a divorce and had recommended that advice be sought from other reformed churches across Europe.[66]

Since all legal change in this sphere had to be authorised by scripture, the attitude of the reformed kirk was cautious and changes to the law were relatively modest.[67] But, at the same time, these must be seen against the backdrop of radical social reform. This was brought about through the imposition and

---

61 E.g., GORSKI, P.S., *The Disciplinary Revolution: Calvinism and the rise of the State in Early Modern Europe* (University of Chicago Press, 2003), pp. 8–19; GRAHAM, M.F., *The Uses of Reform: "Godly discipline" and Popular Behaviour in Scotland and France, 1560–1610* (Brill, 1996), pp. 86–90; 211–215; TODD, *supra* note 33, pp. 291–295.

62 BARDGETT, F.D., *Scotland Reformed: the Reformation in Angus and the Mearns* (John Donald Publishers Ltd, 1989), p. 102.

63 *Records of the Parliaments of Scotland*, A1567/12/2.

64 *Ibid.*, A1567/12/14.

65 *Ibid.*, A1573/4/2; Divorce (Scotland) Act 1938, s. 1(1)(a)-(d).

66 DAWSON, *supra* note 59, p. 164.

67 See Lord GUTHRIE, "The history of divorce in Scotland", 8 (1910/11) *Scottish Historical Review* 46.

gradual spread of a new church organisation which implemented a new structure of ecclesiastical discipline, at the lowest level of which was the local kirk session.[68] Reformers recognised the pressing importance of social change which in their view had to be brought about quickly. Souls were at stake and there was a strong streak of millenarianism in Calvinist thought.[69] Since reformers believed that the world was about to end, people had to be made ready to account for their actions; the state of their soul should be an immediate concern and practices which harmed individual souls, and thereby caused collective harm to society, had to be stamped out. Reformed discipline in Scotland was brought in as quickly as could be achieved but this was done locally; there was no single Reformation in Scotland, but rather there were a series of reformations, in different burghs and regions, and change did not occur at a uniform pace.

Kirk sessions, manned by the ministers and lay elders of the church, often worked hand in hand with local civil government in the baron or justice courts. A number of magistrates, councillors and judges are known to have been elders in the kirk and the privy council in the seventeenth century helped to build the godly society, and to support their vision of family life, by urging the prosecution of moral crimes, particularly adultery. One historian has estimated that in late seventeenth century Aberdeen, taking into account the kirk sessions of each parish plus the local criminal court, there was "roughly one official for every 30 households", active in maintaining godly discipline and correct moral conduct within the neighbourhood.[70] This role was not simply monitory; it could be constructive.[71] Elders might intervene in families in a positive way and the kirk session has rightly been described in relation to family life as "much like a combination of modern social welfare agency, marriage counselling service and police domestic violence unit".[72]

For the first decade of its existence, the General Assembly devoted a great deal of time to questions involving sexuality and marriage.[73] This was seen as an immediate issue and it was one that could unite with powerful force ministers of religion, elders and even closet Catholics: illegitimacy, in particular, led to poverty and vagrancy and had the potential to drain parish resources. Many questions from kirk sessions found their way to the General Assembly for

68 LYNCH, *supra* note 12, p. 250.

69 This is explored in WILLIAMSON, A.H., *Scottish National Consciousness in the age of James VI: the Apocalypse, the Union and the shaping of Scotland's Public Culture* (John Donald Publishers Ltd, 1979).

70 DESBRISAY, G.R., "Authority and discipline in Aberdeen, 1650–1700" (unpublished PhD thesis, University of Aberdeen), p. 397.

71 Evidence from the records of seventeenth century Dumfries is discussed in McDOWALL, W., *History of Dumfries* (A. and C. Black, 1867), pp. 416–424.

72 TODD, *supra* note 33, p. 266.

73 GRAHAM, *supra* note 61, p. 69.

guidance and the General Assembly also lobbied the crown on behalf of the kirk.

The history of the church in Scotland, between 1584 and 1690, was one in which conflict between Presbyterian and Episcopalian factions was endemic; one form of church government gained temporary ascendancy followed by the other until Presbyterianism won out in 1690. But throughout this period the Scots and the Westminster Confessions of Faith, the Larger and Shorter catechism and the activity of kirk sessions maintained the strength of influence of Calvinism. In the process it gave the Scots a rather bleak view of human nature and the weakness of men and women whose natural state inclined them, in the words of the Larger Catechism, "to do the will of the flesh and of the devil".[74] In 1647 the Westminster Confession of Faith, a governing text of the Scottish presbyterian church and a product of what is sometimes called the second, Covenanting, Reformation in Scotland, referred to the "infallible truth, and divine authority" of the Bible and proclaimed the idea that the "infallible rule of interpretation of scripture is the scripture itself".[75]

If theologians were not prepared to go outside the Bible to look for the message of their religion, then they would not think twice about the subordination of a wife to her husband in accordance with their view of plain scriptural teaching.[76] In 1759 MacLaurin was able to state that "no position in law is more indisputable" than that the husband controlled his wife's goods and that she could not administer them without his consent.[77] This *jus administrationis* (a right to manage his wife's estate under the husband's curatorial power) had long been the rule and it went hand in hand with the husband's right of title to his wife's moveable property, the *jus mariti*, conceived in law as an implied assignation to him at the time of the marriage.[78]

It has already been noted, however, that the approach of civil government changed early in the eighteenth century and that most moral offences were no longer punished under the criminal law. These had clearly been set in place as a warning which might be reinforced by sermons from the pulpit, by examples of people being sternly rebuked by kirk sessions and encouraged to repent through

---

74 CAMIC, C., *Experience and Enlightenment: Socialization for Cultural Change in Eighteenth Century Scotland* (Chicago, 1983), p. 19.

75 *Westminster Confession*, I.ix.

76 CAMIC, *supra* note 74, p. 21.

77 McLAURIN, *supra* note 14, p. 29.

78 See WALTON, F.P., *A Handbook of Husband and Wife* (2nd ed.) (W. Green, 1922), p. 136; PATON, G.C.H., "Husband and wife: property rights and relationships" in *ibid.* (ed.), *An Introduction to Scottish Legal History* (Stair Society, 1958), pp. 100–102; 104–105. The *jus mariti* was abolished by the Married Women's Property Act 1881, s. 1(1) and the *jus administrationis* was finally abolished by s. 1 of the Married Women's Property (Scotland) Act 1920.

receiving highly public punishments. In addition, the seventeenth century had seen a number of men and women executed by the state for moral crimes such as incest and adultery. Incest can often be given a clear explanation in early modern societies because of the social context within which it was committed. For instance the dependence of a married woman on being accepted by her husband's family potentially made her vulnerable to abuse by in-laws. As Ulrika Rublack has pointed out in her study of German sources, the family provided a secure arena for sexual abuse because "it so often achieved a conspiracy of silence".[79] A case of alleged incestuous rape in Fife in 1594, discussed by Michael Graham, demonstrates how a local kirk session might hesitate to investigate too closely within a family where the accusers were women and the accused was the male head of the household.[80] Sometimes, incest only emerged because of the failure to hide or explain a pregnancy. But what had been merely an ecclesiastical offence became a capital crime thanks to the Act of 1567 and people could be executed "on the most technical of grounds" if matters investigated by kirk sessions passed to the civil authorities.[81] An example is the beheading of John Weir in 1629 for marrying the widow of his great uncle.[82] In his diary for 15 October 1656, John Nicoll referred to seven "executions" in Edinburgh: two men burned for sodomy and bestiality; a woman executed for mariticide and a mother and daughter for murdering a child who was the product of fornication or adultery. In the other two cases the penalty was corporal only, a man for attempted sodomy and a woman for exposing her illegitimate child on the street so that it died (this may have lacked the necessary intentionality for infanticide).[83] Nicoll certainly felt he was living in a time of "uncleanes and filthynes" but it is clear that as the century progressed kirk sessions increasingly held back from passing cases to the civil magistrate where such heavy penalties would be imposed.[84]

6. THE SIGNIFICANCE OF ROMAN LAW

Despite the continuing influence of ideas from canon law, in cases brought before the courts in post-Reformation Scotland as many, sometimes more, arguments were drawn from Roman law as from biblical or canonist sources.[85] The civilian

79 RUBLACK, U., *The Crimes of Women in Early Modern Germany* (Oxford University Press, 1999), p. 236.

80 GRAHAM, *supra* note 61, pp. 235–238.

81 SELLAR, *supra* note 15, p. 41.

82 *Ibid.*, p. 42.

83 NICOLL, J., *A Diary of Public Transactions and Other Occurrences Chiefly in Scotland From January 1650 to June 1667* (ed. LAING, D.) (Bannatyne Club, 1836), pp. 185–186.

84 *Ibid.*, p. 4.

85 For comment on some of the reported cases, see STEIN, *supra* note 44, pp. 337–340. Cases concerning persons are not particularly prevalent in the session papers, but when they arise arguments from Roman law are fairly common.

influence is a clear challenge to anyone who would argue for the primacy of religion as an influence in the development of family law in Scotland. Nonetheless, case law still provides revealing examples of social and economic contexts that were strongly influenced by the prevailing religious values. The stigma of illegitimacy, for example, was keenly felt. In one case the familial obligations were set out briefly as follows:

> "The general rule of law, with respect to bastards, is, That the father must be at the expence of the birth; the mother is bound to nurse her own child, *mater tenetur lactare infantem*, and is intitled to keep it for *seven* years, on being allowed a moderate aliment by the father, because a woman is more proper than a man for having the custody of an infant, during these its tender years; but the father becomes bound, as well as intitled, at that age, to take it off her hand altogether, and to educate it in some proper manner, by which it may be enabled to do for itself."[86]

That was the general rule, unless the mother was in some sense unworthy of the child (beyond her status as a fornicator). There was plenty of authority amongst lawyers on this point. In the case just quoted, it was said that a daughter should not be influenced by the example of a mother "whom she cannot be supposed to reverence or esteem". While the German jurist Johannes Wissembach's opinion was cited, this point was illustrated by a quotation from the Roman satirist Juvenal rather than medieval or contemporary canonists.[87]

This was a case concerning aliment and it is relatively clear from contemporary case law that while a father may be called upon to aliment his child, the reverse was true should the father fall on hard times.[88] James Rennie, for instance, sued his own adult children for maintenance.[89] The Roman law concept of forisfamiliation, whereby the father was permitted to keep his children at home and took legal title to anything they earned until they were formally emancipated, was also adopted by Scots lawyers.[90] The idea of forisfamiliation was a corollary of paternal power but the doctrine in Scotland was artificial and not clearly understood.[91] Forisfamiliation could not be inferred simply from marriage,

86 ALSP, *The Petition of John Donald junior, Candle-maker in Glasgow*, Arniston collection, vol. 79, no. 12. The Latin means "it is understood that the mother gives milk to her child".

87 JUVENAL, *Satires*, vi, 239.

88 Anton suggests that the position was confused in the seventeenth century: ANTON, A.E., "Parent and child" in PATON, *supra* note 78, p. 121. Stair seems clear, *Inst.* I.5.8–9. Note that a woman could not be obliged to aliment her husband were he in financial need until this was introduced by statute in the Married Women's Property (Scotland) Act 1920, s. 4.

89 ALSP, *Memorial for James Rannis & ors*, Arniston Collection, vol. 80, no. 27.

90 STAIR, *Inst.* 1.5.6, although Stair refers to "parents" rather than the father. ERSKINE (*Inst.*, I.vi.53) cites STAIR and repeats what he says, although he says that parental power is "chiefly" in the father.

91 McLAURIN, *supra* note 14, pp. 37–39 points out how unsatisfactory the law was.

conducting a trade or setting up a separate household, although these were the normal circumstances in which it occurred. Legally, at least from the time of Lord Bankton (writing in the 1750s), it was defined in terms of the express discharge or renunciation of *legitim* (the automatic right, on the death of his father, to receive a share of his moveable estate) by the child.[92] Marriage, or the setting up of a separate household, was merely the normal occasion when such a discharge might be given. *Legitim* in this sense was not itself a Roman law concept. Erskine (as others before him) used language that suggested it derived from natural law, but this seems to confuse the precise rules of *legitim* with the general natural obligation of aliment.[93] He correctly did not attribute it to canon law, although it was a concept that had been supported by ecclesiastical lawyers in medieval Scotland.

A glimpse of the extended family can be found in the practice of interdiction, whereby adults whose youth and inexperience might lead them to protect their property by handing over the administration of their affairs to one or more nominees.[94] These were often a mixture of family members and legal agents who would undertake in effect a guardianship, as in the case of the viscount of Arbuthnot who in 1719 voluntarily interdicted himself for five years, on the basis of "Facility and Easiness of Temper and his not application to Business".[95] For that duration he undertook not to grant any deed without the consent of two out of six named individuals, four of whom bore the surname Arbuthnot. This reflects the fact that it was still often the case men of substance were at the peak of their wealth soon after entering into their inheritance; the youngest male heads of households might often be the wealthiest.[96]

These concepts underline the fact that Scots lawyers after the Reformation often looked to Roman law rather than canon law for rules governing the relationship between persons. Given their civilian education, and the emphasis on examination in Roman law as a means of entry to the Faculty of Advocates, this is not surprising. But it would be misleading to place too much weight on this for

92 MACDOUALL, A., *Lord Bankton, Ane Institute of the Laws of Scotland* (3 vols., A. Kincaid and A. Donaldson, 1751–3), i.155; ERSKINE, J., *An Institute of the Law of Scotland* (ed. J.B. NICOLSON) (Bell & Bradfute, 1871), 3.ix.23.

93 On *legitim*, see ANTON, *supra* note 88, pp. 122–123. The Scots also largely accepted the Roman rule rendering revocable donations *inter virum et uxorem*, until this was removed by the Married Women's Property Act 1920, s. 5.

94 FINLAY, J., *Men of Law in pre-Reformation Scotland* (Tuckwell Press, 2000) p. 225. There are many examples of this in the court records from at least the sixteenth century.

95 ALSP, *Information for the Viscount of Arbuthnot against Mr John Arbuthnot of Forden and Thomas Arbuthnot Merchant in Edinburgh*, 15 July 1723, Hamilton-Gordon collection, vol. 3, no. 8.

96 Cf. HERLIHY, D. and KLAPISCH-ZUBER, C., *Tuscans and their Families: A Study of the Florentine Catasto of 1427* (Yale University Press, 1978), p. 302.

two reasons. First, there was a limit to how many rules from Roman law could be received into Presbyterian Scotland in regard to issues affecting family relationships; and, second, although direct citation of canon law was limited, many rules from the traditional spiritual jurisdiction were simply accepted.

The most blatant example of the limits of Roman law arose in the case of adultery. This was an issue upon which the kirk had had a great deal to say, particularly since adultery related directly to other moral offences. It involved the same behaviour as fornication but was regarded as a far more serious offence (since it threatened to destroy the marital bond central to family life), while the crime of bigamy was regarded simply as aggravated adultery. For religious reformers, in Scotland as elsewhere, adultery was the first and clearest ground of divorce. So clear was it that even at the Council of Trent the introduction of divorce with the possibility of remarriage on the ground of adultery was considered, albeit specifically rejected, by the Roman Catholic Church.[97]

John Calvin supported the death penalty for adultery on the basis of the Old Testament (drawing incidental support from Roman law) and executions are known to have taken place during his lifetime. But it was not until 1566, after his death, that legislation prescribing the death penalty in Geneva was made.[98] Under this law, a married woman who transgressed was simply to be put to death, while a married man committing adultery with an unmarried woman (provided he was not a servant) was only to be whipped and banished. If the man and the woman involved in adultery were both married, both were to be put to death.

In Scotland, divorce for adultery was introduced as a direct result of biblical sanction and not by legislation.[99] In the New Testament, Jesus had condemned adultery but had not endorsed the death penalty for adulterers; instead, he had famously said that he who is without sin should cast the first stone.[100] A different view on stone-throwing was clear in the Old Testament; a number of Protestant reformers, including Martin Bucer, strongly advocated the death penalty for adultery on the basis of Mosaic law and also, at least in Bucer's case, Roman law.[101] Calvin, and Scottish reformers, agreed. An adulterer, it was accepted, was to be regarded as though dead and the innocent spouse free to marry once again

97 BONFIELD, L., "Developments in European Family Law" in KERTZER, D.I. and BARBAGLI, M. (eds.), *Family Life in Early Modern Times 1500–1789* (Yale University Press, 2001), p. 111.

98 KINGDON, R.M., *Adultery and Divorce in Calvin's Geneva* (Harvard University Press, 1995), pp. 116–117.

99 On the early popularity of divorce actions, see SMITH, *supra* note 60, pp. 4–7.

100 John 8:7.

101 GRAHAM, *supra* note 61, p. 19. For Roman law on the penalty for adultery, see ROBINSON, O.F., *The Criminal Law of Ancient Rome* (Gerald Duckworth & Co. Ltd, 1995), pp. 58–68, esp. p. 66.

(whether the guilty spouse could marry again proved to be a much more complicated question). But although they no longer regarded marriage as a sacrament, the reformers remained generally reluctant to set marriages aside. Adultery was a special case and one so clearly warranted on scriptural authority that no legislation was needed to bring about a divorce on the basis of it. As the *First Book of Discipline* put it:

> "Mariage once lauchfullie contracted, may not be dissolved at manis pleasour, as oure maister Christ Jesus doeth witnesse, onles [unless] adulterie be committed; which being sufficientlie proven in presence of the Civil Magistrat, the innocent (yf thei so requyre) ought to be pronunced frie, and the offendar aught to suffer the death as God hath commanded."[102]

Scotland in fact was ahead of Geneva when it prescribed the death penalty for "notour" adultery by statute in 1563.[103] Although Scots Acts can be difficult to interpret, this one appears, unlike the later Genevan ordinance, to have been gender neutral. In 1581, the synod of Lothian asked the General Assembly to crave an act of parliament setting out in more detail what the ambiguous word "notour" meant when applied to adulterers.[104] The parliamentary response was that adultery was notorious when it produced a child, or when it was carried on openly or when it was persisted in despite a warning by the kirk to repent. Any acts of adultery that did not meet these requirements could not be punished with death.

The basic definition of adultery, however, was open to argument and this is where Roman law, and some of its later commentators, might threaten to upset the religiously-based interpretation which the Scots adopted. Their position was, and remained, that if either party to a marriage committed adultery with another person, married or unmarried, this was a ground of divorce and if that conduct was "notour" then the death penalty was appropriate.[105] This was gender-neutral and despite drawing persuasive arguments from Roman law, it was unsuccessfully argued in the case of *Gibson v Hudd* in 1749 that "a married Man lying with an unmarried Woman is not properly Adultery".[106] The Scots rejected drawing any

102 KNOX, *History of the Reformation*, p. 248.

103 *Records of the Parliaments of Scotland*, A1563/6/10; see also A1592/4/29.

104 PETERKIN, A. (ed.), *The Booke of the Universall Kirk of Scotland Buik of the Universal Kirk* (Edinburgh Printing and Publishing Co., 1839), p. 227; MITCHISON and LENEMEN, *supra* note 36, p. 43.

105 Adultery may remain a crime in modern Scots law, albeit one for which prosecution is inconceivable. In 1978 Sheriff Gordon took the view that notour adultery "literally" remained a crime, although his more recent editors do not explicitly say so: GORDON, G.H., *The Criminal Law of Scotland* (W. Green Ltd, 1978), para. 0–04, but cf. para. 1–09 (simple adultery is not a crime).

106 ALSP, *Information for John Hudd Heckle-maker in the Pleasance of Edinburgh against John Gibson Procurator Fiscal for the Shire of Midlothian*, 22 March 1749, *Miscellaneous collection*, vol. xvi (1706–1749), pp. 3–12.

such distinction and the more subtle definitions of adultery favoured by some continental jurists held no sway.[107] In a case of alleged seduction, on the other hand, the judges refused to follow the argument that simply because both parties were "guilty of a sin in the sight of God", and both were punishable in the public interest for fornication, no civil remedy was available to the less guilty female party against the allegedly more guilty male.[108] This argument was based on the Christian doctrine, accepted in Scotland after the Reformation (but not in canon law, the Netherlands or "most Popish countries") that fornication was a crime regardless of the social condition of the woman concerned be she a widow, prostitute or virgin. Particular reference was made to the analogy of the Roman action for corruption of a slave (perhaps curiously since the female pursuer in the case was not married) and also to the French remedy for damages for *rapt de seduction*.[109]

7. THE LANGUAGE OF THE LAW

Religious precepts can clearly be inferred in the language used in Scottish legislation. This is not surprising given that the Law of Moses was the basis for codes of law across Europe. The Bible itself was rarely quoted directly in Scots statutes of the sixteenth and seventeenth centuries, although the Incest Act in 1567 does refer specifically to chapter 18 of Leviticus.[110] But parliament certainly felt free to legislate on the basis of religious fiat in the realm of the family, and in statute the Bible, in particular Mosaic law, often either lies silent in the background or was subsumed under the general phrase "the Laws of God". An example is the Act of 1649 (re-enacted in 1661 after the Restoration) concerning the beating or cursing of parents.[111] Although there is no mention of the fifth commandment or Exodus 21:17, legal commentators like Alexander Bayne, professor of Scots law at Edinburgh, knew exactly what was meant.[112] He referred to the fact that Mosaic Law, like Scots law, punished with death the cursing of one's parents.[113] His counterpart in Glasgow, William Forbes, referred to such

107 E.g. VAN DER MUELEN, J.A., *Statuta et Consuetudines Diocesos Vianensis et Ameydensis* (Johannes Ribbius, 1684), obs. xxx, p. 283.

108 *Elizabeth Linning v Alexander Hamilton*, Mor. Dict. 13909.

109 For *rapt de séduction* in France, see FARR, J.R., *Authority and Sexuality in Early Modern Burgundy (1550–1730)* (Oxford University Press, 1995), pp. 98–110.

110 *RPS*, 1567/12/14.

111 *RPS*, 1649/1/211; 1661/1/263. Along with a statute on blasphemy (1661/1/264) this statute was re-enacted from the legislation of 1649 which was otherwise repealed and not resurrected after the Restoration.

112 "Anyone who curses his father or mother must be put to death".

113 BAYNE, A., *Institutions of the Criminal Law of Scotland* (T. &. W. Ruddiman, 1730), p. 100.

behaviour as "a very great Provocation to God our common father."[114] He pointed out that many wicked persons, "at their ignominious end", had admitted that their evil ways had begun in their contempt for parental authority. But if we trace this through to later commentators, we find the reference in the statute to the "law of God" disappearing. In 1678, Sir George Mackenzie had quoted the statute quite precisely; John Erskine, in his *Institute of the Law of Scotland* published in 1773, referred simply to the fact that "our law" prescribed death for cursing or beating a parent; similarly Baron Hume, in his *Commentaries on the Law of Scotland respecting Crimes* published in 1797, quoted the statute but not the particular reference to "the Law of God".[115] Scotland was not unique in including this particular prohibition in its civil law. As Alan Watson has pointed out, the moral injunction not to curse or beat one's parent can be found in Grotius' *Inleidinge*, his introduction to Dutch law, as a duty "enjoined by the law of nature and the law of God"; through this, and other Dutch writers of the seventeenth century, the provision made its way into France, in the *Code Napoleon*, and through that it appeared in the Dutch civil code where, in the present version, it still remains.[116] But, unlike Scotland, cursing a parent never had the potential to attract the death penalty; nor, in modern practice in the Netherlands, has it actually been enforced.

The evidence for enforcement in Scotland is equally limited; these are provisions which underpinned and reinforced a moral example and affirmed social values that were inspired by religion without necessarily leading to prosecution.[117] Despite the clear terms of the Scottish legislation, not one of the commentators refers to any case where the death penalty was actually imposed simply for beating or cursing a parent. In practice, this was a matter that parents might take to the kirk session where the elders would often work hand in hand with the magistrates who might impose short periods of imprisonment or corporal penalties.[118] This kind of behaviour was often reported to the session by neighbours and there are a number of examples of it in the century after the Reformation. Kirk sessions took it seriously because they regarded it as not only ungodly but also unnatural and it was probably pressure from kirk sessions that had led to the Act of 1661. Abuse of parents can be classified along with parental neglect which, like child neglect, was an issue for the kirk session.

---

114 FORBES, W., *The Institutes of the Law of Scotland* (2 vols., J. Watson, J. Mosman and Co., 1722, 1730), IV.2.2. Cf. ERSKINE, *Inst.*, ii, 1197.

115 HUME, D., *Commentaries on the Law of Scotland, respecting Crimes* (Bell & Bradfute, 1797), ii, 39.

116 WATSON, A., *Failures of the Legal Imagination* (Scottish Academic Press, 1988), p. 474.

117 This is a recognisable historical phenomenon. Some legislation was intended as much to provide moral example in a bid to instil social cohesion and affirm values as for enforcement; cf. BRUNDAGE, J.A., "Sumptuary laws and prostitution in late medieval Italy", 13 (1987) *Journal of Medieval History* 353.

118 E.g. TODD, *supra* note 33, p. 299.

In terms of legal pleading, the Bible was used as a direct source of authority in relevant cases. In *Gibson v Hudd* mentioned earlier, it was cited to defeat arguments from Roman law concerning the nature and consequences of adultery.

> "... the Precepts of the Law of *Moses* are not now binding under the Gospel Dispensation, unless so far as they are agreeable to the law of Nature, and the more recent Declarations of the Will of God, as contained and delivered in the New Testament."

Thus it was suggested that the "Will of God" was, at least to some extent, binding. As a corollary to this notion a further proposition was stated, namely that "nothing that is repugnant to the Principles of Christianity can ... be sustained either as Law or Practice". This was then followed by direct citation of Genesis, Corinthians and the Gospel of St Matthew on the theme of the husband and wife being but one flesh.

In the context of criminal law, the law of God features prominently in indictments which in Scotland took on a syllogistic form.[119] This began with the major proposition "that whereas by the laws of God and of this and every other well governed realm" some kind of behaviour (for example, incest) was a crime. If there was one, the relevant statute would then be set out and, in the minor proposition, the alleged facts would be stated from which the conclusion was naturally to be drawn that the prescribed penalty ought to be inflicted. John Erskine pointed out that since there was no statute against sodomy, the libel for the crime ought to be based directly on divine law, as set out in Leviticus chapter 20, and that the ordinary punishment was burning; generally speaking the sentence being carried out early in the morning.[120]

Religion was therefore of fundamental authority in cases concerning family behaviour. Barbara Shapiro has suggested that in England by the 1670s religious arguments needed to be rational and could no longer simply rely on authority or divine inspiration.[121] This fits with Levack's argument that after 1709 moral offences such as adultery were no longer treated as criminal matters under direct biblical authority and that Scottish prosecutors left them to the sphere of church discipline only.[122] Legal writers continued to classify adultery, for

---

119 For discussion, see CAIRNS, J.W., "Hamesucken and the major premiss in the libel, 1672–1702: Criminal Law in the age of Enlightenment" in HUNTER, R.F. (ed.), *Justice and Crime* (T. & T. Clark, 1993), p. 138, esp. pp. 143–144.

120 ERSKINE, *Institute*, IV.4.57.

121 SHAPIRO, B., *A Culture of Fact: England 1550–1720* (Cornell University Press, 2000), p. 170.

122 LEVACK, *supra* note 3, p. 148. He excepts incest from this charge, since the sole authority for prosecuting incest was the Scots statute which cited Leviticus chapter 18; *idem*, "Sexual crimes in early eighteenth-century Scotland", pp. 173, 185, 189–190.

instance, as a crime, either a crime against the person or, as John Millar (and his student, David Hume) had it, a crime against the religious establishment.[123] But it made little difference in practice. For while Hume preferred classifying adultery as a crime, rather than a civil trespass as in England, because it "breaks so deeply on the happiness of private life, and the welfare of a family", he acknowledged that the crime had not been the subject of a criminal prosecution for many years.[124] Given the lack of legislation in the sphere of Scots private law from Westminster, and prevailing attitudes there, it was unlikely after 1707 that a parliament would ever again be persuaded to legislate for Scotland on the basis of the Mosaic Law. On the other hand, since parliament did not positively repeal legislation by which crimes such as notour adultery continued to be regarded as capital, professors were bound to remind their students that this was the formal legal position even though the prosecutorial background had completely changed.

The attitudinal change between the early seventeenth century and the end of the eighteenth century can be seen in John Millar's analysis of the role of the father within the family. Millar's debt in this section to the moral philosophy of Adam Smith is obvious (he was Smith's pupil in the University of Glasgow and became regius professor of law there in 1761). But his rejection of the analysis of the patriarchalist, Sir Robert Filmer, is telling. Filmer's comparison of the unquestioning submission of children to the submission of a subject to his lawful monarch, was in Millar's view not worthy of the many efforts that had been made to refute it: "To say that a king ought to enjoy absolute power because a father has enjoyed it, is to defend one system of oppression by the example of another."[125]

Millar, as a renowned Whig, was merely one of many who rejected the views of men like Filmer.

In the atmosphere of greater freedom in the eighteenth century, when a moderate party gained the ascendancy in the Church of Scotland, legal theorising developed along new lines under the influence of a distinctive line of philosophical development.[126] Enlightenment thought, particularly in Scotland, strongly emphasised the need for the law to be in tune with the manners of the

---

123 CAIRNS, *supra* note 2, p. 380.

124 HUME, *supra* note 115, I, 453.

125 MILLAR, J., *The Origin of the Distinction in Ranks: Or, An Inquiry into the Circumstances which give rise to Influence and Authority in the Different Members of Society* (W. Blackwood, 1806), p. 138.

126 On the moderate party, the leading work is SHER, R.B., *Church and University in the Scottish Enlightenment: the moderate literati of Edinburgh* (Princeton University Press, 1985); see also DRUMMOND, A.L. and BULLOCH, J., *The Scottish Church 1688–1843: the Age of the Moderates* (Saint Andrew Press, 1973), chapters 3–4.

time and to keep up with the pace of change in a developing society.[127] The mutability of social institutions was recognised by writers, including Adam Smith and Lord Kames, particularly in the context of stadial theories of societal development and they saw the need for Scots law to develop in order to meet the commercial challenges of the later eighteenth century.[128] The importance of sociability in this process was recognised by many moral theorists who emphasised the role of women within the family as a humanising influence.[129]

John Millar built upon Smith's *Theory of Moral Sentiments* and developed original ideas concerning the importance of sentimentality and the "passion of sex" in the development of civilisation.[130] In particular, his work reflects a concern in Scottish philosophy with explanations of society and community and a preoccupation in the eighteenth century with the idea that an increasingly commercial society may degenerate in moral terms under the baneful influence of luxury.[131] For Millar, the danger was that the pursuit of profit and comfortable living may be at the expense of the love and affection that was the foundation of companionate marriage and family life. Not only might this lead men to marry for money, rather than for love, but it may generate an "immoderate pursuit of sensual pleasure" at the risk of destabilising and damaging the institution of matrimony and the concern for rearing children which lay at the heart of civilized society.[132] For all that Millar appreciated the importance of love and sentiment, as a minister's son it was natural for him not only to recognise the separate spheres of husband and wife but also to refer to the Bible for examples of how this relationship should function.[133] A wife's place was most definitely in

---

127 DWYER, J. and MURDOCH, A., "Paradigms and Politics: Manners, Morals and the rise of Henry Dundas, 1770–1784" in DWYER, J. *et al.* (eds.), *New Perspectives on the Politics and Culture of Early Modern Scotland* (John Donald Publishers Ltd, 1982), p. 210.

128 E.g. STEIN, P., "The four stage theory of the development of Societies" in *supra* note 44, pp. 395–410; LIEBERMAN, D., *The Province of Legislation Determined: Legal Theory in eighteenth-century Britain* (Cambridge University Press, 1989), chapter 7; *ibid.*, "The legal needs of a commercial society" in HONT, I. and IGNATIEFF, M. (eds.), *Wealth and Virtue* (Cambridge University Press, 1983), pp. 203–234.

129 See PURVIANCE, S.M., "Intersubjectivity and sociable relations in the philosophy of Frances Hutcheson" in DWYER, J. and SHER, R.B. (eds.), *Sociability and Society in eighteenth-century Scotland* (Mercat Press, 1993), pp. 28–29 and, generally, DWYER, J., *Virtuous Discourse: Sensibility and Community in Late eighteenth-century Scotland* (John Donald Publishers Ltd, 1987), chapter 7.

130 MILLAR, *supra* note 125, p. 184.

131 DWYER *et al.*, *supra* note 127, p. 210. For a useful summary of this theme, see HARRINGTON, D., "Gender, commerce and the transformation of virtue in eighteenth-century Britain", 31 (2001) *Rhetoric Society Quarterly* pp. 34–35.

132 On Millar's views, see DWYER, J., *The Age of the Passions* (Tuckwell Press, 1998), esp. pp. 84–96; 179–182.

133 *Ibid.*, pp. 91–92. On Millar's own attitude to religion, see LEHMAN, W.C., *John Millar of Glasgow, 1735–1801* (Cambridge University Press, 1979), pp. 80–81.

the home (in Millar's case, he and his wife had 13 children, ten of whom survived her death in 1795).[134]

The Union of 1707 linked the Scots more firmly to their southern neighbours whose religious outlook and family law were notoriously different.[135] Since the Union settlement had preserved both Scotland's separate and distinctive religion and private laws, it is not easy to tell what effect, if any, it had on how Scots viewed the family. Certainly it led to economic and social changes but the underlying social development that was ultimately to lead to changes in the pattern of family life, and eventually a different view of family law, was undoubtedly the rise in urbanisation that arose is the more industrialised societies of western Europe. This change can be traced in the first half of the nineteenth century with the establishment in the popular mind of the key and influential model for family structure, that of the wage-earning husband and father and the domestic wife.[136] In its wake developed an increased role for state intervention in the family, leading eventually to the emergence of the welfare state. There is no doubt of the importance of these developments and a number of ideologies have sought to interpret and explain them.[137] The social policy which developed during the twentieth century became, so it has been argued, morally neutral and quite removed from the old Scottish parliamentary tradition by which religious orthodoxy was imposed, if necessary, be means of the criminal law. Morality, institutionalised in the organs of the state, was now based on universal truths disaggregated from individual religious creeds and society was no longer held together by common acceptance of standards laid down by religious authority but through a shared understanding of adherence to the state and its institutions.

8. POST 1800

In Scotland, the first step to explaining these developments must come with the fact that after 1800 local kirk sessions rapidly declined in significance. This was not a consequence of secularisation but came about through the twin influences of urbanisation and industrialisation together with an increasing diversity of religious outlook, the immediate cause of which was the migration of a large

134 LEHMAN, *ibid.*, p. 413.

135 On cross-border attitudes, see LENEMAN, L., *Alienated Affections: The Scottish Experience of Divorce and Separation, 1684–1830* (Edinburgh University Press, 1998), pp. 218–232.

136 DAVIDOFF, *supra* note 19, pp. 20–1; MAYNES, M.J., "Class cultures and images of proper family life" in KERTZER, D.I. and BARBAGLI, M. (eds.), *Family Life in the Long Nineteenth Century, 1789–1913* (Yale University Press, 2002), 195–226.

137 *Ibid.*, pp. 46–47. See the essays in KUHNE, A. and WOLPE, A (eds.), *Feminism and Materialism: Women and Modes of Production* (Routledge and K. Paul, 1978).

number of Roman Catholics to Scotland from Ireland. It has been argued that Presbyterian church discipline reached its height in the middle of the seventeenth century and gradually relaxed during the eighteenth century, a period when a group of clergymen known as the Moderate party gained importance and led the church to a less severe disciplinarian stance.[138] There may be some truth in this hypothesis, but the vigilance of local kirk sessions remained unabated until the end of the eighteenth century.

Scotland urbanised more quickly than anywhere else in western Europe in the late eighteenth and early nineteenth centuries and it was that process which rendered it impossible for kirk sessions to continue to function effectively in the larger cities.[139] They continued to maintain a level of discipline in rural parishes but by 1850 this had also substantially declined. By then, according to Callum Brown, kirk sessions were no longer policing rural parishes but had resorted simply to expelling wayward members from the congregation of the church.[140] The pre-industrial "all-inclusive, communal role of church justice" disappeared during the nineteenth century and, in a phrase, "the inevitability of church discipline" had been removed.[141] The overt local disciplinary role of the church was increasingly taken over by organised police forces.[142]

Despite the views of churchmen like Thomas Chalmers (who believed that religion declined with the growth of cities), and the rise of an active evangelical movement, it has been argued that city-living did not mean the rise of atheism in the nineteenth century.[143] Church discipline was certainly losing its grip throughout that period, and this can most clearly be seen in the decline in the observance of the Sabbath, which one historian has regarded as the "outward and visible sign of the Church's inward and spiritual sway".[144] Sabbath-breaking was a sin, and a breach of the Westminster Confession of Faith, but as people in church congregations began to use trams and buses on the Sabbath, as local shops opened on a Sunday and as people began to use the day for recreation, church ministers were in a difficult position and this only got worse over time. Even so, church attendance – amongst all classes of society – did not seriously diminish in the nineteenth century.

---

138 CLARK, I.M., *A History of Church Discipline in Scotland* (Lindsay, 1929), p. 174.

139 BROWN, C.G., *Religion and Society in Scotland since 1707* (Edinburgh University Press, 2007), pp. 95–96.

140 *Ibid.*, p. 73.

141 *Ibid.*; MITCHISON *et al.*, *supra* note 36, pp. 124–125.

142 CLARK, *supra* note 138, p. 178.

143 BROWN, *supra* note 139, esp. chapter 3.

144 SMOUT, T.C., *A Century of the Scottish People, 1830–1950* (Collins, 1986), pp. 182–183; MACLEOD, J.L., *The Second Disruption: the Free Church in Victorian Scotland and the Origins of the Free Presbyterian Church* (Tuckwell Press, 2000), p. 31.

The nineteenth and twentieth centuries saw cultural attitudes to the concept of the family change and then change again. The significance of the Victorian cult of domesticity, the idea of the family very much consigned to the private sphere as married women came under pressure to withdraw from waged work, has been variously interpreted.[145] Industrialisation certainly had a major impact on work patterns and gendered roles within society, particularly since the workplace and the home were increasingly separated. At the same time, agitation began to improve the position of married women, particularly those gaining new forms of income. Prominent women in 1856 asked "that legal protection be thrown over the produce of their labour" (which might include the proceeds of their intellectual property).[146] Although this call took time to be heeded in England a very limited step, protecting women separated from their husbands, was taken in Scotland in the form of the Conjugal Rights (Scotland) Act, 1861.[147] This was followed by the Married Women's Property (Scotland) Act, 1877, inspired by similar English legislation in 1870. This legislation sought to limit the husband's right to administer his wife's property, specifically by excluding her earnings and investment income derived from them.[148] A more substantial change was brought about by the Married Women's Property (Scotland) Act, 1881.

In terms of religion, the problems and perceived Godlessness in city slums, particularly in Glasgow and Edinburgh, had encouraged the evangelical movement in the early to mid-Victorian era; but evangelicalism, and its ambitious programmes of social and housing reform, was decaying by the 1880s. Certainties were affected by evolutionists, particularly in the period 1890–1910 when debate amongst educationalists in theological colleges leaked out into the popular arena.[149] Confidence in Christian values as an agent of social change was disturbed by this and also by wider social and economic changes. As well as internal divisions in the church of Scotland in the nineteenth century and early twentieth centuries, the significant immigration of Roman Catholics – particularly from Ireland into Glasgow – and the development of industries in the Lowlands, reduced the religious homogeneity of the population. The dominance of a single culture, the traditional culture perpetuated by the kirk session, was disappearing. The last case of church discipline in Rothiemay in Banffshire, for example, is recorded in 1904.[150]

---

145 See DAVIDOFF, *supra* note 19, pp. 26–28. For the narrow range of occupations of women in Scotland in the nineteenth century, see DEVINE, *The Scottish Nation*, pp. 533–534.

146 *The Jurist* (N.S.) 1856, vol. ii, pt. ii, 134.

147 This legislation is discussed in detail by MURRAY, D., *The Law Relating to the Property of Married Persons* (James MacLehose and Sons Ltd, 1891), esp. chapter 4.

148 The Married Women's Property (Scotland) Act 1877, s. 3.

149 BROWN, *supra* note 139, p. 126.

150 BLAIKIE, A., *Illegitimacy, Sex and Society* (Oxford University Press, 1993), p. 208.

Secularisation in Scotland was a process of the later twentieth century. As one historian has put it, "this was the first century when Christian behaviour became unenforceable by the state, with the repeal, liberalisations or effective collapse of traditional Christian-based laws on homosexuality, abortion [and] divorce".[151] Urbanisation did not mean a reduction in church membership or attendance.[152] On a *per capita* basis, church membership actually reached its peak in the Church of Scotland in 1905, and it peaked as a proportion of the population in 1925; a serious decline did not begin until the late 1950s.[153] But social change was gathering pace and with it diminished the ability of religion to form the moral glue capable of maintaining the bonds of an increasingly diverse society.

Secularisation brought with it a tendency toward moral neutrality, particularly in terms of child-rearing and education of the young, which has influenced the direction of legislation and wider social policy. According to sociologists such as Bryan Wilson, an industrialised social system has emerged that proceeded "without recourse, or with decreasing recourse, to morality".[154] The thesis is that modern society is no longer backward-regarding, drawing moral lessons from a communal past, but forward-looking and individualistic: in short, that the pace of social change has quickened so much that the twentieth century saw a wholesale "moral revolution" to mirror Willekens' "revolution" in family law. The important point of this analysis is the emphasis it gives to the idea of roles within society as an agent of social control. The roles of educators and clergymen, for example, underwent change; from attempting to inculcate values and to socialise the young in the moral sphere, their role became detached and professionalised. To perform a technical role in a professional way came to require the absence of personal, individual, moral attributes. The formal roles of public life which, in earlier times depended on "private moral training", therefore have come to depend on neutral, external legal rules.[155] Thus the old moral prohibitions to which society subscribed (including some of those which Forbes identified in the quotation at the start of this essay), the universality of which were expressions of cultural integrity, were superseded by other methods of reinforcing social cohesion.

> "Thus, the state, like the economy, must impose universalistic principles, and must do so not by the slow processes of socialization, education and cultivation, but by

151 BROWN, C.G., *Religion and Society in Twentieth Century Britain* (Longman, 2006), p. 3.

152 *Ibid.*, p. 166.

153 *Ibid.*, p. 163. But membership and actual churchgoing are different things, and affiliation to a church was more resilient than the actual rate of attendance which declined across the twentieth century.

154 WILSON, B.R., "Morality in the evolution of the modern social system", 36 (1985) *British Journal of Sociology* 320. See also the general review by WALLIS, R. and BRUCE, S., "Religion: the British contribution", 40 (1989) *British Journal of Sociology* pp. 493–520.

155 WILSON, *supra* note 154, p. 323.

> political edict: and this is so because, in the modern social system, there is no homogeneous or stable communal base from which cultural and moral consensus can spontaneously arise."[156]

The lack of a socialised moral consensus does not mean that morality in the modern state is irrelevant. But, as Wilson suggests, there has been a "political institutionalization of moral goals".[157] Governments cannot wait for moral consensus to develop through the slow process of socialisation based on the gradual evolution of moral precepts, particularly if they wish to promote formal equality before the law.

Nor, it is argued, can moral action any longer reinforce group identity in a society composed of groups whose values and perspectives are not uniform. The strong sexual taboos, particularly homosexuality, which historically have been used to define and protect ethnic, religious or institutional boundaries can no longer serve this function since the solidarity that underpinned them no longer exists.[158] Adherence to particular religious faith was an important social boundary marker and the tenets of religion normally defined the content and strength of these taboos for entire societies. In societies containing many religions, in which the freedom of "thought, conscience and religion" – particularly the right to change religion – is guaranteed, the power of any one religion to create legal boundaries for all has been removed.[159] Religious diversity, and increasing agnosticism and atheism, has to some degree reinforced the development of legislation based not on morality (which is now conceptualised as variable private morality) but on a more impersonal approach which owes a significant debt to developments in political and economic theory.

Individuals came to be seen as social and economic units by the state bureaucracy, or as customers by commercial actors or as voters and potential voters by political parties, rather than fellow-parishioners whose souls require to be saved. Since the means of production are no longer generally located in the family, and there has correspondingly been an evolution in the shape and function of the household, the state or private organisations have taken on the burden of many functions traditionally associated with the family unit. Beyond the small family business, the laws on family inheritance, as Willekens points out, in practice simply distribute profits rather than the means of production which are now extensively held by legal rather than natural persons.[160]

---

156 *Ibid.*, p. 328.

157 *Ibid.*, pp. 328–329.

158 DAVIES, C., "Sexual taboos and social boundaries", 87 (1982) *The American Journal of Sociology* 1030, p. 1060.

159 European Convention on Human Rights, Article 9(1).

160 WILLEKENS, *supra* note 10, p. 98.

This underlines an important aspect of this development – the idea that life is no longer lived in a close-knit community and that the family or household unit has lost much of its historical power. Life is now lived in the context of society as a whole. The traditional bonds, centred on shared religious understanding within the family, have been replaced by the "impersonal connections of the market, mass media and bureaucracy, and by the anonymity of urban life [which] undermine the context of cohesive, collective faith."[161] The church, so it is argued, has merely become the provider of rites of passage. Marriage has survived but after 1920 the legal status of the parties had changed substantially. In 1950 Lord President Cooper was able to confirm that for a generation a wife had been, in terms of Scots property law, a "free agent"; his language directly contradicted that of Lord Justice-clerk Moncrieff in 1875 in a leading case decided by seven judges which, as a result of legislative change, simply ceased to be followed.[162]

This certainly seems to be the case so far as the Church of Scotland is concerned. By the middle of the twentieth century, while at least 44 per cent of people in Scotland retained a connection to the church, only about a quarter of them actually attended.[163] Secularisation belongs largely to the period from the end of the 1950s since when Scotland as a whole has become a markedly less religious place. Family connection with religious institutions declined and for many was simply lost as one generation succeeded another. New concerns occupied attention – nuclear weapons, issues of equality and the environment – in other words, a bloc of issues with which Christianity is not seen as being particularly connected. This demographic change brought with it changed social practices, increased cohabitation, increased divorce rates, a decrease in stigmatisation of certain social groups and increasing pressure on the legislature to bring about the legal changes in family law mentioned at the beginning of this chapter.

The trends in the last half century have been towards secularisation but also towards an increasingly multi-faith society. In the process of de-Christianisation, the role of women has been particularly stressed in connection to issues such as sexual freedom and sexual equality. In practical terms, it has been argued that a number of men only attended church to accompany their wives or girlfriends and that when fewer women attended men's links to churches also declined. This serves to explain how the revolution in family law which we have seen since the 1980s has been able to take place.

---

161 WALLIS *et al.*, *supra* note 154, pp. 496–497.

162 *Beith's Trs v Beith* 1950 SC 66 at 71; *Menzies v Murray* (1874–5) 2 R 507 at 511.

163 BROWN, *supra* note 139, p. 158.

9. CONCLUSION

The influence of religion in family law in Scotland has not disappeared nor, historically, did it ever remain static. From the ubiquity of the canon law of the medieval church to the growing power of the post-Reformation kirk sessions, from nineteenth-century evangelicalism to the plethora of religious voices which continue to be heard in the framing of social policy within the modern multicultural society, religion has both offered a moral framework and occasionally imposed specific legal rules. It has undoubtedly been an important force in the development of family law in Scotland. Whether its influence came through the collective will of the legislature, or the individual attitudes of advocates, judges and treatise writers, it reflected a general social consensus influenced by direct experience of Christianity as practised in Scotland.

Tracing the decline of religious influence is not an easy task. In the debate over the relationship between church and state which was a marked feature of late sixteenth century Scotland, a clear separation of the kirk from the government emerged. Yet the social control exercised by kirk sessions in the daily life of parishioners remained strong and enduring over generations. After 1707 the British parliament was less active in legislating in Scottish private law than the Scottish parliament had been, and this reflects a general difference between social trends north and south of the border. Compared to the churchwardens of England, the ministers and kirk sessions of Scotland retained a firmer grip on public attitudes.[164] The eighteenth century was important since it fostered thinking that was free from the shackles of religious authority. In 1696 the student John Aikenhead had been executed for expressing heretical beliefs despite recanting them.[165] By 1739 Archibald Campbell, professor of Divinity at St Andrews, could go unpunished by the General Assembly for referring to the Mosaic law not as a divine revelation: but choosing to regard the books of Moses merely "as a history that deserves at least as much credit as any other book of antiquity".[166] For him, deists were to be fought not on the basis of reiterating religious dogma but by stressing the rationality that underpinned public religion. But this is not a simple picture of reason eventually outgunning religiosity and adherence to scripture. The traditional division, between moderates on the one hand and a popular party within the kirk which insisted on dogged adherence to

164 Stone discusses the decline in cases concerning sexual morality in the English church courts, asserting an unwillingness to police such matters after 1660 when the focus shifted to economic, rather than moral, concerns: *supra* note 133, pp. 399–400.

165 CAMERON, J.K., "Theological controversy: a factor in the origins of the Scottish Enlightenment" in CAMPBELL, R.H. and SKINNER, A.S. (eds.), *The Origins and Nature of the Scottish Enlightenment* (John Donald Publishers Ltd, 1982), pp. 116–117.

166 *Ibid.*, 127.

traditional doctrine, is capable of refinement which suggests that reliance on rationality was not solely the preserve of the moderates.[167]

David Hume was unusual in his explicit atheism, but Scots thinkers in general were empiricists who reacted against natural law theories and were able to take an independent view of religion as a causal force in social development. Even within the church, the shift in attitude from a century before was marked, and by the 1770s John Millar was able to bring to bear an historical, comparative and sociological approach that was almost entirely divorced from his own personal faith.[168] Yet the judges were generally more conservative figures. The nineteenth century, with disruption in the Scottish church and an evangelical response to the very difficult urban and domestic circumstances brought about through the industrial revolution, saw important changes to the way in which people thought about the family but there was no obvious decline in religious belief. Indeed, although the First World War may have affected belief in God, it seems that in Scotland a more secular social agenda only began to emerge from the 1950s but proceeded with great rapidity.

Yet while religious precepts often formed the basis of legal rules, and did so in a variety of ways, they were not the only source of such rules nor could they withstand forever changes in social mores. As we have seen, laws outlawing adultery and the cursing of parents remained on the statute book for years, even centuries, without being enforced. Advocates and judges were trained in Roman law and this offered an alternative source of legal rules; indeed *ius commune* commentators did not always offer opinions that were consonant with the view of religious orthodoxy promoted by the church in Scotland. The shifting context of law-making, and the development of different conceptualisations of family life – in particular the role of the head of the household and the position of women – make it difficult to trace in a linear way the interaction between law and religion in the context of the family.

Even in the lifetime of William Forbes, the theological climate had changed and there were the beginnings of a shift from "the moral law", represented by the law of God, towards a new emphasis on the role of religion as moral teaching.[169] This was perhaps the first response to concerted attacks on dogmatic religion and it coincided with wider societal changes that gained pace with the industrial

167 For instance, Ned Landsman has investigated the response of evangelicals in the west of Scotland whose views reflected the dramatic social changes in Glasgow as it developed into a commercial centre: LANDSMAN, N.C., "Presbyterians and provincial society: the Evangelical Enlightenment in the west of Scotland, 1750–1775" in DWYER *et al.*, *supra* note 129, pp. 194–209.

168 LEHMAN, *supra* note 133, pp. 136–137.

169 Cf. CAMERON, *supra* note 165, p. 128.

revolution. An age of secularism had dawned and secularisation – specifically the rejection of any argument for the status quo on the basis that it was the divinely ordained natural order – was the pre-requisite for social change in all aspects of life.[170] But the logic of this, in the development of family law, still took centuries to unfold.

170 CAMPBELL, *supra* note 165, p. 13.

ACCOMMODATING RELIGION TO THE GAY EQUALITY IMPERATIVE IN FAMILY LAW

Kenneth McK. NORRIE

1. INTRODUCTION

God hates fags, according to the Westboro Baptist Church, a small denomination of Christians based in Kansas, USA.[1] The law in the United Kingdom, as elsewhere, until relatively recently shared the sentiment of this sect, if expressing it in less aggressive tones: even after criminal penalties were removed it remained lawful, for example, to dismiss a person from employment because of their sexual orientation;[2] employment benefits available to opposite-sex couples could be withheld from same-sex couples without infringing either domestic UK or European Union law;[3] and limiting the definition of "family" so as to exclude same-sex couples for purposes such as tenancy succession was not inconsistent with European Human Rights law.[4] Religious bodies were not, therefore, out of line with the law, or social attitudes, when they rejected the legitimacy of same-sex relationships. However, from the 1980s onwards, social attitudes have been transformed and the law, particularly in the past ten years or so, has completely reversed its position. In the UK, the most notable consequence in family law of that reversal, as radical in its integrative message as the Catholic Emancipation Act 1829, is the Civil Partnership Act 2004.

> "The enactment of the 2004 Act was possible only because of the profound cultural change which has occurred in most of Europe, within the last two generations, in attitudes towards homosexuality. Many people (and not only homosexuals) would say that that change has taken far too long, and they would be right... In Europe, where the Christian religion has provided the cultural matrix for two thousand years,

---

1 See www.godhatesfags.com.

2 *Saunders v Scottish National Camps Association* [1981] IRLR 277; *Advocate General for Scotland v MacDonald* [2003] UKHL 34.

3 *Grant v South West Trains Ltd* [1998] IRLR 206.

4 *Harrogate Borough Council v Simpson* (1984) 17 HLR 205; *S v United Kingdom* (1986) 47 D&R 274.

male homosexual activity was regarded as a grave sin, at one time punishable as a form of heresy; it was also for centuries a capital crime under the secular law of many European countries; other world religions condemned it, and many still do."[5]

Today, same-sex sexual acts are no longer criminal[6]; equality legislation has been extended in employment, in the exercise of a public function and in the provision of goods and services by outlawing discrimination, harassment and victimisation on the basis of sexual orientation[7]; and access to family law rights and obligations has been ensured not only through the civil partnership legislation but also by redefining the concept of cohabitant[8] and by opening the adoption and artificial reproduction legislation to same-sex couples.[9] In addition, the social unacceptability of prejudice against gay and lesbian people is reflected in the hate crime legislation, by which offences are considered to be aggravated if motivated by homophobia.[10] Some progressive religious groups and individuals, drawing on the strand of Christianity that emphasises the virtues of love, forgiveness and tolerance, have been able to accommodate themselves to these social and legal developments; more conservative religious groups and individuals, however, have found themselves out of tune with both social and legal attitudes and continue to resist the developing consensus that sexual orientation is morally neutral – the foundational understanding that justifies the extension of equality legislation to gay and lesbian people and same-sex couples.

Now, in a pluralist society conflicts of sectional interests are inevitable, and common. It is the central dilemma of any liberal democracy that people must be allowed the freedom to believe what they will, including the belief that people should not be allowed the freedoms associated with liberalism.[11] The solution to this dilemma that western democracies have adopted since the Enlightenment is to protect vigorously the right to believe or hold views and, subject to the laws of defamation and incitement, to express them; but to insist equally vigorously that no individual or group can claim exemption from the general law of the land, or the application of a different system of rules to them, simply on the basis of their

5 *M v Secretary of State for Work and Pensions* [2006] UKHL 11, *per* Lord Walker of Gestingthorpe at para. 92.

6 Sexual Offences Act 1967, s. 1 (England and Wales); Criminal Justice (Scotland) Act 1980, s. 80 (Scotland).

7 The previous discrete statutory provisions covering most of these matters have now been gathered together in the Equality Act 2010.

8 *Fitzpatrick v Sterling Housing Association* [1999] 4 All ER 707; *Ghaidan v Godin-Mendoza* [2004] UKHL 30 and (in Scotland) the Family Law (Scotland) Act 2006, s. 25.

9 Adoption and Children Act 2002, ss. 50 and 144(4) (England and Wales); Adoption and Children (Scotland) Act 2007, s. 29 (Scotland); Human Fertilisation and Embryology Act 2008, ss. 42 and 43.

10 Criminal Justice Act 2003, s. 146 (England and Wales); Offences (Aggravation by Prejudice) (Scotland) Act 2009, s. 2.

11 See SEGLOW, J., "What's Wrong with Liberalism?", (1998) 4 *Res Publica* 229.

beliefs.[12] This is a manifestation of secularism which is, properly, not state atheism but the separation of church and state.[13] It is no surprise, then, to see this approach encapsulated in article 9 of the European Convention on Human Rights: paragraph (1) grants an unqualified right to freedom of religion or belief, while paragraph (2) allows any manifestation of belief to be qualified whenever that is necessary in a democratic society, for example in the interests of others. The paradox inherent in this approach – that a religious belief is protected on its own terms while manifestation of belief is protected only when justified by secular argument[14] – is more apparent than real since religious pluralism (the underlying value of article 9) can exist only in a society that rejects the absolute truth of one theological interpretation of the divine and the absolute falsity of all others. It follows, for example, that an individual is entitled without qualification to believe in the death penalty, and to call openly for its reintroduction,[15] but he or she (entirely self-evidently) is not entitled to execute anyone who merits it according to his or her moral or religious code. Likewise, parents and schoolteachers are entitled to believe that a Christian upbringing of children necessarily includes their physical punishment for misbehaviour[16] – and are entitled not to be discriminated against for holding such beliefs – but they are not entitled to put that belief into effect if the law has prohibited it, for there is no argument beyond "my God says so" that justifies infringing the rights of children not to be subjected to physical violence.[17]

---

12 Western countries, since at least the Treaty of Westphalia in 1648 from which the modern notion of the nation-state is derived, have rejected the ancient idea that law is personal and that different groups within one jurisdiction can be subject to different rules of law. Other countries, such as for example India, Sri Lanka, Malaysia, Israel and South Africa, accept that "personal law" applies in some areas, typically family law, so that the traditional religious rules of marriage apply differently depending upon the religion (or, in the case of South Africa, the customary Tribe) to which the person belongs. See AHMED, F., "Personal Autonomy and the Option of Religious Law", (2010) 24 *Int. J. Law Pol. Fam.* 222; FISHBAYN, L., "Litigating the Right to Culture: Family Law in the New South Africa", (1999) 13 *Int. J. Law Pol. Fam.* 147. (Interestingly, there is biblical support for the rejection of the personal law approach in favour of a unitary law for everyone whether or not they adhere to the majoritarian religion: Leviticus 24:22). Traces of personal law remain, of course, in the rules of international private law.

13 Secularism traces its intellectual origins to Enlightenment thinking and its legal origins to the constitutions that emerged from the American and French Revolutions in the late 18th Century. See MARTIN, D., *On Secularisation: Towards a Revised General Theory* (Ashgate, 2005); SAJO, A., "Preliminaries to a Concept of Constitutional Secularism", (2008) 6 *Int. J. Con. Law* 605.

14 CHAPLIN, J., talks of "justified secularism" whereby public good rather than religious arguments must be put forward to justify any state measure: "The Place of Religious Arguments for Law Reform in a Secular State", (2009) 162 *Law and Just.* 18.

15 And indeed will have little difficulty in finding scriptural support. See for example Exodus 35:2 where death is prescribed for those who work on the seventh day and, pertinently, Leviticus 20:13, where men who have sex with men "shall surely be put to death".

16 Scriptural support may be found in Proverbs 13:24 and 23:13–14.

17 *R (Williamson) v Secretary of State for Education* [2005] 2 AC 246; *Christian Education South Africa v Minister of Education* 2000 (4) SA 757.

The UK courts, particularly since the coming into force of the Human Rights Act 1998, have developed well-oiled mechanisms in a wide variety of areas for dealing with the claims of competing interests.[18] The language of legitimate aim, proportionality and justification has become second-nature to judges and indeed legislators as they seek appropriate balances between different rights. For this reason the courts, when faced with conflicting claims by supporters of gay equality and supporters of religious traditionalism, have not felt the need to develop new ways of reasoning to resolve the particular dispute before them. Yet the clash of these particular interests does present the courts with some unique difficulties. For one thing, the claims of religious traditionalists are based on propositions of the sort that, by definition, are not susceptible to proof, blunting courts' traditional intellectual tools in responding to arguments developed from such propositions. "Blessed are they that have not seen, and yet have believed"[19] is a proposition foundational of faith but inimical to court process and judicial reasoning. Courts are much more comfortable dealing with arguments drawn from secular rationalism than from divine revelation.[20] Let us concede, for the sake of argument, that religious doctrine can itself claim to be rationalist – in the sense of being based on propositions logically deduced from its revelatory origins. I can allow no more generous concession than this, because rationalism, of any sort, requires to be internally coherent and the secularist finds little difficulty in identifying doctrinal incoherences and illogicalities in modern Christian theology. It is, for example, human choice and not divine revelation that determines which of the biblical "abominations"[21] remain condemned by religious traditionalists today. It is political or social choice and not rational deduction that inclines modern Christianity to place Luke's story of the Virgin Birth[22] above Matthew's detailed genealogy of Jesus' descent from Abraham and David – via, of course, his father Joseph.[23] Not for nothing does Luther condemn Reason as the enemy of Religion. Insofar as this is indeed a form of rationalism, we might call it "revelatory rationalism". Its starting point is the truth, from which conclusions are deduced through reason, though neither reason nor evidence can challenge the starting point. Secular rationalism, on the other

18 See EWING, K., "The Human Rights Act and Parliamentary Democracy", (1999) 62 *Mod. LR* 79.

19 John, 20:29. Cf. II Corinthians, 5:7: "For we walk by faith, not by sight" (All biblical quotations in this chapter come from the protestant Authorised King James Version. Roman Catholic equivalents, such as the Douay-Rheims Version, may word matters differently – as may more contemporary translations – but, with the issues discussed in this article, the meanings will substantially overlap).

20 Baroness Hale of Richmond, for example, talked of "the rational behaviour we now expect of government and the state" in *Ghaidan v Godin-Mendoza* [2004] UKHL 30 at para. 132. "If distinctions are to be drawn", she said, "particularly upon a group basis, it is an important discipline to look for a rational basis for those distinctions."

21 See note 117, *infra*.

22 Luke 1:26–35.

23 Matthew 1:1–16.

hand, sees the identification of the truth as the end point, and it demands verifiable origins as well as deductive conclusions. It is this form of rationalism that courts of law, steeped as they are in a liberal/Enlightenment *Weltanschauung*, insist upon from litigants. Courts are discomfited when one or other party eschews such values and they struggle when asked to reconcile the mutually incomprehensible claims of revelation and reason.

Another unique difficulty for courts faced with a conflict of interests between gay equality and religious traditionalism is that the scope for compromise is very much more limited than with other conflicts of rights (such as, for example, the conflict between the right of privacy and freedom of the press). While the democratic process, and the courts, invariably seek some middle ground, or at the very least balance, between conflicting views, this is true only where each view is considered legitimate. Proponents of the views at issue here, however, tend to deny the legitimacy of their opponents' position: gay equality advocates reject the ethical validity of any qualification to their equality claims, while religious traditionalists will deny that the secular law can in any way qualify the God's law by which they seek to lead their lives. Denial of a proposition's legitimacy leads to denial of the very possibility of compromise, with the result that failure to achieve complete victory is regarded as total defeat.[24]

This essay will examine the compromises and accommodations that the law in Scotland and in England and Wales has made as it seeks to reconcile the conflicting claims for gay equality, particularly in family life, where the claim for religious influence is often asserted the loudest, and for religious freedom, in particular the right to discriminate for scriptural/doctrinal reasons. It will attempt to identify the underlying principles upon which this accommodation is based and will offer some assessment of how family law is likely to develop in the future in light of such accommodation. The focus will be on (western) Christianity, not only because this remains far and away the predominant form of faith in the United Kingdom but also and more importantly because the clash

---

24 This is seen clearly in *R (On the Application of Johns) v Derby City Council* [2011] EWHC 375 (Admin) where the court dismissed as "a travesty of the reality" counsel for the claimants' argument that a refusal to accept as foster carers a couple who expressed strongly negative views about gay and lesbian people and same-sex couples amounted to a blanket ban on Christian foster carers, an attempt to de-legitimise Christian belief and a state attempt to force Christians into "the closet". The Council had refused to register the couple as foster carers because of their beliefs relating to homosexuality, and the couple interpreted this as an attack on their religion because it was from their faith that they drew their beliefs about homosexuality. No middle ground was acceptable to either party. The court, refusing to hold that the Council had acted unlawfully, did not seek a middle ground but instead concluded that it was not discrimination based on religious belief to refuse to register the applicants as foster carers because of their attitude towards homosexuality: there was no religious discrimination because the council would have similarly refused to accept a non-religious couple with the same attitude towards homosexuality.

arises world-wide only in countries where that is the predominant form of faith. No country in the world where a majority of its population adheres to eastern (or Orthodox) Christianity, or Islam, or Hinduism, or Judaism has given any recognition whatsoever to same-sex relationships within their own systems of family law[25] and so the clash between law and religion in this area simply will not arise in practice – yet.

2. CHRISTIAN APPROACHES TO GAY AND LESBIAN EQUALITY

Few Christian denominations are today so extreme in their rejection of same-sex sexual orientation, behaviour and relationships as that of the Westboro Baptist Church, but biblical and doctrinal authority for regarding gay and lesbian people as sinners, and for regarding same-sex relationships (whether momentarily sexual or permanently familial) as necessarily unacceptable, is not hard to find. Mosaic law as laid down in the Pentateuch is unequivocal: "Thou shalt not lie with mankind as with womankind: it is abomination";[26] "If a man also lies with mankind as he lieth with a woman, both of them have committed an abomination; they shall surely be put to death; their blood shall be upon them".[27] New Testament authority, however much some glossators seek to present it as more forgiving, more loving of sinners, than the Old Testament, is no less clear. In St Paul's Epistle to the Romans he portrays all sexual acts outwith marriage (by which he meant the sanctified union of one man and one woman) as a rebellion against God and as such a rejection of the Christian way of life:

> "For this cause God gave them up unto vile affections; for even their women did change the natural use into that which is against nature; And likewise also the men, leaving the natural use of the woman, burned in their lust one toward another; men with men working that which is unseemly."[28]

---

25 Curiously, the Supreme Court of Israel has permitted the registration in the marriage registers of same-sex couples who marry abroad: *Yossi Ben-Ari v Minister of Interior* 21 November 2006. And it has interpreted the Israeli employment legislation as prohibiting sexual orientation discrimination: *El Al Israel Airlines v Danielowitz* [1994] Isr SC 48(5). For a general discussion of the issue in a country where religious influences on the polity of the nation are very much stronger than in the UK, see EINHORN, T., "Same-Sex Family Unions in Israeli Law", (2008) 4 *Utrecht L. Rev.* 222.

26 Lev. 18:22.

27 Lev. 20:13. Interestingly, both this passage and Lev. 18:22 is followed by prohibitions on men lying with beasts, and then women lying with beasts. Entirely omitted is any prohibition on women lying with women.

28 Romans 1:26–27. Smith J.A. in the Saskatchewan Court of Appeal does not exaggerate when he says "It is fair to say that religious belief is at the root of much if not most of the historical discrimination against gays and lesbians": *In the Matter of Marriage Commissioners Appointed Under the Marriage Act 1995* 2011 SKCA 3 at para. 145.

Much of modern Christian theology, drawn from the natural law philosophy of St Thomas Aquinas,[29] sees sexual behaviour as justified only by reason of the good – potential creation of new life – that might come from it and not for the selfish reason of the pleasure it gives.[30] This view of sexual behaviour requires the characterisation as sinful, a rejection of God, of all other sexual acts than the potentially procreative, such as masturbation, oral and anal sex, bestiality and same-sex sexual activities, and, for those who question why the scriptural prohibitions cited above should be followed today while so many others are ignored, the view provides an intellectual underpinning to the Christian opposition both to the extension of non-discrimination norms to gay and lesbian people (which presupposes the moral neutrality of sexual orientation), and to the full legal recognition and regulation of same-sex relationships (which presupposes a moral equivalence to married relationships).

Major elements in all the mainstream religious bodies in Great Britain, while tending to claim a distinctly New Testament emphasis on compassion for those whose sexual orientation is not exclusively heterosexual, continue to maintain that, because of the doctrinal traditions adverted to above, same-sex relationships that are sexual in nature (or origin) are, at best, less worthy than opposite-sex relationships of respect, recognition and protection and, at worst, deserving of condemnation and legal punishment. Both the (Presbyterian) Church of Scotland and the (Episcopalian) Church of England have experienced internal disputes of such magnitude as to threaten schism[31] over gay clergy.[32] Neither church

---

29 "Natural law" in post-Reformation thought no longer asserts that human good is found in human nature (which presupposes common understandings of the concepts of "good", "nature" and even "human"). This is what HART, H.L.A. called "the Thomist tradition of Natural Law": *The Concept of Law* (Clarendon, 1961) at p. 152. The Thomist tradition is still adhered to in the Roman Catholic Church, but for protestant adherents to natural law its contribution to thought is that it seeks to unite morals and the law. See ORREGO, C., "HLA Hart's Understanding of Classical Natural Law Theory", (2004) 24 *OJLS* 287. Most natural lawyers (Roman Catholic or protestant) oppose vigorously the very notion of opening marriage to same-sex couples, adopting a "naturalistic" definition (which presupposes what it sets out to prove) of marriage: see CHUE, S., "Catholicism, Natural Law and Same-sex Marriage", (2001) 8 *UCL Juris. Rev.* 84.

30 The argument seems to be that using the body for pleasure alone damages personal integrity by reducing the body to a means to an end: CHUE, *ibid.* at p. 104.

31 Schism is a defining characteristic of organised religion, and its threat may well be the driver of its intellectual life. Within the Christian faith, important schisms have included the Arian Controversy at Nicaea in 325, the Great Schism in 1054 when the Latin (universal) church split with the Orthodoxy of Byzantium, the Reformation of the western church in the 16th Century, and (rather more parochially) the Disruption of the Scottish church in 1843.

32 On 23 May 2011 the General Assembly of the Church of Scotland debated a Report of a *Special Commission on Same-Sex Relationships and the Ministry* and resolved to consider at a later date the lifting of a moratorium on the ordination of persons in a same-sex relationship. The Report found that 19,4% of members would leave the Church if such ordination were permitted, and that 8,5% of members would leave if it were prohibited. On 8 July 2010 it was reported in *The Guardian* that the Church of England had (again) blocked the appointment of

formally approves of its ministers granting blessings to same-sex unions, though only the Episcopalian church positively prohibits them from doing so (perhaps reflecting the hierarchical nature of that church's governance).[33] The Roman Catholic Church, while acknowledging that people "do not choose their homosexual condition" and requiring that "they must be accepted with respect, compassion and sensitivity"[34] denies the acceptability of sexual behaviour between persons of the same sex and, with majestic naivety, concludes: "Homosexual persons are called to chastity".[35] There is no question of sacramental approval of same-sex unions by the Roman Catholic Church.[36] Around the world, where religious fervour burns more fiercely than in the United Kingdom, gay men and lesbians are not just regarded as second class by religious institutions, but are often criminalised and persecuted by the state itself, which frequently founds on religious doctrine for its justification in doing so.[37] There is little doubt that, in world terms, the stronger the influence religion has on the polity of a nation, the more gay and lesbian people (and, it may be said, women in general[38]) are likely to be discriminated against, and even persecuted. The United Kingdom is a classic example of a country where secular liberalism long

---

an openly gay vicar to a post of Bishop. That Church allows both women and gay people to become ministers, but bars them from promotion to leadership roles within its organisation (cutting off for women, incidentally, this route to membership of the legislature, Anglican bishops still having *ex officio* seats in the House of Lords).

33 On 25 July 2005, some months before the coming into force of the Civil Partnership Act 2004, the House of Bishops of the Church of England issued a *Pastoral Statement* to the effect that Clergy of the Church of England should not provide services of blessing for those who register a civil partnership. In addition, it reaffirmed that "sexual intercourse, as an expression of faithful intimacy, properly belongs within marriage exclusively", marriage being a gift from God between a man and a woman. In Scotland, the General Assembly of the Church of Scotland accepted the conclusion of the Special Commission (see footnote 32 above) that the issue was essentially the same as that of the ordination of ministers in same-sex relationships, and that the matter should be considered at the same time.

34 *Catechism of the Catholic Church*, 2358.

35 *Ibid.*, 2359.

36 "Not now, not in the future, not ever, no matter whatever legislation or regulations your government enacts or endorses", in the words the Bishop of Paisley is reported as having written to the Prime Minister, *Herald* 23 July 2010.

37 In *HJ and HT v Secretary of State for the Home Department* [2010] UKSC 31 the Deputy President of the Supreme Court, Lord Hope of Craighead, highlighted "the rampant homophobic teaching that right-wing churches indulge in throughout much of sub-saharan Africa" (para. 2). His use of a political term to describe a religious position is, surely, no mistake.

38 It is not out of place, I think, to recall the strong biblical message of the place of women in society. A typical story, which even if not literally true is presented as an allegory from which lessons on how to lead a good life are to be gleaned, is that of Abraham's nephew, Lot. When angels came to warn him of the imminent destruction of his home town of Sodom, he proved his righteousness by shielding them from the men of Sodom. The sodomites demanded that Lot bring out the men he was sheltering, that they may "know" them (The New International Version rejects the poetic euphemism in favour of sterile literalism: "Bring them out to us so that we can have sex with them"). Lot refused, offering the sodomites instead his "two daughters which have not known man (NIV: who have never slept with a man)... do ye to

ago weakened the political influence of religion and the gains for the gay and lesbian community, and for women, deploying rationalist arguments which can no longer be trumped by divine revelation, have been substantial.

3. THE CHANGING LAW RELATING TO GAY AND LESBIAN PEOPLE

The decriminalisation of male-male sexual activity started a legal revolution in attitudes to sexual orientation. In its terms it did no more than remove one element of direct discrimination, but it had the more profound effect of removing the firewall which had until then existed, providing substantial protection, and secular justification, to discriminatory attitudes and laws: people whose very nature inclined them to criminality were people from whom it was entirely proper to withhold certain civic rights, such as employment protection and relationship recognition. In 1988 the UK Parliament passed legislation designed to restore to some extent that firewall, by prohibiting local authorities from promoting in maintained schools "the acceptability of homosexuality as a pretended family relationship".[39] The legal effect of this provision was minimal[40] but its message was clear: gay and lesbian people were less worthy of respect and legal protection than non-gay and non-lesbian people, and their relationships with each other were not to be regarded as "real".[41] It is, of course, always foolish to build firewalls with combustible materials and, pleasingly, one of the primary effects of this legislation was to galvanise gay-rights activists to seek not only its repeal but in addition real protection from discrimination and, with it, access to the full range of civil rights and protections. Within ten years of the passing of "section 28", equality and non-discrimination had become major political objectives, not only for the new Labour Government that took office in 1997 but also within both the Council of Europe and the European Union.

The European Court of Human Rights held in 1999 for the first time that sexual orientation was one of the prohibited grounds of discrimination under article

them as is good in your eyes" (Genesis 19:5–8). Women have suffered throughout the ages at least as much as gay and lesbian people by religious fervour deduced from revelatory truths.

39 Local Government Act 1988, s. 28, inserting into the Local Government Act 1986 a new s. 2A to that effect. Repealed in Scotland by the Ethical Standards in Public Life etc. (Scotland) Act 2000, sched. 4 para. 1 and in England and Wales by the Local Government Act 2003, sched. 8(1), para. 1. See CUMPER, P. and BELL, M., "Reforming Section 28: Lessons for Westminster from Holyrood", (2003) 4 *EHRLR* 400.

40 Even when it remained on the statute book, the House of Lords felt able to ignore it in holding that a same-sex couple were a "family" for certain statutory purposes: *Fitzpatrick v Sterling Housing Association* [1999] 4 All ER 707.

41 NORRIE, K., "Symbolic and Meaningless Legislation", (1988) 33 *JLSS* 310.

14[42] and it has since been held repeatedly that differential treatment on the ground of sexual orientation, as with sex, requires particularly weighty justifications before being compatible with the European Convention on Human Rights, the state's margin of appreciation being narrow.[43] After some years of resistance, and of founding its otherwise progressive sexual orientation jurisprudence firmly on individuals' right to private life,[44] the European Court finally accepted in 2010 that same-sex couples came within the protection of "family life" under article 8.[45] European Union law has moved in the same direction. Council Directive 2000/78/EC established a general framework for equal treatment in employment and occupation on a number of grounds, including sexual orientation,[46] and in order to meet its obligations under this Directive the United Kingdom passed the Employment Equality (Sexual Orientation) Regulations 2003,[47] which prohibited discrimination on the ground of sexual orientation in employment. In addition, the Equality Act (Sexual Orientation) Regulations 2007[48] prohibited such discrimination in the provision of goods, facilities and services.[49] The Civil Partnership Act 2004 serves the same function for the private sphere as the employment and the goods and services regulations provide for the public sphere: a means of ensuring that gay and lesbian people, and same-sex couples, have access to virtually the same legal rights and liabilities as non-gay and non-lesbian people, and opposite-sex couples, thus allowing them to make public declarations of love, that many waters cannot quench, nor floods drown, as the Song of Songs has it.[50]

---

42 *Da Silva Mouta v Portugal* (1999) 31 EHRR 1055.

43 *Lustig-Prean v United Kingdom* (2000) 29 EHRR 548 at para. 82; *SL v Austria* (2003) 37 EHRR 39 at para. 37; *Karner v Austria* (2004) 38 EHRR 24 at para. 37; *EB v France* (2008) 47 EHRR 21 at para.91; *Kozak v Poland* (2010) 51 EHRR 16 at para. 92; *Schalk and Kopf v Austria* App 30141/04, 24 June 2010 at para. 97.

44 See JOHNSON, P., "'An Essentially Private Manifestation of Human Personality': Constructions of Homosexuality in the European Court of Human Rights", (2010) 10 *H.R.L.Rev.* 67.

45 *Schalk and Kopf v Austria* App 30141/04, 24 June 2010 at para. 94. See SUTHERLAND, E., "A Step Closer to Same-sex Marriage Throughout Europe" (2011) 15 *Edin.L.Rev.* 97.

46 This was made politically possible by the Treaty of Amsterdam, which added a new Article 13 to the EC Treaty (now, after the Treaty of Lisbon, Article 19 of the Treaty on the Functioning of the European Union) which extended the competence of Community institutions to take action in relation to discrimination based on a variety of characteristics including, for the first time, sexual orientation. Both gay and lesbian individuals and same-sex couples must have access to the same level of employment benefits and protections as those afforded to non-gay individuals and opposite-sex couples; *Maruko v Versorgungsanstalt Deutschen Buhnen* [2008] IRLR 450, and *Roemer v Hamburg* CJEU Grand Chamber Case C. 147/08, 10 May 2011.

47 SI 2003/1661.

48 SI 2007/1263. See *Hall and Preddy v Bull* [2011] EW Misc 2 (Bristol County Court) where hotel owners were held to have acted unlawfully in refusing a double room to a same-sex couple.

49 These provisions, and others, are now gathered together into the comprehensive Equality Act 2010, which re-enacts and harmonises the original legislative rules.

50 Song of Solomon, 8:7.

4. ACCOMMODATING RELIGIOUS CONCERNS

Few religious bodies formally welcomed these developments, though Government was by no means insensitive to the fact that the new legal requirements for non-discrimination against gay and lesbian people were likely to cause difficulty to those who chose to interpret the scriptural and doctrinal authority in which they placed their faith as requiring such discrimination. Part of the response, required by the Framework Directive itself, was to extend protection from discrimination to religious believers at the same time as this was granted to gay and lesbian people. The Employment Equality (Religion or Belief) Regulations 2003[51] prohibited discrimination in employment, and the Equality Act 2006 prohibited discrimination in the provision of goods and services, on the basis of religion or belief:[52] both were in similar terms to the equivalent provisions prohibiting sexual orientation discrimination.

More importantly, all the legislation that extends rights (and liabilities) to gay and lesbian people and same-sex couples contain within their own terms qualifications and exceptions in an attempt to ameliorate the fears of religious traditionalists and to accommodate their interests.[53] The employment regulations, for example, contain not only a tightly drawn, but general, exception for posts where being of a particular sexual orientation is a "genuine occupational requirement"[54] but also include an exception (added to the original draft, it seems as a result of representations from religious bodies and in particular the Archbishops' Council of the Church of England[55]) specifically aimed at religious employers and designed to ensure their continued right to ban the appointment or promotion of gay and lesbian individuals as clerics. If the employment is "for the purposes of an organised religion", then the employer may make a requirement that the employee be of a particular sexual orientation if this is necessary either to comply with the doctrines of the religion or in order to avoid conflicting with the strongly held religious convictions of a significant number

---

51 SI 2003/1660.

52 Equality Act 2006, ss. 44–55.

53 There is, of course, nothing new in this approach. The Emancipation Act 1829 (properly, the Roman Catholic Relief Act, 10 Geo. 4, c. 7) was a radical reversal of the civil disabilities of Roman Catholics in the United Kingdom but, to assuage the fears of the protestant majority, the Act did not alter the terms of the Act of Settlement 1701, so that Roman Catholics remain to this day barred from the greatest public office of them all, the Crown. Roman Catholic ex-priests remained barred under the 1829 Act from becoming MPs until, astoundingly, 2001: see House of Commons (Removal of Clergy Disqualification) Act 2001.

54 Employment Equality (Sexual Orientation) Regulations 2003, reg. 7(1). See now Equality Act 2010, sched. 9(1), which talks simply of an "occupational requirement".

55 According to Richards J. in *R (Amicus) v Secretary of State for Trade and Industry* [2004] EWHC 860 (Admin) at para. 90.

of the religion's followers.[56] It is this that allows the Church of England, for example, to explicitly refuse to promote gay clergy to the position of Bishop.[57] The Equality Act (Sexual Orientation) Regulations 2007 contained similar exceptions to the obligation to provide goods and services without discrimination on the basis of sexual orientation.[58]

Within family law, the civil partnership legislation too attempts to accommodate those who fear that the very idea will undermine the religious conception of marriage. It was emphasised throughout the parliamentary passage of the Civil Partnership Act 2004 that while civil partnership would be a means by which the civil law permitted same-sex couples access to virtually all the rights and obligations that are available to opposite-sex couples through the existing institution of marriage, the new institution, though equivalent to marriage, would be entirely separate therefrom, and entirely secular.[59] The separation from marriage is achieved primarily by ensuring that civil partnership is available only to same-sex couples,[60] while marriage remains available only to opposite-sex couples.[61] The secularisation of civil partnership was ensured in a number of ways, in particular by the rule that it can be created only at the hands of a state official, a registrar, and not at the hands of a religious officiant. Indeed the language of "solemnisation", with its sacramental overtones, used even with

---

56 2003 Regs, reg. 7(3) (now Equality Act 2010, sched. 9(2)). These rules survived a challenge to their compatibility with the Framework Directive in *R (Amicus), ibid.* For a discussion of that case, see SAMUELS, L., "Sexual Orientation Discrimination and the Church: Balancing Competing Human Rights", (2005) 8 *Eccl. L.J.* 74.

57 Their legal right to refuse to promote women is traced to the similarly worded s. 19 of the Sex Discrimination Act 1975, as amended by the Employment Equality (Sex Discrimination) Regulations 2005, SI 2005/2467. For a discussion, see RIVERS, J., "Law, Religion and Gender Equality", (2007) *Eccl. L.J.* 24.

58 Religious bodies, particularly the Roman Catholic Church in both Scotland and England, lobbied unsuccessfully for an additional and specific exemption to allow Catholic adoption agencies to continue to limit their services to opposite-sex (married) couples only. They were given instead some extra time to accommodate their practices to the change in the law but have had to comply since 31 December 2008 (Reg. 15), or seek to bring themselves within the terms of the general exception: see *Catholic Care (Diocese of Leeds) v Charity Commission for England and Wales* [2010] EWHC 520 (Ch). On 21 August 2010 the Charity Commission refused to allow Catholic Care to alter its purposes, holding that it was inappropriate to permit charities to exercise deliberate discrimination (decision available under "Final Decisions of the Commission" at www.charity-commission.gov.uk). This decision was upheld by the First Tier Tribunal on 26 April 2011 (decision available at http://www.judiciary.gov.uk/media/judgments/2011/catholic-care-judgment-26042011.

59 Hansard, HL 22 April 2004, col. 388; Hansard, HC 12 October 2004, col. 177.

60 Civil Partnership Act 2004, ss. 3(1)(a), 49(a) and 86(1)(a). This was always the intendment: see DTI Women and Equality Unit, *Civil Partnership: A Framework for the Legal Recognition of Same-sex Couples* (2003) at para. 1.3; Scottish Executive, *Civil Partnership Registration: A Legal Status for Committed Same-sex Couples in Scotland* (2003) at para. 5.6.

61 Matrimonial Causes Act 1973, s. 11(c) (England and Wales); Marriage (Scotland) Act 1977, s. 5(4)(e).

civil marriages,[62] is avoided completely.[63] Also, the location where a civil partnership may be registered must not be "religious premises", that is to say premises which (a) are used solely or mainly for religious purposes, or (b) have been so used and have not subsequently been used solely or mainly for other purposes".[64] This is designed to ensure the separation, even isolation, of civil partnership from both marriage and religion. The place of registration rule will shortly be changed in England and Wales.[65]

5. ACCOMMODATION AS DEFEAT

Religious traditionalists have taken scant comfort from the compromises described above. They have argued that the accommodation of religious interests does not go nearly far enough, and that religious believers may be put in the unwarranted position of having to choose between their faith and their job. In *McClintock v Department of Constitutional Affairs*[66] the appellant was a Justice of the Peace and in that role was required to deal with applications for, and the making of, adoption orders. The Civil Partnership Act 2004 had amended the English adoption legislation[67] to permit adoption applications to be made by couples who are civil partners (previously, only married couples could adopt children jointly). The appellant claimed that he could not, compatibly with his philosophical and religious beliefs, place any child with a same-sex couple, as the law now permitted, and when his employers, the Department of Constitutional Affairs, refused to allow him to recuse himself from any case in which the issue might arise he felt obliged to resign, which he claimed amounted to both discrimination contrary to the Employment Equality (Religion or Belief) Regulations 2003, and a breach of his human rights under article 9 of the European Convention on Human Rights. The Employment Appeal Tribunal had little difficulty in holding that the Department of Constitutional Affairs was

62 "Solemnisation" is the process by which a marriage is created, both for religious and civil marriages: Marriage (Scotland) Act 1977, s. 8; Marriage Act 1949, ss. 1, 5 and 26.

63 The process by which civil partnership comes into existence is through "registration" effected by the registrar, not solemnisation by the registrar.

64 Civil Partnership Act 2004, s. 6 (England and Wales), and s. 93 (Scotland).

65 Under s. 202 of the Equality Act 2010, Regulations may provide for the approval of religious premises for the registration of civil partnership. A consultation on how this is to be achieved was issued by the UK Government: *Civil Partnerships on Religious Premises: A Consultation* (Government Equalities Office, March 2011).

66 [2008] IRLR 29. See also *Matthews v Northampton County Council*, Employment Tribunal, Leicester, 16 November 2010, where a council employee who refused to be involved in the Council's adoption process insofar as it might lead to children being adopted by same-sex couples was held to be lawfully dismissed from her employment.

67 Adoption and Children Act 2002, s. 144, as amended by the Civil Partnership Act 2004, s. 79. The equivalent change was made to the Scottish legislation by the Adoption and Children (Scotland) Act 2007, s. 29(3).

justified in requiring that a magistrate applies the law of the land: a person who has taken a judicial oath does not have the freedom to determine which laws to apply and which to avoid. He had not, therefore, been discriminated against on the ground of his religion or belief but because of his unwillingness to apply the law as Parliament had enacted it. McClintock had attempted to argue that the Civil Partnership Act amendments to the adoption legislation took away his power to determine what was in the interests of the child (the determining issue in adoption), but his prejudgment that it would never be in the interests of a child to be brought up by a couple of the same sex shows his claim to be as preposterous as it was unsustainable. For no judge in a court of law can be heard to say that he will decide a case according to the teachings of his religion, in preference to the verifiable evidence presented to him in an adversarial court process.[68]

The Court of Appeal came to substantially the same conclusion in a case not involving a person subject to a judicial oath but nevertheless exercising public functions. In *Ladele v Islington Borough Council*[69] the claimant had been a registrar of births, deaths and marriages who felt obliged to resign when her employers refused to exempt her from the duty to conduct civil partnership registrations, which she did not want to do on the ground that unions between same-sex couples were contrary to what she described as her "orthodox Christian beliefs", especially her belief in the sanctity of marriage (which she took to mean, following the Thomist tradition, that sexual relations are legitimate only between a man and a woman, and only then when the couple are bound in matrimony). Her claim that she had been subjected to discrimination, on the ground of her religious beliefs contrary to the Employment Equality (Religion or Belief) Regulations 2003, was rejected by both the Employment Appeal Tribunal and the Court of Appeal. The Court of Appeal held that there had been no direct discrimination against the claimant because, by requiring her to undertake civil partnership duties, she was being treated in exactly the same way as all other employees.[70] Nor had there been indirect discrimination, because the Council's legitimate aim was not only to ensure that all couples who wished to register a civil partnership had access to a registrar who would do so but also to ensure that the Council acted consistently with its legitimate policy of fighting discrimination against gay and lesbian citizens, and employees. The Court endorsed the finding of the Employment Appeal Tribunal that:

68 In *T, Petitioner*, 1997 SLT 724 the Lord Ordinary, Lord Gill, was castigated in the Inner House for letting his "own private beliefs" cloud his judgment on the issue of adoption by a gay person. At least McClintock was honest as to where his beliefs came from.

69 [2010] 1 WLR 955. See HAMBLER, A., "A No-Win Situation for Public Officials with Faith Convictions", (2010) 12 *Ecc. L.J.* 3.

70 *Ibid.*, at para. 29.

> "once it is accepted that the aim of providing the service on a non-discriminatory basis was legitimate – and in truth it was bound to be – then... it must follow that [the Council] were entitled to require all registrars to perform the full range of services."[71]

Indeed, the Court of Appeal was willing to contemplate that councils could not lawfully exempt their registrars from civil partnership duties because the Equality Act (Sexual Orientation) Regulations 2007, which prohibit discrimination in the provision of goods and services on the basis of sexual orientation, take precedence over any rights that a person might otherwise have by virtue of his or her religious belief or faith, to practise discrimination on the ground of sexual orientation.[72]

The major problem, from the point of view of the religious traditionalist, with these legislative compromises is that they do not address the true nature of religious objections to gay and lesbian equality and, therefore, they can offer nothing to the traditionalist. A right to believe something internally is, for those who believe they must obey their God in their actions as well as in their thoughts, a worthless right unless it carries the right to external action on the basis of that belief. The secular argument that civil partnership has no effect on the religious concept of marriage has no purchase with a believer who sees the problem as the legitimisation of same-sex relationships. But the legitimisation argument has already been lost. It is easy, from a legal perspective, to dismiss Ms Ladele's claims that civil partnership undermines marriage but the legal answer – that it simply doesn't, because the two institutions are separate – does not address her real concern, which is that same-sex relationships are sinful and should not be sanctioned by the state. "The tree is known by his fruit",[73] and the fruit is legitimisation of same-sex relationships, whatever the tree is called.[74] Ms Ladele's problem is that once the state has taken the position that sexual orientation is morally neutral the law has no option but to reject her real concern, even if in doing so it uses the language of compromise. So while religious traditionalists get virtually nothing (of worth, to them) from the accommodations offered by the law, giving civil partnership to the gay and lesbian community though it asks for marriage is giving it substantially more than it had before and (at least in the United Kingdom) to withhold little of substantive content. It is no surprise, then,

71 *Per* Lord Neuberger M.R. at para. 49, quoting Elias J. in the EAT at para. 111.

72 *Ibid.*, paras. 71 and 74. The same conclusion was reached, for much the same reasons if in a different constitutional context, by the Court of Appeal of Saskachewan in *In the Matter of Marriage Commissioners Appointed Under the Marriage Act 1995* 2011 SKCA 3.

73 Matthew 12:33.

74 See HUMPHREYS, J., "The Civil Partnership Act 2004, Same-sex Marriage and the Church of England", (2005) 8 *Eccl. L. J.* 289; BAMFORTH, N., "The Benefits of Marriage in All but Name? Same-sex Couples and the Civil Partnership Act 2004", (2007) 19 *CFLQ* 133.

that religious traditionalists see compromise as defeat. In truth, they are fighting battles that they have already lost.

6. THE PRINCIPLES UNDERPINNING ACCOMMODATION

One of the reasons why there is a dissonance between the expectations of the parties in terms of accommodation, and what the law actually offers, is that different accommodations apply with different statutory provisions with the result that the principles underlying and justifying the very concept of accommodation are obscure. The cases do, however, show a marked undercurrent of Enlightenment values, in particular secularism, and this helps to explain why the law puts the onus on those seeking to use a religious basis in order to justify qualifying the civil rights of gay and lesbian people in some way. Gay equality advocates have been successful in large part because, in the absence of forensically acceptable evidence that homosexuality is socially (or even personally) harmful, they are able to structure their arguments on the secular rationalist basis that underpins human rights law. Religious traditionalists, on the other hand, eschew the need to provide evidence of social harm and, by founding instead on revelatory injunction against homosexuality, are denying the very basis upon which a secular legal system operates. The courts consistently reject arguments derived from revelatory rationalism[75] and have, overwhelmingly, accepted the accommodations that the democratic process has produced.[76] This reflects, at

75 Perhaps, however, this proposition needs to be limited to UK courts. The US Supreme Court was content to grant an exemption to the criminality of the use of hallucinogenic drugs to members of a church whose beliefs included the revelation that their God could only be understood by users of such drugs. The decision was built upon a refusal by the Court to challenge the revelatory starting point: *Gonzales v O Centro Espirita Beneficiente Uniao Do Vegetal* 546 US 418 (2006). The previous year the same Court had demanded verifiable evidence of the medicinal benefit of cannabis when health care providers sought to use it in treatment. The providers argued not from a revelatory but from a scientific basis, and they lost when the Court held the evidence to be insufficient: *Gonzales v Raich* 545 US 1 (2005). It is reported by KEENAN, C., "Lessons from America? Learning from Child Protection Policy in the USA", (2006) 18 *CFLQ* 43 that some 30 states in the US have express statutory provision to the effect that a parent who withholds medical treatment from a sick child is not to be found guilty of child neglect if he or she chooses to seek a cure through prayer. The policy would seem to be that the parent is not to be blamed for the failure of God to answer the prayer and cure the child.

76 The only UK case in which a challenge to a sexual orientation equality provision was successful is the Northern Irish case of *Re Christian Institute's Application for Judicial Review* [2008] IRLR 36, but the claim that was upheld there was that proper consultation had not taken place rather than that the rules at issue were disproportionate to their aim. For a discussion of this case, see SANDBERG, R., "Gods and Services: Religious Groups and Sexual Orientation Discrimination", (2008) 10 *Eccl. L.J.* 205.

least partly, a normal judicial deference to the democratic process[77] and an acceptance that determining where the balance is to be struck between opposing interests requires (rational) policy choices to be made which, subject to the requirements of the European Convention on Human Rights, Parliament is better placed than the courts to make. The choices Parliament has made exhibit in turn a clear acceptance that the law should reflect the changed social attitudes to homosexuality, the very thing that religious traditionalists seek to resist.

The clash between revelatory rationalism and secular rationalism can be seen at its most explicit in *McFarlane v Relate Avon Ltd*,[78] which, like *Ladele*, involved an employee unwilling to provide the services offered by his employer to same-sex couples. On being dismissed he claimed that it was he who was being discriminated against, on the ground of his religion. A witness statement was offered in support of the claimant by Lord Carey of Clifton[79] disputing that the manifestation of the Christian faith in relation to same-sex unions was discriminatory,[80] and warning that it was "but a short step from the dismissal of a sincere Christian from employment[81] to a 'religious bar' to any employment by Christians".[82] Both the claimant and his noble supporter were arguing that the court should respect the position taken by the claimant, as a rational deduction from his scripturally founded beliefs. Laws L.J. adopted the orthodox liberal/Enlightenment approach in response: in a secular society reliance on religious belief is not, indeed *cannot* be, enough to establish the validity of any particular position.

> "The conferment of any legal protection or preference upon a particular substantive moral position on the ground only that it is espoused by the adherents of a particular faith, however long its tradition, however rich its culture, is deeply unprincipled. It imposes compulsory law, not to advance the general good on objective grounds, but to give effect to the force of subjective opinion. This must be so, since in the eye of everyone save the believer religious faith is necessarily subjective, being incommunicable by any kind of proof or evidence. It may of course be *true*; but the ascertainment of such a truth lies beyond the means by which laws are made in a reasonable society. Therefore it lies only in the heart of the believer, who is alone bound by it. No one else is or can be so bound, unless by his own free choice he accepts its claims.

77 See FREDMAN, S., "From Deference to Democracy: The Role of Equality Under the Human Rights Act 1998", (2006) 122 *LQR* 53.

78 [2010] EWCA Civ B1.

79 Previously, as Archbishop of Canterbury, the head of the Anglican Communion.

80 Of course it is discriminatory if it seeks to treat same-sex couples differently from opposite-sex couples. The crucial question is whether the differential treatment can be justified or not.

81 This ignores the crucial factor of *why* the person is dismissed.

82 Something that both EU law and ECHR law clearly prohibits.

The promulgation of law for the protection of a position held purely on religious grounds cannot therefore be justified. It is irrational, as preferring the subjective over the objective. But it is also divisive, capricious and arbitrary. We do not live in a society where all the people share uniform religious beliefs. The precepts of any one religion - any belief system - cannot, by force of their religious origins, sound any louder in the general law than the precepts of any other. If they did, those out in the cold would be less than citizens; and our constitution would be on the way to a theocracy, which is of necessity autocratic. The law of a theocracy is dictated without option to the people, not made by their judges and governments. The individual conscience is free to accept such dictated law; but the State, if its people are to be free, has the burdensome duty of thinking for itself."[83]

This reasoning is orthodox, and persuasive, and Munby L.J. and Beatson J. in *R (On the Application of Johns) v Derby City Council*[84] said that they "respectfully and emphatically agree with every word of that".[85] Munby L.J. in that case had earlier pointed out:

"We sit as secular judges serving a multi-cultural community of many faiths. We are sworn (we quote the judicial oath) to 'do right to all manner of people after the laws and usages of this realm, without fear or favour, affection or ill will'. But the laws and usages of the realm do not include Christianity, in whatever form. The aphorism that 'Christianity is part of the common law of England' is mere rhetoric; at least since the decision of the House of Lords in *Bowman v Secular Society Limited*[86] it has been impossible to contend that it is law."[87]

The arguments put forward by gay equality advocates have been in large part successful precisely because they resonate so well with this liberal/secular orthodoxy; equally the arguments of the religious traditionalists have failed because by asserting the validity of subjective truths they deny the very basis upon which court cases are, and can only be, decided.

Some commentators, while welcoming the gains achieved by the gay and lesbian community, are nevertheless uncomfortable with the law's heavy reliance on a secular rationalist approach as the basis for the accommodation of religious concerns, seeing it as leading not to accommodation but to the complete rejection of a different conception of truth, and rationality. Carl Stychin,[88] for example,

83 *McFarlane v Relate Avon Ltd* [2010] EWCA Civ B1, *per* LAWS L.J. at paras. 23–24. The claimants in both this case and *Ladele* have applied to the European Court of Human Rights claiming an infringement of their right to freedom of religion: applications 51671/10 and 36516/10.

84 [2011] EWHC 375 (Admin).

85 At para. 55.

86 [1917] AC 406.

87 [2011] EWHC 375 Admin at para. 39.

88 "Faith in the Future: Sexuality, Religion and the Public Sphere", 2009 *OJLS* 729.

prefers the value of tolerance, which he correctly identifies as an essential prerequisite to pluralism.[89] He is deeply sceptical of the public-private divide inherent in the action/belief dichotomy captured by article 9 of the European Convention and embraced by the UK courts. He warns that confining religious beliefs to the private sphere is to reject the pluralism that modern society must embrace and, worse, to relegate those of faith to the closet from which gay and lesbian people have so recently emerged.[90] The decision of the UK Supreme Court in *HJ and HT v Secretary of State for the Home Department*[91] is a startlingly uncompromising rejection of the proposition that gay and lesbian people should accommodate themselves to a hostile environment by leading their lives "discreetly" and, though writing before this decision, Stychin argues that people of faith should be no more required than gay people are to lead lives that do not openly challenge majoritarian values or political elites. He suggests that to regard faith as a matter of rational choice with people being free to choose to follow their beliefs, or not, is to misunderstand the very nature of faith. While faith may be a matter of choice in the eyes of the secularist[92] it is, he says, a matter of obligation in the eyes of the faithful, who will subsume the verifiable in favour of the unknowable. True pluralism, Stychin argues, requires that this be accepted on its own terms and that, therefore, the law should seek means of making public space available to believers to exercise their faith – more space, he proposes, than was made for the likes of Ms Ladele and Mr McFarlane.[93] Mutual tolerance of the irreconcilable is the key, and the limits of religious tolerance should be determined, he suggests, by an examination of the core values of the believer and an assessment of the extent to which the claimed compromise would truly offend

89 In *Baczowski v Poland* (2009) 48 EHRR 19 the European Court pointed out that "referring to the hallmarks of a 'democratic society', the Court has attached particular importance to pluralism, tolerance and broadmindedness" (at para. 63) and it had earlier stated that "pluralism is also built on the genuine recognition of, and respect for, diversity and the dynamics of cultural traditions, ethnic and cultural identities, religious beliefs, artistic, literary and socio-economic ideas and concepts. The harmonious interaction of persons and groups with varied identities is essential for achieving social cohesion" (at para. 62).

90 The High Court in *R (On the Application of Johns) v Derby City Council* [2011] EWHC 375 (Admin), though not directly quoting Stychin, dismissed with some disdain the same claim when made by counsel.

91 [2010] UKSC 31. Here the Supreme Court accepted that gay people from countries where they have a well-founded fear of persecution as a result of their sexual orientation are not to have their asylum claims rejected on the grounds that they could avoid persecution by hiding their sexuality.

92 It is interesting to note that the European Court of Human Rights clearly conceives the freedom of religion protected by Article 9 as a protection of choice: see for example *Refah Partisi v Turkey* (2003) 37 EHRR at para. 128: "[The Court] reiterates that freedom of religion… is primarily a matter of individual conscience".

93 See also KOPPELMAN, A., "You Can't Hurry Love: Why Antidiscrimination Protections for Gay People Should have Religious Exemptions", [2006] 72 *Brooklyn L. Rev.* 125; SANDBERG, R., "Laws and Religion: Unravelling *McFarlane v Relate Avon Ltd*", (2010) 12 *Ecc LJ* 361.

these values. The example Stychin offers, citing a Canadian decision,[94] is of a Christian printing company being permitted to refuse to print anti-Christian literature but not being able to refuse to print pro-gay literature. This would require a contextual analysis of the competing interests that are, in reality, at stake and envisages different solutions in different contexts.

However, not only is the distinction between core and peripheral belief which underpins Stychin's argument difficult to draw in all but the most obvious cases (and it is not clear, to me, that the example he offers is a particularly obvious case), but the attempt to elevate the aspiration of tolerance into a workable tool capable of resolving actual disputes between the gay and lesbian community and religious traditionalists is ultimately unpersuasive for at least three reasons.

First, the concept of "core belief" (that which is always to be tolerated) is not one that any body outside the religious organisation itself can delineate,[95] and so the level of tolerance required would be defined by those claiming it, and in any case would always remain obscure. It would be impractical for courts or employment tribunals to undertake an examination of how "core" to the individual's belief structure any particular position on gay equality (or any other religious/political/social matter) was.[96] It is not for a court of law to explain, say, to a committed Anglican who opposes gay bishops, women vicars and blessings of civil partnerships that he has misunderstood the core tenets of Anglicanism[97] (though it may, after hearing evidence, conclude that his beliefs are not sincerely held).

---

94 *Ontario Human Rights Commission v Brockie* (2002) 222 DLR (4th) 174.

95 See *Catholic Care (Diocese of Leeds) v Charity Commission for England and Wales* [2010] EWHC 520 (Ch) where the court held that, without compelling reasons to do otherwise, it would have to accept the evidence from the appropriate bishop as to whether or not disapproval of same-sex relationships was a core belief of Roman Catholicism: *per* Briggs J. at para. 106.

96 In *R (Williamson) v Secretary of State for Education* [2005] UKHL 15 Lord Nicholls said this at para. 22: "But, emphatically, it is not for the court to embark on an inquiry into the asserted belief and judge its 'validity' by some objective standard such as the source material upon which the claimant founds his belief or the orthodox teaching of the religion in question or the extent to which the claimant's belief conforms to or differs from the views of others professing the same religion. Freedom of religion protects the subjective belief of an individual... The European Court of Human Rights has rightly noted that 'in principle, the right to freedom of religion as understood in the Convention rules out any appreciation by the state of the legitimacy of religious beliefs or of the manner in which these are expressed': *Metropolitan Church of Bessarabia v Moldova* (2001) 35 EHRR 306, 335, para. 117. The relevance of objective factors such as source material is, at most, that they may throw light on whether the professed belief is genuinely held."

97 Cf. the UK Supreme Court's palpable discomfort at being asked to determine how 'Jewish' a person had to be to be eligible for a place at a Jewish school: *R (On the Application of E) v J.F.S.Governing Body* [2009] UKSC 15.

Secondly, though tolerance is a virtue whose social benefit should not be underrated, nor should it ever be forgotten that some views and many practices are, quite simply, intolerable to any democratic society. Anti-semitism, racism, ought not to be, and is not, tolerated and clothing such views in religiosity cannot make them any more acceptable. There are limits, in other words, to acceptable tolerance and these limits must be determined on grounds of social good and not divine revelation.[98] The genocides against the Canaanites and the Gibeonites ordered by God and carried out by Joshua[99] were abominations that are as tolerable today as the Holocaust. Ms Ladele's employers, in deciding whether to tolerate her wishes to be exempt from civil partnership duties, were required to take into account not only their own non-discrimination policy but also whether it was reasonable to demand that Ms Ladele's gay and lesbian co-workers tolerate alterations to their own shift patterns in order to allow her to express her disapproval of homosexuality. Neither she nor her supporters were ever able convincingly to distinguish the position she was claiming from that of the (hypothetical) registrar unwilling, for example, to conduct mixed-race or mixed-religion marriages.[100]

Thirdly, tolerance might be a suitable starting point for the accommodation of mutually incompatible views if the opposing views are, themselves, internally coherent and consistent. But religion speaks with as many voices as there have been languages since the people were scattered from the city of Babel where the whole earth was of one language,[101] and the existence of such conflicting voices if they are all to be tolerated would require exemptions from the general law for anyone who believes that, for non-legal reasons, they are entitled to be exempt. It

98 Munby L.J. pointed out in *R (On the Application of Johns) v Derby City Council* [2011] EWHC 375 (Admin) at para. 44 that "Some cultural beliefs and practices are simply treated by the law as being beyond the pale. Some manifestations of religious practice will be regulated if contrary to a child's welfare… And some aspects of mainstream religious belief may even fall foul of public policy", referring to *Westminster City Council v C* [2008] EWCA Civ 198 where a marriage recognised by the *lex loci celebrationis* and by sharia law was held to be manifestly contrary to public policy and therefore not recognisable in the United Kingdom.

99 Joshua 6:21 and 10:40–41.

100 The Court of Appeal of Saskatchewan addressed this point in *In the Matter of Marriage Commissioners Appointed Under the Marriage Act 1995* 2011 SKCA 3. Smith J.A. pointed out, at para. 102, that if religious belief justified discrimination in the provision of marriage services, the state would be able to permit any individual to discriminate against same-sex couples in the delivery of any public service. He also dismissed (at para. 107) as irrelevant the argument that the risk of a same-sex couple not being able to find a state official willing to conduct their marriage was minimal: "Knowing that legislation would legitimise such discrimination is itself an affront to dignity and worth of homosexual individuals". At issue, he concluded, was not merely or even primarily the right of same-sex couples to marry, but "the right of this vulnerable group to be free from discrimination and prejudice in the delivery of a public service, available without discrimination to all other members of society" (para. 108).

101 Genesis 11:1–9.

is for this reason that no secular court can afford to concede the validity of subjective truths. In attempting to accommodate irreconcilable views courts have no option but to adopt a secular rationalist approach, for that is the only approach that is capable of providing solutions that it would be justified to impose on everyone, believer and non-believer alike.

It is submitted for these reasons that, however attractive it is, tolerance alone is too protean a concept to provide a sound basis for deciding whether to accommodate the claims of those who seek the legal right to treat people of different sexual orientations differently. It is a virtue to be aspired to, not a tool to be used. A more robust tool may be found, it is suggested, in more traditional legal concepts, such as autonomy and dignity. Lord Nichols in *R (Williamson) v Secretary of State for Education*[102] reminds us that to engage the article 9 right to freedom of religion or belief, the belief must be one that is "consistent with basic standards of human dignity and integrity".[103] At its crudest, the belief that gay and lesbian people ought to be harassed and bullied and driven from their jobs and homes, and have their relationships put asunder, would not meet that test, but in *Re Christian Institute's Application for Judicial Review*[104] Weatherup J. refused to accept that a belief in the inherent wrongness of homosexuality would necessarily fail that test.[105] Nevertheless dignity is, it is submitted, a suitable principle against which to test whether and how accommodation between conflicting claims should be sought. As Moon and Allen have shown, dignity is more than a respect for autonomy, but is inherent in all humanity (whether individuals choose it or not), something that reflects "the perceptions of ordinary members of society as to what is dignified".[106] Dupré sees dignity as something that concerns the autonomous individual's place in society.[107] So it requires the law to show respect to individuals not only for the choices they make but also for the people they are. This makes dignity a particularly attractive starting point for accommodation since it is as claimable by religious believers, whether faith is a matter of choice or of being, as by gay and lesbian people.

Dignity, though less visible in British constitutional doctrine than it is elsewhere,[108] can nevertheless claim to be one of the underlying values of

102 [2005] UKHL 15.
103 *Ibid.* at para. 23.
104 [2008] IRLR 36.
105 *Ibid.* at para. 50.
106 MOON, G. and ALLEN, R., "Dignity Discourse in Discrimination Law: A Better Route to Equality?", [2006] *EHRLR* 610, at p. 628.
107 DUPRÉ, C., "Unlocking Human Dignity: Towards a Theory for the 21st Century", [2009] *EHRLR* 190, at p. 196.
108 See O'CONNELL, R., "The Role of Dignity in Equality law: Lessons from Canada and South Africa", (2008) 6 *Int. J. Con. Law.* 267.

democracy,[109] the principle indeed from which the notion of equality is itself derived. As Baroness Hale of Richmond put it:

> "Democracy is founded on the principle that each individual has equal value. Treating some as automatically having less value than others not only causes pain and distress to that person but also violates his or her dignity as a human being… such treatment is damaging to society as a whole. Wrongly to assume that some people have talent and others do not is a huge waste of human resources. It also damages social cohesion, creating not only an under-class, but an under-class with a rational grievance."[110]

More importantly, for our purposes, dignity can serve as a practical tool that helps in the resolution of clashes between equality claims and religious liberty claims.[111] Moon and Allen see cases like *Ghaidan v Godin-Mendoza*,[112] where legislation designed to confer the benefit of tenancy succession on opposite-sex cohabitants was interpreted to include same-sex couples, as an example of the application of the underlying principle of dignity, in that it enhanced the dignity of the tenant without affecting the dignity (as opposed to the pocket) of the landlord. They suggest that focusing on dignity in equality law recognises that both sides in a dispute have the right to respect for their positions, and that any victory for one side ought not to be disproportionately burdensome on the dignity of the other side. But, unlike the virtue of tolerance, a dignity analysis is able to contemplate that, in particular cases, compromise is inappropriate and full victory for one side or the other may be the only socially acceptable outcome. It is this aspect of dignity that makes it so useful when the clash of interests is between irreconcilable positions.

A dignity analysis could be applied to the clash of interests at issue here by identifying whose dignity would be harmed most by not granting them what they ask for. This is, as McCrudden points out,[113] very close to the "proportionality" approach long demanded by the European Court of Human Rights, and is

109 It is a constitutional right in many countries, appearing for example in article 1 of the German *Grundgesetz* and Article 10 of the South African Constitution. Article 1 of the Universal Declaration of Human Rights states: "All human beings are born free and equal in dignity and rights. They are endowed with reason". Though the European Convention on Human Rights does not explicitly refer to "dignity", the "very essence" of the European Convention, the European Court has said, is "respect for human dignity and human freedom": *Pretty v United Kingdom* [2002] 35 EHRR 1 at para 65. The Charter of Fundamental Rights of the European Union opens with the declaration that "human dignity is inviolable".

110 *Ghaidan v Godin-Mendoza* [2004] UKHL 30 at para. 132.

111 McCRUDDEN, C., in an important article "Human Dignity and Judicial Interpretation of Human Rights", (2008) *EJIL* 655, traces the historical notion of dignity as status through the religious perception of human dignity derived from man being made in the image of God to a means of human rights interpretation and adjudication, and he concludes that dignity is at its most valuable today as a process rather than as a substantive right with definable content.

112 [2004] UKHL 30.

113 McCRUDDEN, *supra* note 111 at p. 716.

explicitly the approach in the equality jurisprudence of the South African Constitutional Court.[114] It is unlikely that this approach would give any different result from the accommodations the British Parliament settled upon in the legislation discussed above, but it may well provide an explanation for them. *Ladele* and *McFarlane*, for example, can thus be explained in this way: a same-sex couple's dignity is necessarily harmed by the refusal of a person of faith to recognise them as a legitimate couple, and this is a hurt that goes to the most personal and intimate aspects of their human existence. It is, in the words of Ackermann J. in the Constitutional Court of South Africa,[115] a "crass, blunt, cruel and serious invasion of their dignity". The question becomes whether this is a hurt of a higher order than the hurt to a religious traditionalist's dignity in being required not to discriminate against such a couple when she offers services to the public. Even if religious belief is as central to a believer as sexual orientation is to a gay or lesbian person (which I concede only for the sake of this argument), individual tenets of belief are unlikely to be as definitional of the individual as one's sexual orientation. This, together with the fact that the law all the time requires religious believers to accommodate themselves to the disjunction between the secular law and their own moral code,[116] and they are, in large part, happy to do so[117] means that the answer that the Court of Appeal gave in *Ladele* must be correct.

---

114 "The crucial determinant will always be whether human dignity is enhanced or diminished and the achievement of equality is promoted or undermined by the measure concerned": *per* Sachs J. in *Fourie v Minister of Home Affairs* 2006 (1) SA 524 at para. 152.

115 *National Coalition for Gay and Lesbian Equality v Minister of Home Affairs* 2000 (2) SA 1 at para. 54.

116 So for example the devout Roman Catholic registrar is obliged to perform marriages of divorced people notwithstanding that this is contrary to the doctrines of his or her faith. (Perhaps, however, the registrar's protestant friend will help reconcile him or her with God by reminding him or her of the divorces in the Bible, such as those in Deuteronomy 24:1–4 and Jeremiah 3:8. When the Pharisees challenged Jesus with these examples, he replied by allowing a man to put away his wife only for fornication: Matthew 19:9. It was this passage that allowed divorce for adultery into Scotland, immediately on that country's Reformation in 1560, and which inclines non-Catholic religious traditionalists to seek to limit divorce to fault grounds).

117 While Lev. 20:13 says "If a man also lies with mankind as he lieth with a woman, both of them have committed an abomination; they shall surely be put to death", the religious traditionalist protects himself from accusations of religious fundamentalism by accepting the proposition but choosing to reject (or to ignore) the consequence. Yet if the foundation of revelatory rationalism is the unquestioned acceptance of the word of God, its rationality can be maintained only by a rational explanation of why the New Testament message of love and compassion acts to qualify the second part of the passage but not the first. Other biblical "abominations", almost universally ignored today (even by those who claim to abominate homosexuality on the basis of the revelation in Leviticus), include men wearing skirts (kilts?) (Deuteronomy 22:5), remarrying one's divorced wife if she had remarried in the interim (Deut. 24:4), lying (Proverbs 12:22) and, famously, eating shellfish (Lev. 11:10–12).

7. THE COMING OF MARRIAGE

Dignity, as the driver of any accommodation between the gay and lesbian community and religious traditionalists, is regarded with grave suspicion by the latter, for it is the very concept that underlies the reasoning in many of the same-sex marriage judgments from courts around the world.[118] The compromise of offering same-sex couples civil partnership instead of marriage has been under constant attack, and it has been unable to withstand challenges in a number of jurisdictions which have held that a "distinct but equivalent" approach is in reality a "separate but equal" approach, that is to say one that hides rather than addresses continuing inequalities.[119] The inequality that most of these cases focuses on is the social status that marriage brings, a status that is claimed to be absent from civil partnership regimes.[120]

An English domestic court held soon after the coming into force of the Civil Partnership Act 2004 that creating civil partnership for same-sex couples as opposed to opening marriage for them was an appropriate policy choice for the UK Parliament to make and one that the court could not interfere with.[121] The European Court has held more recently that, at least in the absence of a Europe-wide consensus that a civil partnership approach is unacceptable, individual States have the right within their margin of appreciation to respond to the need to ensure a non-discriminatory family law by this means rather than by opening marriage to same-sex couples; it did, however, envisage the possibility that such a consensus might eventually develop.[122] Given the nature of the Coalition Government that took office in 2010 in the United Kingdom, the issue may well become of greater political import here, for while it is not Conservative Party policy to hug a homosexual, the opening of both marriage and civil partnership to couples of any gender mix became official policy for the Liberal Democrats in September 2010. No doubt some religious traditionalists will oppose vigorously any move to repeal the same-sex bar on marriage but they have already seriously

---

118 See in particular *Halpern v Canada (Attorney General)* (2003) 65 OR (3d) 161 (Ontario Court of Appeal); *Goodridge v Department of Public Health* 798 NE 2n 941 (2003 Massachusetts Supreme Court); *Fourie v Minister for Home Affairs* 2006 (1) SA 524 (Constitutional Court of South Africa); *Kerrigan v Commissioner of Public Health* 957 A2d 407 (2008 Connecticut Supreme Court); *In Re Marriage Cases* 189 P3d 384 (2008 Supreme Court of California); *Varnum v Brien* 763 NW 2d 862 (2009 Iowa Supreme Court).

119 "Historically the concept of 'separate but equal' served as a threadbare cloak for covering distaste for or repudiation by those in power of the group subjected to segregation": *per* Sachs J. in *Fourie v Minister for Home Affairs*, *ibid.*, at para. 150.

120 I have previously argued that gay and lesbian people do themselves a disservice by asserting that civil partnership is less worthy than marriage. It becomes so, because we say it is so: see NORRIE, K., "South Africa's Civil Union Act 2006: A Scottish Perspective", 2010 *JR* 21.

121 *Wilkinson v Kitzinger* [2006] 2 FLR 397.

122 *Schalk and Kopf v Austria* App 30141/04, 24 June 2010 at para. 61.

weakened themselves by previously arguing that no accommodation at all, not even a civil partnership regime, is acceptable: having lost that argument they have no additional arguments against same-sex marriage other than the proposition that marriage is an institution where the taking into account of religious doctrine is peculiarly apt. There is some, but limited, validity to that argument in countries with established churches, or where religious officiants are entitled to create the legal institution of marriage,[123] but this has never been allowed in the past to prevent changes in the law of marriage that were deemed socially expedient even although contrary to some doctrinal interpretations.[124] The question then becomes whether, when marriage in Scotland or England and Wales is to be opened to same-sex couples (for it surely will be[125]), there is anything that can – or should – be done to meet the concerns of religious traditionalists.

One accommodation might be to limit same-sex marriage to civil ceremony: in other words such marriages could be solemnised by registrars only, and never by religious officiants. Such a compromise would emphasise the secularity of (one form of) marriage but that tactic, when adopted with civil partnership, satisfied neither religious traditionalists who objected to equalising same-sex couples with opposite-sex couples, nor gay and lesbian people of faith who saw no rational basis, in a legal system that eschews favouring one religious doctrine over another,[126] for using religion A's opposition to its officials sanctifying same-sex couples as the justification for denying religion B's right to permit its own officials from doing so, if it so wished. A more acceptable accommodation would be to remove such obligation as presently exists on ministers of religion from acting as state officials in the conducting of marriage ceremonies, making it effectively a matter of individual choice subject only to internal rules in hierarchically organised religions.[127] The matter is of some consequence in

123 Marriage Act 1949, Pt II; Marriage (Scotland) Act 1977, s. 8(1)(a)(i).

124 For example, the Marriage (Prohibited Degrees of Relationship) Act 1986 substantially altered the rules on the forbidden degrees of relationship, bringing them up to date and divorcing them from the Biblical degrees set out in Leviticus.

125 In March 2011 the UK Government Equalities Office issued a consultation on the registration of civil partnerships in religious premises. It affirmed (at p. 6) "the [UK] government's commitment to consult on further developments in legislation, including progress towards equal marriage and partnerships". In the Scottish elections in May 2011 all parties, except the Conservative and Unionist Party, gave manifesto commitments either to open marriage to same-sex couples or to consult on the issue. The victors in that election, winning an overall majority in the Scottish Parliament, pledged a consultation on the issue. The countries that have opened marriage to same-sex couples are: The Netherlands (2001), Belgium (2003), Spain (2005), Canada (2005), South Africa (2006), Norway (2008), Sweden (2009), Portugal (2010), Iceland (2010), Argentina (2010), and, in the United States of America, Massachusetts, Iowa, New Hampshire, Vermont, Connecticut and the District of Columbia.

126 See *Manoussakis v Greece* (1997) 23 EHRR 387; *Metropolitan Church of Bessarabia v Moldova* (2002) 35 EHRR 13.

127 The Californian Supreme Court in *In Re Marriage Cases* 189 P 3d 384 (2008) at pp. 451–452 found that opening marriage to same-sex couples did not infringe the right of religious

England and Wales where the Anglican churches there are presently obliged to marry people in their parishes, but conscience exemptions already exist for marriages permitted by the secular law while inconsistent with how Anglicans choose to interpret scripture[128] and these provide a useful model.[129]

Perhaps, however, it is not accommodation that is needed but a radical rethinking of the very nature of marriage. In a secular legal system there always has been something distinctly peculiar about permitting ministers of religion to solemnise marriages, that is to say to create a legally defined institution that has only secular effects. Religion, of course, has long had strong cultural claims on the important moments in family life – birth, marriage and death – which even for those whose connections with religion are otherwise tenuous or even non-existent continue to take comfort from. Yet only with marriage does a religious ceremony have the potential to have legal effect. This has the effect of confusing the sacred and the profane aspects of the institution and has led us to forget that what marriage is to a minister is something very different from what marriage is to a lawyer. A major reason why the so-called marriage "debate" is so frustratingly sterile is that the protagonists, though using the same language, are not engaging in the same argument. Marriage to the secularist is a relationship registered with the state that acts as the signifier of various civil rights and obligations; marriage to the religious is a sacrament defined and governed by divine rule. The gay equality advocate is asking for one thing and the religious traditionalist is denying the other thing. The religious traditionalist is demanding dignity for their sacraments and the gay equality advocate is denying the right to discriminate. They are talking past each other and the word "marriage" (but only the word) is the name of the small intersection in the Venn diagram of their debate. Only by a clear and absolute separation of church and state, including in particular the removal of the power of ministers of religion to create civil status, can the two separate conceptions of marriage be isolated, and understood, and dealt with appropriately in their own contexts.[130] Believers, of course, (including

---

freedom because there was no requirement in Californian law for any religious officiant to solemnise a marriage contrary to his or her religious beliefs.

128 Marriage Act 1949, s. 5A, as inserted by the Marriage (Prohibited Degrees of Relationship) Act 1986, allows Church of England and Church of Wales clergy to refuse to marry a couple within the biblical degrees of relationship while being outwith the legal degrees. Section 5B, as inserted by the Gender Recognition Act 2004, similarly allows these clergy to refuse to marry anyone who has changed gender. Scriptural authority on transsexualism is, it may be noted, sparse.

129 The problem does not arise in Scotland where, already, ministers of the established church (and all other churches) are free to refuse to marry any person on the basis of their religious conscience.

130 It is not only atheists who might find some good in this suggestion. Ekklesia, whose website presents itself as "The religion and society think tank at the cutting edge of culture, spirituality and politics" puts forward the proposal in a research paper by BARROW, S., "What Future for Marriage?" (2006), accessible from www.ekklesia.co.uk.

gay and lesbian believers) would still be able to walk down the aisle in their fine clothes and become "married" in the eyes of their God, if it pleases Him, just as a baby is baptised in the eyes of its parents' God, and just as a Hindu couple become married in the eyes of their pantheon by performing the *saptapadi* irrespective of when they go through the legal formalities. Religious traditionalists are unlikely to regard disestablishment as any "accommodation" of their wishes. But the complete secularisation of family law may well be the only way to achieve true equality for families based around same-sex couples, while at the same time allowing religious organisations the autonomy to decide themselves whether love, toleration, or hatred of such couples is demanded by their rules and sacraments. Each will have their own dignity, whether or not they tolerate each other.

8. CONCLUSION

The major problem in seeking to accommodate the wishes and interests of religious traditionalists to the gay equality imperative is that the competing rationalities of the protagonists – one secular, one relevatory – are alien to each other. Religion and the (secular) law are simply not engaging in the same argument, because they are talking about entirely different things, even while using the same words (such as "equality", "respect", and "marriage"). This is not surprising since religion and law serve very different functions in modern society. Religion, whose authority is traced to a supernatural being (or beings) whose existence is by definition unprovable and whose wishes can only be known through human (therefore fallible) interpreters, offers a model for people to live their lives by, with enforcement by conscience only; law, whose authority comes from the sovereign power of the state (the governance of all, whether believers or not), provides responses to situations, and a police power of enforcement. It is entirely legitimate for religion to offer a model of life based upon monogamous relationships between a man and a woman, sanctified in a religious ceremony with the presumed blessing of a divine being; it is illegitimate for religion to seek to enforce its model on those who do not believe. It is legitimate for the law to allow legal consequences to follow from the fact that two people register their personal (sexual) relationship with the state; it is illegitimate for the law to differentiate its consequences depending upon the individual's beliefs, or sexual orientation.

There seems little doubt that in Great Britain today the starting point of the law is one of equality, which is qualified by the liberty interests of those who can show reason why they should not be subject to non-discrimination requirements. The burden, in other words, is clearly on those seeking exemptions and to their palpable frustration religious traditionalists have signally failed to satisfy that burden, beyond the very limited concessions described above. Religious traditionalists may well have made a tactical error in focusing so much of their attention on the issue of same-sex relationships and turning that into a shibboleth of doctrinal purity, for history is not on their side, and will be unforgiving. The influence of religion has been waning in Great Britain since at least the Enlightenment and it will not be reasserted if traditionalists continue to cling to their revelatory certainties about homosexuality, like small boys clinging to their mothers, hoping to be protected from the complexities of the adult world. The cultural grip of religion weakens in all societies that embrace the moral neutrality of sexual orientation, as surely as the weakening of its political influence allows that very embracing. Not everyone will see that as a bad thing, but traditionalists are unlikely to take comfort from the thought that they are bringing about their own cultural, as well as political, demise. The warning in Ecclesiastes remains as apt today as it was when it was first written: "Be not righteous over much; neither make thyself over wise; why shouldest though destroy thyself?"[131]

131 Ecclesiastes 7:15.

RELIGION, FAMILY VALUES AND FAMILY LAW

Michael Rosie and Fran Wasoff

1. INTRODUCTION

Recent decades have seen major and interrelated changes in family life and structure. These have comprised later marriage, more cohabitation, more visible same-sex partnership, later parenthood, lower fertility, higher levels of relationship breakdown, more lone parents, non-resident parents and solo living, and greater labour market participation of married women. The so-called "traditional" nuclear family has variously been seen as under attack, breaking down, or undergoing transformation possibly in tandem with other modernising social trends such as secularisation. Accompanying such wider structural and demographic changes have been debates around what might loosely be termed "family values": whether demographic changes are to be celebrated or denounced; what rights and obligations should be carried over from "traditional" forms of the family into the "new"; and attitudes towards the propriety or morality of "new" family forms. Debates about family values often run along social "fault-lines" such as age, gender and religiosity. Family law reform is at the centre, and often the subject, of debates about family values. In this paper we focus on secular/religious social divisions and examine the extent to which there is an association between religion and views on obligations and attitudes towards family life. We also consider whether any fault lines run along a denominational cleavage, or a broader cleavage between the religious and the secular.

Scotland offers a promising environment to explore the links between religion and "family values". Modern Scotland was religiously mixed between a Presbyterian majority and a sizeable Catholic minority, with very small non-Christian minority populations. Contemporary Scotland has travelled far down the Northern European road of secularisation but denominational cleavages persist. Its historical trajectory, and the establishment of a devolved Scottish parliament in 1999, has led to increased interest and debate about the place of religion in Scottish society, and an upsurge in the amount of official and semi-official data collected on religious belonging and attitudes. The Scottish Executive has a keen interest in the demographic changes taking place in Scotland,[1] and, to support its recent family law reform resulting in the Family Law (Scotland) Act 2006, commissioned, jointly with the Nuffield Foundation, a family attitudes module in the Scottish Social Attitudes Survey 2004.[2] In this contribution, we look at data from this module in relation to religion and how attitudes towards family life and sexual morality vary by religious difference, whether that is in terms of differences between secular and religious people, denominational differences or in different levels of religious attendance. We then consider the alignment of family attitudes and family law and the implications of these patterns for family law reform.

2. RELIGION AND THE TREND TOWARDS SECULARISATION

In terms of a formal engagement with religion, there can be little doubt that the last four decades have seen a major shift in behaviour across most of Western Europe. Whether in terms of membership of religious bodies, attendance at religious services, number of baptisms, or proportion of weddings celebrated religiously, the downward trend of all indicators has been relatively recent, but clear. In Scotland there is broad agreement that such a decline is underway, but debate over its historical starting point. For Callum Brown,[3] the mid 1960s proved the key turning point whilst others, such as Bruce & Glendinning,[4] argue that decline can be traced to the wartime 1940s. Crockett & Voas,[5] on the other hand, argue for a decline across the whole twentieth century. Regardless of precise timings, most commentators agree that by mid-century the decline was significant, and that "From then until the present, the slide in all indices has been very severe for most Protestant churches."[6] Institutional decline is not exclusively Protestant: Catholic Mass attendance in Scotland halved between 1950–2000,

1 MORRISON, A., HEADRICK, D., WASOFF, F. and MORTON, S., *Family formation and dissolution: trends and attitudes among the Scottish population* (Scottish Executive, 2004); WASOFF, F. and MORRISON, A., *Family Formation and Dissolution in Europe: Scotland in a European Context* (Scottish Executive, 2005).

2 WASOFF, F. and MARTIN, C., *Scottish Social Attitudes Survey 2004 Family Module Report* (Scottish Executive, 2005).

3 BROWN, C., "Religion and Secularisation" in A. DICKSON, A. and TREBLE, J.H. (eds.), *People and Society in Scotland*, Vol. III, 1914–1990 (John Donald, 1992); BROWN, C., *The Death of Christian Britain: Understanding secularisation 1800–2000* (Routledge, 2001).

4 BRUCE, S. and GLENDINNING, T., "When was secularization? Dating the decline of the British churches and locating its cause", (2010) *British Journal of Sociology*, 61 (1), pp. 107–126.

5 CROCKETT, A. and VOAS, D., "Generations of decline: Religious change in 20th century Britain", (2006) *Journal for the Scientific Study of Religion*, 45 (4), pp. 567–584.

6 BROWN (1992), *supra* note 3, p. 54.

closely matching the pattern found in England.[7] The Scottish experience has been unexceptional and mirrors a phenomenon found across much of the "developed" world. Although its speed and extent may differ between societies "the direction of change in all indices of involvement in institutional religion is the same: downwards."[8]

Despite these trends, secularisation is a contested concept and religious ideas are strongly persistent. Critics, while accepting institutional decline, point out that religious *beliefs* remain widespread. For Grace Davie people are "believing without belonging", the key issue a "drifting of belief… nominalism remains a more prevalent phenomenon than secularism."[9] However, whilst belief in God remains high throughout Western Europe, it too is falling and disbelief rising.[10] Secularisation has impacted upon the culture of religious institutions themselves, with many reducing "the specifically supernatural in their product" and downplaying major aspects of traditional orthodoxy.[11] A 1987 "lifestyle survey" of Church of Scotland members found that 13 per cent did not describe themselves as Christian; 13 per cent did not state a clear belief in God; and 47 per cent did not believe in, or were unsure about, life after death.[12] More recently, a study of Scottish Christian clergy found that only one-third believed in Hell.[13] A key critic of the secularisation thesis, Peter Berger, rejects the notion of a "secularised world" arguing that our "world today, with some exceptions… is as furiously religious as it ever was". But even Berger notes a crucial exception: "In Western Europe, if nowhere else, the old secularisation thesis would seem to hold."[14]

7 ROSIE, M., *The Sectarian Myth in Scotland: Of Bitter Memory and Bigotry* (Palgrave MacMillan, 2004).

8 BRUCE, S., *Religion in the Modern World: From Cathedrals to Cults* (Oxford University Press, 1996), p. 31.

9 DAVIE, G., *Religion in Britain since 1945: Believing Without Belonging* (Blackwell, 1994), pp. 74–76.

10 ASHFORD, S. and TIMMS, N. (1992), *What Europe Thinks: A Study of Western European Values* (Dartford, 1992).

11 BRUCE, *supra* note 8, p. 36.

12 ROBERTSON, A., *Lifestyle Survey* (Church of Scotland Board of Social Responsibility, 1987).

13 STODDART, E., "Church of Scotland Ministers as Representative of the Theological Outlook of Scotland's Clergy", (2006) *Journal of Contemporary Religion*, 21 (1), 69.

14 BERGER, P., "The Desecularization of the World: A Global Overview", in BERGER, P. (ed.), *The Desecularization of the World: Resurgent Religion and World Politics* (Ethics and Public Policy Center, 1999), pp. 2–3 and 9.

3. THE POLITICS OF FAMILY LAW REFORM AND THE VOICE OF FAITH GROUPS

Despite the declining number of adherents, the voice of faith groups in Scotland has been prominent in public debates and consultations throughout the lengthy period of family law reform culminating in the passage of the Family Law (Scotland) Act 2006. The main objective of the 2006 Act is to: "... update family law to provide legal protection and safeguards for children and adults in today's family structures".[15]

This legislation has had unusually ample opportunity for public consultation, beginning with the 1989 and 1992 documents of the Scottish Law Commission, *Report on Reform of the Grounds for Divorce* (1989) and *Reform of Family Law 135* (1992). In 1999 the Scottish Office published a family law Green Paper, *Improving Scottish Family Law*, which was followed in 2000 by the Scottish Executive White Paper, *Parents and Children*. A further stage of consultation about options for family law reform followed the White Paper "with green edges", and another stage of consultation to "refresh" ministerial thinking took place in 2004 with the publication of the Scottish Executive's *Family Matters: Improving Family Law in Scotland* (2004).

Consultation responses in all three rounds were analysed by Nicolson.[16] There were 304 responses to the 1999 Green Paper, most of them from individuals (219). Nicolson comments[17] in relation to the large proportion of responses from individuals:

> "... a significant minority of responses from individuals contained a degree of identical wording of phrases and sentences, indicating the likelihood of various campaigns and lobbying of views amongst some communities. From some of the comments made in such responses, it could perhaps be deduced that some respondents had not had sight of the consultation paper itself but had based their submissions on information provided to them by a third party."

Of the organisational responses, 14 (16 per cent) were from bodies classified as faith groups.[18]

---

15 Scottish Parliament (2005) Family Law (Scotland) Bill Policy Memorandum www.scottish.parliament.uk/business/bills/36-familyLaw/b36s2-introd-pm.pdf.

16 NICOLSON, L., *Improving Family Law in Scotland: Analysis of Written Consultation Responses* (Scottish Executive, 2004); www.scotland.gov.uk/Resource/Doc/26350/0025007.pdf.

17 *Ibid.*, p. 13.

18 *Ibid.*, p. 78.

A similar pattern was replicated in responses to the Scottish Executive consultation, *Parents and Children* (2000). Almost three-quarters (73 per cent, n=251) of responses were from individuals, the great majority of which (90 per cent): "... came from individuals, clergy or church groups as a result of a leaflet published by the Christian Institute, an evangelical group. All made similar points [in response to one question only]".

The final round of consultation included seeking responses to the consultation document (over 300 responses were received), holding focus groups with key constituencies, and events hosted by the Scottish Civic Forum, plus a debate in June 2004 in the Scottish Parliament. Faith groups were a key constituency of respondents.[19]

4. THE FAMILY MODULE OF THE SCOTTISH SOCIAL ATTITUDES SURVEY 2004

Formal consultation is just one means of gauging opinion about policy reform options, and it is a selective one at that, securing responses from individuals and organisations with a particular interest in the topic. We cannot infer from this what the population in general think. Thus, to produce evidence of public opinion that would complement the responses received through its consultation processes, the Scottish Executive, in collaboration with the Nuffield Foundation, commissioned a module on family attitudes and knowledge of family law in the Scottish Social Attitudes Survey (SSAS) 2004.[20] This is an annual survey conducted by the Scottish Centre for Social Research, and in 2004 involved face-to-face interviews with a representative sample of 1,637 adults aged 18 or over living in Scotland, of whom 1,514 also returned self-completion questionnaires. The module explored public knowledge of and attitudes towards issues addressed by the Family Law (Scotland) Bill, such as unmarried fathers, cohabiting couples (including same-sex partners), step-parents and grandparents, as well as attitudes to marriage and sexual relationships. Further details of the respondent's own familial circumstances and biography were sought in addition to the standard information collected in the main survey. Many of the questions took the form of vignettes and some replicated questions asked in earlier surveys conducted in both Scotland[21] and Britain.[22] Data were weighted in the analysis to correct for

---

19 Scottish Executive, *Family Matters: Improving Family Law in Scotland* (Scottish Executive, 2004).

20 WASOFF and MARTIN, *supra* note 2.

21 BARLOW, A., "Attitudes to cohabitation and marriage" in CURTICE, J., MCCRONE, D., PARK, A. and PATERSON, L. (eds.), *New Scotland, New Society* (Polygon, 2002).

22 BARLOW, A., DUNCAN, S., EVANS, G. and PARK, A., "Just a piece of paper? Marriage and cohabitation in Britain" in PARK, A., CURTICE, J., THOMPSON, K., JARVIS, L.,

overrepresentation of adults living in single households and rural areas, to ensure that the resulting sample was representative of the Scottish population from which it was selected.

5. OPERATIONALISING "RELIGION" – AFFILIATION AND (CLAIMED) PRACTICE

The *Scottish Social Attitudes Survey 2004 Family Module Report*[23] and subsequent related papers analysed the variation in survey question responses across a standard range of socio-economic variables, such as age, gender, marital status, household income group, and housing tenure.[24] Minimal attention was given to religion, to which we now turn. The Scottish Social Attitudes Survey contains various indicators that capture different dimensions of the broad concept of religion, and these measures are usually repeated in the survey every year. One useful measure in respect to religion and secularisation is the labels individuals use when asked in surveys to identify to which religion, if any, they belong. Table 1 shows the trends in religion (or religious affiliation) in Scotland since 1992 in large scale representative social surveys, as measured by responses to the question "Do you regard yourself as belonging to any particular religion?"

Table 1. Religious affiliation, 1992–2009

% by column	1992	1997	1999	2002	2004	2006	2009
Church of Scotland	46	39	35	32	29	27	22
Catholic	16	14	14	15	12	12	12
Other Christian	12	14	10	10	9	13	12
Other religion	1	1	1	2	2	3	2
No religion	25	32	40	42	48	46	52
Base	*952*	*882*	*1482*	*1665*	*1637*	*1594*	*1482*

Sources: Scottish Election Surveys 1992 & 1997; Scottish Social Attitudes Surveys 1999–2009.

Two aspects of the data are immediately apparent: the very steep decline of the Church of Scotland sample in less than 20 years (from almost half, 46 per cent in

BROMLEY, C. and STRATFORD, N. (eds.), *British Social Attitudes: Public Policy, Social Ties. The 18th Report* (Sage, 2010).

23 WASOFF and MARTIN, *supra* note 2.

24 DEY, I. and WASOFF, F., "Protection, Parity, or Promotion: Public Attitudes to Cohabitation and the Purposes of Legal Reform", (2007) *Law & Policy*, 29 (2), pp. 159–182; WASOFF, F., "Public attitudes and law reform: extending the legal framework for child contact to unmarried fathers, grandparents and step-parents?", (2009) *Journal of Social Welfare & Family Law*, Vol. 31 (2), pp. 159–172.

1992, to just over one-fifth, 22 per cent in 2009), and the broadly mirrored increase in the "no religion" sample over the same period. This latter group has grown from one-quarter to just over one half of the sample. There is little evidence to suggest that a "return" to religious identification (let alone religious activity) is likely in the foreseeable future.[25] It appears more likely that the "no religion" category will grow even further, since the trend is closely associated with age. Table 2 shows the proportion of two broad age groups (those aged under 40, and those aged 40 or more) who describe themselves as having no religion across the same range of surveys as described in Table 1:

Table 2. Proportion of individuals who state they have no religion by age group, 1992–2009

	1992	1997	1999	2002	2004	2006	2009
	%	%	%	%	%	%	%
18–39	37	47	53	56	62	60	66
Over 40	17	21	32	35	40	37	44

Sources: Scottish Election Surveys 1992 & 1997; Scottish Social Attitudes Surveys 1999–2009.

Three aspects of this table are notable. Firstly, respondents in the younger group have consistently been, and remain, more likely to choose "no religion" than respondents in the older group. Secondly, the relative gap is declining – at the beginning of the trend table the younger group were more than twice as likely to say they are of no religion; by the early years of the twenty first century the gap had reduced markedly. Thirdly, the trend in both age groups is unmistakably upwards, to the point that the proportion of no religion in the older group by 2004 is very close to the proportion of no religion in the younger group at the start of the trend table in 1992. Irreligion – the claim of having no religious affiliation – now accounts for a clear majority of the younger group and, unless these trends are reversed, is likely to account for a majority in the older group in the next decade or so.

It may be that the "no religion" group is united only negatively, by an absence of a religious affiliation, rather than positively by any commonality of beliefs, attitudes, or behaviour. However the "religious" are no more united or coherent, since they represent a variety of different faith and denominational groups, as well as differing in their degree of religious observance. We can divide the "religious" into two distinct sub-groups: the "active" who say they regularly attend religious services (defined here as at least once a month), and the "nominal" who say they attend less often or not at all. Such a subdivision creates

[25] ROSIE, M., "Death by Committee", *Theology in Scotland*, IX (2), (2002), 21.

three categories which will inform much of the foregoing analysis. Table 3 shows these three categories for the period 1992–2009.

Table 3. Degree of religious observance, 1992–2009

% by column	1992	1997	1999	2002	2004	2006	2009
Religious, active (attends ≥ monthly)	24	24	26	17	19	22	20
Religious, nominal (infrequent or non-attender)	51	44	34	41	33	33	27
No religion	25	32	40	42	48	46	52
Base	*951*	*871*	*1477*	*1665*	*1634*	*1591*	*1474*

Sources: Scottish Election Surveys 1992 & 1997; Scottish Social Attitudes Surveys 1999–2009.

From this table it appears that much of the decline in the proportion of people willing to assign themselves to a religious affiliation relates to a "falling off" of respondents in the "nominal" group who, whilst thinking of themselves within a religious category, did not regularly bring that category into practice (as measured by attending religious services). Whilst the proportions who are both religious *and* regularly attending show a slight downward trend, this is far less marked than the sharply decreasing proportion of the "nominal". Secularisation, in this context, seems to have eroded the "softer" part of the religious constituency leaving an active "core" relatively unchanged, and comprising around one fifth of the current population.

An important question for our analysis is whether each of these three groups is characterised by more than its claims to religious identity and observance, and whether each group is distinguished from the others in terms of its attitudes and beliefs. In other words, will the differences *within* each group be greater than (or at least equal to) differences *between* it and the other groups? We now examine this in relation to a range of "family values" relevant to recent family law reform, and informed by three questions:

- (In what ways) are attitudes on, and responses to, issues of "family values and obligations" associated with religion?
- Do those from different religious/denominational groups differ in their attitudes and beliefs on family values?
- Are there differences in attitudes and beliefs between the religious and the non-religious?

Where such differences exist, we shall also consider the extent to which they can be explained by other differences (such as age, gender or socio-economic position) between the groups.

6. RELIGIOUS ADHERENCE AND FAMILY VALUES

Looking at how family attitudes vary by the degree of religious adherence, respondents were asked to indicate their level of agreement with a range of attitude statements about marriage, cohabitation, sexuality and family life. The first set of statements, relating to marriage, were:

- "People who want children ought to get married."
- "Married couples make better parents than unmarried ones."
- "Even though it might not work out for some people, marriage is still the best kind of relationship."
- "It is a good idea for a couple who intend to get married to live together first."
- "Gay or lesbian couples should have the right to marry one another if they want to."

Responses were given in a five point Likert scale (strongly agree, agree, neither agree nor disagree, disagree, strongly disagree). We have combined agree/strongly agree and disagree/strongly disagree, and omitted the neutral responses. All of the data that follow presents associations that are statistically significant.

6.1. MARRIAGE AND COHABITATION

In Tables 4 to 8 below it can be seen that the secular "no religion" group are consistently less traditional than the religious group, and within that group, the actively religious are consistently more traditional in their attitudes towards the centrality of marriage for family life. In all of these tables, the nominal religious group occupy an intermediate position in their family attitudes, and the differences between the actively religious group and the secular group are large.

Table 4. "People who want children ought to get married."

% by column	Any religion	Religious - Active	Religious - Nominal	No religion
Agree	**64**	73	59	**30**
Disagree	**15**	13	16	**40**
Base	*793*	*300*	*493*	*707*

Table 5. "Married couples make better parents than unmarried ones."

% by column	Any religion	Religious - Active	Religious - Nominal	No religion
Agree	**30**	38	25	**13**
Disagree	**33**	31	35	**58**
Base	*783*	*298*	*485*	*696*

Table 6. "Even though it might not work out for some people, marriage is still the best kind of relationship."

% by column	Any religion	Religious - Active	Religious - Nominal	No religion
Agree	**69**	76	65	**44**
Disagree	**11**	11	12	**25**
Base	*796*	*300*	*496*	*708*

Table 7. "It is a good idea for a couple who intend to get married to live together first."

% by column	Any religion	Religious - Active	Religious - Nominal	No religion
Agree	37	28	43	**65**
Disagree	22	32	15	**9**
Base	*787*	*297*	*490*	*699*

Table 8. "Gay or lesbian couples should have the right to marry one another if they want to."

% by column	Any religion	Religious - Active	Religious - Nominal	No religion
Agree	27	18	32	**53**
Disagree	**48**	55	45	**22**
Base	*784*	*295*	*489*	*693*

6.2. AGE EFFECTS

While these data show a clear difference between those who are religious and those who are not, these patterns could well be age-related, since members of the younger cohort are also more likely to state they have no religion. To control for age effects, we divided the sample into two broad age groups: those aged below 40 or aged 40 or more, and looked at variation within each of these two age cohorts. Table 9 shows that the differences seen above, and especially within each group, are, to an extent, age related. Across each question and across each religious group, the younger cohort is less traditional than the older cohort. Likewise across each question and across each cohort, the religious are more traditional than the non-religious. Clearly, therefore, *both* age and religiosity are associated with more traditional views.

Table 9. Percentage in each age group of those agreeing with attitude statements by religious affiliation

% who agree	Any religion	Religious - Active	Religious - Nominal	No religion
People who want children ought to get married				
Aged 18–39	**41**	49	36	**17**
Aged 40+	**71**	80	66	**42**
Married couples make better parents				
Aged 18–39	**18**	27	12	**5**
Aged 40+	**34**	41	30	**20**
Marriage is still the best kind of relationship				
Aged 18–39	**41**	50	35	**28**
Aged 40+	**79**	85	76	**58**
Good idea ... to live together (before marriage)				
Aged 18–39	**59**	41	69	**81**
Aged 40+	**30**	23	34	**52**
Gay/lesbian couples should have the right to marry				
Aged 18–39	**49**	32	58	**64**
Aged 40+	**19**	13	23	**44**

6.3. THE TRADITIONAL MARRIAGE SCALE

These five questions were used to construct a scale of attitudes towards "traditional" marriage. This has been done by standardising the responses. The scale thus ranges from those who hold the "most traditional" attitudes towards marriage, represented by the value "1" (i.e. those who *strongly agree* that: people who want children ought to get married; married couples make better parents; marriage is still the best kind of relationship, and *strongly disagree* that it is a good idea to live together before marriage; Gay/lesbian couples should have the right to marry), to those with the "least traditional" attitudes (who strongly disagree with the first three statements and strongly agree with the final two).

In the sample as a whole the mean score is 2.97 whilst the median is 3.00. Table 10 shows the mean scores for the traditional marriage index for different subgroups of the whole sample across age, gender and various measures of religion, ranked from the most to the least traditional. All "religious" categories lie below the mean score for the population (*i.e.* on the more traditional side) whereas the mean for the "no religion" group is above the mean. Indeed, the only groups whose mean scores are above the sample mean are women, the "no religion" group and the youngest age group. Mean scores differ substantially by age, with the oldest group (65+) closest to the "most traditional" pole, and the youngest group (under 35) closest to the "least traditional" pole. The middle-aged group lie precisely in the middle. Gender differences are weaker, though women appear less traditional than men.

All measures of *religion* point the same way: there is a sharp division between the religious and the non-religious, regardless of whether we look at all those with a religious affiliation, those who are active or nominal, or whether we look at particular religious denominations. Each of these groups falls clearly below the mean, in contrast to the "no religion" group which falls clearly above it.

Table 10. Mean scores for the Traditional Marriage Index by age, gender and religion

	Mean Score	(weighted) N =
Most "traditional"		
65+	2.16	*241*
Active religious	2.42	*266*
Non-Christians	2.55	*20*
Presbyterians	2.57	*377*
Other Christians	2.61	*135*
All religious	2.64	*694*
Nominal religious	2.78	*428*
Catholics	2.86	*161*
Men	2.88	*603*
35–64	2.97	*745*
ALL SAMPLE	**2.97**	***1361***
Women	3.05	*759*
No religion	3.32	*667*
18–34	3.51	*376*
Least "traditional"		

Of course there will be overlaps (and interactions) between these variables. We know, for example, that the "no religion" group (mean age = 43) is much younger than the actively religious group (mean age = 55), and that Presbyterians are, on average, rather older than Catholics (mean age 58 as compared to 47). The relative weight we can place on religion, religiosity and age remains, therefore, unclear. In order to examine the impact of religious affiliation and (non) attendance on family attitudes whilst controlling for socio-economic variables such as age and gender, we present a logistic regression analysis that identifies which characteristics are most likely to predict a more traditional marriage scale score than the average.

We created a dichotomous variable which divides the sample into those whose score falls on or below the overall mean (2.97) – thus having an average or more than traditional score – and those who fall above it (with less traditional than average scores). Parallel exploratory models were constructed, each containing measures of age, gender, social class and education. In one set of models we also included the three way distinction explored above – that is, separating respondents into the actively religious, the nominally religious, and those of "no religion". In the other, we included a variable containing a range of denominations (those outlined in Table 1) and a dichotomous variable recording whether or not the respondent was a regular religious attender.

Crucial in such models is the calculation of odds ratios – each explanatory variable has a baseline or reference category against which all other values of the variable are compared. For example, in our first model the reference category for "religious group" are those who are of "no religion". Here, the odds ratios will show the relative likelihood of taking a more traditional view of marriage, holding the effects of all the other variables constant, of the other categories – the actively and nominally religious. An odds ratio of 1.0 indicates *no difference* in likelihood; an odds ratio greater than 1.0 indicates how much *more likely* a person in that category is to claim to be *more traditional*; an odds ratio of less than 1.0 how much *less likely*.

In the first model on the likelihood of taking a more traditional view of marriage, the *only* statistically significant effects were found within age, gender, and religious group. The other variables – education and social class[26] – do not have any significant effect either way. Table 11 shows the significant effects found in the model – once education and class were removed – in terms of beta values, standards errors, statistical significance, and odds ratios.

26 These are measured by highest qualification held, and by the Goldthorpe-Heath educational schema.

Table 11. Model A: Statistically significant effects in a traditional view of marriage

	Beta	S.E.	Sig.	Odds ratio
Age (in years)	.075	.005	.000	**1.078**
Sex (*Women*)				
Men	.622	.140	.000	**1.938**
Religious group (*No religion*)				
Actively religious	1.877	.195	.000	**6.534**
Nominally religious	1.071	.153	.000	**2.917**

Source: SSA 2004. Reference groups in parenthesis.

Crucial here is the impact of the age category – whilst the odds ratio at first glance appears to be close to equalling "no difference" it should be stressed that the effect relates to each *year* a particular person is older than another. Thus the odds ratio the model produces for two individuals a decade apart in age is very substantial indeed. In age, gender and religious group we find significant and positive effects. That is, older people, men, and both types of religious respondent are more likely (all other factors being held constant) to take a "more traditional" view of marriage than younger people, women, and those of "non religion". The odds ratios show that the magnitude of these differences is substantial. The religiously active, for example, are – by this measure – more than six times more likely to take a traditional view of marriage than those of "no religion". Men, meanwhile, are almost twice as likely as women to take a traditional view.

The parallel model incorporating denominational differences produced very similar results. Again both education and class offered no statistically significant predictive value, and again gender, age and the religious variables provided significant and positive effects. Table 12 shows the significant effects found in the model once education and class were removed.

In this model both the magnitude and direction of the age and gender effects are almost identical to those found previously. The cumulative effect of religious affiliation and religious attendance are also similar, though two points are noteworthy here. First, the most powerful effects are found in the "Other Christian" and "Non-Christian" categories. We should be cautious here since both of these are of course heterogeneous constructs containing a number of quite different denominations and faith traditions. Further, the latter of these groups is numerically modest, with just 24 respondents. The second point relates to the supposed divide in Scotland between Protestants and Catholics – this is certainly not borne out by attitudes towards marriage. Once we control for age, gender and religious attendance we find the differences between these groups are very modest indeed. Thus the observed differences between religious denominations are small, particularly when compared with religious affiliation.

Table 12. Model B: Statistically significant effects in a conservative view of marriage

	Beta	S.E.	Sig.	Odds ratio
Age (in years)	.079	.005	.000	**1.082**
Sex (*Women*)				
Men	.699	.142	.000	**2.012**
Religious affiliation (*No religion*)				
Presbyterian	1.000	.171	.000	**2.718**
Catholic	.986	.246	.000	**2.681**
Other Christian	1.280	.248	.000	**3.597**
Non-Christian	2.826	.519	.000	**16.879**
Religious attendance (*Irregular/none*)				
Regular	.706	.205	.001	**2.025**

Source: SSA 2004. Reference groups in parenthesis.

This analysis shows the value in modelling and controlling for key socioeconomic variables: we find that social class and educational differences do not predict differences in attitudes towards marriage. On the other hand age and gender, and religion do predict such differences. Whilst there are some nuances and differences within religion, it is clear from our analysis that two cleavages are crucial: first the secular/religious divide is a key predictor in "more traditional" attitudes towards marriage; secondly knowing whether a religious respondent is "active" or "nominal" helps to predict the extent of that "more traditional" view.

7. RELIGIOUS ADHERENCE AND SEXUAL MORALITIES

The second set of attitude questions relate to sexual moralities. The four questions elicit the respondent's view as to how far certain types of sexual relations are wrong, along a five point scale (always wrong; mostly wrong; sometimes wrong; rarely wrong; not wrong at all). The questions were:

- If a man and woman have sexual relations before marriage, what would your general opinion be?
- What if it was a boy and a girl who were both still *under 16?*
- What about a *married person* having sexual relations with someone other than his or her partner?
- What about sexual relations between two adults of the *same sex?*

Tables 13 to 16 report attitudes towards these four scenarios regarding sexual moralities by levels of religious adherence. As above, we have combined the two "wrong" and the two "rarely/not wrong" categories, and excluded the more ambiguous "sometimes wrong" response.

Table 13. If a man and woman have sexual relations before marriage, what would your general opinion be?

% by column	Any religion	Religious - Active	Religious - Nominal	No religion
Always/Mostly wrong	**19**	31	12	**4**
Rarely/Not wrong	**64**	44	75	**88**
Base	*858*	*322*	*536*	*774*

Table 14. What if it was a boy and a girl who were both still *under 16*?

% by column	Any religion	Religious - Active	Religious - Nominal	No religion
Always/Mostly wrong	**80**	95	87	**90**
Rarely/Not wrong	**5**	1	4	**2**
Base	*857*	*322*	*535*	*774*

Table 15. What about a *married person* having sexual relations with someone other than his or her partner?

% by column	Any religion	Religious - Active	Religious - Nominal	No religion
Always/Mostly wrong	**89**	94	89	**91**
Rarely/Not wrong	**4**	*	3	**2**
Base	*858*	*322*	*536*	*774*

Table 16. What about sexual relations between two adults of the *same sex*?

% by column	Any religion	Religious - Active	Religious - Nominal	No religion
Always/Mostly wrong	**54**	58	51	**27**
Rarely/Not wrong	**33**	26	37	**58**
Base	*857*	*322*	*535*	*774*

Attitudes towards two of the scenarios – underage sex and adultery – are very clearly *not* divided across religion. Most people, regardless of their religious beliefs, state that adultery and under-age sex are wrong. It is with regard to the two remaining scenarios that there are substantial differences in attitudes. In relation to pre-marital sex the clear difference is between the actively religious and the others, rather than across religion *per se*. Thus, whilst clear majorities of the no religion group (88 per cent) and the nominally religious (75 per cent) think pre-marital sex is "rarely wrong" or "not wrong at all", only a minority of the actively religious, albeit a substantial one (44 per cent), think so. In relation to premarital sex, the actively religious are very clearly less permissive in their attitudes than the other two groups.

We find a quite different pattern with regard to same-sex relationships. Here differences of opinion are most marked across the religious/secular divide, with 54 per cent of the religious group, but only 27 per cent of the secular group considering that homosexual sex is always or mostly wrong. To some degree these attitudes will be mediated through other variables such as gender and, especially, age. In a logistic regression that controls for these and other socioeconomic factors, we can see that, even when controlling for these, the religious groups are less permissive and more homophobic than the non-religious.

For this model we created a dichotomous variable contrasting those who feel that same-sex relationships are "always" or "mostly wrong" (41 per cent of respondents) with everyone else. The model is thus seeking to identify the statistically significant predictors of *disapproving* of same-sex relationships. Again we constructed parallel models containing the four background variables noted above, with some models using a three-way division of religiosity, and the other looking at denominational affiliation and attendance separately.

The first thing to note is that again social class proved to have no predictive value, and was omitted from subsequent elaboration of the models. Education, however, did play a statistically significant role with a clear division between those with intermediate and advanced qualifications – who were significantly *less* likely to hold disapproving views – and all those with elementary or no qualifications. There were no statistically significant differences between those with no qualifications, and those with elementary ones (this in denoted, in the following table, as "n.s." for "not significant"). The models also found consistent age and gender effects, with older respondents and men more likely to disapprove than the younger and than women.

Of key interest here, however, is the role of the religion variables. In the parallel exploratory models similar effects were uncovered, which suggested that the key division was between the religious and the secular. Indeed we found that religious attendance had no appreciable impact on the explanatory utility of the model: the underlying difference in attitude is best explained by whether or not a respondent claims a religious affiliation *regardless* of whether they are "active" or "nominal". Again whilst there are differences between denominations, these are relatively modest amongst the three Christian categories, with Presbyterians and Catholics almost equally as likely – other things held constant – to disapprove of gay and lesbian relationships.

Table 17. Model C: Statistically significant effects in disapproval of same-sex relationships

	Beta	S.E.	Sig.	Odds ratio
Age (in years)	.042	.004	.000	**1.043**
Sex (*Women*)				
Men	1.025	.142	.000	**2.012**
Education (*No qualifications*)				
Degree	-1.205	.192	.000	**.300**
Other higher education	-.733	.214	.001	**.480**
Higher/A level	-.626	.194	.001	**.534**
Standard Grades 1–3/GCSE	-.512	.194	.008	**.599**
Standard Grades 4–7/CSE			n.s.	
Foreign/other			n.s.	
Religious affiliation (*No religion*)				
Presbyterian	.855	.143	.000	**2.351**
Catholic	.882	.184	.000	**2.416**
Other Christian	1.159	.209	.000	**3.186**
Non-Christian	2.558	.466	.000	**12.904**

Source: SSA 2004. Reference groups in parenthesis.

7.1. GAY AND LESBIAN ADOPTION

It is not only same-sex partnership where a religious/secular difference is evident, but also in relation to same-sex parenthood. Respondents were asked their opinion about whether or not a settled same-sex couple should be allowed to adopt children, with the sample divided evenly between those asked about a male and female couple:

> "Now think about two (men/women), both in their early thirties, who have been living together for five years as a couple. Should it be possible for them to adopt a child in exactly the same way as a married couple?"

As we have seen in relation to same-sex partnerships, both religious groups were more critical of the prospect of gay and lesbian adoption than the secular group. Interestingly, all groups were less critical of the idea of lesbian than gay male adoption. A majority in all groups thought gay male couples should not be allowed to adopt, compared to a smaller majority of the religious groups who thought the same for a lesbian couple, and only just over one third of the secular group stating that a lesbian couple should not be allowed to adopt. Differences are clearly between the religious group and the secular group in the case of gay male adoption, whilst there are some intra-religious differences with respect to lesbian adoption, with a less disapproving attitude associated with those of nominal religion.[27]

Table 18. Attitudes to adoption of children by same-sex couples

% by column	Any religion	Religious - Active	Religious - Nominal	No religion
Gay male couple should	23	23	23	37
Should not	73	73	74	57
Base	*419*	*165*	*254*	*407*
Lesbian couple should	37	28	41	56
Should not	57	68	52	35
Base	*437*	*157*	*280*	*362*

8. FAMILIAL OBLIGATIONS

Family values, and family law, are not confined to family structure and sexual moralities, they also concern familial obligation. Indeed, much of the recent family law reforms both in Scotland and elsewhere has focused on extending the range of partnership and parental relationships to which care and support obligations apply, particularly when those relationships end by separation or death. A number of scenarios relating to financial obligations between partners at the end of relationships were presented to respondents. Four of these relating to property are summarised in Table 19 which shows the percentage of respondents answering "definitely" or "probably should" to the question posed. The scenarios concern issues addressed by the Family Law (Scotland) Act 2006. Bearing in mind the scale of religiosity differences in relation to norms and moralities discussed above, it is striking here how much smaller the "religious" differences are in relation to familial obligations with regard to the redistribution of property when a heterosexual relationship ends either by death or separation.

[27] It should be noted, however, that the differences we see between the actively and nominally religious are statistically significant only at the 5% threshold (.015).

Table 19. Views on familial obligations regarding property by religiosity

% answering *definitely* or *probably should*	Any religion	No religion
I would like you to think of *an unmarried couple* who have been living together for ten years. The man dies. He worked for a company whose occupational pension pays a pension to the surviving husband or wife in the event of death. Do you think the surviving partner should or should not be entitled to receive a pension on the same basis?	84	89
Imagine *another unmarried couple* without children who have been living together for ten years and live in a house bought in the man's name. Say he dies without making a will. Do you think the woman should or should not have the same rights to keep the home as she would if she had been married to the man?	87	92
Still thinking about these *two men* who have been living together for ten years as a couple. One of them owns the house they live in. Say he dies without making a will, do you think his partner should or should not have the same right to keep the home as he would if they were a married couple?	66	81
Still thinking about these *two women* who have been living together for ten years as a couple. One of them owns the house they live in. Say she dies without making a will, do you think her partner should or should not have the same right to keep the home as she would if they were a married couple?	70	85

Larger differences between the two groups are evident in relation to same-sex couples, whether male or female. The great majority of religious respondents do not draw a sharp distinction in their attitudes towards the claims of heterosexual married or cohabiting partners on separation or death, favouring parity of treatment. However, considerably fewer support identical claims for a share in the family home upon the intestate death of a same-sex partner, though parity of treatment with heterosexual couples is nonetheless favoured by a majority of this group. In contrast, a large majority of the "no religion" group consider that the partner of a person who dies intestate should be treated in the same way as a married spouse, whether they were heterosexual or homosexual cohabitants, and with a higher level of support for parity of treatment of homosexual partners than found in the religious group.

A further difference between religious groups relates to their views on ongoing financial support from the other partner for an economically disadvantaged partner in a childless marriage or cohabitation of long duration upon divorce or separation (Table 20). Both groups gave rather weak support to such claims even where the couple was married (54 per cent for the religious; 46 per cent for the secular). Such claims from unmarried heterosexual cohabitants attracted weaker support, at 43 per cent for the religious and 38 per cent for the secular. Weaker still, particularly from religious respondents, was the level of support for claims by former unmarried homosexual ex-partners. Those who are not religious draw a lesser distinction between whether married, cohabiting and same-sex partners should be able to claim financial provision on separation or divorce than do religious respondents. However, the differences between the two groups are smaller than found in relation to norms about marriage and sexual behaviour outside marriage.

Table 20. Views on familial obligations to financial support by religiosity

% answering *definitely* or *probably should*	Any religion	No religion
I would now like you to think about a *married couple* who have been together for ten years. They have no children, but one of them has a much higher income than the other. They then split up. In these circumstances, do you think the partner with the lower income should be able to claim financial support from the other partner?	54	46
Still thinking about an *unmarried couple* who have been together for ten years. They have no children. One of them has a much higher income than the other. They then split up. Do you think the partner with the lower income should or should not be able to claim financial support from the other partner?	43	38
And now I would like you to think of *two men* who have lived together as a couple for ten years. One of them has a much higher income that the other. They then split up. Do you think the partner with the lower income should or should not be able to claim financial support from the other partner?	34	36
And now I would like you to think of *two women* who have lived together as a couple for ten years. One of them has a much higher income that the other. They then split up. Do you think the partner with the lower income should or should not be able to claim financial support from the other partner?	29	37

9. DISCUSSION AND CONCLUSION

Throughout our analyses religion emerges clearly as a social division that explains differences in attitudes towards non-traditional family life, and sexual behaviour outside marriage. There is a hierarchy between those who state they have both a religious affiliation and regularly attend religious services, those with an affiliation but who are infrequent or non-attenders and those who state they have no religious affiliation. This hierarchy applies across a wide range of family issues, including marriage, cohabitation, sexual moralities outside marriage and unmarried parenthood. The scale of difference between those who are religious in both affiliation and attendance, those who state a religious affiliation but are not frequent or regular church attenders, and those who state they have no religion differs according to the issue in question. However, the *ranking* amongst these groups is constant. Those who are regular church attenders have the most "traditional" family attitudes, and those who state they have no religion have the least traditional attitudes, with those who state a religious affiliation but who are not regular church attenders always in the middle. This pattern is evident even when controlling for key socioeconomic variables such as age and gender, both of which modify the scale of religious difference but do not explain it away. Interestingly, social class differences are not associated with differences in family attitudes. So there is a religiosity divide when it comes to family values about the centrality of marriage for family life and sexual behaviour outside marriage – a divide reflected in public debates about "the family", with religious institutions on one side and secular voices on the other. Thus, these data show that family values debates are mirrored by differences in attitudes in the population at large in relation to the centrality of marriage for parenthood and family life, and sexual activity.

But the picture is more complicated if one factors in public attitudes towards familial support obligations, particularly when partnerships end either in separation or death. While views about familial norms and moralities may differ substantially between the religious and the secular elements of Scottish society, their differences in relation to a wider conception of familial support obligations are smaller, and largely supportive of the direction recently taken by the Civil Partnership Act 2004 and the Family Law (Scotland) Act 2006.

Here the differences between the religious and secular are not so great and the voice of the religious lobby in public debates about family values seems to be somewhat out of tune with the views of its constituency, whether that constituency is seen as those who espouse a religious affiliation or those who are regular church attenders. For example, the argument is made by some faith groups that giving cohabitants rights to claim financial provision on separation or death of a partner undermines marriage. However, the great majority of those with any religious affiliation think a cohabitant *should* be able to claim financial provision on the intestate death of their partner.

In making evidence-based policy, family law reformers can look to the knowledge base generated not only in public consultations but also through social attitudes surveys. The process of family law reform is often a controversial one, sparking family values debates that are never far below the surface, and it is important for policy makers to be able to quote good evidence in response to claims and counter claims. Furthermore, in anticipating the reception of a new policy, such evidence enables policy makers to assess the extent to which the proposed direction of policy change will go with the grain of public opinion.

The 2004 Scottish Social Attitudes module identified one area of family law in which public opinion was, at best, divided, and only weakly supportive of the direction of change. This concerned whether one partner should be able to claim financial provision from the other upon separation in the case of a childless marriage, civil partnership or heterosexual or same-sex cohabitation, when the other partner has a much higher income. Only about half (just below for the non-religious and just above for religious respondents – the difference was small) agreed such claims should be possible in the case of marriage, with weaker support for same-sex partners and heterosexual cohabitants. This contrasts with the legal position in Scotland where a married person has long been able to claim financial provision on divorce from an ex-spouse. Section 9 of the Family Law (Scotland) Act 1985 sets out a framework of principles by which an award of periodical allowance can be justified. The equivalent right was given to (same-sex) civil partners in 2005 by the Civil Partnership Act 2004 (after this survey was carried out). And a more limited right to claim financial provision on separation in the case of economic disadvantage was given to both heterosexual and same-sex cohabitants by section 28 of the Family Law (Scotland) Act 2006. However, if these attitudes do not accord with section 9 of the 1985 Act, perhaps they align with the principle in the 1985 Act that adequate financial provision should be achieved, where possible and reasonable, by a clean financial break. The most recent evidence, now somewhat dated, found that the award of periodical allowance to a childless spouse was infrequent, whether by the courts or by a separation agreement.[28] More recently, research on the cohabitation provisions of the Family Law (Scotland) Act 2006 found the number of cases family lawyers dealt with that involved any of the these provisions since the Act came into force has been small.[29]

Nonetheless, the evidence produced by the family attitudes module during the law reform process culminating in the Family Law (Scotland) Act 2006, will be of some comfort to policy makers, such as the strong level of support found from both religious and secular respondents to allowing claims by an unmarried (particularly heterosexual) partner for a share in the assets of a deceased partner. The analysis of such data along religious lines, in addition to analyses involving more ubiquitous socioeconomic divisions, shows that a religiosity divide in Scotland remains salient in relation to many family issues, not between different religious denominations but rather, between those who are active church

[28] MORRIS, S., GIBSON, S. and PLATTS, A., *Untying the Knot: Characteristics of Divorce in Scotland, 1989–1991* (HMSO, 1992); WASOFF, F., "Mutual consent: separation agreements and the outcomes of private ordering in divorce", (2005) *Journal of Social Welfare and Family Law*, Vol. 27 (3–4), December, pp. 237–250.

[29] WASOFF, F., MILES, J. and MORDAUNT, E., *Legal Practitioners' Perspectives on the Cohabitation Provisions of the Family Law (Scotland) Act 2006* (Centre for Research on Families and Relationships and the Nuffield Foundation, 2010).

attenders, those with a religious affiliation but irregular or non-attenders and those who have no religious affiliation. Religiosity matters where family values are concerned, but the degree to which it matters depends on whether those values refer to the role of marriage in family life, the acceptability of sexual activity outside marriage or family obligations beyond marriage.

ASSESSMENT

THE PLACE OF RELIGION IN FAMILY LAW: A COMPARATIVE SEARCH

Jane MAIR

1. WHY SEARCH FOR RELIGION IN FAMILY LAW?

At times of uncertainty, change and crisis, it is common for individuals to turn to religion for guidance, insight and comfort. It might be suggested that similar motivations lie behind the current notable and rapid growth in academic interest in religion and law. Within the last few years there has emerged a significant body of debate and writing on the interaction of law and religion which, although wide ranging in terms of specific religions, particular legal issues and theoretical frameworks, nonetheless converges in its shared analysis of how law and religion intersect. This shared focus is hardly a coincidence and can be linked to various common trends and developments and to a number of specific key events. Within a UK context, the now notorious speech of the Archbishop of Canterbury, Rowan Williams,[1] was a significant catalyst, sparking controversial debate specifically with regards to the relationship between Shari'a law and civil law. The range and level of debate which has ensued is,

> "due not only to disparate views about the nature and attractiveness of Shari'a, but [has] also exposed subterranean unease about the identity of the West itself, especially given its mixed inheritance of humanistic, religious, and post-modern elements."[2]

The repercussions of this speech have spread to many other European countries and have helped to open up discussion on a wider range of issues surrounding

---

1 The Archbishop of Canterbury The Rt Rev Dr Rowan Williams, *Civil and Religious Law in England: a Religious Perspective*: text of the Foundation Lecture at the Royal Courts of Justice delivered on 7 February 2008. The full text of the speech is available at www.archbishopofcanterbury.org/1575.

2 AHDAR, R. and ARONEY, N., "The Topography of Shari'a in the Western Political Landscape" in AHDAR, R. and ARONEY, N. (eds.), *Shari'a in the West* (Oxford University Press, 2010), p. 11.

law and religion, whether Islam, Christianity or Judaism, contributing to the current situation where it can be said that:

> "Everyone today agrees on the new prominent role religions have acquired in politics, law and economics, not to mention other fields of public life. Nevertheless we still miss the necessary instruments to decipher and understand the causes and effects of this re-enchantment of the world."[3]

It is as part of that process of deciphering and understanding, within the specific context of religion and family law, and with a view to exploring some of that "subterranean unease", that this book was conceived.

The current interest in religion and law is inspired by a range of concerns and reflects the convergence of various distinct trends. Migration and the consequent establishment of ethnic minority communities within predominantly Christian societies have led to growing awareness of, and demands for recognition of, cultural and religious differences. Human rights, and in particular protection against discrimination on the grounds of religion and belief, have given rise to debate over the complexities of ensuring religious freedom and religious tolerance.[4] Increasing secularisation of many liberal Western legal systems has highlighted those who have strong religious beliefs which do not always fit with the majority view. Concern about a lack of meaning in postmodern law and society have encouraged renewed interest among some to search for meaning within religious or other belief systems. There are many explanations for the current shared interest in religion and there is a range of different legal issues arising specifically in respect of particular religions.

Although, traditionally, family law has not been a key area for comparative study, that has changed significantly in recent years.[5] The belief that family law is embedded in cultural specificity, previously hindered comparative[6] analysis but much recent work has begun to challenge that perception.[7] In conjunction with religion, family law is a highly appropriate area for consideration. The personal nature of the family and the close ties between emotions, individual

---

3 FERRARI, S. and CRISTOFORI, R. (eds.), *Law and Religion in the 21st Century: Relations between States and Religious Communities* (Ashgate, 2010), Preface, p. xvii.

4 See e.g. RIVERS, J., "Law, Religion and Gender Equality", (2009) 9 *Ecc LJ* 24.

5 Similarly, until recently, there has been relatively little comparative analysis of the interaction of law and religion: see, e.g., BERMAN, H.J., "Comparative Law and Religion" in REIMANN, M. and ZIMMERMANN, R., *The Oxford Handbook of Comparative Law* (Oxford University Press, 2006), 739, at p. 740.

6 For discussion of this argument see ANTOKOLSKAIA, M., *Harmonisation of Family Law in Europe: A Historical Perspective* (Intersentia, 2006), pp. 3–47.

7 See e.g. BOELE-WOELKI, K., "What Comparative Family Law Should Entail?", (2008) *Utrecht Law Review* 1.

personality, affective relationships and religious beliefs make it an ideal aspect of law in which to trace the influence of religion. Family and religion may each be classified as private and yet are frequently the subject of debate in terms of the interaction of public and private. Love, which is often cited as being at the heart of modern familial relationships, is also a key element of religious teaching and faith. Our aim in this book was not to focus on any particular religion, or to adopt in advance a specific theoretical or thematic approach, but instead to embark on a search for incidents of the place which religion has or might have within family law.

2. RELIGION AND FAMILY LAW: VIEWS FROM THE PAST

The primary focus of our search is family law within Europe and therefore, historically, the key religious influence is Christianity, as mediated through the principles and institutions of canon law. It has been argued that "[t[he medieval uniform canon family law of the Roman Catholic Church was the common cradle from which all Western European countries started their evolution."[8] The extent to which this universal source was similarly implemented in different countries and regions is debated[9] but nonetheless it is widely acknowledged that, throughout Europe, there was a certain level of commonality based on canon law, as it related to the family. There are significant shared elements: the origins of Western legal systems in canon law, the liberalisation and individualisation of family law which followed from the Reformation and the more recent trends towards secularisation and declining levels of personal religious belief and conformity. Although the speed and timing of change may be different in each of the systems considered, there is nonetheless considerable common ground. There is no straightforward graph to be drawn, showing a clear trend from a time when canon law was largely synonymous with family law to a time when it has little remaining influence. Instead there is a much more nuanced picture of the complex relations between the two. In this comparative assessment, our aim is to highlight juxtapositions and intersections rather than to identify disappearances or to discover complete and conclusive patterns.

2.1. CHURCH AND STATE

One of the key issues to emerge from historical analysis of family law and religion, within a western European context, is the interaction between church

8 ANTOKOLSKAIA, *supra* note 4, p. 154.

9 See, e.g,. discussion by FINLAY, in this volume, *supra* at p. 276.

and state; the relative importance of canon law being to a great extent a reflection of the shifting relationship of power between church and state. The Reformation was obviously a significant moment of change in this power struggle but there were other relevant factors and influences. The Catholic Church exercised power, not only by influencing the principles and rules of family law, but also through education of the lawmakers and judges. The simple enactment of a legal and political separation between church and state was unlikely to result in a strict divide between matters religious and secular. The recognition of certain churches, as established churches or as state churches, provided for ongoing links and ensured a special place for those religious bodies within the society. In the absence of a radical change, such as, for example, that which occurred with the coming into being of the Soviet Union, there was unlikely to be a clean break with religious law of the past and therefore its influence continued long after the formal separation of religious establishments and the state.

Although formal, legal reform indicates a break from religion at various points in history, the accounts in several of the essays in this volume highlight the resilience of religion and the ingenuity of legislators and judiciary in maintaining and adapting religious principles, particularly where they have strong support from society. Where a break has been made in one respect between religion and family, its connection may later be detected in a new and surprising context. Speaking of the Reformation in England, Lawrence Stone observed that,

> "the household was the inheritor of many of the responsibilities of the parish and the Church; the family head was the inheritor of much of the authority and many of the powers of the priest. Thus the Word of God was to some degree removed from the parish church and transferred to the private home: the Holy Spirit was partly domesticated."[10]

The interaction between canon law and state was in itself complex and therefore the Reformation, while signalling a significant change in the church's relationship with the secular state and its legal rules, did not amount to the removal of religion from the equation. In tracing the developing impact of religion in family law, we should not restrict our vision to a single church or religious body and its formal relationship with the state.

---

10 STONE, L., *The Family, Sex and Marriage in England 1500–1800* (abridged) (Penguin, 1979), pp. 104–105.

2.2. SCRIPTURE AS LAW

Religion was influential in family law not only through institutional structure but also in terms of the creation and formation of rules; recognising the fact that the "canonists ... were expert in developing legal principles from scripture".[11] Canon law was particularly influential in the development of a modern legal model of marriage: the domesticated, nuclear marriage which was to form the basis for family life. It is argued that this was not a given, a direct consequence of scripture, but instead a carefully developed model of the medieval Roman Catholic Church. There are examples, in some systems of family law, of the express incorporation of passages from scripture but, often, the reliance was more subtle:

> "The Bible itself was rarely quoted directly in Scots statutes ... But parliament certainly felt free to legislate on the basis of religious fiat in the realm of the family, and in statute the Bible, in particular Mosaic law, often either lies silent in the background or was subsumed under the general phrase 'the laws of God'."[12]

The skill of jurists and judges is evident in Harding's discussion, for example, of the Irish law on nullity, where, guided by pragmatism, they attempted to preserve the tenets of canon law but in ways which would not unduly alienate the non-Catholic sections of the society.

Throughout the various historical accounts in this volume, and in discussion of current issues,[13] the flexibility of scripture and its openness to interpretation is clear. Not only within Christianity, but also in terms of Judaism and Islam, there is evidence that, despite what may at times be taught, there is considerable room for difference of opinion and interpretation. This has undoubtedly assisted religion in remaining relatively resilient and adaptable throughout historical change. It also lies behind some of the key differences between the substance and development of different European family law systems. The treatment of marriage as a sacrament by some legal systems but not by others, and the schism between those Christian systems which adopted a consensual approach to marriage formation and those which did not, requiring either consummation or priestly declaration in addition to individual exchange of consent, are examples of how the same passages of scripture can lead to quite distinct legal rules. This scope to interpret and mould the same words into different models should offer some

---

11 FINLAY, in this volume, *supra* at p. 276.

12 *Ibid.* at p. 288.

13 See in particular the essays of DE BLOIS and NORRIE, in this volume, *supra* at pp. 232 and 304, where they highlight the different interpretations of liberal and traditional, or orthodox, religious groups.

hope to those who seek to reconcile what may seem to be intractable clashes of dogma.

2.3. THE CHURCH IN THE COMMUNITY

Following the Reformation in Scotland, the direct link between the Roman Catholic Church and family law was broken but, in other ways, the church continued to play an important role. As the church's role as lawmaker and lawgiver declined, there was evidence of its considerable power as law enforcer. In Scotland,

> "[t]he kirk regarded itself, in the service of a godly community, as having an interest not only in preserving individual souls but also having a licence to interfere directly in household life in the name of protecting the wider interests of the parish."[14]

This support, and consequent interference, could be seen, for example, in the context of the provision of parish support for the poor. Kirk sessions operated a far reaching network of local policing, not only controlling and enforcing but supporting too, "much like a combination of modern social welfare agency, marriage counselling service and police domestic violence unit."[15] The blurring of boundaries between, on the one hand, religious doctrine and faith and, on the other, religious community as a source of social support or control can also be seen, for example, in the ongoing influence of the Swedish church in social life and the breadth of social services provided by the Roman Catholic Church in Malta.

Just as there may be a perception of a declining role for religion in society and in the individual lives of many people, so there is a perception that there has been a shift from a time when religion played a central and defining role in family law to the present situation where religion may be relevant in specific aspects of family law or for particular groups and communities but of much less impact on family law in general. This decline reflects the changing relationship between state and religion, a diminishing legal reliance on a particular religious family model and a weakening in individual religious belief and observance. Tracing the changing relations between religion and state, individuals and religious authority and religious belief and law highlights the complex and fragmented channels by means of which the church, or other religious body, governed, instructed, inspired, infiltrated and enforced. Both historically, and in terms of

---

14 FINLAY, in this volume, *supra* at pp. 279-280.

15 *Ibid.*, at p. 281.

current analysis, greater enlightenment may come from awareness of new intersections rather than disappearing links.

3. RELIGION AND FAMILY LAW: CURRENT DILEMMAS

Our search for the place of religion in family law does not aim or pretend to be comprehensive but instead seeks to highlight current instances of the interaction of religion and family law. Some of these reflect ways in which family law and religion are linked because of the functions and forms of each. Others highlight specific issues which arise because of clashing or competing values, in particular legal systems, between state and religion. We have grouped individual contributions to our search into four themes, to assist in identifying shared concerns and contrasting approaches. Clearly, however, there is considerable overlap between these themes, and consideration of individual contributions should not be confined within a single classification.

The first focuses on Accommodating a Place for Religion: dealing specifically with issues which arise in respect of the treatment of a particular religious group within a larger society, which does not share its religious values or laws. The concept of "accommodation" is also considered, however, in many of the other papers, in a variety of ways: the accommodation of tradition and culture within laicism;[16] an "accommodationist approach" to the right to freedom of thought, conscience and religion within the context of the provision of education;[17] the accommodation not only of law to religion but also of religion to law, as evidenced by the accommodation of "religious groups and individuals" to "social and legal developments" in respect of same-sex relationships.[18] The second theme focuses on Denying a Place for Religion; considering states which have specifically adopted a principle of secularism and, by so doing, may be said to "deny" a place for religion within the legal system. While secularism does not ignore the existence of religion, it does deny it a formal place within state policy and law. The third looks at instances in which the legal system may be seen to be Supporting a Place for Religion, either on a wide scale basis or in respect of a particular issue. Finally, we explore the extent to which legal systems, and particular aspects of family law, may be viewed as Reflecting a Place for Religion, by analysing the roles which religion and religious beliefs or values may play.

16 ÖRÜCÜ, in this volume.

17 McCARTHY, in this volume.

18 NORRIE, in this volume, *supra* at p. 304.

3.1. ACCOMMODATING A PLACE FOR RELIGION

Much of the current interest in religion and law stems specifically from the treatment of religious minorities within jurisdictions which do not share their particular faith or belief system. This is the challenge, identified by the Archbishop of Canterbury within the UK context, which is posed by "the presence of communities which, while no less 'law-abiding' than the rest of the population, relate to something other than the British legal system alone."[19] This is not an entirely new challenge to the extent that, in many countries where there has been a dominant, or established church or religious body, migration and social trends have from time to time raised the issue of how to accommodate non-conformists or non-believers. To a large extent, however, issues previously faced by European countries related to the accommodation of other churches or sects but still within a broadly Christian framework: the accommodation of different views but within an essentially common frame of reference.[20] The most obvious challenge which is now emerging is how to deal with a Muslim community, which wishes to live and be regulated according to Shari'a, within a civil legal system which is either loosely based on Christianity or which is secular.

Various approaches as to how to deal with minority communities have been considered and may be summarised as ranging from assimilation to accommodation. Within these choices, there is further flexibility, with accommodation in particular being described as "an elastic term".[21] Two contributions in this volume directly address the extent to which minority religious laws and practices are, or should be, "accommodated".[22] Crawford and Carruthers trace the development of rules of international private law, and their judicial application, and in so doing demonstrate a well-established and accepted means by which to "accommodate and resolve issues of cross-cultural diversity".[23] The rules of international private law, and their application within the UK, clearly fit within a model of accommodation,

> "seen as a gracious *concession* conferred by the framers of the single overarching law for all citizens and decidedly not the acknowledgement of a rival legal order that some citizens, by virtue of their faith, can avail themselves of."[24]

---

19 *Supra* note 1.

20 For further discussion, see BHANDAR, B., "The Ties That Bind: Multiculturalism and Secularism Reconsidered", (2009) 36(3) *Journal of Law and Society* 301.

21 AHDAR *et al.*, *supra* note 2, p. 24; BUDZISZEWSKI, J. in AHDAR *et al.* (eds.), *supra* note 2, pp. 181–206.

22 MENSKI, and CRAWFORD and CARRUTHERS, in this volume.

23 CRAWFORD and CARRUTHERS, in this volume, *supra* at p. 37.

24 AHDAR *et al. supra* note 2, p. 24.

The approach supported by Menski comes much closer to "acknowledgement of a rival order." He firmly rejects the assimilationist approach as overly simplistic and as failing to take account of the two way process on which it is based: "Simplistic assumptions about assimilation of migrants like 'salt into water' are manifestly wishful thinking, because simple common sense suggests that the water itself changes quality when the salt dissolves."[25]

Both of these contributions share substantial focus on Muslim communities and Shari'a,[26] and issues are specifically raised in that context. One aspect of current debate is substantive, in that it relates to the content of particular rules and practices within Shari'a, and it is recognised that some of the hostile reaction to the suggestions made in the Archbishop of Canterbury's speech, and much of the debate which has followed, focuses on the substance or alleged substance of specific rules.[27] Our focus here is more on the structural possibilities for accommodation rather than on critique of the substance of Shari'a in respect of family law. Menski argues that the current attitude of most lawyers, judges and academics towards "new ethnically and ethically pluralising developments in our midst"[28] is to ignore them or to pretend to have no knowledge of them. In so doing they fail to take account of "others", risk creating unfair and discriminatory outcomes and cling to an unjustified belief in the existence of or need for a fixed and settled legal code. This narrow perspective is being sustained in the face of "emerging scenarios of 'superdiversity' and even of 'plutopia,' an emerging condition where no single community has absolute control."[29] The reluctance to acknowledge or to engage with the religious, and often informal, laws of minorities within our society may spring partly from hostility towards those religious or ethnic groups and perceptions of their rules and practices but also from a fear of unfamiliar, alien and complex procedures, systems and frameworks.

The open and fluid approach advocated by Menski contrasts sharply with the more traditional and clearly defined application of the rules of international private law as a way of dealing "with diversity, principally legal diversity, and subsidiarily cultural and religious diversity" and of accommodating "that diversity as the forum from time to time sees fit".[30] The distinctions and divisions in the latter approach are much more clearly drawn and the relevant place of the

---

25 MENSKI, in this volume, *supra* at p. 16.

26 Although Crawford and Carruthers deal with a wider range of religions and Menski acknowledges that the issues he discusses do not arise only in the context of Islamic law.

27 See e.g. SHACHAR, A., "State, Religion and the Family: The New Dilemmas of Multicultural Accommodation" in AHDAR *et al.* (eds.), *supra* note 2, pp. 115–133.

28 MENSKI, in this volume, *supra* at p. 16.

29 *Ibid.*, at p. 17.

30 CRAWFORD and CARRUTHERS, in this volume, *supra* at p. 68.

domestic and secular legal system and the role of "secular judge" within it are firmly established. The way in which UK courts have developed over time, and adapted to accommodate aspects of the personal laws of individuals, reflects a clear legal structure although at the same time a growing awareness and understanding of the foreign law.

A key issue which Crawford and Carruthers highlight, although do not further explore, in their essay is the fact that, "[i]n international private law, religious law typically has been encountered under the banner of 'foreign law'. This assumes that foreign law starts at the border."[31] It is here that the difference is evident between the treatment of an individual who acts in compliance with the rules of foreign law when outside the UK and an individual who complies with these same rules but when territorially within the UK.[32] For those legal systems which have previously accommodated ethnic, cultural and religious diversity primarily through recognition, in appropriate cases, of the foreign law, the establishment and settlement of substantial ethnic minority communities within their own territory increasingly highlights the difference in treatment based on location. The sharp contrast between these two contributions may begin to alight on some common ground in their shared acknowledgement that there can be resulting unfairness from the recognition of personal law where it is foreign law but not in the situation where the foreign territorial element is missing.

3.2. DENYING A PLACE FOR RELIGION

Several of the legal systems considered in this book have adopted an expressly secular system of family law and the principle of secularism features to some extent in most of the contributions. Three examples in particular are explored, each of which has an apparently secular system of family law. Sweden is well known for being the ultimate secular state; a system which developed gradually over a period of time. Turkey has a principle of laicism which it imported to replace, and modernise, a previously pluralist system. Russia has experienced both religious and secular systems of family law, with sudden shifts between them as a result of political change. In each analysis, there is an opportunity to consider the nature of secularism while at the same time exploring the fit between that express principle and the role of religious establishments, private religious belief and behaviour within the particular society.

The term "secular" is used widely to describe a legal system which is quite separate from organised religion and religious principles, and it is often posited

31 *Ibid.*

32 See for a recent example their discussion at p. 52 of *Sulaiman v Juffali* [2002] 2 FCR 427.

as the opposite of religious. This distinction is increasingly questioned and the nature and effect of "truly" secular laws challenged.[33] The very notion of secularism, and its claim of separateness from religion, is argued to be "itself derived historically from Western Christian religious beliefs."[34] In the examples considered in this volume, a range of meanings and effects of secularism can be seen.

For Sweden, "by reputation ... one of the most secularised countries in the world",[35] secular family law is a legal framework which reflects "exclusively secular values" and which has evolved largely in line with its other Nordic neighbours.[36] Swedish secularism has become associated with modern, liberal family laws which emphasise equality and neutrality and the principle has been presented confidently as fitting well with Swedish society. Turkish laicism, by contrast, appears far out of line with the views and expectations of a large part of Turkish society, and its adoption, as part of the borrowed Swiss legal code, marked an abrupt split with the previously pluralist system. During the Ottoman Empire, "there was no one language, no single distinct culture, no one religion and therefore no one law."[37] Pluralism was firmly entrenched within the previous legal system "both as to substantive law to be applied and the courts which had jurisdiction to apply the law"[38] and family matters were governed by the personal, and in many cases religious, laws of individuals.

These two secular systems outwardly have little in common but both Jänterä-Jareborg and Örücü refer to structural imbalances in the operation of the secular principle. In Sweden, there is a state recognised church, the Church of Sweden, which continues to have a relatively high level of membership, whilst in Turkey, laicism is described as being "one-sided" due to the fact that, although "the interference of religion into state affairs and politics is not permitted, the interference of the state into religious affairs is."[39] In both countries, what is clear is that, while there should be no direct influence of religion in law that does not mean the absence of a role for religion.

In Russia, there have been sharp swings from religion to secularism; from a position where "Russia had no family laws other than religious ones" to a period,

---

33 See e.g. BHANDAR, *supra* note 20.
34 BERMAN, *supra* note 5, at p. 742.
35 JÄNTERÄ-JAREBORG, in this volume, *supra* at p. 73.
36 For discussion of the Church of Sweden and those of the other Nordic countries, see CHRISTOFFERSEN, L., "Not Even Believing in Belonging: States and Churches in Five North-European (Post-) Lutheran Countries" in FERRARI *et al.*, *supra* note 3, pp. 187–197.
37 ÖRÜCÜ, in this volume, *supra* at p. 118.
38 *Ibid.*
39 *Ibid.*, at p. 122.

following the Bolshevik Revolution, of "militant atheism".[40] Russia, as with Sweden and Turkey, has a population, a high proportion of which, adheres to one single religion or church and therefore, until recently at least, the issues have not been further complicated by pluralist claims. In Russia, although there has been a strong revival in the Russian Orthodox Church and in individual religious belief post-independence, the legal principle of secularism remains. For the time being, Antokolskaia comments that church and state exist in relative harmony, although it may be questioned to what extent this is a reflection of their recently troubled past and the current period of re-emergence and tolerance.

In Sweden, there is a sense that secularism as a legal principle has developed largely in line with the views of the population, although with relatively little impact on the role of the Swedish Church in the life of the population; in Turkey, laicism represented a political "aspiration",[41] adopted almost without regard for the views of Turkish society and in Russia, the secularism of the Soviet Union was a much more extreme attempt not only to remove the church from society but to change the beliefs of individuals: "to roll back the influence of religion – the Bolsheviks' greatest ideological rival."[42] These three different examples offer some insight into the different meanings of secularism and its differing implications for state religion, cultural religion and individual faith. While for the time being, religion and religious belief appear to be providing relatively little difficulty for secular Russia, in Sweden and in Turkey, the secular state is to some extent being challenged by issues of multiculturalism, strong personal Islamic belief and by the difficulties inherent in distinguishing religion from culture.

3.3. SUPPORTING A PLACE FOR RELIGION

In contrast to legal systems which have adopted an expressly secular attitude, there are others which support religion, either by giving a particular religion or church special protection within the Constitution or by recognising or incorporating specific religious concepts, rules or procedures within aspects of the family law framework. We have included papers considering Ireland and Malta, in both of which the Roman Catholic Church has had a privileged role or privileged status. We have also included consideration of the Jewish *get* and various ways in which this form of religious divorce has been recognised or "supported" in different legal systems. Provision for, or accommodation of Jewish law in respect of the *get*, although apparently a relatively minor aspect of a family law system, constitutes a significant instance of legal support for religious law.

40 ANTOKOLSKAIA, in this volume, *supra* at p. 97.
41 ÖRÜCÜ, in this volume, *supra* at p. 121.
42 ANTOKOLSKAIA, in this volume, *supra* at p. 105.

The treatment and protection of faith schools, particularly within the UK context, is another example of an otherwise secular legal system supporting religion, by making special provision for religious education.

Malta offers the most overt and wide-ranging support for religion, by means of its Constitution which "proclaims the Roman Catholic Apostolic Religion as the religion of Malta".[43] Despite some historical changes in the relationship between the church and the state, Roman Catholicism has a long, and relatively unchallenged, position within Malta, and its teachings, laws and traditions not surprisingly have been highly influential in the "ethos" of family law.[44] What is notable, however, is the way in which the Maltese courts have attempted to accommodate the demands of European human rights within the confines of the domestic, religious family law; albeit with the significant exceptions of same-sex relationships and divorce. The latter are instances of challenge to the dominant Catholic model of marriage-based family which, to date, have been beyond the stretch of what has otherwise been shown to be a relatively flexible model.

Flexibility and responsiveness to change and to diversity are similarly evident through the judicial decisions of the Irish courts, which demonstrated that, by means of a "'catholic' approach to Church doctrines", they have been able in the past to "find a way to reflect a prevailing liberal morality even if they must use the tools of an inherently conservative framework."[45] Ireland's support of a specific family model, which is clearly, if not always expressly, moulded on Roman Catholicism, has been moderated through awareness of the need to accommodate a range of religious and other social views. There is no direct line between canon law and Constitutional provision, but an astute pattern of interpretation, with a clear objective in mind but also with awareness of the need for accommodation. Harding suggests that it is the lack of such a clear objective, now evident "in the absence of homogenous religious values", that is resulting in the more recent inconsistency of "the constitutional protection of marriage".[46] The success of constitutional protection of religion or a religious model is to a large extent dependent on the strength of the majority belief and the careful accommodation of other influences, whether religious, moral, cultural or social.

Jewish family law, and in particular the *get*, has been considered by several jurisdictions in recent years. While Jewish law is expressly supported in Israel, with at least part of Israel's family law being based on religious law, other secular jurisdictions have also provided support for the *get* by recognising or

43 FARRUGIA, in this volume, *supra* at p. 187.
44 *Ibid.*
45 HARDING, in this volume, *supra* at p. 161.
46 *Ibid.*, at p. 184.

incorporating it in various ways into their secular divorce laws. Whereas there is considerable diversity in the individual approaches of legal systems towards accommodating this clash between civil and religious requirements, and there are other jurisdictions which have chosen not to recognise the *get*, this stands out as an area of religious law which has attracted a relatively supportive reaction from several legal systems. This recognition of extra-judicial divorce by some secular states stands in contrast to the more widespread resistance to recognition of Shari'a divorce provisions and raises questions as to the level and consistency of support for any or some religious family laws.

The continued support within the UK for religious education may be simply a reflection of a relatively high level of support for faith-based education but it may also, to some extent, be due to the fact that it has not always been identified as an issue of central importance in the religious/secular debate. From one view, education is at the outskirts of family law, but teaching and guidance is central to the relationship between parent and child and, as McCarthy points out, "religion is built into British schools from the foundations." Support for religion in education can therefore be seen as central both to the development and continuation of family relationships and to the place of religion within the state. There are obvious tensions between secular state, parental responsibilities and wishes and children's rights; tensions which are underlined if a further distinction is made between "education" and "religious education".[47]

3.4. REFLECTING A PLACE FOR RELIGION

In the final section, we have included discussion of ways in which religion, and religious values or beliefs, may influence and be reflected in family law, regardless of the particular commitment of the overall legal system to either a religious or secular principle. Just as it might be argued that the decline in public stature of religion and church within many societies has been balanced to some extent by the internalisation of religious based beliefs and models, so there is evidence of the continuing reflection of religion in outwardly secular laws.

Historical analysis tends to indicate that, although for most of Europe, the Reformation signalled a split between church and state, there was not necessarily such a clear shift in direction within family law. Although canon law ceased to be directly enforceable and the system of enforcement itself changed from church based to civil courts, the tenets of canon law in many areas continued to exercise strong influence. This is particularly evident in respect of marriage and adult

---

47 As seen, e.g., in Turkey where the parents have the sole right to decide on the religious education of their children: discussed by ÖRÜCÜ, in this volume, *supra* at pp. 138–139.

relationships, where the Christian model of marriage has continued to exert control. Where the debate is between "formal" marriage and "marriage-like" relationships, the barriers to change have been relatively weak; not surprisingly perhaps, as, for many European jurisdictions, the canon law consensual model had already accepted that it was the consent of the parties rather than any third party intervention or declaration which created the bond. Of all of the reflections of religious law and teaching in family law, those relating to the inherently heterosexual nature of Christian marriage have been most obvious. Only in Russia, during the Soviet period of atheism, was there evidence at a relatively early stage in the twentieth century of some legal acceptance of non-marital and same-sex relationships. In some states that legal acceptance has not yet been secured and in many countries, even where same-sex partnerships have been legally recognised and treated as being equal to marriage, gender neutral marriage has remained out of reach. Unlike in other areas, where more progressive and obviously secular developments in European human rights provided an impetus for domestic change, the slowness of the European Court of Human Rights to accept a same-sex family model has allowed domestic legal systems to remain relatively unchallenged.

While the influence of religion has remained strong within the context of adult intimate relationships, in other areas of family law its grip is much weaker. In the historical account of religion and family law within Scotland, Finlay highlighted the relatively modern nature of "family law" and the lack of universal applicability of canon law to all aspects of what we might now conceive of as family law. In particular, there was a split between issues of status and family relationships, centred on marriage, and regulation of matrimonial property. In the empirical analysis of recent social attitudes in Scotland, a similar split can to some extent be detected with regard to questions relating to relationships, where the apparent reflection of religiosity was strongest, and those relating to familial obligations, where there was much less evidence of a divide.

In looking for reflections of religion in law, there is a risk of misinterpretation. Finlay argues that,

> "[i]solating religion as a causal force is ... potentially to misunderstand the fact that there were many causal forces, social, economic and psychological, which influenced the development of the idea of the family and also the law which regulated its place in the social structure of the community."[48]

It is a risk also highlighted in Rosie and Wasoff's interpretation of current Scottish attitudes but, even taking account of other influential factors such as

[48] FINLAY, in this volume, *supra* at pp. 270–273.

age, social class and education, they conclude that, "[a]ll measures of *religion* point the same way: there is a sharp division between the religious and the non-religious."[49]

Whereas much of the focus in the individual contributions in this volume, and more widely in the current debate on religion and law, is on diversity and pluralism, analysis of Scottish social attitudes towards family values and family law indicates a different divide: "a religiosity divide".[50] In many aspects, there is more that unites those with some form of religious belief or connection than divides them in terms of specific affiliation or practice. Although,

> "there is a hierarchy between those who state they have both a religious affiliation and regularly attend religious services, those with an affiliation but who are infrequent or non-attenders and those who state they have no religious affiliation,"[51]

the authors nonetheless conclude that "religiosity matters" even where that takes the form of a religious affiliation without accompanying religious practice; a conclusion which lends weight to the paradoxes highlighted in the context of Sweden. Whether it is a case of "believing without belonging" or "belonging without believing",[52] the message is clear; religion continues to be reflected in family law and, in searching for the place of religion in family law, we should cast our net wide.

4. SHOULD THERE BE A PLACE FOR RELIGION IN FAMILY LAW: CONTINUING DEBATES?

Current debates surrounding religion and law reflect changes in population, human rights, family law and religious beliefs and practices, but while the immediate motivation behind the interest is "change", the issues that emerge show consistency with long-established concerns. Previous struggles between church and state, religious and secular, private and public, function and form, unity and diversity re-emerge in new guises. An "eternal conflict of interests and values, with victory swaying back and forth between the various contestants for priority"[53] has the consequence that, while the details of current issues are new, there is resonance with existing debates within family law and in particular with the Western enlightenment tendency towards dichotomies.

---

49 ROSIE and WASOFF, in this volume, *supra* at p. 342.

50 *Ibid.*, at p. 353.

51 *Ibid.*, at p. 351.

52 For further discussion of these different approaches to religious belief and religious affiliation, see e.g., CHRISTOFFERSEN, *supra* note 35 and DAVIE, G., *Religion in Britain since 1945: Believing Without Belonging* (Blackwell, 1994).

53 STONE, *supra* note 10, p. 425.

4.1. RELIGION AND FAMILY LAW: A PUBLIC/PRIVATE DICHOTOMY?

A classic academic debate, within family law, concerns the position of families and their legal regulation in the context of a public/private dualism.[54] Family life and familial relationships are often presented as part of the private sphere, governed by values of individualism, freedom, emotion and love, whereas the regulation of families and the effectiveness of services provided by and within them are clearly identified as being of considerable public importance. Religion too occupies a difficult and unsteady place within this dichotomy: at times identified with the state, at others relegated to the private sphere. Love, which is often presented as central to both family relationships and to religious belief, is viewed as a concept to be kept in private.[55] Lacking in the rationalism necessary for the public sphere, it is contained and nurtured within the private. Many aspects of the discussion of family law and religion resonate with this well-established framework of public and private.

4.1.1. *Public space for religion*

There is an initial split between those legal systems which retain a space for religion within the public state and those which have adopted, in public, a policy of secularism. Questioning of this split, however, quickly demonstrates inconsistencies: those states which are publicly secular may nonetheless recognise, and to some extent support, an established church or religious body.[56] By so doing they give public status to that organisation which may in turn result in unequal treatment of other religious bodies which do not share its recognised position. Even in a system which appears strongly secular, such as Sweden, a continued role for the church, in the public celebration of family relationships, gives it a legal and social status which is to some extent paradoxical.[57] A number of European countries operate a dual system of marriage celebration, giving equal legal status to religious and civil marriage. Aside from issues of diversity and equality, which may stem from state control of those religious bodies which are permitted to solemnise marriage, questions may also be raised as to the dividing line between "religious" celebrants and "others":

54 See e.g., O'DONOVAN, K., *Sexual Divisions in Law* (Weidenfeld and Nicolson, 1995); OLSEN, F., "The Family and the Market: A Study of Ideology and Legal Reform", (1983) 96 *Harvard Law Review* 1497.

55 For some thoughts on love, both romantic and Christian, and its unsuitability to the public sphere, see ARENDT, H., *The Human Condition* (University of Chicago Press, 1958) and discussion of this in CHIBA, S., "Hannah Arendt on Love and the Political: Love, Friendship and Citizenship", (1995) *The Review of Politics* 505, especially pp. 524–531.

56 In the case of Turkey, the *Diyanet*. For discussion, see ÖRÜCÜ, in this volume, *supra* at p. 123.

57 See JÄNTERÄ-JAREBORG's discussion of the "Swedish paradoxes", *supra* at pp. 77–80.

what of those who hold strong beliefs but which do not fit within a traditional theist model, as in the case of humanists?[58] In Sweden, the continued strength in practice of the public celebration of marriage within a church may also challenge the neutral, inclusive legal provisions for same-sex and opposite-sex relationships which are enshrined in the secular legal framework. Control of access to the church or religious building, as a public space, to some extent questions the secular nature of the state.[59]

In other systems, although religious belief appears firmly relegated to the private sphere, it might be argued to have remained or re-emerged under the guise of "public" culture. In Turkey, the courts have shown adaptability towards religious belief by transforming it into culture and in that way gaining flexibility to accommodate it within the strict framework of laicism. In similar ways, the Irish courts are described as having incorporated elements of canon law in the form of culture. In Sweden, the folk and cultural significance of the Swedish Church has resulted in it retaining a surprisingly public significance. The place of religion and religious bodies is to some extent dependent on what we view as religion and how we distinguish it from broader notions of cultural identity. Declining levels of personal religious adherence mask the continuing and strong public presence of religion in the form of public buildings and cultural space.[60]

4.1.2. The private nature of belief

One view of religion identifies it in terms of personal faith; religious belief. A principle of freedom of religion and religious tolerance may provide a negative right to individuals to private belief and to personal adherence to that belief but may not fully address the interaction of that private belief with civil law and state.[61] Many western legal systems adopt a position similar to that set out in *Sulaiman v Juffali*, to the effect that "[r]eligion … is no doubt something to be

---

58 For some discussion of these issues within a Scottish context, see MAIR, J., "Public Ceremony and Private Belief: the Role of Religion in the Scots law of Marriage", (2007) *Juridical Review* 280.

59 Further evidence of these tensions can be seen in the attempts to reform the UK's Civil Partnership Act 2004 which originally prohibited civil partnerships from being registered within religious premises. For discussion, see NORRIE, in this volume, *supra* at pp. 314–315.

60 There are, of course, also examples of the removal of religious signs and symbols from public space. See, e.g., BIRNBAUM, P., "On the Secularization of the Public Square: Jews in France and in the United States", (2008–2009) 30 *Cardozo L Rev* 2431; RORIVE, I., "Religious Symbols in the Public Space: In Search of a European Answer", (2008–2009) 30 *Cardozo L Rev* 2669.

61 Issues arising from the interaction, within a European context, of freedom of religion, tolerance and non-discrimination are explored in TULKENS, F., "European Convention on Human Rights and Church-State Relations: Pluralism vs. Pluralism", (2008–2009) 30 *Cardozo L Rev* 2575; EVANS, M.D., "The Freedom of Religion or Belief and the Freedom of Expression", (2009) 4 *Religion and Human Rights* 197.

encouraged but it is not the business of government or of the secular courts".[62] Secular legal systems choose to contain religious beliefs within the context of the private sphere but that division, it is argued, is itself the product of a specifically Christian perspective.[63] Speaking particularly of Judaism, de Blois observes that "in religious law, there is no 'public' and 'private' distinction"[64] and this holistic approach is also firmly grounded in Islam. To construct a place for religion within the context of a public/private divide is in itself to deny recognition of some religions and religious law. Speaking specifically of Islam, it has been commented that "religious identity tends to blur the border between what is political and what is not political, as well as what is 'private' and what is 'public'"[65] and rejection of this classic dichotomy is particularly appropriate within the context of family law, where attempts to divide public from private and personal from political have often been criticised.

4.1.3. Personal meaning of public relationships

Regardless of the secular nature of a state, private religious belief may be tolerated, or even welcomed, particularly if it reinforces publicly agreed values and contributes to a sense of shared and sharing community. The individual nature of family relationships has been acknowledged as precluding a necessarily shared understanding of the shape of the personal interaction[66] but, arguably, this lack of common purpose has been exacerbated by changing legal regulation of marriage, with greater emphasis being placed on personal affect and emotional satisfaction than on a single, state imposed model of spousal relations. This opening up of legal marriage has allowed for inclusion of unmarried cohabitants within the legal framework and, to some extent, of same-sex couples, but it has consequently shaken whatever certainty there might previously have been as to the legal nature of marriage and, more broadly, as to why family law chooses to regulate certain types of relationship. As de Blois comments, "[i]t is remarkable that the whole idea of marriage as a legal concern is, in general, not questioned in even the most liberal of states."[67] The interaction of personal meaning with publicly recognised and regulated family relationships is most evident in the context of marriage which has, "long been regarded as both a legal and a spiritual

62 [2002] 2 FCR 427, *per* Munby J. at p. 439, as quoted and discussed by CRAWFORD and CARRUTHERS, in this volume, *supra* at p. 38.

63 Although this is not always fully acknowledged: BERMAN, *supra* note 5, at p. 740.

64 DE BLOIS, in this volume, *supra* at p. 209.

65 GAUDREAULT-DESBIENS, J.-F., "Religious Courts' Recognition Claims: Two Qualitatively Distinct Narratives" in AHDAR *et al.* (eds.), *supra* note 2, at p. 68.

66 For an interesting discussion of the "subjective" nature of intimate relationships in contrast to commercial contracts, see WIGHTMAN, J., "Intimate Relationships, Relational Contract Theory and the reach of Contract", (2000) 8(1) *Feminist Legal Studies* 93, particularly pp. 105–107.

67 DE BLOIS, in this volume, *supra* at p. 227.

institution – subject at once to special state laws of contract and property and to special religious canons and ceremonies."[68] With the declining certainty of a public legal conception of intimate relationships, space is being opened up for greater attention to focus on the "spiritual institution". Strong private belief may gain greater influence over the public framework, where the public model lacks clear and agreed foundations.[69] Much focus in the law and religion debate has been on the challenges posed to legal systems by religious beliefs of "others" but these challenges also provide opportunities to reconsider and redefine the nature of family relationships and family law.

4.2. RELIGION AND FAMILY LAW: FORM OR FUNCTION?

Another familiar framework employed in analysis of families and family law is that which seeks to distinguish between form and function. All European jurisdictions have seen similar trends during the twentieth century, and into the twenty first, away from emphasis on the form of relationships, dictated by compliance with legal rules and religious models, towards increasing recognition of the similar functions of a variety of differently constituted relationships.[70] This has been particularly evident within the context of the regulation and recognition of adult relationships: demonstrated by a move away from heterosexual marriage towards inclusion of informal relationships of cohabitation and of same-sex partnerships, both formal and informal. There is, however, no clear consensus in terms of the legal and political preference for either form or function and their interaction is complex. So too, it appears, when a similar analytical model is applied to religion.

4.2.1. Form of family relationships

In discussion of religion and family law, it is clear that the area which has attracted most attention is marriage. The Christian model of the family, based on a monogamous, opposite sex, permanent union, has exerted strong and lasting influence throughout the European jurisdictions considered. Several of the particular issues discussed in individual essays in this collection relate to this

---

68 WITTE, J., "The Future of Muslim Family Law in Western Democracies" in AHDAR *et al.* (eds.), *supra* note 2, at p. 281.

69 See e.g. the contrasting approach to the formation of marriage in the Scottish Outer and Inner House decisions in *SH v KH* 2006 SC 129. Is marriage a civil status entered into by compliance with the statutory provisions for formation or does it require personal consent to an underlying model of commitment to act as husband and wife? For further discussion of this issue in a Scottish context, see MAIR, J., "Marriage: Legal Status or Personal Relationship", (2007) *Edin LRev* 117.

70 See e.g. McCLAIN, L., "Love, Marriage and the Baby Carriage: Revisiting the Channelling Function of Family Law", (2006) 28 *Cardozo L Rev* 2133.

model: recognition of unmarried cohabitation; grounds for nullity; acceptance of divorce and, most recently, legal recognition of same-sex partnerships. Even where the biblical origins of modern family law are not openly acknowledged, the continuing force of their influence is clear, as can be seen, for example, in the Swedish reaction to a proposal, "to transform the legal institution of marriage into a gender-neutral concept, thus permitting also same-sex marriages", a reaction which "clearly demonstrated how deeply intertwined marriage is with religion."[71]

Religion has impacted on the form of family relationships, not only within the context of Christianity, but also when broadly Christian, albeit formally secular, legal systems come into contact with family forms of other religions. In the case studies presented by Menski, differing rules and understandings of family form clash. Particularly within the context of Ahmadi marriages in Pakistan, the variety of form and formation, according to the personal law of the individuals, further exacerbates "legal insecurities"[72] and the resulting reluctance of lawyers and officials to engage with the legal validity of various types of relationship.

4.2.2. Function of family relationships

In discussion of international private law developments, there is evidence, particularly within the context of polygamous marriages, of the UK courts developing a greater openness towards recognition of such marriages, not "in general or in the abstract", but in the context of a particular purpose and with focus on the incidents of marriage, rather than the status of marriage itself.[73] Although subsequent developments led to a much more widespread recognition of polygamous marriage, it is noteworthy that recognition was easier in the early stages where it could be linked to the function and consequences of marriage rather than to its inherent form. It might similarly be argued that when the focus is on function rather than form, it becomes more acceptable to acknowledge the Jewish *get* despite a legal system's requirement otherwise of judicial divorce. The unfairness to the "chained wife" of *get* refusal has clearly been of considerable influence in persuading legislators or courts to recognise the particular function, within religious family law, of this form of divorce. Evidently, however, focus on function is maintained at best inconsistently in most legal systems, as the accommodation of the Jewish *get* is a relatively isolated incident of willingness to take into account "religious" divorce.

71 JÄNTERÄ-JAREBORG, in this volume, *supra* at p. 74.

72 MENSKI, in this volume, *supra* at pp. 29–34.

73 CRAWFORD and CARRUTHERS, in this volume, *supra* at p. 39.

The function of family relationships is of concern not only to the state but to religious organisations and communities. The symbiotic nature of interaction between families and faith is highlighted particularly in the issue of religious education, where the function of parents as guardians and guides for their children overlaps with their duty as individual members of a faith community to broadcast and promote their religious beliefs. Commitment, support and obligation are values at the heart of both family and faith and the interaction of both can be seen as central to their respective maintenance.

4.2.3. Form of religion

It has not been a principal aim of this work to consider in detail, or to criticise, the differing form of individual religions or religious beliefs but some distinctions clearly emerge between religious beliefs which are more, or less, acceptable within broadly secular legal systems. Partly that might be explained within the context of a human rights analysis although, as de Blois, for example, has highlighted, in discussion of many aspects of religion and family law there are arguments on both sides.[74] It is clear that some forms of religion appear to be less threatening and more easily accommodated than others and this has had an inevitable impact on the extent to which they are resisted or incorporated.

The form which religion takes within a particular society has emerged as a point of some interest. Is it religion as a source of rules, as a form of culture, as individual belief, or as a way of life? A high level of religious belief amongst individual citizens does not necessarily correlate with legal protection for that religion or reflection of the religious rules and concepts within the provisions of family law. In fact, in some systems it is quite the opposite.[75] In other systems, a very low level of individual religious adherence or faith is ironically situated within a society in which the church has a central cultural role. This is most obviously evidenced in Sweden where,

> "Scandinavians belong to the State Churches without even believing in belonging, since faith is only partly the function of the Churches, alongside ensuring arrangements for the central institutions of life, the family, national heritage and nation-building."[76]

The form, or formulation, of religion or certain religious practices or beliefs as culture or tradition can be seen either to mask the apparent secularism of a

[74] DE BLOIS, in this volume, *supra* at pp. 228–233.
[75] Most obviously Turkey.
[76] CHRISTOFFERSEN, *supra* note 35.

society or to assist in the accommodation of personal religious faith into a system which otherwise allows no place for religion.[77]

Attempts to step away from individual beliefs and differences and to look for some common ground may help to highlight what is shared and may facilitate better and more productive communication. The concept of "civil religion" emphasises common ground and casts light not only on what is shared between different religions but also between religion and law.[78]

4.2.4. *Functions of religion*

Differing forms of religion and religious belief within various societies raise questions as to the function of religion. Historical accounts give some indication of a range of functions which religion and church may fulfil: a source of rules; a system of moral principles and beliefs; a structure of courts and judges; a framework for regulation and registration of relationships; a method of social control. In modern comparative analysis too, it is clear that religion can fulfil a variety of functions. In practical terms, the role of the Roman Catholic Church within Malta can be seen not only as providing much of the substance of family law rules but also as upholding principles of the Christian family model and providing practical support in the community. The social benefits, it might be argued, to some extent help to balance what some at least will view as the conservative restrictions which continue to apply. The relatively high levels of church membership within Sweden's strongly secular society, may reflect strong cultural and national ties rather than any "religious" affiliation. As Jänterä-Jareborg comments, "to *renounce* one's membership in the Church to which one was born and which continues to be well-established in society, requires taking a position on what religion is about."[79] Just as family lawyers are aware of the need to challenge an assumption of a universal understanding of "family" so we need to question our understanding of religion.

While civil courts are much happier with "arguments drawn from secular rationalism than from divine revelation"[80] and religion, perceived as strong, or even extreme, individual faith, may struggle for accommodation within secular law, the support which religion and religious thought can provide to family relations should not be overlooked.[81] The functions of religion are not necessarily

77 See in particular, in this volume, ÖRÜCÜ and HARDING.

78 See in particular BERMAN who discusses the concept of "civil religion" as identified by Jean-Jacques Rousseau: BERMAN, *supra* note 5, particularly at pp. 744–746.

79 JÄNTERÄ-JAREBORG, in this volume, *supra* at p. 78.

80 NORRIE, in this volume, *supra* at p. 306.

81 See e.g., BROWNING, D.S., "Modern Law and Christian Jurisprudence on Marriage and Family", (2008) 51 *Emory LJ* 31.

far removed from the functions of law, both of which communicate their values through "ritual", "tradition", "authority" and "universality".[82] While secular legal systems are likely to fear or mistrust strong expressions of faith or belief, preferring more "rational" behaviour and scientific motivation, the common ground inhabited by faith in religious belief and belief in affective relationships should not be overlooked.

4.3. RELIGION AND FAMILY LAW: CERTAINTY OR CHAOS?

The aim of much modern family law is to design and implement a clear and consistent set of principles and rules which foster certainty and limit discretion. Against that stated aim, however, is posited the pragmatic view that families and relationships are by their very nature chaotic and that we should expect nothing different of family law.[83] For modern, secular systems of family law, which have attained a relatively certain framework of legal rules, the prospect of recognising religious pluralism is a disturbing thought, whether in terms of particular religions or of tolerance of personal religious meaning in the context of legally established relationship models. Ironically, however, the clear, modern rules of secular family law may mask a lack of certainty and shared understanding of meaning; a certainty which is, in turn, associated closely with religious faith.

4.3.1. Clear laws but chaotic meaning

A driving force behind much family law reform in recent decades has been to clarify and simplify the legal framework. Replacement of discretion with clear rules or principles and the development of consistency and certainty are key objectives of modern family law. Civil rules for marriage and registration of relationships have replaced earlier systems allowing for informal constitution of marriage; restriction of the availability of declarators of nullity in favour of simplified divorce and detailed provisions for establishing parentage can all be seen as driven by a desire for clarity and coherence.

As legal rules have moved towards definition and administrative certainty, however, there has been a simultaneous fragmentation of meaning. What does it mean to say that a couple live together as husband and wife, except that they have the outward evidence of marriage in the form of an extract from a legal register; what does it mean to be the legal "parent" child when there is no necessary connection between those who appear on the legal birth certificate and those who "parent" the child? Emphasis on personal freedom and individual

---

82 BERMAN, *supra* note 5, at p. 746.

83 DEWAR, J., "The Normal Chaos of Family Law", (1998) *Modern Law Review* 467.

satisfaction within relationships has contributed to the demise of any shared notion of what it means to be "husband and wife". As soon as we accept the possibility that marriage need not be between a man and a woman, then the potential for diversity and fragmentation is clear. Modern family law may be set out in clear, formal terms but what it means in any deeper sense is increasingly chaotic. Legal rules have developed to define in detail the wide range of scientific or social paths to becoming a parent, but these clear legal rules overlay an underlying chaos as to what it means to be a parent. Simply seeking to protect the clarity which has been achieved in the formal provisions of modern, secular family statutes, against the messy invasion of diverse and complex religious beliefs, overlooks the chaos of meaning which lurks beneath these formal rules. Increasingly it is clear that some reconsideration of underlying concepts is needed and here again it is the interaction between apparent opposites, rather than their separation, which provides an opportunity "to explore ... conceptual deserts ... more thoughtfully."[84]

4.3.2. Clear belief but chaotic laws

When Menski says that many lawyers may not want to know about diverse personal laws, at least part of the explanation lies in a reluctance to open up an outwardly clear, secular legal framework to the operation and influence of a myriad of personal laws. He recognises that "we often instinctively desire more uniformity and certainty"[85] and, measured against that desire, the complex and, to our eyes, chaotic web of formal and informal practices, subject to regional variation and multiple interpretation, of shari'a appears entirely contradictory. To permit the operation of personal religious law, within a system of universal, civil rules, gives rise to an image of chaos. The extent to which many secular, family law systems currently operate, however, according to clear rules of general application, is questioned when we examine the place within these systems of private ordering. Increasingly legal systems offer a pick and mix approach to family regulation, with opportunity for, and state encouragement of, privately negotiated modification and settlement. Public systems of matrimonial property, from which individuals can choose to opt out through private contract, and principles of child welfare, which may evade public scrutiny as a result of private parental agreement, result in limited application in practice of the general rules. Alternative dispute resolution, family mediation and private ordering play an increasingly significant role in the day-to-day regulation of family relationships and operate beside or beneath the outwardly universal system of family law. While such private ordering takes place to a greater or lesser extent within the

---

84 BERRY, P., "Postmodernism and post-religion" in CONNOR, S. (ed.), *The Cambridge Companion to Postmodernism* (Cambridge University Press, 2004), 168, at p. 179.

85 MENSKI, in this volume *supra* at p. 17.

shadow of the law, it significantly undermines an image of modern family law as a coherent system of defined principles and provisions.

That is not to challenge such private agreements in themselves but simply to highlight that family law is already well accustomed to the incorporation or substitution of private rules into a public system. "[W]e have long known that many aspects of human life import dynamic and inherently messy legal dimensions"[86] and increasingly, secular family law systems leave those aspects to private regulation by means of personal agreement. As with each of the dualisms considered here, the interaction of religion and family law can shed light on both sides. Legal acceptance of civil private ordering, but not of religious based alternative dispute resolution, highlights an inconsistent approach. While there is considerable concern expressed in current debate about potential unfairness and inequality, particularly towards women, which may result from settlements mediated through faith, there is much less voiced concern about the implications of civil, negotiated settlements; although there is significant underlying unease as to their gendered impact.

5. THE RESULTS OF OUR SEARCH

Our search for the place of religion in family law was not undertaken with any real hope or expectation of "finding" but it was instead an attempt to explore, to highlight and to encourage discussion. The very mention of religion and the suggestion that it might have a place in secular family law, or that conflicts between different religious beliefs might require to be addressed within the context of monolithic legal systems, are uncomfortable thoughts for those who feel secure within the framework of a clear, modern, secular system. Part of our purpose was to consider possibilities as to how religion does, or could, infiltrate or integrate with family law: to begin to open up connecting channels between religious and secular. By doing so we were only following two well-known principles of good relationships: fostering open communication, in which we seek to "speak with one another" and not "merely about one another",[87] and accepting the possibility of compromise.

There have been many insights into particular issues involving religion and family law and into specific impact within the context of individual legal systems. Perhaps the strongest lesson is that strict distinctions, between church and state, between private belief and public policy, and between faith and rationalism, are

[86] *Ibid.*, at p. 19.

[87] HABERMAS, J., "An Awareness of What is Missing" in HABERMAS *et al.*, *An Awareness of What is Missing: Faith and Reason in a Post-secular Age* (Polity Press, 2010), at p. 16.

unhelpful and far from clear. We should learn from previous misconceptions which have resulted from false dichotomies and challenge the notion that religious and secular are, or should be, in opposition. Doing so is not simply an academic exercise in finding out more about other legal and religious systems of family law. Nor should it be viewed negatively in terms of necessity: an enforced accommodation of differing values. While competing requirements of plural belief and belief-based systems pose challenges for legal frameworks, they also offer opportunities. The aim of this volume was to search for the place of religion: a search embarked upon with confidence from within the citadel of family law, with religion quite clearly placed in the position of challenger. Admitting the possibility of another, however, inevitably demands self-reflection. Searching for the place of religion may in turn lead to questioning the role of family law.

www.ingramcontent.com/pod-product-compliance
Ingram Content Group UK Ltd.
Pitfield, Milton Keynes, MK11 3LW, UK
UKHW051925100926
8556IPUK00022B/1382

9 781780 680156